# Families

# Families

## PRACTICAL ADVICE
## FROM MORE THAN 50 EXPERTS

### EDITED BY JERRY B. JENKINS .

**MOODY PRESS**

# Table of Contents

# Foreword

Our family was racing through a torrential downpour to get under the overhang at the airport entrance. I led the pack carrying the heaviest suitcase, and Martie and the kids were following single file, jumping over, stepping into, and trying to dodge the deep puddles between us and our destination. As I jumped the curb, I noticed a man standing under the protective covering, directly in my path. Both my momentum and protective paternal instincts caused me to blurt out as I nearly knocked him over, "Look out, family coming!" He responded with a measure of disdain. "Big deal."

We finally made it to our seats, and as I settled in, hoping to dry off, his comment echoed in my mind. It seemed to me that the whole culture had stood up and said what they thought about the family.

## Under attack

On every front, the primacy and value of the family is under attack. Special interest groups lobby hard, both in the political arena and through well-placed, powerful influence brokers in the media, to redefine "family" as any societal group of individuals who happen to live together and who give a sense of meaning to one another's lives. The culturally elite seek to call these groupings legitimate families, thus devaluing the unique importance of a family where husband and wife commit themselves to each other and together rear a productive cluster of children for the next generation.

Materialism has invaded the family fabric. A surging sense of greed and the opportunities affordable to us draw fathers and mothers alike into the workplace, where competitive forces and quickly fulfilling rewards have kept lots of us dads away from our families – physically, mentally, and emotionally – during those years when they needed us to be there to mentor and model for them.

The moral decline of our country has not helped to strengthen our homes. The values that define right from wrong and uphold lifelong commitments in marriage are long gone from our society. The resultant shattering of our families through parental breakup and a parallel increase in abusive patterns have had a devastating impact on the homes of America.

## Debilitating influence

Those of us who have grown up and continue to live in contexts where the truths of Christ and His Word are proclaimed are not exempt from these debilitating influences. The voices of those who would devalue family are far too creative and far too prevalent in our living rooms through the mediums of television, music, and magazines to allow us to be complacent about what families are and ought to be. Those of us whose children go to public schools recognize that they will be under a steady barrage of input that redefines family and promotes values that undercut their capacity to develop a godly and constructive home. Surprisingly, the inculturation of values that are counter to productive families is so prevalent that even some places of higher education most of us would consider to be Christian in mission and in nature may not always be safe havens.

Do we need a new look at families? Absolutely. We need something that's definitive, fundamentally biblical, remedial, culturally relevant, and helpful. For years, we at Moody have been committed to serving the cause of Jesus Christ through His church. We are becoming increasingly aware that to serve the church effectively, we must also serve the cause of good and godly families. For it is from godly families that the church of tomorrow will find the strength and capacity to carry the torch for Christ into its generation.

We also recognize that many of our brothers and sisters in Christ carry deep wounds and scars from family experiences. We, the church of Christ, must learn how to put our arms around these precious ones with the grace and mercy that heals.

This book comes to you with the prayer that its contents will shore up the foundations of our homes. Read it with an open heart and transfer its pages to the transforming power of Christ for you and those who make up your family.

**Joseph M. Stowell**
*President, Moody Bible Institute*

# The Future of the American Family

*George Barna*

Drive past the houses in your neighborhood. In days gone by, you could fairly well predict what types of families resided within those homes. Today our culture is changing rapidly, and predictability is a rare commodity. Yet, when we speak about *family*, there is at least one prediction you can make about the typical household.

The Cleavers don't live there anymore.

In the sixties, the made-for-TV Cleaver family (of the "Leave It to Beaver" series) provided a weekly portrayal of some of the realities facing the American family. Addressing those issues were the working father, the homemaker mother, and the two children under the age of eighteen who lived in that home. This family configuration represented 60 percent of American households in 1960. Today, that same configuration represents just 3 percent of all American households.

Clearly, the same whirlwind of change that has redefined modern life over the past three decades has also transformed the American family. It would be difficult to overstate the significance of this transformation to the stability and definition of our culture. The family unit has served as the fundamental building block of our nation since the Pilgrims first set foot on the shores of America. Family has consistently served as a central means of determining and disseminating personal values, societal mores, and community relationships. Changes in the health and contour of the family unit have generally presaged important transitions in the direction and nature of the American people.

Consider the myriad of challenges to the traditional family structure and mentality: Divorce. Cohabitation. Births outside of marriage. Gay couples. Abortion. Working women. Multigenerational households. Single parents. The deterioration of the extended family. Rampant sexual promiscuity. Bearing fewer children. Changes in childrearing attitudes. Physical abuse in the family. Rising sterility. Put all of these changes together and you find a crucial social institution that is being wholly reshaped.

## New views of reality

Somewhere along the way adults began to realize that their codes of conduct were self-imposed and could be altered as their situation dictated. Consequently, over the past three decades, an experimental mind-set has characterized American lifestyles. Absolute truth was replaced by relative truth. Long-term relationships, either at the personal or career level, were replaced by relationships of convenience or benefit. Even the core values to which people ascribed have been redefined

> *Put all of these changes together and you find a crucial social institution being wholly reshaped.*

and reprioritized.[1]

Consider the shifts in attitude regarding family matters. Today, nearly half the adult population defines a family as any combination of people who have a close, personal relationship. They need not be married or related by blood. To millions of Americans, simply "having a good relationship," "enjoying the time spent together," or "feeling emotionally bonded" are sufficient criteria to define the people involved as a family.[2]

But old attitudes die hard. The vast majority of adults believe that marriage remains a viable practice in our society, that a legal, formal marriage between adults is important for family stability, and that marriage is intended to be a long-term relationship. The concept of marriage remains widely accepted as a reasonable, if not typical, lifestyle decision.[3]

However, those enduring views are softened by newer, more self-centered perspectives. For instance, two out of three adults contend that "marriage should be used by people to help them cope with life more effectively, but should not limit people's activities or opportunities in any way." In other words, as long as marriage meets one's personal needs, it is useful; as soon as the bond requires compromising one's own time, energy, or experiences, the union ceases to be viable.

Consider the fact that one-third of all adults now believe that "people who get married these days are fighting the odds; it's almost impossible to have a successful marriage these days." Psychologists point to this philosophy as a self-fulfilling prophecy. If marriage is intended to be a lasting mutual commitment between people, the assumption that marriage will not last prevents the couple from truly making the depth of commitment necessary to persevere through the inevitable tough times. The result? The expected result.

Attitudes toward sexual behavior have also continued their radical transformation. While the AIDS epidemic has put a new twist in the game, the underlying belief remains that a person is sexually accountable only to him- or herself. One-third say that sexual relations outside marriage are acceptable behavior. More than two-thirds of the adults who get married this year will have had sexual intercourse before their marriage – and see no moral incongruities in that behavior. Among adults who have never been married, fewer than one in four is still a virgin, and relatively few adults defend the virtue of remaining a virgin until marriage.

# Patterns in marriage

Fewer people are making the walk down the aisle these days. Among those who do, an increasing proportion are individuals who are being remarried after a divorce.

In 1960, almost three-quarters of all adults twenty-five or older were married. Today, barely half of that group are married. People are not only less likely to get married these days, but those who make the commitment are doing so later in life. The median age of a person's first marriage was twenty-one years in 1960. Today, the median age has jumped to twenty-five.[4]

Divorce is now an expected part of life for many people. There is virtually no social stigma left in relation to divorce, except among certain leadership positions (e.g., clergy and political leaders). Since 1960, the rate of divorce has quadrupled; nearly half of all marriages end in divorce. In fact, about one out of every four adults in the nation has experienced at least one divorce. Among

> *Since 1960, the rate of divorce has quadrupled; nearly half of all marriages end in divorce.*

## About the author

*George Barna, M.A., is founder of Barna Research Group, specializing in marketing research, and has written many books, including* Vital Signs (Crossway), The Frog in the Kettle, User Friendly Churches, *and* The Power of Vision (Regal).

those adults who divorce and remarry, the probability of going through another divorce is even higher: in excess of 60 percent of all divorced adults who remarry will divorce again.

Cohabitation has become the norm among today's couples. Three out of every five couples who get married this year will live together for some period of time before tying the knot. That constitutes a fivefold increase in just the last two decades. Among the Baby Bust generation (adults twenty-seven years or younger), it is widely accepted that cohabi-

tation is a precursor to marriage.

Interestingly, the impact of cohabitation on marital longevity appears to be of little interest to most of the adults who live together prior to marriage. While the usual reason for cohabitation is that individuals wish to have a "trial period," studies of such couples show that those who live together before marriage are 80 percent more likely to wind up getting divorced than are those couples who did not share living quarters before marriage.[5]

Different types of marital relationships are also on a sharp growth curve. Homosexual couples are increasing rapidly, although these liaisons represent less than one out of every twenty households. Nevertheless, notice that Americans are more accepting of gay couples and homosexual behavior than was true in the past. Today, one-quarter of adults believe that gay couples are families. One out of five believe that "there's nothing wrong with two people of the same sex getting married to each other."[6]

Another change in marital patterns is interracial marriages. In the last two decades, we have seen nearly a tripling of the number of newly married couples who are interracial.

# Evolving roles of women

While June Cleaver stayed home all day and tended to household and family duties as a full-time endeavor, fewer and fewer women are following in her footsteps. Today, more than two-thirds of all women are in the work force. Even among mothers of preschool children, 59 percent are in the labor force.[7]

Women have proven to be capable in the marketplace. Three out of ten businesses in the nation are owned by women, and the majority of new businesses started this year will be initiated by women. They have taken on greater positions of leadership in government, both in elected offices and appointed positions. Their impact is also being felt on

> *We have grown from less than 150,000 children enrolled in child care in 1960 to more than 2 million in 1990.*

college campuses, where approximately half of all graduate degrees are now being awarded to females.

Yet, for all the remarkable advances made in our society by women, one expectation has remained virtually unchanged: if a woman bears a child, caring for that child is primarily her responsibility. Even in this era of revised priorities and values, there are relatively few Mr. Mom's in place. And, though six out of eight adults concur that the responsibility for raising children should be equally borne by fathers as well as mothers, only one out of eight is actually doing so.

One of the vexing challenges to America today is how—or whether—to facilitate mothers juggling the multiple stresses and responsibilities of being mother, wife, employee, friend, and citizen. Surveys indicate that the anxiety produced by this balancing act is the most frustrating aspect in the lives of working women.

Many mothers, faced with competing demands for their time and energy, have turned to child care for assistance. This in turn has led to concerns about the quality of care received by the child, the bonding process between parent and child, the values transmitted to the children by the care providers, and the cost of such care.

To gain perspective on the magnitude of the situation, realize that we have grown from less than 150,000 children enrolled in child care in 1960 to more than 2 million in 1990. During the same period, there has been more than a tenfold increase in the number of child care centers, and a 600 percent increase

in the proportion of companies providing child care benefits to employees as an inducement to women to remain in the work force.[8] Families spent more than $14 billion on child care in 1989.[9]

# The downtrodden

Single parents are perhaps the most beleaguered heads of households. Not only are we seeing rapid growth in the proportion of households headed by single parents, but the emotional toll of managing the family as a single parent is overwhelming for many.

It is expected that among all of the children born this year, 60 percent will live in a single-parent household at some point before they reach their eighteenth birthday. The vast majority of those children will live with their mother, and most of them will experience severe economic hardships as a result of the family dissolution. Even more disturbing is the recent finding that such children are several times more likely to experience developmental, learning, and emotional problems before leaving home to initiate their own careers and living arrangements than youths from intact families.[10]

# The state of children

We recently passed a milestone: for the first time in our history, America has more elderly people than teenagers. That shift is reflective of a changing emphasis upon age groups in the nation's psyche. Despite the minor baby boom of the late eighties and early nineties, our focus is no longer on childhood but upon adulthood.

The average family size has decreased substantially. The typical family now has 2.6 people. Women have an average of two children apiece, just half as many as was the case in 1960. The fertility rate of American women has actually dropped below the population replacement rate for the first time in the country's history.

> *The typical parent spends less than one hour per week in meaningful interaction with each of his or her children.*

Factors such as increasing numbers of single adults, an aging population, and the high rate of divorce also contribute to the decreasing family size.

Children these days are being asked to do more at an earlier age, with less emotional support. Children seventeen or younger will spend an excess of $200 billion this year, much of it on purchases made on behalf of their parents or family. The typical American adolescent will spend more money in the coming twelve months than more than 1 billion adults in other nations of the world.

While parents place financial burdens on their youngsters, they frequently do not provide the necessary emotional support to undergird that responsibility. Most adults believe that the *quality* of time spent with others is more important than the *quantity* of time spent in those relationships.[11] This is certainly evident in parent-child relationships. The typical parent spends less than one hour per week in meaningful interaction with each of his or her children.[12] Although a substantial proportion of parents admit to this failing, few seem committed to rearranging their priorities to alter that circumstance.

Sadly, the street gangs that have attracted so many youths, especially in urban areas, are simply a surrogate family for youngsters in search of meaning, respect, and acceptance. The experience of people who work with gang members, the research related to parentless children, and the statistics regarding criminal activity among children from broken homes all suggest that there is no substitute for parental time and concern.

**The family still has a future.**

# Challenges for the future

Family is certainly not dead in America, but it looks and behaves very differently than it used to. We can expect the changes that are in progress to continue during the remainder of this decade and beyond.

For those who wish to have a positive impact on the family, there are several potential services that could be performed toward the enhancement of successful family systems and healthy individuals.

First, people are struggling with the very definition and purpose of family. Providing a benchmark of understanding on this pivotal issue would go a long way toward eliminating the confusion and discontent that exists in regard to family affairs.

Second, millions of Americans lack insight into how they might gain support from or provide support to those who need such encouragement in family matters. Parenting has never been an easy job, but the complexities of today's world make it even more difficult than in the past. Building a strong marriage is difficult in a society where selfishness is accepted and communication skills are all too rare.

Third, how helpful it would be for Americans to have a philosophy of life that assists them in understanding the value and role of the family! Without such a worldview, it is difficult to make decisions that reflect the best interests of anyone other than oneself. Armed with a comprehensive philosophy, such decisions can be more consistent and positive.

1. For a fuller discussion of these changes, see Barna Research Group, Glendale, Calif., "There's No Truth Like Your Own Truth," in *Ministry Currents*, July-September 1991, pp. 1–4; George Barna, *The Frog in the Kettle* (Ventura, Calif.: Regal, 1990); George Barna, *What Americans Believe* (Ventura, Calif.: Regal, 1991); Charles Colson, *Against the Night* (Ann Arbor, Mich.: Servant, 1989); and Carl F. H. Henry, *The Christian Mindset in a Secular Society* (Portland: Multnomah, 1984).
2. Barna Research Group, Glendale, Calif., "Family, Marriage, and Ministry," in *Ministry Currents*, April-June 1992.
3. *Family in America*, a national research study conducted by the Barna Research Group, February 1992.
4. Data from the U. S. Census Bureau.
5. Data provided by the National Bureau of Economic Research.
6. *Family in America*.
7. David Popenoe, "Flight from the Nuclear Family," *The Public Perspective*, March-April 1991, pp. 19–20.
8. *National Policy Quarterly*, Winter 1990, p. 23.
9. *Monthly Labor Review*, December 1989, p. 49.
10. "Developmental Learning and Emotional Problems," Nicholas Zill and Charlotte Schoenborn, Advance Data #190, U.S. Department of Health and Human Services, 1990.
11. George Barna, *What Americans Believe*, pp. 110–12.
12. Research conducted by the Barna Research Group, Ltd., for Josh McDowell Ministry in connection with the "Why Wait?" program.

## Further Reading

George Barna. *The Future of the American Family.* Chicago: Moody, 1993.

James Dobson and Gary L. Bauer. *Children at Risk: The Battle for the Hearts & Minds of Our Children.* Dallas: Word, 1990.

Bernie A. Schock. *Remodeling the Family: A Radical Plan for Restoring the Home.* Nashville: Woglemuth & Hyatt, 1989.

Fran Sciacca. *Generation at Risk, Revised & Expanded.* Chicago: Moody, 1990, 1991.

# YOUNG LOVE AND MARRIAGE

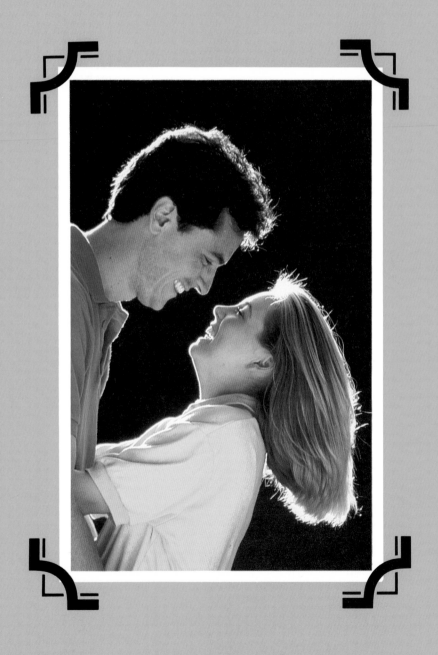

# How to Know When you are Really in Love

*Max and Vivian Rice*

"I know it's love," you say.

"I think about her all the time; I get butterflies in my stomach; I can't eat; I can't sleep; my heart pounds anytime she's near—of course it's love!"

But the question is, Are you in love with the person, or are you in love with love? Would it surprise you to know that most people who think they are in love are not really in love with the person? They are in love with the *idea* of love.

## In love with the idea

You can see this almost any day at school. Our girls came home one day telling us about a guy who had asked a girl to go steady with him; she said no. He asked a second girl to go steady with him; she rejected him. A third and a fourth girl both said they were not interested. He asked a fifth girl to go steady with him, and she said yes! And now he is completely and totally in love with that girl. She is everything to him. She is the only girl in all the world. Why? Because they were truly meant only for each other? No. Because he needed a girlfriend, and she was available.

We have a strong, inborn need to love and to be loved. This has been proven in hospitals where infants without parents receive the best of medical care. However, if they are not held and fondled, they do not develop properly.

In addition to this natural desire, there is strong social pressure to have a steady. If you do not, people wonder what is wrong. We search for someone to meet this need for belonging. Some, for one reason or another, are unacceptable to us. Others, whom we like, may not like us. But finally we find someone who meets our needs. We meet his needs. We get together and call it "love." All the symptoms follow. We are in love with love.

Haven't you seen this happen among your friends? Last year a boy was madly in love with a girl. They had an electric relationship. She was the one and only girl for him. Now they couldn't care less for each other. Each one loves someone else as much as they used to love each other.

It isn't so bad when you have a close relationship with a person for a while and then break it off. The tragedy comes when you marry and then find that you do not love the person anymore. If you think that could not happen to you, remember that most people who marry feel the same way. They think that what they have is real love. But the climbing divorce rate proves that many are sadly mistaken.

This is not written to scare you away from love but, rather, to encourage you to seek the real thing. The Hollywood or *Playboy* version of love just does not work. Biblical love does.

## Three kinds of love

As we search the Scriptures to discover what love really is, some of the precepts may sound silly to you. True love is so foreign to the modern counterfeit that you may be tempted to reject it as unreal, unless you are convinced that God is wiser than you are.

What, then, is real love? How do you know when you have it? How can you tell if the other person really loves you?

The Greeks had several words for love. Unfortunately, in the English language we try to make do with one. This causes confusion because there are three important types of love, represented by the Greek words *agape*, *phileo*, and *eros*.

*Agape* is the word normally used for God's love for man, man's love for God, and man's Christian love for his fellow man. *Phileo* means intimate friendship and indicates that you enjoy the company and fellowship of the other person. These two words are used in the Bible.

The other principal Greek word for love is *eros*. It refers to physical, sexual love, usually tied to the emotions. The word itself is not in the Bible. But this does not mean that the Bible is silent about sexual love. After all, God invented it. More about this later.

You may be wondering which of these three kinds of love is necessary for a happy marriage. The answer is easy: all of them. It is like a three-legged stool. If any leg breaks, the stool collapses.

## Agape love—true love

Agape love considers the object of love to be infinitely precious. Agape desires the very best for the one loved. It is a self-sacrificing love. It must be the foundation upon which the other loves are built. Agape love, in its purest form, is of God. It is part of the fruit that the Holy Spirit produces in those who are God's children (Galatians 5:22).

Agape love is not a matter of the emotions. It is something we should have for all people, though, of course, we should have it to a much greater degree for the one we marry. You may think that this is not what you are interested

### About the authors

*Max and Vivian Rice are founders and directors of Look-Up-Lodge, located in South Carolina. They have written four books, including* You Can Be First String on God's Team *(Here's Life). The Rices have three daughters.*

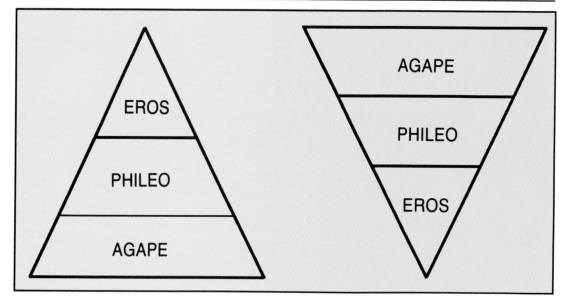

in. You are interested in romantic love for a particular person. But unless you have agape as a foundation, the other loves will not last.

Think of love as a pyramid. Agape is at the base; phileo is next; and eros is at the top. If we try to turn it upside down, the whole thing topples.

The Egyptian pyramids have stood storms and winds for thousands of years because they had a proper foundation. If it were possible to have built them upside down, the slightest breeze would have toppled them.

A marriage will also stand all the storms and stresses of life if it is built on the proper foundation. However, most couples build a relationship with eros as the foundation. Therefore, their marriage cannot endure the storms that are sure to come. They discover too late that phileo and agape cannot be built on the foundation of eros.

Some time ago our daughter Carolyn, then a college freshman home for the weekend, visited with several friends who are high school seniors. She was distressed over hearing the news that one of her high school classmates, who got married last year, was already divorced. The couple stayed together only five months.

In explaining the situation to her friends, the girl said, "He simply was not capable of real love." She was not talking about eros, or sexual love. That was the big attraction in the first place. And there was certainly a little phileo, or liking, there. They liked to go to basketball games together. They enjoyed listening to music together. So what kind of love was she talking about that was missing? Obviously, the kind that lasts: agape love.

How do you know if you are capable of agape love? How do you know if the one you intend to marry is capable of it? How do you develop it? God has given us a wonderful training and testing place. It is called the home, the family you live with now.

## The test of love

If you cannot exhibit agape love in your home before marriage, you will not be able to once you are married. You may be thinking that the object of your affections is different from the members of your family. But just remember that your parents thought that about each other, and the ones who marry your brothers and sisters will think that about them. The problems are not with the particular people with whom you live. The problems are in living close to someone.

It is in the selfish interest of the person you are going with to act lovingly toward you now. But when the drudgery and routineness of marriage set in, her basic nature will come through. If she is selfish in her present home, she will be selfish in your new home. The same is true of you. If you cannot exhibit true love at home, you cannot exhibit it in marriage.

In fact, people generally treat their spouses worse than they do other people. All the jokes about married people are not so funny when they come true in your marriage. One of the big tasks of marriage counselors is to get partners to treat each other with the same consideration they do others. Don't think that you and your mate will be the exception.

One of the biggest mistakes people make is to get married because they cannot stand to live at home. Until you learn to live at home, accepting and loving the other members of your family, you are not ready for marriage.

# What is true love?

What is involved in agape love? First Corinthians 13 tells us. Listed below are love's characteristics. The phrases are taken from *The Living Bible*, with portions from the J.B. Phillips translation in parentheses.

Applications of these verses to everyday life are limitless. We can suggest only a few, some dealing with your relationships at home now, some with the person you may be considering for marriage. Some examples use feminine pronouns, others masculine. They all apply to both.

If you will memorize 1 Corinthians 13:4–8 and ask the Holy Spirit to teach you how

> *If you cannot exhibit true love at home, you cannot exhibit it in marriage.*

to live these verses, you will find hundreds of other examples. You will also be able to tell whether these qualities appear in your friends.

**Love is very patient**

Suppose a boy says to a girl, "I love you so much I can't wait until we are through school. Let's drop out and get married now." This is not agape love. If he really loves her, he will say, "I love you so much that I want the very best for you. I want our children to have educated parents. I wouldn't think of ruining our chances by getting married now."

The Bible gives an example of this kind of love: "Jacob served seven years to get Rachel, but they seemed like only a few days to him because of his love for her" (Genesis 29:20).

Are you and your true love patient with each other? Are you each patient with other members of your families? It may be possible for you to be patient with each other under the rather artificial circumstances of dating. But if you are not patient now at home, you will not be patient in marriage after the original excitement wears off.

The Bible specifically warns us "do not make friends with a hot-tempered man, do not associate with one easily angered" (Proverbs 22:24). Many broken homes are tragic examples of failure to heed this advice. Do either of you display short tempers at home now?

**Love is kind** *(Looks for a way of being constructive)*

Proverbs 31:10–31 is a wonderful portrait of a virtuous woman. One of the characteristics it mentions is that "the teaching of kindness is on her tongue" (v. 26, NASB). True love leads a person to say the kind thing, to perform the thoughtful deed.

In one of the great love stories of the Bible, Boaz was drawn to Ruth because of the way she treated her mother-in-law (Ruth 2:11). When Abraham's servant sought a wife for

> *Real love puts the happiness of the other first.*

Isaac, the test he used was that the girl displayed kindness beyond what was called for (Genesis 24:14).

## Love is never jealous or envious *(Is not possessive)*

Suppose there is a party planned where the guests are coming in couples. You are unable to attend. Would you want the one you love to go with someone else and have a good time or to stay at home and be lonely? Real love puts the happiness of the other first. In talking with teens, this point usually brings more disagreement than any other, until they think about it.

Some are afraid that they might lose their steady if they allow the person to go with someone else. But think for a moment. Suppose the one you love would be happier with someone else? When is the best time for you to find out? Do you want to wait until after you are married? Of course not! The sooner you find out, the better. If the only way you can hold someone is by not letting that one compare you with others, you do not have a very firm foundation for marriage.

Another reason for going out with others is that each of you will mature and develop more broadly if you relate to a number of different people. Real love will lead you to want to become the best possible mate for the person you will marry someday. A wide range of wholesome Christian fellowship will better prepare you for marriage.

I am glad my wife and I each dated numbers of others before we got together, because, when we did, we knew it was right and have never had the slightest doubt since.

Jealousy not only limits associations with the opposite sex but often keeps teens from meaningful relationships with others of their own sex. Jill used to enjoy fellowship with a group of Christian girls. She is no longer able to be with them, however, because her boyfriend monopolises all her time. When he is not with her, she wants to be at home in case he calls on the telephone.

Real love would lead a person to say, "Although I want to spend time with you, I also want each of us to spend time with others." Real love, according to the Bible, is not possessive or jealous.

Henry A. Overstreet, psychologist and philosopher, had this to say:

*The love of a person implies, not the possession of that person, but the affirmation of that person. It means granting him, gladly, the full right to his unique humanhood. One does not truly love a person and yet seek to enslave him by law or by bonds of dependence and possessiveness.*

*Whenever we experience a genuine love, we are moved by this transforming experience toward a capacity for goodwill.*[1]

## Love is never boastful or proud *(Anxious to impress)*

Have you ever seen anyone display her sweetheart like a trophy? By her actions, she seems to be saying, "Look what I caught. He's mine. I got him." She is anxious to impress people with how much she and her catch love each other.

Our daughter came in one day quite tickled over an incident that illustrates this point. In order to jump on the trampoline at our camp, it is necessary to have four spotters. There were five people there, which should have been ideal: one to jump and four to spot. However, no one could jump because two were seemingly glued to each other and had to be considered as one. What they called love would not let either one move four or five feet away from the other so that all could enjoy the trampoline. Doubtless they thought they were impressing people that their love was the real thing. Not so, says the Bible. Real love is not anxious to impress others.

**Love is never haughty or selfish** *(Nor does it cherish inflated ideas of its own importance)*
Since we are in love, members of our family, our friends, and all others should make whatever adjustments are necessary in order that our love should have central place. Right? *Wrong!*

**Love is not rude** *(Has good manners)*
The basis of manners is thoughtfulness for other people. Lack of good manners indicates self-centeredness. A person who does not show respect and consideration for others now will not have respect for his mate after marriage.

**Love does not demand its own way** *(Does not pursue selfish advantage)*
Often when a person says "I love you" he really means "I love me and want you." For example, suppose a boy says, "I love you," then by his actions says, "Because I love you, I'm going to ruin your character, your reputation, your chance for a happy marriage, your self-respect, and your relationship with God. And I'm going to do all this because I love you so much." Does he really love you? Do you want to build a home on that kind of foundation?

If anyone really loves you, he will try to make you a finer, sweeter person. When anyone tries to push you down instead of lift you up, you can be sure he loves himself and is using you.

This does not mean that we are to neglect ourselves or that we cannot enjoy the other person. It does mean that we do not hurt others to gratify our own desires.

**Love is not irritable or touchy**
Do you or your true love overreact to instructions from your parents? Do you resent the

> *The basis of manners is thoughtfulness for other people. Lack of good manners indicates self-centeredness.*

way others act? Are you easily upset? If so, you are not yet capable of the kind of love that leads to a happy marriage. Work on this at home.

**Love does not hold grudges and will hardly even notice when others do it wrong** *(Does not keep account of evil)*
If the person you go with is very critical of other people, you can be sure he will be critical of you. Maybe not now. Maybe not to your face. But all the jokes about nagging will cease to be funny if you marry a critical person.

**Love rejoices when truth wins out.**

**Love is never glad about injustice** *(Or gloats over the wickedness of other people)*
Many people, for one reason or another, refrain from certain bad things themselves. However, they seem to enjoy thinking about these things and talking about those who do them. Others rejoice in naughty acts and think there is something cute or clever about mischief. The Bible says, "Doing wickedness is like sport to a fool" (Proverbs 10:23, NASB).

One reason some people gloat over the wickedness of others is that it gives them such excuses as, "Everybody is doing it," "Other people do things just as bad," "It's just the style."

**Love rejoices whenever truth wins out**
Paul said, "Finally, brothers, whatever is true, whatever is noble, whatever is right, whatever is pure, whatever is lovely, whatever is admirable — if anything is excellent or praiseworthy — think about such things" (Philippians 4:8).

How do the two of you check out on this? You can tell by what you enjoy reading, watching, listening to, and talking about.

**If you love someone you will be loyal to him no matter what the cost** *(No limit to its endurance)*
The Bible says, "Be completely humble and gentle; be patient, bearing with one another in love" (Ephesians 4:2). Here again, the home is the ideal training and testing ground.

**You will always believe in him** *(No end to its trust)*
In 2 Peter 1:5–7, we are told that faith is the foundation on which all other virtues are built. Love, the greatest virtue, is the last one added. Anyone who does not believe the truths of God will be incapable of true love. This works both ways. Many young people do not believe God's truth because through lack of love, they are rebelling against their family. In order to justify their behavior, they doubt the Bible.

**You will always expect the best of him** *(No fading of its hope)*
In light of the startling statistics about the high rate of unhappy marriages, most people have very little hope of happiness. Those who trust God, however, have tremendous hope, which will be evidenced by their following the scriptural pattern. "For everything that was written in the past was written to teach us, so that through endurance and the encouragement of the Scriptures we might have hope" (Romans 15:4). "Everyone who has this hope in him purifies himself, just as he is pure" (1 John 3:3).

**(Love can outlast anything)**
In marriage, you will be called on to endure inconveniences, hardships, and misunderstandings. Do you have the love that endures?

**Love goes on forever** *(Never fails)*
The love we have been talking about never fails. The Hollywood or *Playboy* version often fails before the honeymoon is over. Which do you want?

Perhaps you are discouraged by now. You were interested in romance, and we have not even got there yet. Many people have experienced the same thing in watching a new home being built. They were anxious to see the house go up, and instead the workmen dug down. Builders know the importance of a firm foundation.

Any good football team spends most of its time on fundamentals. Those who master the fundamentals are the ones who experience the thrills later on.

> *In marriage, you will be called on to endure inconveniences, hardships, and misunderstandings.*

**It is important to cultivate friendship with people of both sexes.**

# Phileo love – friendship love

Christians should develop agape love for all people. We do not have phileo love for all, however. We have phileo love for a much smaller group, some of our own sex and some of the opposite sex. This is the group that we enjoy being with. Phileo is closer to our word "like." The pyramid illustrates how the objects of our affection grow fewer in number when it comes to phileo love. As we think of narrowing further to the one we will share eros with, it is extremely important that we are certain that we have phileo love for this person *first*.

Do you enjoy doing things together – other than making out? Do you enjoy working together, talking about important things together, discussing spiritual things together, and playing together? Do you have some common interests?

If you enjoy only physical intimacy, you have a very poor foundation for marriage. It is much more likely that you are in love with love than with each other.

This is one reason it is so important to have a wide variety of meaningful relationships with people of both sexes. If we single out one too soon, we fail to develop the capacity for a strong phileo relationship.

Some may want to work on phileo and eros at the same time. "Why not spend part of the time making out," they reason, "and part of the time talking and doing other things to develop phileo love?" It won't work. To understand why, we must examine the nature of eros.

# Eros love – blind love

Since *eros* is not used in the Bible, we turn to the Greek writers to learn its meaning. The following list contains some typical quotations from several Greek authors to describe

> ## For Plato, eros was "an ecstasy which transports man beyond rationality."

eros: "passionate love which desires the other for itself"; "sensual"; "intoxication"; "sets all the senses in a frenzy"; "no choice is left, nor will"; "ecstasy"; "sensual intoxication and the supreme form of ecstasy."

For Plato, eros was "an ecstasy which transports man beyond rationality."

The modern way of saying much of the above is simply, "Love is blind." If you retain your common sense, you do not have a real case of eros. Remember, this is the opinion of the romantic writers, not that of some stuffy old theologian.

The conclusion should be obvious. If we become blind as soon as eros sets in, we must be sure that we have agape and phileo love first. The answer to the question "How can I know if it is really love?" is simply that you cannot if eros develops before you are certain about the other types of love.

Under the influence of eros, you will think that you have phileo and agape for each other. This is one reason for postponing physical intimacy.

To illustrate, suppose you are planning to go out one night. The power company calls and informs you that the lights will be turned off in fifteen minutes. You need to choose socks to match your clothes. Would you want to make your choice before or after the lights go out?

Likewise, if you want to be sure you have agape and phileo love for a person, when do you need to decide? Before the lights go out. As soon as eros sets in, the lights go out. You become blind.

Surely you have seen this in others. You have wondered why one of your friends likes a particular person. What could he possibly see in her? Actually, he is unable to see any-thing in her. He is blind. Everybody knows it except him. Think for a moment, and you will probably recall many incidents like this.

How do you keep it from happening to you? Postpone physical relationships that would result in eros until after the other relationships are thoroughly developed. This, of course, takes time.

Youth often ask about kissing on an early date. If a person realizes that eros may very well set in with the first kiss, the answer should be obvious. If this seems far-fetched, look again at the high percentage of unhappy marriages. Do you want to join them?

Remember, most of them "just knew" theirs was the real thing. They never thought they would be blind. Too late they found out that they were really in love with love.

This chapter is taken from *When Can I Say "I Love You"?* (Chicago: Moody, 1977).

1. Henry A. Overstreet, *The Mature Mind* (New York: Norton, 1969), p. 103.

## Further Reading

Kevin Leman. *Were You born for Each Other?* New York: Delacorte, 1991.

Max and Vivian Rice. *When Can I Say "I Love You"?* Chicago: Moody, 1977.

M. Blaine Smith. *Should I Get Married?* Downers Grove, Ill.: InterVarsity, 1990.

Walter Trobisch. *Love Is a Feeling to Be Learned.* Downers Grove, Ill.: InterVarsity, 1968.

# Leaving Home: A Prerequisite to Cleaving

*John Trent*

Couples stand at the altar with great expectations of a loving, lasting relationship. Yet without realizing it, many are setting themselves up for deep hurt and disappointment. Instead of the intimacy they really want, they find only frustration and a gnawing emptiness. And in place of a close-knit family, they find themselves destroying each other, and later their children, with their words and actions.

What is it that can ruin a couple's relationship? How can they allow their commitment to succumb to "friendly fire"? It begins when they fail to practice a biblical necessity — truly "leaving" home as a prerequisite to "cleaving" to their spouse.

## The command to "leave"

In nearly every wedding, you hear this familiar verse: "For this cause a man shall leave his father and his mother, and shall cleave to his wife; and they shall become one flesh" (Genesis 2:24, KJV). Many couples do not realize that these words are not simply ceremonial but constitute a command.

"Leaving home" is clearly identified as the first step on a ladder to higher levels of intimacy. First we are to "leave," then comes the emotional bonding of "cleaving." Both provide the basis for sexual oneness — becoming one flesh.

## About the author

*John Trent, Ph.D., is vice president of Today's Family. With Gary Smalley, he has coauthored* The Blessing *and* The Gift of Love *(PUB),* The Two Sides of Love *and* The Language of Love *(Focus on the Family), and* Love Is a Decision *(Word). He and his wife, Cynthia, have two daughters.*

You can find a great deal of advice about "cleaving" and how to have a positive physical relationship. Yet until recently very little emphasis has been given to the first step necessary for intimacy — leaving home in a healthy way. Skipping the work of "leaving" can keep a newly-wed couple on the ground floor, with emotional and physical intimacy always out of reach.

Like so many couples, Mark and Susan entered marriage with high hopes and a strong commitment. Yet in only two years those dreams turned into a nightmare and their commitment had worn paper thin.

# From dreams to a nightmare

Susan grew up in a home where her mother had dominated nearly every aspect of her father's life. When it came to the children, finances, social events, or vacations, her mother called the shots. After years of watching her father become more passive and distant and her mother more dominant and assertive, Susan made an unswerving decision. By high school she had decided what kind of man she would marry. He would not be passive like her father but a strong leader — someone who would take charge as well as take care of her. That's why Susan was convinced that Mark fit the bill. He was a handsome college football player, captain of the defense, leader in the campus ministry they both belonged to, and a hard-working student.

Susan looked so closely at what he was like, she ignored his past. She never questioned the environment Mark would have to "leave" in order to set up a successful family of his own. If she had, she would have seen a home strikingly similar to her own.

Mark's father was a workaholic. Mark's mother had inherited almost all responsibility at home. Mark grew up without a biblical example of what a husband's role should be.

Mark exhibited leadership and drive in sports, in the classroom, and at work; but when it came to personal relationships, he kicked into neutral. From his father he learned how much time and energy it took to ·be a leader in the business world but not in the home. After the wedding Mark focused on his

> *Susan never questioned the environment Mark would have to "leave" in order to set up a successful family of his own.*

career, not on Susan. He did not come home to relate. He came home to relax — just like his father.

It does not take a psychologist to see what this couple was headed for. Susan found herself having to take charge at home — just like her mother — and resenting every bit of it. What's more, she found herself exploding at Mark the same way her mother had so many times.

Susan's constant pleas that he be a leader echoed the cries his own mother had made — and brought the same result. Mark became more and more emotionally distant and spent longer hours at work to avoid the heat at home — just like his father. After all, he knew his role at work but was uncertain about his role at home.

In two short years this couple had reproduced the painful patterns their parents had taken years to perfect. All Susan's work to find someone "different" from her father had netted her someone just like him. Exhausted and unfulfilled, they were at the brink of divorce. Fortunately, they stopped arguing long enough to see a counselor and came to understand that you cannot short-cut the growth process God has set up. You must "leave" home in a healthy way if you are ever to attain a fulfilling relationship.

# How to "leave" home

While "leaving" home is a subject worthy of an entire book, there are several first steps any couple can take — no matter how long they have been married.

## Work at establishing a "peer relationship" with your parents

This isn't always easy. I think of Jana, for example — bright, intelligent, hard-working, forty years old, a college graduate, and the mother of three children. She was a responsible adult in every way — save one. In her parents' eyes, she was still the "little princess" that commanded all their love and attention. When Jana visited her parents, her father still wanted her to sit on his lap. He would hide candy for her to find and would talk to her at a school-girl level — not as a fully-functioning adult.

There is a part in all of us that loves to be babied. Just wait till our next cold or crisis. But couples who want to reach the high ground of intimacy are committed to growth. And genuine growth means graduating from childlike ways of responding to others — even to our parents.

If a friend called and asked Jana to do something, she would make a decision based on what was best for her and her family. That's healthy. But when her parents called, she would always cave in and let them set her schedule — even when it greatly inconvenienced the rest of the family.

It is hard to break patterns from the past. In most Christian homes, parents rightfully (and biblically) start their relationships with a vertical power structure. Dad and Mom are on top, and the children are on the bottom. But in the healthiest homes, as the children grow older, the power base in the home tends to shift. By adulthood, there should be a horizontal sharing of power in the relationship — a side-by-side friendship with great respect given the parents and yet great responsibility and independence given the children. This does not deny honor to a parent — another command from Scripture — it affirms it. Shifting the power base merely recognizes that preteen children are called to "obey," whereas adult children are called to honor.

The power orientation of Jana's home

**"Leaving" home is a vital step.**

never changed as she grew up. She remained the baby even as she neared midlife. Without fully realizing it, her parents used their powerful positions to control and manipulate her.

If you asked them (as I did), they would tell you that every draining request for her time and energy were made out of love. But healthy love frees people to become all they can be; it does not make them slaves. Jana did not have the emotional strength and courage to confront the problem and bring a change in the relationship until her husband told her to make up her mind to either move back in with her parents or stay married to him.

Building a peer relationship with parents can begin with something as simple as going Dutch for dinner instead of having Mom and Dad pay. It can also mean saying no to them when appropriate, not equating every one of

> *Viewing ourselves at age five, eight, or twelve will bring back full-blown memories.*

your vacations with "a visit to the relatives," or simply asking them to talk with you on an adult level.

### Take a long, honest look at your past
Your past influences you. And your spouse sees that most acutely. But how do you begin to tackle the past?

An exercise we do with couples in counseling is to have them gather together as many old family photos as possible. Over a long afternoon or evening we discuss why the situations in the pictures were photographed. Take note of who was always in the pictures and who was usually left out. What memories, patterns, or emotions emerge as you view your life through the years. Viewing ourselves at age five, eight, or twelve will bring back full-blown memories. And therein lies a problem.

Memories access our emotions, and emotions trigger more feelings. We may be uncomfortable with this exercise because it can surface feelings we may have avoided for years. Perhaps we will see all over again how favored our sister was or how all the photos featured the athlete of the family, not the band member. Perhaps your father was never in the picture because he always held the camera or because he never took time to be with you.

Whatever the pictures reveal, the truth of John 8 needs to be your guide: "you will know the truth, and the truth will set you free" (v. 32). For those with a background full of hurt, it is only by honestly facing their past that they will ever be free from its control.

Hating abusive parents will not "overcome" them. Nor does ignoring them or their memory give us emotional breathing room. For-giveness, understanding, even compassion, is possible to those who honestly seek to see how the past can control the present.

For some, such a process may involve a skilled Christian counselor. The Scriptures tell us "to listen to advice and accept instruction, and in the end you will be wise" (Proverbs 19:20). You are not weak or foolish to seek help, and it may be necessary for those who have suffered sexual or physical abuse to receive counseling before taking any further steps toward intimacy.

### Be careful not to equate leaving home with simply doing the opposite of what your parents say
Sometimes doing the opposite can be profitable. There is a form of financial investing called "contrarian theory," which says that, when everyone else is selling, you buy, or, when everyone else is bailing out of a plunging market, you dive in.

In personal relationships, both two-year-olds and teenagers often adopt this strategy when dealing with parents. Saying, "Don't touch the stove!" to a two-year-old often entices him to do that very thing. "Clean up your room!" can cause a teenager to throw another layer of clothes on the floor. However, as adults, doing the opposite of what our parents say simply to establish our independence does not work.

Esau, the wayward twin of Jacob in the Old Testament, took such a tack. Esau knew Isaac's clear instructions concerning the marriage of his sons. They were to take wives from those in the land of Isaac's father, wives who believed in God and were of the household of faith (Genesis 26:3). Esau, however, desired to set up his own home in his own way. "Esau ... married Judith daughter of Beeri the Hittite, and also Basemath the daughter of Elon the Hittite [both pagan women]. They were a source of grief to Isaac and Rebekah" (v. 34).

Isaac and Rebekah are not alone in their

heartache. Many parents have a child whose quest for independence has meant tossing aside parental values for the sake of "launching out" on his or her own — like Andi, who saw her parents' counsel as intrusion, their values as obsolete. To be her own person she married a man they warned her against. He had been married three times before. When he divorced her to hunt for a fifth wife, she had two preschool children.

In a healthy peer relationship, we should evaluate our parents' counsel to see how it squares with Scripture and common sense — and honor their advice if we can. That makes for healthy "leaving" and joyous "cleaving."

## Further Reading

Gary Chapman. *Toward a Growing Marriage.* Chicago: Moody, 1979.

Frank B. Minirth, Brian Newman, and Robert Hemfelt. *Passages of Marriage.* Nashville: Oliver-Nelson, 1991.

Larry and Nordis Christenson. *The Christian Couple.* Minneapolis: Bethany House, 1977.

Walter Trobisch. *The Complete Works of Walter Trobisch.* Downers Grove, Ill.: InterVarsity, 1987.

# Falling in love

I remember the first time I fell in love. I was ripe for it. It was the summer before my junior year in high school. I had had girl friends, someone to walk to class or talk on the phone to till my parents threatened to bill me. But I had not been in love.

A family moved to town, and somehow I was enlisted to help them move in. Their daughter, who just had to be in college, was a leggy, fresh-faced, quick-smiling girl who loved to talk and listen and looked you right in the eyes, especially if she thought you were in college too. It emerged that we were the same age.

Fifteen. She would be a high school classmate.

## Smitten

The first time we shared a ride home from a church activity and held hands, I was smitten. What a boon to self-confidence! A girl everyone could see was a knockout was "going" with me! For days I could think of nothing or no one else. I doodled her name, found reasons to call her, wrote her notes, hung around with her.

The night we'd sat holding hands in the car for all of six or seven minutes was heavenly. That was better than any athletic success I'd ever had!

I was in love. How could anything be more beautiful, more perfect?

For me it was fun while it lasted, and remains a harmless memory. But here's the problem with my all-too-common story: *being in love* is not love.

## An act of will

Love is not a feeling or even a state of being. Cold and unromantic as this may sound, I am not "in love" with my wife. I love her. It's an act of the will. It's something I do. Love is a verb, not a noun.

That first time I fell in love, what or whom was I in love with? I thought I loved the girl. I didn't know the girl! She looked great, and she smiled a lot. I don't even know whether I liked what she said as much as that she said it to me. I was in love with being in love.

That wasn't the last time I fell in love. By the time I met my wife, I had learned little about avoiding infatuation. I did know this, however: it would pass. It always does. I'm happy to say that the crush, the rush, the warm fuzzies I felt for my wife were light years ahead of what I had ever felt for anyone before, but if they weren't, that would have been OK too. I wasn't about to marry someone with whom I was hopelessly in love, because that's not a good basis for marriage.

Though I dated my wife for less time than anyone else I had ever dated, and though we were engaged within a few months and married inside a year, ours was the most open and honest and probing relationship I had ever had. This was a woman I knew I would want to love even after I had no choice. You see, when you're in love, you have no say in the matter. Your head and heart tell you that you, among all men, have finally found that perfect vision of looks and personality and character. You think of her all the time, your heart races when you talk to her, you want to melt when you touch her.

You don't know her yet.

**Jerry Jenkins**

# A Sexuality Primer for Newlyweds

## *Brian and Deborah Newman*

Holly could not believe what was happening. Here she was on her honeymoon night, locking herself in the hotel bathroom on purpose.

Tim tapped on the door. "Holly, I'm sorry. Can you come out so we can talk?"

She pulled her robe tightly around herself and emerged, tears falling.

"I'm really sorry," Tim said. "I should have been more gentle. It's just that I was getting frustrated. It's been a long day. Let's just lie down and hold each other and unwind."

"I'm sorry too, Tim. I feel like a failure. I really want to have a good relationship. I didn't think it would hurt so bad."

## A journey

Tim and Holly endured what some couples experience on their honeymoons — and most couples experience at some point in their marriage. Marriage launches a journey of intimate sexual union. But no worthwhile journey is without challenging twists and turns. Some experience a bump immediately; for others the unexpected dips surface later. Learning how to love and excite each other sexually is part of developing intimacy in marriage.

Premarital preparation should include planning for the sexual union God designed for couples. Many couples feel so passionate about each other they assume that they will naturally have a blissful sexual experience. The truth is that achieving mutual satisfaction requires work, time, and patience. That's the beauty of it. When the sexual experience is

### About the authors

**Brian K. Newman**, D.Phil., *is the clinical director of inpatient services for the Minirth-Meier Clinic in Richardson, Texas. He was named to* Who's Who Among Human Services Professionals, *has spoken before many groups, and led training seminars in the use of the* Personal Fathering Profile. *He has coauthored several books, including* The Man Within. **Deborah R. Newman**, D.Phil., *practices at the Minirth-Meier Clinic in Richardson, Texas. She was named to* Who's Who Among Human Services Professionals *and is a frequent speaker. She and her husband Brian coauthored* Day by Day Love Is a Choice, Love Is a Choice Workbook, *and* Passages of Marriage (PUB). *She is also coauthor of* The Thin Disguise (PUB). *She and Brian have two children.*

seen as a journey that will include peaks and valleys, it helps maintain lifelong interest and satisfaction. From beginning to end, sexual intimacy is a dynamic, growing experience of learning how to please and love your partner.

Even if you have been married or sexually active for a long time, there may still be many things you do not know that keep you stalled at one of the bends in the journey of intimacy. Issues from your sexual past may become barriers to enjoying the full degree of intimacy God wants for you. Issues such as sexual abuse, rape, or a promiscuous lifestyle need to be acknowledged and addressed, because they affect beliefs about sex.

# Feelings of inadequacy

Many people suffer feelings of inadequacy about their sexual anatomy and fear that they will not be a good enough sexual partner because they do not have the right size or shape. In fact, however, sexual anatomies differ as much as facial characteristics. The psychological effect of holding a negative view of your body and sexuality can hinder you from enjoying all the pleasure God wants you to have. As you read about sexual anatomy, recognize characteristics about your body that you feel shame about. Several good guides to sexual anatomy are available (see "Further Reading"), and we recommend that couples study these — and their partners — carefully in order to become fully aware of each other's sexuality.

# Sexual physiology

Sexual arousal and release occur in four basic stages: desire, excitement, orgasm, and resolution.

## Desire

The first stage involves the most important sex organ, the brain. How you think and feel about sex affects your responsiveness. Inhibi-

tions you may have about your body or the pain you may have suffered from previous encounters will affect sexual desire and, thus, the other stages of sex. Also, any resentment you may hold against your partner will affect your interest in sex. If you experience a lack of desire for intimacy, you may consider discussing this with a counselor to discover the root of your inhibitions.

## Excitement

This is where the body begins to respond and prepare for intercourse. Stimulation in this stage is both sexual and psychological.

For the female the first sign of sexual excitement is vaginal lubrication; an erection is the most obvious sign for the male. Some equate the amount of lubrication with the woman's degree of sexual responsiveness. The truth is, however, that the amount of lubrication varies. The need for an outside lubricant should not be viewed as an inadequacy or as evidence of a lack of interest on the woman's part.

Another myth is that the presence of natural lubrication signals that a woman is ready for intercourse. A woman requires at least ten to fifteen minutes of sexual stimulation before she is ready to have an orgasm. The woman should signal the man when she is ready. A caring, loving husband will want to proceed only when it is most comfortable for his wife and should not feel that he will be able to sense this without input from her. Other female responses during the excitement phase vary also, so there is value in mutually studying and discussing them together.

Premature ejaculation may be a problem for some men. Ed Wheat's book *Intended For Pleasure* addresses this issue with exercises to help the man experience more control.

## Orgasm

When stimulation continues though the excitement stage and creates sexual tension, it peaks in what is called an orgasm. It lasts for only a few seconds and is followed by rapid relaxation. The orgasm itself consists of rapid, rhythmic contractions. Some describe an orgasm as soothing and relaxing, whereas others describe it as explosive and dramatic.

There are many myths surrounding orgasms. One is that a male will always know when the female's orgasm has occurred. In fact, he may be so caught up in his own experience that he does not recognize his wife's orgasm. It is not healthy for a wife to say she has had an orgasm or pretend to have an orgasm to make her husband feel adequate. A husband should not judge his sexual potency by his wife's orgasm. This leads to psychological or emotional pressure that may block her orgasm. It is best to be patient and understanding about each other's sexual pleasure.

Some believe that women should always have more than one orgasm. Though women are capable of multiple orgasms, whereas men are not, without a refractory period a woman may not desire to have more than one orgasm. This should not be considered abnormal.

It is thought that a woman should only have an orgasm during intercourse. Some estimate that as many as half of women will not experience orgasm during intercourse unless there is manual stimulation at the same time. A woman's orgasm does not have to occur during intercourse to be pleasurable and intimate.

Another myth is that mutual orgasm is the peak of sexual experience. Mutual orgasm can be exciting, but working toward this can take away the enjoyment and spontaneity of intimacy. In some cases the pressure to achieve mutual orgasm results in poor sexual experiences. Mutual orgasm should not be viewed as the ultimate sexual experience but, rather, as one stop on your journey to intimacy.

Women may consider doing the Kegel exercise to help them become more orgasmic. The exercise was named after the doctor who discovered that tensing and releasing the muscles that start and stop urination to help

> Plan for your honeymoon to include times of ▶
> learning to love each other.

women with bladder control problems also improved their enjoyment of sex. These are the same muscles that contract during orgasm. To identify where the muscles are, start and stop urination. After you have identified the muscles, you can do the exercise by contracting and releasing these muscles anytime or anywhere. The exercise should not hurt or become tiresome, if you are doing it correctly.

### Resolution

This is the period of return to the unaroused state. If there has been a considerable amount of excitement, but orgasm has not occurred, it will take longer to return to this state. The resolution period is a time where some couples enjoy holding each other or talking about their experience. It is an important part of sexual intimacy. It has been called "afterglow," where the couple enjoys the closeness and pleasure they have just experienced.

Along with a basic understanding of sexual function and anatomy, it is also helpful for couples to study positions for sexual intimacy. Choosing a position is up to the couple. There are no set patterns or standards, and it is important that both partners feel comfortable. A couple will probably find a position they enjoy most, but they might also enjoy experimenting with different positions.

# The honeymoon

Engaged couples should talk about their expectations for the honeymoon. Do not set yourself up for disappointment by thinking that this will be the most blissful moment of sexual pleasure of your lives. If that were true, what would you have to look forward to?

Your expectations should include a time of learning how to love each other in a sensuous and emotional way.

### Advance planning

Before our honeymoon we talked about how we would like things to go. We decided to spend the first night a short drive away from where we were married and near the airport so we could catch a plane the next day. We planned to check into our hotel, eat our dinner, relax, and talk about our special day. Then we planned to get ready for our lovemaking.

A few weeks before our wedding we also drove over to the hotel so that we could see what it looked like. Whatever you choose to do for your honeymoon, we recommend that you spend it where there is privacy and plenty of time for relaxation. Don't plan a long trip the first night together.

Another suggestion is to bring along lubrication. Many couples have sex frequently during their honeymoons, and plenty of lubrication is essential for pleasure. Most likely, manual stimulation guided by the female will be the most pleasing on the honeymoon.

Before the honeymoon, it is important for the woman to have a gynecological check-up. During this check-up she should discuss birth control methods and procedures. She could ask that her future husband be present to discuss birth control with the doctor, or the couple could have already decided what is best for them and have this confirmed by the doctor. A woman should be aware that she needs a pap smear and gynecological check-up annually, if she is not already doing so.

### Honeymoon cystitis

Janet was so mad! Here she was on her honeymoon in a beautiful Caribbean village, but instead of taking in the sights, she was visiting a foreign emergency room because of pain in her bladder. Janet's problem is common in the first year of marriage. The urethra may get bruised by thrusting during intercourse and infection sets in. The condition is characterized by blood in the urine, pain in the bladder, and pain during urination. It is treated with antibiotics. To best avoid this condition, it is helpful for women to urinate after intercourse. This flushes the area and helps prevent infection. Do not douche as this may further create an environment for the problem.

# Communicate

A couple may be married a number of years and not know what pleases each other. Do not be afraid to tell your partner what you feel — good and bad. The wife should tell the husband what feels good to her. And she should feel free to instruct him about where and how to touch her to be most pleasing. The husband should not feel as if he has to know this instinctively. Likewise, the husband should tell his wife what he enjoys most.

The wife should tell the husband when she is ready for intercourse. Remember a man can experience orgasm in two to three minutes after excitement. For women it takes at least ten to fifteen minutes. Don't build up resentments by enduring a pleasureless (or even painful) ritual. Sexual intimacy is a special part of your marriage relationship. You will not learn how to love and excite each other unless you communicate openly about your feelings.

Many couples wonder how often they should have sexual intercourse. Two to three times a week may be fine for many happily married couples, but others experience sex multiple times each day.

Some couples wonder whether they should tell their future mates about their sexual past. It is essential to inform a fiance of any sexually transmitted diseases, previous children, or abortions. Openness about your sexual past is helpful, but it is not necessary or good to go into details.

Lastly, educate yourself about sexual intimacy. There are several books and tapes

> *Our honeymoon was the most wonderful time of our lives.*

available that are not erotic or sexually suggestive. Both partners should read or listen to this material. Consult the "Further Reading" list for suggestions of books and tapes.

Our honeymoon was the most wonderful time of our lives. It was a week of learning how to love and excite each other, and to relax and grow more intimate. Our ensuing time has continued to be a growing and delightful experience. Our journey has met with twists and turns that increased our understanding of each other. Pregnancies, work stress, even control issues, have affected our sexual experience. We have made adjustments that in the long run have drawn us closer as a couple. Proverbs 5:18–19; Genesis 2:25, 26; and 1 Corinthians 7:3–5 have all encouraged us to develop a strong healthy sexual union. It is a special part of any marriage.

## Further Reading

James Dobson. *Dr. Dobson Answers Your Questions About Marriage and Sexuality.* Wheaton: Tyndale, 1986.

Mike Grace and Joyce Grace. *A Joyful Meeting: Sexuality in Marriage, Revised.* St. Paul, Minn.: Int. Marriage Encounter, 1981.

Frank Minirth et al. *Sex and the Christian Marriage.* Grand Rapids: Baker, 1988.

Ed Wheat and Gaye Wheat. *Intended for Pleasure, Revised.* Old Tappan, N.J.: Revell, 1981

## Tapes

*(available from Scriptural Counsel, Inc., 130 Spring St., Springdale, AR 72764)*

"Before the Wedding Night." Ed Wheat. 1982.

"Sex Techniques and Problems in Marriage." Ed Wheat. 1981

# Marriage in Urban America – God's Style

*Anthony T. Evans*

The disintegration of the family is the most devastating internal issue facing our nation in general and urban America in particular. Families touch every area of society; their strengths and weaknesses to a large degree determine the strengths and weaknesses of churches and communities. If there is weak male leadership in the church and in society, if children are rebellious in the home, the same will be true in schools and on the streets.

Foundational to strong families are strong marriages. Put another way, failed marriages cannot produce the unified, enduring families needed to support our troubled society. When children grow up in loveless homes, they don't learn the crucial lessons necessary to develop good self-images now and to build strong marriages for themselves later. When children see their fathers coercing submission from their mothers through fear and intimidation, they learn a warped definition of manhood and womanhood, which often results in poor behavior and communication. When a father abandons his family, a son learns that this is an option for him in the future, and a daughter learns to fear a similar desertion by the man she marries. These and far too many other situations like them are especially devastating in urban settings, where, coupled with many other problems, there is a massive destruction of the family.

If urban America is going to rebuild its communities morally, socially, and spiritually, it is going to have to begin by rebuilding families. To do that, marriages must function as God

## About the author

*Anthony T. Evans (Th.D., Dallas theological Seminary) is president and founder of The Urban Alternative, a teaching ministry targeted to urban America. He is also the senior pastor of Oak Cliff Bible Fellowship in Dallas.*

intended. That is particularly important for Christian marriages, because the church is the most potent force for community change. If the church is to be properly equipped to bring about that change, it needs to be central to building strong families. Christian marriages must be solid so that the family unit – and thereby the church – can do its job effectively.

> *The church is the most potent force for community change.*

## Maybe I do

Many men and women tell their biggest lie on their wedding day. He (or she) stands before a minister, family, and friends to commit his life to a partner and says, "I promise to love, honor, and cherish you in sickness and in health, for richer or poorer, for better or worse, for as long as we both shall live." Then, before long, he is divorced – or wishes he were.

Maybe you are one of those people in an unhappy marriage. You may sit in a pew every Sunday morning singing that your God is so high you can't get over Him, so low you can't get under Him, and so wide you can't get around Him – but back at home you and your spouse have agreed that even God can't put your marriage back together. What a contradiction! In fact, that's more than a contradiction – it's sinful. Given the fact that our own strength is limited, it's not hard to understand why marriages aren't surviving the pressures of the twentieth century. But we don't have to rely on our own finite powers. With Christ as our enabler, we can do all things through Christ who strengthens us (Philippians 4:13). When Paul wrote those encouraging words to the church at Philippi, he wasn't saying that he could fly on his own power if he chose to, but he was promising that everything Christ commanded him to do, Christ would enable him to accomplish.

If I had the athletic ability of Cecil Fielder, I could hit many home runs. If I had the musical ability of Mozart, I could create beautiful music. If I had the mind of Einstein, I could solve difficult equations. In other words, if I had the ability those men had, I could do what they did. That is what Paul was saying. Christ gave Paul the ability to do everything that He commanded. Because Christ commanded that marriages be permanent, each believer has the ability to accomplish God's will for marriage. The problems and challenges that marriage involves should cause us to implement and apply the power of God, not divorce our spouses.

I serve as chaplain for the NBA's Dallas Mavericks. One day I played basketball with the star forward Mark Aquirre (now with Detroit). When I play by myself I'm absolutely unstoppable. I can make any play and shoot any shot. But when I played one-on-one with Mark, I wasn't good anymore. My ability isn't tested when I play without opposition; the test of my ability is how good I am when the opposition steps in. When I went up to shoot with 6 foot 6 inches' worth of opposition in front of me, the true measure of my ability was revealed.

So it is with marriage. Conflicts shouldn't destroy the union; they should show the power of Christ within us. Because Christ never asks us to do what He has not already given us the ability to do, marital conflict can be the area in which we show the difference Christ makes.

I become discouraged when I see men shirk their responsibilities to marriage and family and use social issues as an excuse. Although problems such as racism, injustice, and unemployment are painfully accute, they are no more overwhelming than those our great-grandparents faced in slavery. Because of their faith in and obedience to God, they overcame seemingly insurmountable obstacles to give their children, grandchildren, and great-grandchildren a precious family heritage. We need to follow the tradition of our ancestors if

> *Each believer has the ability to accomplish God's will for marriage.*

> *Conflicts should show the power of Christ within us.*

we are going to withstand Satan's attack on the family. We can avoid divorce, but, like our ancestors, we need to rely on God's strength.

Did you ever notice that Satan never bothered Adam before Eve was created? As long as Adam was single Satan left him alone, but as soon as he was united with Eve the attack was on. Why? Because Satan's long-term goal is to destroy the whole human race, not just one man. Satan's attacks are focused on the husband-wife relationship, because by destroying that he destroys children as well. Making marriage work is a matter of spiritual warfare that involves defeating Satan in his attempt to overcome us, our families, and our communities.

# Making a mess of marriage

There is no area in which God's power needs to be more graphically demonstrated than in marriage. Today one out of every two marriages ends in divorce. Wife and child abuse is on the rise in families of every class and color. Nearly 60 percent of all black families are headed by single females—and that figure continues to climb. Compounding this tragedy is the fact that not only are the marriages of non-Christians being destroyed, but believers are streaming into divorce courts as well. For Christians to experience such defeat is an embarrassment to the kingdom of God and an insult to the Creator of marriage.

The Bible tells us that God has the power to do anything He wills. Although God is all-powerful, many Christians don't believe He can keep their homes together. Christians often don't recognize God's power to heal their hurts and repair the damage in their marriages

and families. Instead of running to God for for help, they accept defeat and sometimes adopt loose living because "everyone is doing it." It is not unusual to hear Christians excusing their immorality with statements such as, "But I'm only human." They have bought Satan's lie that failure in one's personal life and in one's marital life is to be expected. One woman summed up the contemporary attitude this way: "When I got married I was looking for an ideal, but marriage has become such an ordeal that I want a new deal."

In some Christian homes battle lines are drawn. Husbands are looking at their wives and saying, "If I hadn't married you, I'd be successful and important by now." And wives are looking at their husbands and saying, "If I hadn't married you, I wouldn't be stuck at home with four kids while you're out having a good time." Negative, selfish attitudes like those are bringing tension in many homes to an explosive level. The fact is, many people simply don't know how to be married. They have never studied God's instruction manual on marriage. The Bible provides clear guidelines for making good, stable marriages, but too many people are looking for directions in other places — and ruining their marriages in the process.

Many people subscribe to the popular version of love and marriage that begins when two young people fall in love — an emotional experience identified by chills, thrills, and butterflies in their stomachs. With eyes only for each other, the infatuated pair promise undying love and rush to the altar to pronounce their vows. Unfortunately, soon after they say "I do," they don't anymore. Their relationship looks as if the secretary of war married them instead of the justice of the peace. Divorce seems the only way to forge a truce.

I once came across an interesting illustration of the way marriages deteriorate over the years. The comments are those of a husband whose wife had caught a cold during the successive years of their marriage.

**Year 1** – *"Sugar dumpling, this cold is making you mighty uncomfortable. Won't you let your lover boy take his baby to the doctor to get rid of that nasty cough?"*
**Year 2** – *"Darling, that cold seems to be getting worse. Call Dr. Miller."*
**Year 3** – *"You'd better lie down, dear, and rest with that cold before the baby wakes up."*
**Year 4** – *"Be sensible now and take care of that cold before it gets any worse."*
**Year 5** – *"You'll be all right. Just take some aspirin. By the way, how about ironing these pants for me?"*
**Year 6** – *"Would you do something about that cough, instead of barking like a seal?"*
**Year 7** – *"Woman, do something about that cold before you give me pneumonia!"*

Husbands aren't the only ones guilty of the kind of thing in that illustration. When the honeymoon is over, both husbands and wives often, consciously or unconsciously, begin to change their behavior toward their spouses.

How can things fall apart a week after the honeymoon? And why do marriages break down after ten, fifteen, and even twenty-five years? The root cause is the failure to understand God's design and purpose in marriage. Genesis 2 provides instruction in marriage God's style.

# Mankind and marriage

Genesis 2 contains the detailed account of God's creation of mankind and marriage. In this dual event God provided a model of things to come. The earthly marriage of Adam and Eve in the past is an illustration of Christ's union with the church in the future (Ephesians 5:32). To help us understand this heavenly mystery, God gave us marriage to demonstrate what it is going to be like when we gather at the second coming of Christ and are united with Him. In this life men and women are married to one another, but when we are gathered together in heaven, there will be no marriage between husbands and wives (Mark 12:25). Instead, every member of the church will be wed to Christ.

Knowing that marriage is a model of the eternal union of the believer and Christ in heaven gives us a second reason for improving the quality of our marriages. Everyone agrees that a good marriage is more pleasant and beneficial than an unhappy one. But equally important, a good marriage is a model for the heavenly union of God with the believer. In other words, your marriage might win someone to Christ – or cause him to turn away from God's offer of salvation. That in itself should be reason enough for us to learn to be godly mates and live the abundant life in the context of a Christian marriage.

As we review the details of the first union of a man and woman, a great deal can be learned about what God had in mind when He created marriage. When God made man, three Persons were involved – the Father, Son, and Holy Spirit. They created man in their image, imparting their nature to him so that man in a sense had their nature. Before the Fall, Adam was able to walk and talk with God in the way two friends might do on a summer evening. During those talks God made His will clear to Adam in the garden and appointed him to be its overseer, a pleasant job in a fertile garden where there were no weeds, no destructive insects, and no droughts. Then God gave Adam instructions to enjoy all the fruit of the garden, with one exception: the fruit of the tree of the knowledge of good and evil. God gave Adam lessons about work and following instructions even before He created a mate for him.

The first lesson we can draw from this is a warning for single women. Women, when you consider a man for marriage, remember that before God gave Adam a wife He gave him responsibility. It's clear from the order in which these events took place that God wants a husband to work and to be responsible. That shows us that a lazy and irresponsible man –

no matter how handsome — is not a good choice. Marriage won't make him a responsible provider and leader. God wants the best for each of His daughters, so consider your choice of a mate carefully, and follow God's standard by marrying only a man who demonstrates while he is single that he can and will take care of you in marriage.

The second lesson, based on verses 16 and 17, indicates why so many marriages break up. "The Lord God commanded the man, saying, 'From any tree of the garden you may eat freely; but from the tree of the knowledge of good and evil you shall not eat, for in the day that you eat from it you shall surely die'" (NASB). God gave Adam work to do in the garden, and with those instructions He prepared Adam to live there. That conversation with Adam points us to the weakness in most homes: most husbands don't know what God has said. If you ask the average man what God has said about his responsibility to his wife, to his children, and to himself as the head of the home, he will either admit he doesn't know or give an answer that demonstrates he doesn't know. And instead of looking to God for answers, these husbands either listen to their friends on the corner or adopt standards from TV. Because they don't know God well enough, they base their personal identities on clothes, cars, relationships with women, and money. That reduces manhood to a primitive level, which suggests that manhood is nothing more than the ability to put on one's pants correctly.

God's definition of manhood is the ability to put divine truth into action at home and on the job. Any man can look good on the outside, but unless he knows and follows the commands of God, he cannot do anything inside or outside his home for the kingdom.

# Making a mate for man

It is important for us to recognize that God didn't bring a woman into Adam's life until he had a job and divine insight. Only when Adam

> *God wants your marriage to succeed.*

met those two requirements was he ready for marriage, and only then did God provide a mate for him. In verse 18 God says, "It is not good for the man to be alone; I will make a helper suitable for him" (NASB). Creating a mate for Adam was God's idea, not Adam's. That reminds us that all of God's plans, every aspect of every design, are perfect. If you're in a bad marriage, it's not because God had a bad idea. Marriage is ideal; it's the people who are bound together in the relationship who make it good or bad. (If you're in a difficult relationship, don't let this discourage you. God wants your marriage to succeed and is ready to help you and your mate as soon as you are willing to do things His way.)

God brought to a responsible, godly man a woman who was to be his helper. The word *helper* means one who is brought alongside to assist. Throughout the Bible women were given one basic responsibility — to help. After Eve plucked the forbidden fruit and shared it with Adam, God sought out Adam. God put the burden of the responsibility for the home on Adam, not Eve. Woman was created to come alongside man to assist him; she was never meant to bear the burden of responsibility for the home and family. Whenever a husband shifts that burden over to his wife, he makes a serious mistake. Generally speaking, that gives the wife a level of responsibility that God never planned for her to have. God intended — and still intends — for the husband to carry the weight of the responsibility of the home. We see the results of failure to follow God's direction in black households where women are forced to be mother/father and breadwinner because there is no husband present. The destructiveness of this arrangement is obvious from the crisis in which the black family is trapped. God made man to head the

**God made man to head the household.**

household, and no other plan devised by man is a good substitute for God's plan.

I can hear some of you complaining, "You sure are hard on men." You're right. But that's only because men are to be the leaders. As leaders, men must be willing to bear the brunt of the burden for marriage in the same way that Adam had to when God came looking for him in the garden, even though it was Eve who opened the door to sin after her dialogue with Satan (Genesis 3:1–6).

That does not absolve women, however, from responsibility. Did you know that God did not command women to love their husbands? God *expects* wives to love their husbands and expects older women to teach younger women how to love their husbands (Titus 2:3–4), but His command is for women to *respect* their husbands (Ephesians 5:33). Because men have strong egos, they have a great need for recognition. Just as women have a need to be loved, men have a need to be respected. That is why Peter tells wives not to use the tongue to turn around disobedient husbands but rather to use reverence (1 Peter 3:1–2). A man wants to feel like a king, so when his wife gives him that respect, he is more likely to keep his wife happy so that she can keep him feeling like a king. That is why Paul teaches that husbands must love their wives and wives must loves their husbands. If each spouse follows the command given to them, the pair will become the unit God intended.

The greatest thing a wife can do for her husband is to follow Sarah's example. Sarah called Abraham "lord," recognizing his position as head of the household and as a demonstration of sincere respect (1 Peter 3:6). That pleased Abraham, but, more important, it pleased God. In fact, God honored Sarah so much that He closed the wombs of the women of a whole household in order to protect her (Genesis 20:18).

Respect is particularly needed by men in the black community. Often black males don't receive respect at their jobs. In a society where many black men are still looked at as "boy" no matter what their age, there needs to be a place they can go and know they are respected. That place should be the home. Because their dignity is often diminished outside the home, black men in particular need their wives to respect them in the home.

The church has historically played a critical role in the black community. A man could be known as "boy" all day in the cotton fields, but on Sunday he became Deacon Jones. The church gave him dignity. That is why being a preacher is significant in the black community. It has been and still is (although to a lesser extent) the highest position of dignity in the black community.

Demonstrating respect involves submission. I know that submission is an unpopular word. But when women understand submission from a biblical perspective, they will see that it is a positive force to accomplish good, not a negative force to subject them to an inferior status. The Greek word for submission, *hupotosso,* means to place oneself under the authority of another. That does not involve coercion but rather a willingness to take who and what God made you and submit it to the authority of another. Biblical submission in marriage reflects a willingness to use your talents, opportunities, and gifts to achieve the goals established jointly for the good of your marriage.

The perfect illustration of submission is Jesus Christ Himself, who "although He existed in the form of God, did not regard equality with God a thing to be grasped, but emptied Himself, taking the form of a bond-servant, and being made in the likeness of men. And being found in appearance as a man, He humbled Himself by becoming obedient to the point of death, even death on a cross" (Philippians 2:6–8, NASB). Although Jesus was equal with God, He put aside the independent use of

His attributes and placed Himself under the absolute authority of His Father for the good of the redemption plan for mankind. At no point did Jesus stop being equal with the Father. That's clear from His miracles and claims to deity. But He did submit them to His Father so that the goal of providing salvation could be achieved. If Christ had not been willing to submit, there could be no salvation for mankind.

We profited by Christ's submission, but was that submission a losing proposition for Christ? Philippians 2:9–10 says, "Therefore also God highly exalted Him, and bestowed on Him the name which is above every name, that at the name of Jesus every knee should bow, of those who are in heaven, and on earth, and under the earth" (NASB).

The point is that the wife must reverence her husband, and the husband must exalt his wife in love so that they mutually meet the needs of one another for the good of the whole relationship. Whether your mate is supportive of you in respect or love or is totally unsupportive, be the mate God designed you to be. You won't be sorry.

The mate God gave you was created to fit together with you in marriage. When God created Adam, He knew that the man needed a partner, because he was lonely and in need of someone similar to himself. Genesis 2:18 says God decided to make "a helper suitable for him." A suitable helper was one who made man complete, one that helped him fulfill all God intended him to be. God made woman to complete man. That tells us that man alone could not be all that God wanted him to be. The woman was necessary to complete him and enable him to fulfill the role God gave him. Whenever a man says, "I have achieved so much," he ought always to include, "because at home I have someone who has enabled me to." He needs to acknowledge the part his wife has played and

*Be the mate God designed you to be.*

> *Adam needed a helpmate. He couldn't make it by himself.*

make sure he climbs no rung of the ladder without taking his helper along to be with him.

# Readying man for marriage

In order to prepare the first man for marriage, God began to lead Adam toward the idea that he needed companionship. To help him discover that need, God told Adam to name the animals. When Adam began naming the animals he saw that for every ram there was a ewe, and for every rooster there was a hen. For all of the world's animals there were corresponding mates, but for the man there was no one who could fulfill his needs.

There is a tremendously important lesson for us here, so I'd like to address the women first, then the men. Women, if you are single and dating a man who never says he *needs* you, who never lets you know he knows he needs your help through life, think twice before you marry him. If he ever tells you in the heat of anger, "I don't need you," watch out. The whole point of creating Eve was that Adam needed a helpmate. He couldn't make it by himself, and that is still God's plan.

Men, do you know what that means to you? Manhood is not the ability to make it without a woman, and it's not the ability to have sex with every attractive woman you meet, either. In the first case, God planned for each man to be made complete through marriage to a *specific* woman. And in the second case, no man should be proud of himself or believe he is more masculine because he is sexually active – every animal God created is capable of that. Genuine manhood is the ability to see your need for a specific helpmate and to com-

mit the rest of you life to her alone. Monogamy – dedicating yourself in marriage to one woman – and lifetime commitment are basic to happy marriages as well as to the growth and development of men. Recognizing that isn't a sign of weakness. It's just the opposite – a sure sign of strength.

# Complementing

In light of God's plan for wholeness in marriage, one of the most uninformed statements that a husband or wife can make is, "We are not compatible." Sometimes it's expressed, "We don't have anything in common," or, "We are as different as night and day." Of course you are – if both of you were the same, one of you would be unnecessary! The reason you need each other is because you're different. One likes coffee; the other likes tea. One goes to bed early; the other stays up late. One of the sweetest blessings God has given me is a woman who has a personality totally different from mine. I'm an outgoing, exuberant, public personality whereas my wife is sedate and serene. We are different, and that is according to God's plan. Because our personalities are in contrast, when I'm too outgoing, her reserve pulls me back, and when she is too reserved, my enthusiasm pulls her forward. Occasionally this causes friction because I become a little irritated when she's too sedate, and she becomes a little ruffled when I'm too outgoing. But the issue is not our differences; we're supposed to be different. The issue is making those God-given differences work *for* us instead of *against* us.

Since sin entered the world, we have lost our understanding of how to make differences complement one another. If we would simply look for what God is trying to teach us through the mate He has given us, we would be growing rather than griping. You may say, "I don't believe God gave me my mate." It's too late for that conclusion! God will teach you how to love and learn from the one you're

> *God made marriage, and He can make it work.*

with, anyway. You and your mate don't have any problems as a result of differences that cannot be solved by applying God's guidelines for making them complementary rather than conflicting.

## A union of three

In marriage, we experience a glimpse of the Trinity. The Trinity is made up of three coequal Persons who are One: God the Father, God the Son, and God the Holy spirit. Marriage is an earthly replica of this divine Trinity — three persons who are one: a man, a woman, and the Lord. You cannot leave God at the altar and expect to have a happy marriage. God wants to join you in your home, instructing you in how to make a house a real home. Christ's resurrection power operating in your life is the only power that can save your life, your marriage, and your home. When Christ arose from the dead, He gave mankind access to the power of His resurrection. That power can enable you and your mate to live together, love one another, trust each other, and share life with one another until death parts you. God alone has given mankind the ability to do that.

You may say, "Wait a minute. What about the divorce rate? What about all the broken homes?" The divorce figures in the United States are astronomical and the number of broken homes heartbreaking. The fact is that people don't know God. The problems in these homes are ultimately a reflection of men's and women's estrangement from God. But there is good news. God sent His Son Jesus Christ to earth to die on the cross as a substitute for mankind's sin. Whenever men or women respond to Christ in faith, trusting Him alone as Savior, He not only forgives them but empowers them to live new resurrection lives as they live in obedience to Him.

It's this power of God operating in your life that makes marriage work. If you haven't made that personal decision to turn the totality of your life over to Jesus Christ, you don't have that resurrection power. But you can have it if you believe Christ rose from the dead to give you power to be the kind of husband or wife that He has called you to be. When you give Him your life, then you will experience marriage as God planned it. God made marriage, and He can make it work. I challenge you to commit yourselves to God. Let Him remake your marriage into a marriage God's style.

This chapter is taken from *Marriage God's Style* (Chicago: Moody, 1988).

### Further Reading

George Barna. *The Future of the American Family.* Chicago: Moody, 1993.

Anthony T. Evans. *America's Only Hope: Impacting Society in the '90s.* Chicago: Moody, 1990.

H. Norman Wright. *Holding On to Romance.* Ventura, Calif.: Regal, 1992.

# What Makes a Home "Christian"?

*Kenneth and Elizabeth Gangel*

Discipleship and leadership begin at home. Both Old and New Testament Scriptures indicate that prospective church leaders must have proved records of godliness within their families before they qualify for service in the church. There are those who dismiss the recent evangelical emphasis on the family as faddism, but a strong emphasis on the home has been characteristic of believers since the first century.

The typical family no longer resembles two-parent-two-kid stereotypes. The single adult population is burgeoning, and the number of unmarried men and women living together is in the millions worldwide.

But what *may* happen is primarily of interest to those who study sociology and anthropology. Biblical Christians concern themselves with what *ought to be,* because they base their lives on God's unchanging Word and unwavering standards. The family may be different, but it is not dead. Sin may stain its potential, but the Savior can salvage its purpose.

## Biblical people

Christian homes are created by biblical people. We can discern a clear pattern — biblical *people* become biblical *partners,* who can then become biblical *parents.* Only believing people can enter Christian marriage, otherwise the marriage is not Christian. And the process requires us to become partners before we become parents.

### About the authors

**Kenneth Gangel**, Ph.D., is vice president of academic affairs and professor of education at Dallas Theological Seminary. His books include The Family First *(BMH),* The Gospel and the Gay *(Nelson), and* Christian Education *(Moody). He and his wife,* **Elizabeth Gangel,** *coauthored* Building a Christian Family *(Moody). Elizabeth taught elementary school for fifteen years and operated a preschool for five. The Gangels have two children.*

What kind of people is God seeking to create and sustain Christian homes in the frenetic final years of this century?

One of the most important aspects of the Christian home is an unselfish attitude of loving and giving. Marriage is not like a coat one puts on but, rather, like a flower that grows. Its life depends on the healthy love of each partner for the other and on creative self-giving in which patience, kindness, and gentleness produce growth in both partners. False love tries to find the perfect person on latch on to. True love commits itself to another despite the flaws in his or her character.

In Philippians 1:9–10, Paul writes, "that your love may abound more and more in knowledge and depth of insight, so that you may be able to discern what is best and may be pure and blameless until the day of Christ." He speaks of spiritual love to Christ and the church, but the same holds true of marital love between a husband and wife. Popular songs would have us believe that romantic love can be sustained endlessly, but that is a juvenile myth. Love must grow and be protected in a marriage relationship. As Larry Christenson has said, it is not the love that sustains the marriage, but the marriage that sustains the love.

*The Living Bible* rendition of 1 Corinthians 13 offers some standards of life-long love, and the following "love test" is based on that passage. How does your love measure up?

*Love is a responsiveness to the total self of the one loved.*

*Love is a feeling of pleasure but also of reverence.*

*Love is a quality of self-giving.*

*Love is a willingness to take responsibility as well as to accept joy.*

*Love is an unusual joy in the company of the other and pain in separation.*

*Love is a mutual joy and enjoyment of each other without need of physical expression.*

*Love is a protective attitude evidenced by care for the other person.*

*Love is a feeling of longing for the loved one.*

*Love is an inner knowledge that you understand the loved one well.*

*Love is a growing consistence and maturity and stability.*

When difficulties come in a marriage relationship (and they always do), we are tempted to retreat into selfishness, to seek and protect

> *It is not the love that sustains the marriage, but the marriage that sustains the love.*

our own happiness. But biblical people ask the ultimate question: "What does God want us to do?" The Holy Spirit witnesses inwardly about our salvation, and He can certainly affirm God's will regarding family decisions and marriage relationships. Biblical people don't look first to the sociologists or the psychologists – they look to the Father.

# Biblical purpose

Have you ever wondered why God created marriage in the first place? Has God designed any priorities for the relationship? What does the pastor mean when he says, "Whom God hath joined together, let no man put asunder"? We not only believe God has given us biblical purposes for marriage but that there may even be an order of importance that, if violated, could account for some of the family problems we see all around us.

### Complete companionship

Companionship stands as the primary purpose of marriage. In spite of all the wonderful things God had created in the Garden of Eden, Adam lived in inadequacy. None of the animals, as splendid as they must have been before the Fall, could provide a fitting companion for the man. At that point the Lord created the first family. Here's how the *Amplified Bible* captures the impact of Genesis 2:18: "Now the Lord God said, It is not good (sufficient, satisfactory) that the man should be alone; I'll make him a helper meet (suitable, adaptable, completing) for him."

The strategic role of fellowship in marriage provides the bull's-eye on the family target.

# Model parents

We were playing a game of cards with our school-aged children. One of them looked at the hand I had dealt him, threw a tantrum, and walked away from the game. I made that little person come back, pick up his hand, and play it out. He needed to learn about winning with whatever hand he'd been dealt – that's an important lesson for life. Some people are dealt a pretty lousy hand. Their parents are a mess and their lives are damaged. Other folks are dealt a pretty good hand, and still others are dealt a wonderful one. I am writing to testify to the wonderful "hand" I was dealt by my parents.

**Faith**

My parents had a simple, private faith in Christ. They believed in His salvation, and they put Christian principles into operation in our family as best they knew how. We didn't go to church, but we were taught that God does not live in a churchshaped box to be visited like a sick relative on Sunday. Our parents showed us a present-tense God who would hear our prayers, treat us kindly, and hold us accountable to them and to Him at the end of the day. They gave us what they knew, and for me, it was enough to lay a foundation for faith and make it easy for me to accept Christ when I was presented with the gospel.

**Jill Briscoe**

> *Companionship stands as the primary purpose of marriage.*

Everything else is secondary. Everything else takes a lower place of esteem, because if companionship isn't working, the family isn't working.

**Sexual fulfillment**

The early chapters of Genesis contain no account of the sexual attitudes and activities of Adam and Eve. But throughout the pages of Scripture it seems clear that in Christian marriage physical sharing flows from spiritual sharing. The mutual responsibilities of husband and wife are obvious in Scripture:
*The husband should fulfill his marital duty to his wife, and likewise the wife to her husband. The wife's body does not belong to her alone but also to her husband. In the same way, the husband's body does not belong to him alone but also to his wife. Do not deprive each other except by mutual consent and for a time, so that you may devote yourselves to prayer. Then come together again so that Satan will not tempt you because of your lack of self-control.* (1 Corinthians 7:3–5)

Sexual fulfillment in marriage is a part of God's design and is never to be used as a ploy or tool of manipulation. Such "defrauding" opens our lives to temptation by Satan. Biblical people practicing biblical purposes understand the meaning of Hebrews 13:4: "Marriage should be honored by all, and the marriage bed kept pure, for God will judge the adulterer and all the sexually immoral."

**Planned parenthood**

How interesting that in a perverted society a good expression like *planned parenthood* should take on negative connotations and get dragged into the horrors of abortion. The crowning glory of children in marriage pro-

vides the theme for a song of praise often sung in the pages of Holy Scripture. In two consecutive psalms (127 and 128) we learn that children are a reward from the Lord; they will be "like olive shoots" around the family table. The command to "be fruitful and increase in number and fill the earth" came to both Adam and Noah. God's miracle of procreation continues as a mystery of His grace to expectant parents.

But this purpose cannot be filled by every parent. In some cases God wills parents to be childless, and we must not pass judgment on His will. What seems clear in Scripture is that in most families God designs people to be loving partners and then loving parents.

**Family unit**

Shortly before his death Moses reiterated the law for his nation and emphasized their responsibility as parents (Deuteronomy 6:4–25). The home has always been God's primary place of nurture and growth. In designing marriage the heavenly Father created a place where children could be nurtured in holy wisdom and faith. God doesn't give children to school systems or church congregations but to families. The very process of reproduction stamps on parents the responsibility to nurture their children through growth and development until they become adults and the cycle begins all over again.

**Church symbolism**

Certainly the primary metaphor for the church in the New Testament centers in the human body (Romans 12; 1 Corinthians 12). But in the well-known verses from Ephesians 5, Paul draws a comparison between the husband-wife relationship and Christ and His church. What is the church like? Like a family. How do we understand what the church is supposed to do? We watch godly husbands and wives relating to each other and to their children, and we learn what God intends in the church.

**Christian families can demonstrate their faith publicly.**

Some Christian families become the only "church" unsaved neighbors ever see. As they watch a husband nourishing and cherishing his family they learn something about the way the Lord nourishes and cherishes the church. As they see a wife respond in submission, and children treat their parents with respect, honoring them with obedience, they learn how God's people respond to the Lord of the church. Your family is a microcosmic demonstration of the Body of Christ in the world.

We recall often a time when our children were very small and we were eating in a restaurant. Another couple, sitting at a nearby table, went unnoticed until they got up to leave and stopped as they walked by our table. They commented about the behavior of our children, calling it a pleasant exception to what they commonly saw in restaurants.

After the initial shock, we took note of the fact that someone watches and observes the relationships in our family every time we're in public. We were communicating without even being aware of it.

As anyone would, we experienced a slight case of pride that we were such wonderful parents. But God showed us that we were just being His people in the world, demonstrating in living color what the Lord can do in and through His church.

> *Some Christian families become the only "church" unsaved neighbors ever see.*

# Biblical principles

Marriage is for adults only. Part of being biblical people ready to embark on a biblical purpose means maintaining a level of maturity ready to handle the different tasks of family relationships and apply biblical principles of those relationships. One could make an endless list of biblical principles for marriage and family living, but let us name just two.

## Monogamy

What are we to make of Old Testament passages telling us that David and others had multiple wives and yet were greatly loved and blessed of God? Indeed, David is called a man after God's own heart! In looking at the flow of God's truth through both Old and New Testaments we see the initial design as God created it — one man and one woman in the Garden. Then sin entered the world, and all kinds of aberrations became common in human experience. In speaking to the Greeks about idolatry Paul said, "in the past God overlooked such ignorance, but now he commands all people everywhere to repent" (Acts 17:30). As the New Testament opens and the church takes form, it almost seems as though God is starting again with His plan for Christian families. Joseph and Mary offer the purity and beauty of monogamous godly marriage, the spiritual Adam and Eve of the New Covenant. In the midst of the paganism of Graeco-Roman culture, the church stands out as committed to several basic and absolute truths — among them is the purity of the marriage relationship.

## Fidelity

What ever happened to "till death us do part"? In Romans 7 Paul uses that concept as an illustration of the role of the law in Christian living. His illustration reminds us of the finality of the marriage bond: "For example, by law a married woman is bound to her husband as long as he is alive, but if her husband dies, she is released from the law of marriage" (Romans 7:2). Sometimes we talk about marriage being "eternal," but that is not a biblical concept. In heaven there is no marriage (Matthew 22:30) — the termination is a part of God's plan.

This chapter is taken from *Building a Christian Family* (Chicago: Moody, 1987).

### Further Reading

Larry Christenson. *The Christian Family.* Minneapolis: Bethany House, 1970.

Kenneth and Elizabeth Gangel. *Building a Christian Family.* Chicago: Moody, 1987.

Gordon MacDonald. *There's No Place Like Home.* Wheaton: Tyndale, 1990.

Edith Schaeffer. *What is a Family?* Tarytown, N.Y.: Revell, 1982.

# PARENTS AS ROLE MODELS

# Love is Spelled T-I-M-E

## *Josh McDowell*

A little over thirteen years ago, I learned something about time management from my two-and-a-half-year-old son, Sean, and my wife, Dottie. The lesson they taught me is permanently engraved on my mind, and it happened while I was in my study, busily engaged in one of several projects that I usually have going at once. In this case I was right in the middle of a chapter for a new book when in wandered Sean.

"Want to play, Daddy," he chirped expectantly.

As an "experienced" parent (we had already been through the two-year-old stage with Kelly) I should have realized that basically, Sean just wanted a hug, a pat, and a minute or two to show me the new ball he was carrying. But I was working on an important chapter and I felt that I just didn't have even two minutes right then.

"Son, how about a little later? I'm right in the middle of a chapter."

Sean didn't know what a "chapter" was, but he got the message. Daddy was busy and he would have to leave now. He trotted off without complaining, and I returned to my manuscript. But my relief was short-lived. In a minute or two Dottie came in and sat down for a "little chat." My wife never tries to nail me; she has much gentler — and more effective — methods.

"Honey, Sean just told me you were too busy to play with him. I know that this book is important, but I'd like to point something out."

"What is that?" I asked a bit impatiently because now my wife was keeping me from my all-important project.

"Honey, I think you have to realize that you are always going to have contracts and you

## *About the author*

*Josh McDowell, Ph.D., is founder and president of Josh McDowell Ministry in Dallas, Texas, and promoter of the "Why Wait" campaign. He is the author of many books, including* Answers to Tough Questions, Evidence That Demands a Verdict, More Evidence That Demands a Verdict, The Myths of Sex Education, The Secret of Loving, *and* The Resurrection Factor *(Here's Life). He has also written* Find the Treasure in You *and* Josh McDowell's Easy Guide *(Tyndale), as well as* How to Help Your Child Say "No" to Sexual Pressure *and* Love, Dad *(Word).*

*You can't schedule
a small child
the way you schedule
a committee meeting.*

are always going to have deadlines. Your whole life you will be writing and doing other projects, but you're not always going to have a two-year-old son who wants to sit on your lap and ask you questions and show you his new ball."

"Honey, I think I hear what you're saying and you make a lot of sense as usual. But right now I've got to get through with this chapter."

"All right, Josh, but please think about it. You know, if we spend time with our kids now, they'll spend time with us later."

## A child is two only once

I did think about it. And the more I thought the more Dottie's gentle words were like a knife slicing into the core. She was right. I'd always have deadlines. There would always be contracts to fulfill, phone calls to answer, people to see, trips to take. But my boy would be two only once, and soon that year would be gone and then he would be three, and four, and five — and would I have any more time for him *then*?

I knew what the answer would be if I didn't change my ways. Quietly, without any big speeches or fanfare, I made my decision. Ever since, I have tried to place my children ahead of contracts, deadlines, and the clamor of a world that wants me to get back "ASAP." Since then I have had an understanding with publishers that my family and my children must come first. If not, I would have to be constantly telling my child that "a book is more important than you are."

As I learned with my own two-year-old, you can't schedule a small child the way you schedule a committee meeting, or a doctor's appointment. The attention span of a small child is very, very short. And when you are willing to be available according to the child's agenda, you give the child permission to have that short attention span.

Often a child will want to play a game or whatever, but after a few minutes he wants to do something else. He may wander off to play with his own toys or see if it's time for Sesame Street.

I sometimes talk to parents who get frustrated, because their young children don't want to "finish what we start." I try to help them understand that it's OK to leave a game unfinished or to leave play undone. Play isn't something you finish, it's something you and your child enjoy.

Yes, all this takes patience. In our seminars, Dick Day often likes to point out that we parents just can't wait for our children to do certain things because we get impatient. We jump in and finish their prayer for them, or we take the hammer or saw away saying, "Here, let me help you."

The chief hallmark of being able to enter into a child's agenda is patience. We must be able to wait them out, hear them out, let them try it themselves, and if they don't quite get it right or don't finish it, we don't worry about it.

I believe it was John Wesley who said, "If you don't know how to teach children, then get children's tracts and read them until you know how to teach children."

All John Wesley was saying is that if you want to deal with a child, you must learn how the child thinks and be able to get on the child's

*Play isn't something you
finish, it's something
you and your child
enjoy.*

wave length. Then you can start to see life through his eyes, according to his agenda, and that's when you will start to communicate.

## Teens need time, too

Fortunately, the lesson I learned when Sean was two has stuck with me over the years. Just recently, I was in the middle of writing a children's book in our favorite vacation retreat in Mexico, right on the coast of Baja. One morning I was "on a roll" with the ideas really flowing when Kelly, my sixteen-year-old, walked in and said, "Daddy, would you take me to get my nails done?"

My first thought was, *Man, this is the last thing I need right now.*

My second thought was, *Josh, practice what you preach about being available.*

My third thought was, *Lord, give me a joyful spirit.*

You see, I could have looked glum and said impatiently, "OK, I'll go." But then I might as well have given her the money for a cab and sent her on by herself.

Instead I said, "Honey, I'll be glad to. I'll be right with you."

I folded up my chapter, hoping that later I could "catch the roll" I had been on, and with joy I took my daughter to get her nails done. It wasn't just a matter of being her personal taxi driver to get her somewhere. What she really wanted was time with me, and we did have a good talk on the way down and back.

Kelly has thanked me at least three or four times since that day. Why? Because my actions said to her, "Honey, you are of such tremendous worth to me that I'm willing to interrupt what I'm doing, no matter how important it might be, and spend some time with you."

That's what acceptance and appreciation are really all about! They just aren't buzz words to throw around when you are trying to sound like a profound parent. Acceptance and appreciation tell the child that he or she is

> *God loves your children through you, but if you're not available, how can He love them?*

of tremendous worth. And I can only express my acceptance and appreciation through being affectionate — and *available.*

## What availability says

When we're available to our children it says, "You are important." And when we're not available it says, "Oh, yes, I love you, but other things still come ahead of you. You are not *really* that important."

To help dads, in particular, internalize this concept, I will often call a man out of a parent seminar audience and present the following situation:

> Suppose you are a good friend of the boss at your company. It's Friday and you have a need to see him on short notice, so you go over to his office and ask his secretary if you could possibly talk to him for just a few minutes. But the secretary tells you, "I'm sorry, but he's totally booked up until next week on Tuesday — you'll have to come back."
>
> Because you really need to see your boss now, you tell the secretary, "Look, I won't take much of his time. Please just tell him I really need to see him, it'll only take a minute."
>
> And then suppose the secretary tries to call your boss and tell him you're there. She mentions your name, but all she hears back is, "I'm sorry — I simply can't see him now. He'll have to come back next Tuesday."

At this point, I ask my volunteer from the audience the key question: "If this happened to you, how would you feel?"

Invariably, the man replies that he would feel less important or not very important at all. He would begin to think, *If only I were a vice president or somebody who really mattered around here. . . .* The bottom line is that he would go away thinking, *I'm not important enough.*

And then I simply point out to everyone in the room: "That's exactly how your child feels when you tell him the equivalent of, 'Sorry, come back next Tuesday.'"

It takes effort — and time — to make people feel important. It means inconvenience to make yourself available when you're right in the middle of something. Granted, there are those times when you simply can't stop what you're doing. You can't drop everything to take off with your child or go play a game of catch. But the point is this: *There are many times when you can stop if you really want to bother.* Stopping on those occasions will help your child realize that you do think he or she is important and, when one of those times comes when you simply can't stop, it won't have the same negative impact that it might have if the child consistently gets the message, "I'm too busy — I can't talk to you or play with you now."

# If I have not time . . .

A major reason why it's crucial to have time for your children is that, if they feel important to you, they will feel important to their Heavenly Father. Another lesson I learned along the way — probably from Dick Day — is that each one of us earthly fathers models God the Father to our children. You see, God loves your children through you, but if you're not available, how can He love them?

As the title says, *Love Is Spelled T-I-M-E.* You spell acceptance and appreciation the same way. If I say I accept you and love you without conditions, if I say I appreciate you and want you to feel significant, but I spend no time with you, I am exactly like the "sounding brass" the apostle Paul talks about in 1 Corinthians 13:1. In other words, I don't ring true.

Unfortunately, many parents are falling into the trap of not ringing true to their children, and in many cases it's happening by default. Parents wind up being unavailable to their kids because they are too busy. Everyone makes jokes about the hectic pace at which we all seem to be living, but it isn't funny. Parents complain of "having too much to do," and then they tell me about their work schedules, their church schedules, their social schedules. For many people their commuting schedule alone is incredible. They spend several hours a day on the freeway just getting to and from their jobs.

As parents dash through life, too busy to spend time with their children, their children watch and take mental notes. After all, they want to be just like Mom and Dad. And as the years go by Harry Chapin's song, "The Cat's in the Cradle," comes true. They grow up just like us.

And then our children marry, have families of their own, and slip into the same mode, failing to spend enough time with their children, who will be our grandchildren. I often talk to grandparents who have realized their mistake and are now spending more time with their grandchildren than they did with their own children. I believe one of the greatest forces for building better family relationships in our country today is grandparents. I talk to junior high students and ask, "Who can you talk to?" Do you know what they say? Many of them don't mention Mom or Dad. They say, "My grandparents — Grandma or Grandpa."

There are different reasons for this in different families, I'm sure, but one basic reason that kids talk to grandparents more than parents is that Grandma and Grandpa have more time. They're more available.

# Better parents?

According to one study I've seen, fifty years ago the average child had three or four hours a day of interaction with parents or extended family members. But that was in the days when many people lived on farms and the entire family worked together. That was in the days when extended family members lived just down the road.

Today, with our "upwardly mobile" society, people have moved in from the farm to the city or, more correctly, the suburbs. In a typical family, both Mom and Dad dash out the door to work each morning and come dragging back home at night to get ready for the next day. The result is that children have only about fifteen minutes of interaction with parents each day. And, according to some experts, twelve of those minutes are spent in a setting where the children hear only critique, instruction, or criticism. That leaves three minutes for fun, laughing together, or enjoying quality moments when real communication occurs.[1]

Today's baby boomer generation of parents likes to talk about spending "quality time" with their kids. The concept of quality time is based upon the idea that, although they have an overpacked scheduled, they can "zero in" and not waste a moment as they relate to and communicate with their children.

According to a report published by *USA Today* the baby boomer generation (those born between 1946 and 1964) believe that they are doing a better job of parenting than their parents did.[2] Still, study after study shows that these parents are spending far *less* time with their kids than their parents spent with them.

One study of three hundred seventh and eighth graders revealed that children would spend an average of 7.5 minutes a *week* in "focused conversation" with their fathers. Focused conversation means eyeball to eyeball where both people are talking to each other and both people are listening and really exchanging ideas. That's barely *one minute a day* spent really communicating with their fathers. And for mothers, it's not much higher.

Several years ago, I did a conference for six hundred junior high and high school students in one of the largest churches in the United States. The number one question I heard that week was, "Josh, what can I do about my dad?"

"What do you mean?" I would ask.

"Well, he never talks to me. He never takes me anywhere. He never does anything with me."

I spoke sixteen times from Monday noon to Friday noon that week and had forty-two half-hour counseling situations. I could have had three hundred if I had the time, but I handled all I could. At every one of these forty-two sessions, I asked the same question: "Can you talk with your father?"

One student said yes. Forty-one said no.

# Quality or quantity?

I'm convinced that one of the biggest myths we have going today is the myth of "quality time." Of course we all want those quality moments with our kids. But you don't get them by appointment or on some kind of tight schedule. You get quality moments by spending larger quantities of time with your children. Out of the quantity comes the quality.

One of the biggest advantages of quantity time with children is that you are able to serve as a role model for them. Whenever I go downtown, whenever I run an errand, I try to take one of my children with me. If I don't, I miss an opportunity to model for them.

It's when they're with me that they can see how I respond to the world: how I act when another driver cuts me off or when somebody irritates me in some other way.

How do I act when I get cheated, delayed, or

> *One of the greatest forces for building better family relationships in our country today is grandparents.*

frustrated? How do I act, for example, when I put a quarter in the newsstand container and I can't get the door open to get my newspaper? Do I hammer on the thing and call it a few choice names? Or am I patient and able to handle being "ripped off"?

My kids will never know unless they're with me, watching me, experiencing these same frustrations with me. Write this down and seal it in your mind:

*To be a hero to your kids — a good role model — you have to spend quantity time. And out of that quantity will come the quality that will communicate your acceptance and appreciation of them.*

**Being your kids' role model is a full-time job.**

# Disneyland experiences

Another myth we fall victim to is the one that says, "It's the big moments that count." I call them the Disneyland Experiences — those major excursions that take all day and usually cost a lot of money. I used to believe that it was the big moments that counted, and I would haul my family to Disneyland or wherever with "great enthusiasm." Finally, Dottie got through to me in her quiet, but laser-accurate way: "Honey, it's not the big times they're going to remember. It's those consistent small moments with them that will mold them, and that's what they're really going to remember."

As you can tell, I make it a habit to think about Dottie's remarks. I "check them out" in my mind, and I usually decide that she's right. She wasn't saying that we discontinue the big moments. Disneyland is still on our schedule,

but it's not nearly as big as it used to be. Big moments are necessary, but they can never replace the consistent little moments, because it is there that heroes are made and children feel loved and accepted.

# Teenagers need parents

For those who are parents of teenagers, I'd like to mention still another myth: "The formative years are past." It's amazing how the Roman Catholic motto, "Give us a child until he is seven" dominates the thinking of society. There is good reason for this, because it's true that the first seven years of life (actually the first three) are very formative ones in many crucial ways. That's why Dick and I emphasize the need for acceptance and building trust and autonomy into a child when he or she is very young.

But recent research is telling us that there is another set of formative years for every child — adolescence, which begins around the age of eleven or twelve. As a child moves into the teenage years, the myth has it that he doesn't need his parents as much, because he is branching out and becoming independent. Again, there is truth to this, but it's not the whole truth, by any means.

I can recall talking with James Dobson not long after he published his excellent book, *Preparing for Adolescence* (Bantam, 1984). I mentioned that I had run across so many fathers who thought it was good to spend time with their kids when they were small, but once they got into adolescence, it wasn't that necessary. Dobson's reply was to the effect, "No, that's not right. According to my research, when children reach puberty, they need their parents — especially their father — just as much if not more than they ever did."

That little conversation with Jim Dobson gave me new motivation to spend as much time as I could with my own teenagers and to keep encouraging other fathers to do the same. Yes, I realize this isn't always easy. In fact, in many cases it can seem impossible. When I mention that teenagers need time with their parents, many moms and dads give me a frustrated look and shrug their shoulders.

"How can we spend time with our teen-agers?" they want to know. "They have their own schedules, their own friends, their own lives. They're almost too busy to talk to us."

I understand, and that's one reason why I urge parents of younger children not to be too

> "When children reach puberty, they need their parents — especially their father — just as much if not more than they ever did."

Is being a parent a major priority for you? ▶

busy for their kids. You see, if you start making time for your children when they are very young, you will have many more opportunities — and requests — to spend time with your children when they are teenagers. Earlier I mentioned Kelly, my sixteen-year-old, who interrupted me while I was writing and wanted me to take her to get her nails done. Many parents would look on such a request as an impertinence or at least a thoughtless imposition. Don't teenagers know that we parents have better things to do than haul them around?

The answer to that question is "yes and no." Obviously, parents can't sit around and be available on demand every moment of a twenty-four-hour day. There is work to be done, there are chores to take care of. There is a certain schedule to maintain or a family would simply disintegrate into chaos. But at the same time, there are plenty of moments when we can make ourselves available and can allow ourselves to be "imposed upon" if we really are interested in spending more time with our kids. The question every parent must ask is this: "Is being a parent a major priority for me?"

I'm not talking about taking an approach to parenting that makes it as a life sentence — a daily duty that every mother and father has to perform. I'm talking about being a hero to your kids — someone who wants to accept, appreciate, and nurture them at every opportunity. Spending time with your children is absolutely imperative if you want to be a believable, credible hero who builds your child's security and sense of significance.

*How can you really accept or appreciate your child if you are not available? How can you show your child affection if you are not there?* What follows may sound extreme, but we fear that it is all too true:

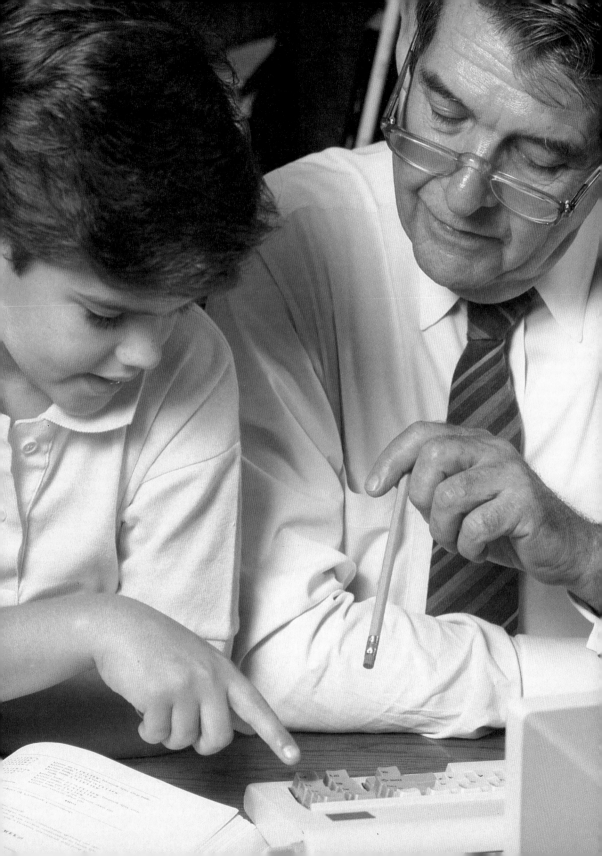

> *If you are not willing to make time for your children, then every other piece of advice you get is meaningless.*

# He lost his kids

Some of the saddest words that parents ever say is, "If only I had spent more time . . . if only I had listened to my kids more . . . if only . . ."

The wife of a senior vice president of a huge construction firm heard me speak at a local church about being available to your children. Later, I ran into this woman in a restaurant. She mentioned hearing my talk, and then she started to cry.

"I have to share something with you," she said hesitantly. "My husband just died. He was a million-dollar-a-year man. He traveled all over the world building and constructing things, but he never took time for his children, even when he was home. All his children turned against him, and when they were grown, they would have nothing to do with him. On his deathbed he confessed to me that he was dying one of the saddest men in the world. He told me, 'I gained prestige, but I lost my family. If only I had spent more time with my children.'"

This widow's words remind me of what Jesus said: "What good will it be for a man if he gains the whole world, yet forfeits his soul? Or what can a man give in exchange for his soul?" (Matthew 16:26).

Making time for your children will not gain you salvation, but it does indicate how seriously you take the clear advice from Scripture about being a faithful, loving, and nurturing parent. This executive died an unhappy man because he had gained the whole world and forfeited his children's love. He made a great deal of money, but he had been unavailable to the most important people in his life. He had bought them things. He had given them birthday cards saying, "I Love You," but they weren't fooled. He should have known: "You can con a con, you can fool a fool, but you can't kid a kid."

As I left that restaurant, memories of that day when I turned my little two-year-old away because I was too busy flooded back. And as I thought of that dad who died without his family's love, Dottie's words took on extra meaning: *If we show an interest in our children now, they will show an interest in us later.*

This chapter is taken from Josh McDowell and Dick Day, *How to Be a Hero to Your Kids* (Dallas: Word, 1991).

1. See Josh McDowell, *How to Help Your Child Say "No" to Sexual Pressure* (Waco, Tex.: Word, 1987), p. 19.
2. Anthony Casale, *Teaching Tomorrow's Friends* (Kansas City: Andrews, Mcmeal & Parker, 1986).

---

## Further Reading

Jorie Kincaid. *The Power of Modeling: Hope for the Imperfect Parent.* Colorado Springs: NavPress, 1989.

Kevin Leman. *Smart Kids, Stupid Choices, Revised.* Edited by Kathi Mills. Ventura, Calif.: Regal, 1987.

Josh McDowell and Dick Day. *How to Be a Hero to Your Kids.* Dallas: Word, 1991.

Bernie A. Schock. *Remodeling the Family: A Radical Plan for Restoring the Home.* Nashville: Wolgemuth & Hyatt, 1989.

# The Power of Words in a Family

*Chuck and Winnie Christensen*

❝ Listen, my son, to your father's instruction and do not forsake your mother's teaching. ❞ (Proverbs 1:8)

Learning to listen and to speak God's language begins in the home, the place where impressions and discipline make the strongest impact on children. When a parent talks, an infant's attention follows that familiar voice. A child's comprehension grows. The parent gives simple instructions at first, and the child responds. He experiments with words, then phrases, and finally concepts and ideas. In the normal verbal give-and-take in a home, the child usually develops positive or negative attitudes in response to what he hears.

## Respect

Parents teach respect by speaking to their children with respect. Chuck worked with children for years in church, in camps, and at a radio station in Chicago. He constantly treated children with respect. (He wouldn't write this about himself, but his wife can.) He didn't talk down to them or belittle them, and children responded positively. He showed the same respect to our own children, and the pattern continues with our grandchildren.

Sometimes, however, children have to learn respect for authority the hard way. When one of our sons was seven, he took a dare to write a note to "Bozo" with some smart remarks and put it on the school principal's windshield. He naively signed his name before placing it under the windshield wiper. He and his friends giggled at the fun until the principal went to his car, read the note, and

### About the authors

*Chuck Christensen, Ed.D., served for twelve years as chairman of the Department of Communications at Moody Bible Institute. His wife, **Winnie Christensen,** is a speaker, author, and registered nurse. Together they have written* How to Listen When God Speaks *(Shaw) and* Careful! Someone's Listening *(Moody). They have four children and four grandchildren.*

strode across the street to our house. A thoroughly chagrined little boy had to face the principal that day, and he learned a valuable lesson about respect, appropriate speech, and accountability for his words.

Having mutual respect in a family does not mean there can't be strong discussions. Our dinner table frequently became an open forum about various issues. We discussed politics, religion, boyfriends, sports, girlfriends, every subject in the school curriculum, sex, prejudice, feminism, and theology. The discussions were animate, sometimes argumentative. Someone was always playing the "devil's advocate" — usually Chuck. Sometimes we had to fight for the floor, but we also learned to listen to one another, to cooperate. We allowed the children to exercise their freedom of speech.

# Ninnyolatry

No subject was off-limits, unless the conversation degenerated into what we labeled "ninnyolatry," or worship of the immature. That term cropped up frequently, especially in the telling of jokes. We liked to laugh, and we enjoyed jokes within limits, but maybe Paul had ninnyolatry in mind when he said, "Do not let any unwholesome talk come out of your mouths" (Ephesians 4:29). We also did not allow swearing and crude language. We told the children that people who have to resort to dirty words reveal their own paucity in vocabulary. We hear Christians use such expressions as "Oh, my God!" with alarmingly increasing frequency. It is so easy to carelessly imitate the world about us.

# Roast sermon for dinner

Even in open discussion among family members, derogatory statements about other people should not go unchallenged. It is important for children to learn the difference between attacking an idea or philosophy and attacking the person espousing it. We wanted

> *Having mutual respect in a family does not mean there can't be strong discussions.*

to build positive attitudes toward other people, and particularly toward fellow Christians. We might have "roast sermon" for Sunday dinner, but we tried not to chew up the preacher. We didn't always succeed, but we tried.

Because such discussions were encouraged in our home, the kids themselves continued them on a more informal basis. Sometimes one of our teenagers would materialize in the bedroom doorway after we had turned off both the light and our minds and say, "Can I ask you a question?" At that time of night there was seldom a simple yes or no answer. Those deep topics rarely came up during planned discussion times. They crept up unexpectedly, usually one-on-one, at odd hours. Those occasions allowed us to make a practice of praying with the children about any issue.

# Everyday talk

When Moses prepared the people of Israel to enter the Promised Land he said,
*Love the Lord your God with all your heart and with all your soul and with all your strength. These commandments that I give you today are to be upon your hearts. Impress them on your children. Talk about them when you sit at home and when you walk along the road, when you lie down and when you get up.* (Deuteronomy 6:5–7)

The parents in the nation of Israel were charged with the responsibility of communicating the facts and principles of God's teaching. They had to learn God's language within the context of the normal activities of everyday life. A parent's life was to reflect a

# No regrets

Before we had children I worked for a publishing company where it was my job to interview people for first-person stories. In a brief period, say a couple of months, I happened to interview five men whose children were grown. I was talking to each about something different. With one it was his testimony, with another his business, with another an interesting anecdote, and so on. But with each I got to the point where I asked if he had any regrets.

They all had one thing in common. It was almost as if they had conspired to send me a message. Each said he wished he'd spent more time with his family. None of them had kids who went off the deep end or were away from the Lord in serious rebellion. They simply wished they had spent more time with their children.

**Decision**

My wife and I discussed it at length and made a decision. Though we wouldn't be having children for a couple of more years, we set a policy. From the time I got home from work until the time the kids went to bed, I would not do any writing or any work from the office.

That allowed for some interesting bonding. I gave baths, changed diapers, spoon fed, crawled, wrestled, ran, and did all those things babies and toddlers do. I saved my free-lance writing for late at night and usually had between two and three hours each day with the kids.

**Jerry Jenkins**

personal relationship with God. For any parent who truly loves God, that is neither a duty nor a chore but a privilege.

The family is a microcosm of the world and society. What children learn at home is what they will take with them when they are grown. A woman we know only as Lemuel's mother understood this.

# Straight teaching

Proverbs 31:1–9 records some straight teaching that the mother of Lemuel the king gave him. His respect for her is immediately apparent in his reference to her words as an "oracle." Oracles were usually considered to be equal to prophetic utterances in the Old Testament. Most children today do not give parental instruction such respect.

We heard a preacher tell a story about a little boy who wandered away from home. His mother frantically searched for him but to no avail. She finally called the police, and headquarters notified a police helicopter that happened to be flying in that area at the time. The flying officer began a low circuit around the boy's neighborhood, and every few minutes he called out over a loudspeaker, "Johnnie Smith, go home." Soon Johnnie appeared on his own doorstep.

His mother discovered that he had been at a neighbor's, and she asked, "What made you come home?"

In great seriousness and awe he replied, "God told me to!"

# The right to be heard

Lemuel's mother addressed her son with great warmth and tenderness: "O my son, O son of my womb, O son of my vows [answer to my prayers]" (31:1). Lemuel and his mother obviously had a close relationship. She took her role as a mother seriously. As the queen mother she did not exploit her son's position and power for self-gratification or

> *What children learn at home is what they will take with them when they are grown.*

self-promotion. She had prayed for this son, and over the years she had earned the right to be heard. Lemuel's mother did not say to him, "Now hear this and do as I say because I'm your mother." Instead, she built up credibility with her son over the years.

She communicated two basic life principles to her son: do not give in to excesses, and treat others fairly. Parents would do well to learn from her wise example of communicating with her son.

### Live your life with self-control

Lemuel's mother warned her son that although his position gave him power, it also carried a great weight of responsibility. "Do not spend your strength on women, your vigor on those who ruin kings," she said (v. 3).

"It is not for kings, O Lemuel – not for kings to drink wine, not for rulers to crave beer, lest they drink and forget what the law decrees and deprive all the oppressed of their rights" (v. 4). A king was responsible for the welfare of his subjects. If he allowed his mind to be controlled by any substance, he would not be able to rule wisely. The people depended on the king to make good decisions, to execute justice.

This principle has not changed. Irresponsible living affects the lives of other people. The more people for whom a person is responsible, the greater the impact of his personal choices. Our minds are precious gifts from God. They are not to be wasted or destroyed. "Instead, be filled with the Spirit" (Ephesians 5:18).

Some years ago Winnie was invited to lead a Bible study for women in Alcoholics Anonymous. It was a great learning experience.

## Irresponsible living affects the lives of other people.

One mother told Winnie that one of her teenage daughters had asked her to lie for her. The woman said, "My daughter had skipped school and gone to the beach with some of her friends. She asked me to write an excuse to her teacher saying she was sick that day. If she had come to me just a few weeks earlier with that request I probably would have done it. I would have thought, *My life is so messed up, who am I to say to my daughter that it's wrong to tell a lie?* However," she went on, "I have hit a crisis in my own life. I'm dealing with my alcoholism. I am also working on my relationship with Jesus Christ. My life is turned around. So I said to my daughter, 'No, I can't lie for you. You'll have to take the consequences of skipping school.' Winnie," she concluded, "it felt so good to be right!"

That was precisely the point Lemuel's mother was trying to make. There is strength in moral integrity. A parent or leader's words will carry weight if they are backed by a disciplined life.

### Treat others fairly

Lemuel's mother further charges, "Commit yourself to justice and to defending the rights of the poor." She taught her son to speak for those unable to speak for themselves. A leader sets the direction, and people listen. Lemuel's position as a leader was to serve the needs of the people. That is still what true leadership means: serving. "He who oppresses the poor shows contempt for their Maker, but whoever is kind to the needy honors God" (Proverbs 14:31).

Behind every person, no matter how lowly, is his or her Creator. Jesus reinforced that truth when He said, "I tell you the truth, whatever you did for one of the least of these brothers of mine, you *did for me*" (Matthew 25:40, italics added).

Lemuel's mother knew that the quality of her son's reign as king would not be determined by successful military conquests. Rather, it would be judged by his personal strength of character and his endeavors to help the weakest and poorest in his kingdom.

What is your primary goal in your conversations with your children? Do you encourage them to develop into the best that God has created them to be? In what ways can you incorporate the concept of learning a new language into your home?

This chapter is taken from *Carefull Someone's Listening* (Chicago: Moody, 1991).

### Further Reading

William Backus. *Telling Each Other the Truth*. Minneapolis: Bethany House, 1985.

William Lee Carter. *Family Communication*. Houston: Rapha, 1992.

Gary Jackson Oliver and H. Norman Wright. *When Anger Hits Home: Taking Care of Your Anger Without Taking It Out on Your Family*. Chicago: Moody, 1992.

H. Norman Wright. *The Power of Parents' Words*. Ventura, Calif.: Regal, 1987.

# Improving Communication Within Marriage

*Gary Smalley*

### About the author

*Gary Smalley is president of Today's Family. He has written* If Only He Knew *and* For Better or for Best *(HarperCollins), and* The Key to Your Child's Heart *(Word). He has coauthored several other books with John Trent. He and his wife, Norma, have three children.*

Whenever I survey couples at my seminars on what would improve their marriages, without exception the majority answers "better communication." In nearly thirty years with my wife and children, I have found the same thing to be true. Better communication means an improved relationship.

Of all the methods you could use to improve communication, two have worked best for me, my family and friends, and my counselees: first, active listening by repeating what someone has said, and, second, word pictures to show empathy.

## Active listening

This first came to me at our Today's Family national board meeting in Dallas. Our last session together involved a time of praying for each other and expressing those qualities we would love to develop. As an exercise we mentally went to a local department store and purchased one character quality.

I selected a greater quality of softness, mostly toward my wife but also toward my family and friends. I also sought wisdom to know when and how to use that quality. I said that it would be a great year for me if my wife said that I had learned to listen, learned to be soft.

My wife Norma said that her goal was to be more bold, share her feelings, and be more confrontive. One of the board members asked Norma how bold she would rank herself. Surprisingly, she said about three on a scale of one to ten. I look at her as the head of our ministry. She leads, directs, and confronts when necessary several employees.

Someone else asked Norma, "How bold are you to confront Gary in areas that he needs to improve." Again, she said about a three. I've always thought of Norma as very open, very able to confront me. I thought she was doing great. But everyone who really knows us looked as if they agreed with Norma, that she was way too soft on me.

I said, "Let me say this out loud to make sure I have heard correctly."

I asked her if she was saying that she would like to have greater skill in sharing what she considers to be areas that other people need to work on to have a better relationship with her. She said "Yes, that is what I'm saying."

I asked her if she believed she was about a three in her ability to share with me the things she felt I needed to hear. She said yes. All this happened in front of my board and staff! I thank God they care only about what is best for each of us and were very encouraging. I appreciate the scriptural principle that we should accept counsel, reproof, and correction. So I was open to feedback regarding how I needed to improve.

## Using word pictures

Shortly after that the second communication-building technique came into play. Norma and I woke up in a hotel room in Waco, Texas, where my son goes to college. Norma was a little down because our "baby" was growing up and was away from our control. What did I do? I exhorted her.

"Oh, come on, you'll get over it. Let's have a good day. Let's go to the fair and not be down."

She looked at me and said, "Gary, you never let me be a woman, never allow me to just feel what I feel, to be sad if I want to be sad or happy if I want to be happy. Let me be myself!"

**Active listening will improve communication.**

I asked, "Do you feel like a rose petal?"

"Yes! I feel like a rose petal that has just fallen off my supporting stem to the ground."

She was in a position to be trampled on, and her beautiful color and fragrance could be lost in a hurry. I made a decision on the spot: I should not have exhorted her. She did not need that. What she really needed was a husband who heeded the admonishment of 1 Peter 3:7: "Be considerate as you live with your wives, and treat them with respect as the weaker partner." That word "weaker" in Greek means "sensitive, soft, fragile."

There are times when, no matter how strong they appear, women can feel vulnerable and sensitive; their hormonal changes can bring on a fragility. I told myself, "Gary, you know who you are living with, that although she is a mature CEO and handles tough problems at work and appears to be strong and independent, right now she is extremely vulnerable. She is sensitive. What she needs is comfort, your sensitivity, your arms around

> *When you actively listen, an instant compassion is felt. There is an instant bonding and understanding.*

her. She needs you to actively listen to her."

I sat next to her, put my arms around her, let her put her head on my shoulder, and with her nestled up against me told her how sorry I was that she didn't feel great today, how sorry I was that she was sad, but that I was going to be there for her. I asked her if she felt like a storm had hit. She said that it felt like a rainy day, with thick, dark clouds and a wind that chilled to the bone. I just held her, listening as she talked and talked. Slowly I saw a transformation in her.

Although I teach marital communication, I still mess up and tend to lecture my wife. I am, however, open to her saying that she doesn't need that right now. I need her to keep me accountable.

## Understand one another

A friend of ours, Dallas Dimet, is the world's expert on active listening and has written much on the subject. Dallas has taught me to hear what others are really saying. We solve many problems by this method.

When my board was actively listening, repeating aloud what Norma was saying to me, we were truly communicating. We honor the people we are listening to by looking at them, giving them our full attention, leaning toward them. Hours of unnecessary arguments are avoided. When you actively listen, an instant compassion is felt. There is an instant bonding and understanding.

Emotional word pictures bring instant understanding. When I asked Norma about feeling like a cloudy day or like a rose petal, I was trying to paint pictures. I said, I did not want to trample her and that I need all the help I can get. Word pictures let others know that, yes, we do understand. They increase honor and understanding in our relationships.

## Breaking down walls

Recently I counseled a family and employed active listening. The older children and I repeated what we heard their mother say. These adult children would say, "Mom, I didn't know you felt like that!"

I asked her if her father's leaving her when she was growing up made her feel rejected and therefore she was still looking for her father's approval. She said out loud, "Yes, that is what I'm saying."

Her kids gaped at her because they had never heard this. Her eyes filled with tears because she still had that nine-, ten-, or eleven-year-old little girl still inside, fragile as a rose petal, wanting someone to care for her. I asked if she wanted that same acceptance and approval from her husband and children. That broke any walls that had built up over time. The tears flowed freely, and she wept. Her husband held her, her children saw something they had never seen. All four kids saw her in a way they had never seen before. One by one, they hugged her gently and tenderly and told her how much they loved her, how they accepted her, and that she did not have to earn their love and acceptance. I was moved by the power of that woman's family truly hearing her.

When we were born, our little hearts were designed by God to grow to a certain size and shape. When that woman's father walked out on her, a big hole was left in her heart. I told her husband that some of the behavior that irritated him was coming straight out of that vacuum in her heart. His and his children's disapproval, attacking those qualities in her had only enlarged the hole. They apologized and told her they accepted her, hole in her heart and all. There were many tears and much understanding. The mother said she was going to go for help, that she was going to seek counsel on how to get help from the Lord, to get over her problems with His power and with the guidance of His Holy Spirit. For the first time she was ready to assume responsibility for that hole and get help.

I have seen the power of people using these two communication methods, richly improving their relationships. Active listening simply involves repeating what you think you have heard and getting a yes signal from that person. Using word pictures illustrates what a person is trying to say so that it touches feelings and emotions. Use them both to improve your marriage!

## Further Reading

Gary Chapman. *The Five Love Languages: How to Express Heartfelt Commitment to Your Mate.* Chicago: Moody, 1992.

Gary Smalley and John Trent. *The Language of Love.* Colorado Springs: Focus on the Family, 1988, 1991.

Nancy Van Pelt. *How to Talk So Your Mate Will Listen and Listen So Your Mate Will Talk.* Tarrytown, N.Y.: Revell, 1989.

H. Norman Wright. *How to Speak Your Spouse's Language.* Tarrytown, N.Y.: Revell, 1988.

# The Importance of Marital Fidelity to Children

*Gary Chapman*

### About the author

Gary Chapman, *director of adult ministries at* Calvary Baptist Church, Winston-Salem, North Carolina, *is the author of* Hope for the Separated, Toward a Growing Marriage *and* The Five Love Language *(Moody).*

Infidelity, sexual or otherwise, not dealt with by repentance and forgiveness will lead to divorce — emotional or legal. Divorce means disunity. Only fidelity can maintain unity.

We now have a society in which marriage can be terminated at any time for any reason. We retain the phrases of permanency in our ceremonies — phrases such as "so long as we both shall live," but those in the audience are wondering, "How long this one will last?" The gap between what we proclaim and what we practice is incredible. The intent of divorce is to get out of a bad situation and to create a better one. Divorce is supposed to give the partners a second chance, but what about the children? Hardly ever do children perceive divorce as giving them a better life. Inevitably, they see it as taking something away from them. Divorce is a price they pay for their parents' new opportunity.

Listen to the perspective of a fifteen-year-old girl who wrote the following poem two days after her father walked out on her mother for another woman.

### I Never Thought*

*I never thought it would happen to me.*
*How could I have been so naive?*
*There weren't any hints, no problems at all —*
*At least not any that I saw.*
*No one can help you, no one can know.*
*How hard it is to watch your daddy go.*
*When I feel so powerless in all this mess*
*I have to remember this is just a test.*
*God picked me out of all the rest —*
*To see how strong I can really be.*

*It's so hard to see your hero slip away.*
*Then it happened on that terrible dark day.*
*He said, "I'm sorry, I have to go,"*
*Then his emotions began to show.*
*Your world collapses, you feel defeated.*
*Why did my family have to be cheated?*
*As he turned to go away*
*He said he had just one more thing to say.*
*With sadness in his eyes he said, "I love you,"*
*But how can this be true?*
*He wants to leave us, but wants my love, too.*

*The emotions I feel for him are so confused.*
*Sometimes I love him; but then I hate him, too.*
*But the emotion I feel that's the strongest*
*    of all*
*Is the one that's so strong it could cause me to*
*    fall . . . FEAR.*
*Fear of what will happen to me.*
*I fear, as I grow older, this might happen to*
*    my own family.*
*I know that it's all right to cry,*
*Sometimes it's the only thing that helps me*
*    get by.*
*But when I begin to feel this way,*
*I have to stop and think and pray —*
*And ask God for a brand new day.*

## Children suffer most

A commonly held assumption is that the effect of marital infidelity on children will be short-lived, but listen to this same girl at age twenty-one as she writes an essay for her English class. "My name is Shannon, and I come from a broken home — 'broken' in the respect that my father left us; or as psychologists would rather it be said — left my mother. But nonetheless he broke my heart in the process. I would like to be able to say that it gets easier with time and the hurt begins to fade, but that wouldn't be completely honest."

She goes on to say that after reading every-

> ## Divorce is supposed to give the partners a second chance, but what about the children?

thing she could find on the subject of the children of divorce, she is in counseling to "continue my healing process." Contemporary research has shown that these emotional struggles are not abnormal. Marital infidelity is almost always more devastating for children than for their parents. Children initially respond to a marital breakup according to their age and developmental stage.

Preschoolers totally dependent for physical care will likely fear abandonment: if one parent left, the other parent may also. Their reaction may be manifested in not wanting to go to bed, bed-wetting, thumb-sucking, unusual attachment to security objects. They may become more aggressive toward siblings or playmates. If the child must also move, all these reactions may be exaggerated.

Younger elementary school age children will likely experience deep feelings of loss, guilt, rejection, and abandonment. They fear they will never again see the parent who left. They fear that their parent will get a new child, and they will no longer matter. They may cry more, be more irritable, express anger, be unable to concentrate on studies; school grades may decline; they may even complain of physical pain rooted in emotional loneliness. They often view the marital conflict as a fight and wonder which side they should be on.

Children nine to twelve typically exhibit intense anger toward their parents for divorcing and are especially furious with the parent they blame. They have an acute sense of loneliness and helplessness. They may align themselves with one parent in an effort to control the other parent. On the other hand, they may try to comfort both parents. This puts tremendous emotional strain upon a child. Petty stealing, lying, and manipulating their peers may also be expressions of their desire to control their lives or to get their parent's attention.

Marital breakup is particularly devastating to teenagers. People sometimes think that teens are old enough to understand, but teens still need structure, order, and discipline. With the breakup of the marriage, family discipline and order is often diminished. Teenagers are also terrified that they may repeat their parents' failure. Normal adolescent anxieties are heightened. Angry, hurt, and lonely, these teens may become sexually active in an effort to find love and security.

Divorce-prone couples sometimes decide to stay together until the children get into college. They reason that by then their divorce will not affect the children. When I lecture on college campuses, however, I encounter these children. The people from whom they learned their values and who gave them the foundation for life have now split, and their worlds fall apart.

"I don't even want to go home this Christmas," said a freshman whose parents had separated since she left for school. "There's no home to go to." College is the normal time to evaluate the morals, values, and worldview with which one grew up. When the parents who taught these have now violated their own values and morals, tremendous confusion results in the mind of the student.

## Time does not heal

It would be comforting to believe that the emotional fall-out of marital infidelity would be short-lived and that children at every age level would be back to normal within a year or so. The facts, however, reveal something quite different. The most extensive research to date on the effects of divorce upon children has been done by Judith S. Wallerstein, founder and executive director of the Center for

> ## Divorce lingers forever with the children.

the Family in Transition in Corte Madera, California. Her research is based on 60 divorced couples and their 131 children. She followed these families over a fifteen-year period and has reported the level of emotional and social adjustment after two years, five years, ten years, and is in the process of compiling data from her fifteen-year study.

Wallerstein discovered that divorce lingers with the children forever. Almost all children of divorce feel they have lived under a shadow and that the divorce has radically affected their lives. Sadness, loneliness, fear, anger, and frustration follow many children throughout their lives. As adults, many children of divorce delay having children until they are sure their own marriage will work. They often feel deprived economically, socially, and psychologically. They feel less protected, less cared for, less comforted than others. As adults they desperately want a marriage that will last forever, but they are filled with anxiety and fear that this will not happen. This fear, coupled with the lack of a positive marital model, predisposes many of them to marital failure.

Many of these children enter adolescence and adulthood with unresolved anger and resentment toward their parents. There is no evidence that time alone heals these wounds. In Wallerstein's study, "almost half of the children entered adulthood as worried, under-achieving, self-depreciating, and sometimes angry young men and women. Some felt used in a battle that was never their own. Others felt deprived of the parenting and family protection that they always wanted and never got."[1]

The effects of divorce on our children stand as a reminder of why God was so dogmatic in His statements about marital fidelity. "For this reason a man will leave his father and mother

# Lifestyle of love

My father had wonderful blue eyes. They could hold warmth and love and teasing – but they could also be piercing. I remember how he looked at me when he had to correct. He didn't raise his voice, though it held authority, but instead he fixed on me those cool, probing eyes, and I knew instinctively that I'd better obey – and quickly!

"He ruled with his voice and his eyes," one of my sisters commented as we waded our way through a box containing his little mementos. She was right – but he also ruled with his love.

I would never have challenged my father – not because I greatly feared the consequences, but because I did not want to jeopardize in any way the love relationship we had. As a small child, I knew without a doubt that he loved me. I also knew that I was always welcome on his lap to snuggle up closely against his firm chest. He wasn't in the house two minutes before I had claimed my rightful position. So it was the great love that I felt for him that made me respond quickly to his commands.

### Gentleman
But Dad also ruled by example and expectation. His mother had taught him to be a gentleman, and for that, I will always be grateful to the grandmother whom I scarcely knew. She had raised my daddy to doff his cap when greeting a lady on the street, to rise from his chair when a woman entered the room, to give up his seat quickly and without comment, and to put the comfort of others before his own. I was proud of my daddy.

And Dad expected no less from his offspring. Selfishness, pettiness, and rude and improper behavior were not acceptable. We knew that by his example. We also knew that he had higher expectations for his children.

My father, in his quiet, gentle way, made it awfully easy for me to accept a heavenly Father who expected both love and obedience from his children. After all, I had learned that love and obedience fit together naturally.

### Daring and giving
My mother – and we are thankful to still have her with us – is a totally different personality. From things that I have gathered, she must have been an outgoing, vibrant, pert, and sometimes saucy child and teenager. She was the kind who brought home strays – both animal and human. She was daring and giving and people-oriented. She was quick to speak her mind and just as quick to share anything that she had with others.

She carried the same qualities into her marriage. There were never so many in her home or around her table that she couldn't make room for one more or two or. . . . She was never too busy that the task couldn't be set aside to make a cup of tea for a drop-in neighbor or a complete stranger.

People were always coming to our house and taking away my mother to nurse the sick, to comfort the mourning, to minister to the dying, even to prepare the dead for burial. As a child, I suppose I resented this at times, but that's just the way she was, and it was to be accepted.

**Janette Oke**

and be united to his wife, and they will become one flesh" (Genesis 2:24). "You shall not commit adultery" (Exodus 20:14). "I tell you that anyone who divorces his wife, except for marital unfaithfulness, causes her to become an adulteress, and anyone who marries the divorced woman commits adultery" (Matthew 5:32). "Husbands, love your wives, just as Christ loved the church and gave himself up for her" (Ephesians 5:25). "Wives, submit to your husbands as to the Lord" (Ephesians 5:22).

# Reversing the trend

With secular research speaking so loudly about the detrimental, long-lasting results of marital infidelity, will we see the trend begin to change in Western society? The latest research shows that the divorce rate is no longer rising. From the Christian perspective we know that the trend is only likely to change when we rediscover the biblical admonition: "Do nothing out of selfish ambition or vain conceit, but in humility consider others better than yourselves. Each one of you should look not only to your own interests, but also to the interests of others" (Philippians 2:3–4). As long as we continue to exalt personal happiness above all else, we will continue to sacrifice our children's emotional, social, financial, and spiritual future on the altar of parental selfishness.

1. Judith S. Wallerstein and Sandra Blakeslee, *Second Chances* (New York: Ticknor and Fields, 1989), p. 299.

---

## Further Reading

Debbie Barr. *Caught in the Crossfire: Children of Divorce, Revised.* Grand Rapids: Zondervan, 1992

Dave Carder. *Torn Asunder: Recovering from Extramarital Affairs.* Chicago: Moody, 1992.

Jerry Jenkins. *Loving Your Marriage Enough to Protect It.* Chicago: Moody, 1993.

Judith S. Wallerstein and Sandra Blakeslee. *Second Chances: Men, Women and Children a Decade After Divorce.* New York: Ticknor & Fields, 1989.

# The Importance of Family Involvement in Church

*Zig Ziglar*

### About the author

**Zig Ziglar** *is chairman of the board of the Zig Ziglar Corporation and has authored nine books, including* Top Performance *(Berkeley),* Raising Positive Kids in a Negative World *(Nelson), and* Ziglar on Selling *(Oliver-Nelson). He likes to be known as "motivational teacher and author."*

"The family that prays together, stays together" is much more than a cliché! And when the family adds the dimension of praying together *in church,* the truth becomes even stronger.

At the age of forty-five, faith became a fact of life for me, and my life changed dramatically. My health improved, I became happier, and I felt more real security and more peace of mind than I ever dreamed possible. My relationship with my wife and children became better than ever (and it had always been good). I am convinced that the primary reason I was prepared to make a profession of faith later in life was due to the seeds that were planted in my youth. God's Word, we are assured, does not return void!

## Number one

Few parents today would deliberately deny their children food, shelter, clothing, or a reasonable amount of time, attention, and love. These are obviously important to a child's physical, mental, and emotional well-being. However, a parent's number one responsibility is to help his child establish a personal relationship with Jesus Christ.

> *If neither parent took the children to church, only 9 percent became active Christians.*

Let's face it. Each of us will be dead a great deal longer than we will be alive. Eternity is such an incredibly long time that loving parents will want to carefully consider the best overall, long-range plan for their child. The church should be a part of this plan.

Several years ago a survey revealed that when Mom and Dad took (not sent) their children to church, 76 percent of the children followed their parents in their faith. If only the father took the children to church, the percentage dropped to 55 percent. Interestingly enough, if only the mother took the children to church, the percentage dropped to 15 percent. If neither parent took the children to church, only 9 percent became active Christians. Any plan that is successful in helping children develop a personal relationship with Jesus Christ must include church.

## A child's perspective

As one of twelve children who lost not only his father but also his baby sister in less than a week in the heart of the Depression, I had a chance to view first-hand how church involvement can lead to faith in God, and what a God-based belief system can do for an individual and a family.

On Sunday morning, without fail, the Ziglar family would hear a horn sound in front of the house, and we knew it was Mrs. L. S. Jones in her old, dark blue Dodge. Every Sunday she would pick us up and take us to First Baptist Church in Yazoo City, Mississippi, where we would attend Sunday school and church. The routine was always the same: the horn blew, my mother sang out "Let's go, children," and we went. My mother's face shown brightly with the love of Jesus.

It never occurred to any of us to challenge Mother as to whether we would go to church. She had spoken, and we went. Not only were we there on Sunday morning, but we were also there on Sunday evening and Wednesday evening as well. I'm delighted to say that my mother lived to see each of her children come to know Christ as his or her personal Savior.

At church we learned many of the great hymns of the faith, and my mother kept them vivid and real for each of us. I can still hear her beautiful, clear voice softly singing as she sat on the screened-in back porch of our home, churning milk by hand. Everything from "Sweet Hour of Prayer" to "The Old Rugged Cross" and "Jesus Loves Me" poured beautifully from her lips. How well I remember waking in the middle of the night to go to the bathroom, having to cross that back porch on the way and glancing into the long hallway where my mother was busy quilting by the light of a kerosene lamp. Often she softly hummed or sang "Onward Christian Soldiers" or "How Great Thou Art." What an inspiration she was!

## Drawing strength

The church was very real to the Ziglar family. When our Dad, John Silas Ziglar, died in 1933, we were living about eight miles outside Yazoo City in the country. Dad had been an overseer for a large farm. Lila Ziglar lost her husband and twelve Ziglar children lost their father on Thursday; on the following Tuesday the youngest daughter, our baby sister passed away. Two of my older sisters were very ill at that time, one of them seriously. Mrs. R. J. Koonce, a very active member of the church and wife of the superintendent of Yazoo City Schools, heard about our plight. She and Dr. Webb Brame, the pastor, came to see us. They showed with their words and actions that the love of Christ is very real. The church moved us to town, paid our first month's rent ($10), and bought us a big grocery order with emphasis on the staples. They also provided warm clothing for the smaller children. Even as a five-year-old, somehow I knew that the church was made up of nice people who really cared about us.

Just a few years ago, I was visiting with

Mrs. Koonce after she had been stricken with cancer. As she recalled this event she shared something I remember with deep gratitude: "The thing that amazed both Dr. Brame and me the most after the death of your father and sister was that, though sparsely furnished, your home was absolutely spotless and all the children were clean and had on clean clothing."

One day about a month later, the Red Cross came by with blankets for us. My mother met them at the door and expressed her gratitude, but told them there were probably families who had a real need for them and that she was in the process even then of finishing all the necessary quilts we would need to keep warm for the winter. My mother was the hardest-working person I ever knew and managed to raise her children, six of whom could not work at the time of her husband's death, during the toughest Depression our country has ever seen. To the best of my knowledge the kindness shown by First Baptist Church of Yazoo City was the only time during the Depression that our family ever accepted any charitable help.

In those days the word of a dedicated pastor carried a great deal of weight in the business community. As my brothers and sisters and I sought jobs, entrance to college or the service, references were always needed and we knew we could get excellent ones from the pastor of our little church, because he knew each of us well.

## A practical approach

One of the great things I learned from our family's involvement in the church and one of the reasons I'm so enthusiastic about my own faith is that Christianity is such a practical approach to life. For example, the Lord's Prayer teaches us to ask for our daily bread even before we ask forgiveness for our sins. That's practical. Christ knew that if a person was starving, he would have difficulty believ-

> *Christianity is such a practical approach to life.*

ing there was an unseen but loving heavenly Father who was deeply concerned about him. Two-thirds of the parables of Christ deal with our physical or financial well-being, indicating He knew then, knows now, and understands our needs.

The biblical principles our families learn at church have always worked. A survey conducted by Korn-Ferry International (a New York executive search firm) in conjunction with the UCLA School of Management revealed that in a group of 1,361 vice presidents of major corporations, 89 percent of them were active in their faith. Eighty-seven percent were still married to their one and only spouse, and 92 percent were raised by two-parent families.[1]

The church is interwoven in every facet of our life. In the corporate world those who have faith do better than those who do not. The April 28, 1986, issue of *Fortune* magazine revealed that 91 percent of the CEOs of the "Fortune 500" companies claimed a church affiliation, indicating that to a degree their accomplishments were the result of the values they learned either in church or from the Bible. Since 54 percent came from lower-middle-class or poor families, the evidence is good that the church played a role in their accomplishments.

## Immediate benefits

In this day of divorce, violence, alcoholism, drug abuse, promiscuity, wife-beating, child abuse, and a host of other social, economic, and family problems, the church's role in the family takes on critical importance. The need for support groups, counselors, companions, and prayer partners is growing. The need for role models, mentors, and friends is greater than ever.

> *When these two godly institutions — the family and the church — unite, God is there to make miracles happen!*

The family that goes to church together receives an incredible number of immediate as well as eternal benefits. Just the physical act of getting the family together and preparing to go to church establishes a bond and a direction that brings it closer. Hearing the inspiring words of the pastor as well as the beautiful music of people raising their voices in praise to God has an uplifting impact on a family. You know you're part of something big and that, though God created the sun, the moon, and all the stars and planets, man is His greatest creation. When we fully understand that the Creator of the universe loved each of us so much that He sent His only begotten Son to die on the cross so that we might have eternal life, it is an awesome and humbling thought.

There's enormous comfort to the child as he or she watches Mom and Dad hand in hand, with heads bowed, praying to their heavenly Father. That child clearly understands that the parents respect authority and is far more likely to respect the authority of parents as well as the authority of the police and other governmental bodies. The benefits from a genuine worship of God in a church are transferred into love and affection.

The church and the family are so interwoven that it is impossible to separate them. Our Lord's first miracle was performed at a wedding where he obviously placed His blessings on marriage and the family. When our children grow up seeing our reliance on God, knowing there is a heavenly Father who loves them even more than their earthly father, it gives them stability and confidence, as well as peace of mind.

The church is not mortar or bricks, the church is the family, and the family is vitally important to the church. There are many empty buildings professing to be churches, and there are many empty houses professing to hold families. When these two godly institutions — the family and the church — unite, God is there to make miracles happen!

1. *Korn-Ferry International's Executive Profile: A Survey of Corporate Leaders of The Eighties*, October 1986

---

### Further Reading

Richard Dobbins. *The Family Friendly Church.* Altamonte Springs, Fl.: Creation House, 1989.

John C. Howell. *Church and Family Growing Together.* Nashville: Broadman, 1984.

Charles M. Sell. *Family Ministry: Enrichment of the Family Through the Church.* Grand Rapids: Zondervan, 1981.

# PARENTS AS LEADERS

# Parenting Styles

*Dave Wyrtzen*

My sons and daughter are learning in elementary school things I learned in college. State-of-the-art media flashes everything before their eyes from Michael Jackson to the explosion of the space shuttle *Challenger*. The Star Wars generation has an air of technical sophistication, but does it have a clear grasp of spiritual realities or moral standards? Does our children's broadened exposure through media and quicker acceptance of new technology guarantee that they have a clear idea of how to live a skillful life?

The scandal of powerful preachers caught sleeping with prostitutes while moneyed Wall Street brokers go to jail for acting illegally on inside information and magazine headlines that read "What Ever Happened to Ethics — Assaulted by sleaze, scandals and hypocrisy, America searches for its moral bearings" (*Time*, May 25, 1987) suggest that computer chips are not giving young people or adults the right moral programs.

As a dad, I feel an intense desire to protect my kids from all the immorality, deception, substance abuse, and violence of contemporary America. Sometimes I dream of isolating them in a monastery where they would be safe from the seduction of evil.

## The monastery parent

As I counsel, I find many parents who identify with my feelings of wanting to isolate our kids from the influence of the secular world. I refer to this philosophy of raising kids as "monastery parenting." Fred and Mary repre-

## About the author

*David Wyrtzen, Th.D., is pastor of Midlothian Bible Church in Midlothian, Texas, a frequent conference speaker, and author of* Raising Worldly-wise but Innocent Kids *(Moody). He is the son of Jack Wyrtzen and has four children of his own.*

sent this approach.

In their college days during the sixties they experimented with drugs and "free love" lifestyles. In the midst of their search for meaning, a friend challenged them to consider the person of Jesus Christ. After reading the gospel of John, they both opened their lives to Him. Their pasts make them painfully aware of the power of evil, and they know the scars sin can cause. They fear for their ten- and eight-year-olds. Over coffee in their living room Fred shares his concerns.

"I thought things were coming apart in the sixties, but things have deteriorated even more today. Last night Lance asked me if they had 'crack' when I was growing up. And last Friday he brought home a piece of paper covered with occult pentagrams. One of his classmates told him they were nice designs. I fear for my kids, and I intend to protect my family by creating a Christian environment. The rules concerning dress, music, and entertainment will be strict. I'll make sure they never come into contact with the influences that seduced me. I'm going to build a wall around my children which will guarantee that no corrupting influences can pollute their innocent minds."

I empathize with Fred and Mary's concern, but I question their "ignorance is bliss" solution. Will turning back the clock to the days of "Father Knows Best" and "Leave It to Beaver" conquer evil's internal and external blitz against our kids?

Too often I hear the cries of monastery parents after the reality of evil has scaled their protective walls:

"We attended a gospel-preaching, Bible-teaching church, but now our fifteen-year-old is pregnant."

"Our kids were never allowed to touch a drop! How could our John be expelled from school for having beer on the campus?"

"We sent Debbie to a good Christian college. How could she be so cold concerning spiritual things now that she has graduated?"

> *I'm going to build a wall around my children which will guarantee that no corrupting influences can pollute their innocent minds.*

"Our pastor exhorted against perversion each Sunday. How could he have been having affairs with so many women?"

Nostalgic reruns from the fifties will not equip us or our children to face the sophisticated temptations of the nineties. We cannot turn back the clock. Ecclesiastes 7:10 warns us against yearning for the good old days: "Do not say, 'Why were the old days better than these?' It is not wise to ask such questions."

In reality, the monastery approach was thoroughly tested in the "good old days." It failed!

The first-century Pharisees were Super Bowl champions at trying to conquer temptation by isolationism and rigid rules. They critically attacked Jesus because His disciples did not honor the traditions passed down by their learned religious teachers (Mark 7:5) — traditions skillfully designed to erect a wall around the moral law of God so human passions could be controlled and the individual protected from yielding to evil.

Jesus' reply to these religionists reveals the internal inconsistency whenever any of us tries to generate morality by locking people into an external behavior pattern. The monastery approach fails because it attempts to clean up internal, moral filth with an external bath.

*Isaiah was right when he prophesied about you hypocrites; as it is written: "These people honor me with their lips, but their hearts are far from me. They worship me in vain; their teachings are but rules taught by men."* (Mark 7:6–7)

The monastery philosophy of raising children cannot generate a deep intimacy with God, which alone yields a wise and moral lifestyle. It mislocates the problem of evil in external influences rather than in internal conditions. Walls cannot be built high enough to keep evil away from our kids. It has already infected their internal nature from the beginning. The isolationist technique is an impotent religious tradition that can never check the virility of evil. Jesus labeled this legalism stupidity.

*Are you so dull? Don't you see that nothing that enters a man from the outside can make him "unclean"? . . . For from within, out of men's hearts, come evil thoughts, sexual immorality, theft, murder, adultery, greed, malice, deceit, lewdness, envy, slander, arrogance and folly. All these things come from inside and make a man "unclean."* (Mark 7:18, 21–23)

Jesus discerned the weakness of the monastery approach: it mislocates the enemy and is powerless to turn a rebel into a trusting child of God.

Children raised in monastery-style environments — where devotion to God is equivalent to attending church services, giving a few coins in the offering, memorizing Bible verses, and having the correct haircut — tend to grow up and flee those restrictions. Regretfully, they often rebel against the spiritual values of their parents and experiment with evil. When they marry and have children, they often vow there will be no rigid rules in their home. Their children will be free to discover their own standards. Thus, in reaction to rigidity, the pendulum swings to the opposite extreme — the laissez-faire approach.

## The laissez-faire parent

Laissez-faire is a philosophy that deliberately abstains from giving direction. Its adherents focus on noninterference and stress individual freedom of choice and action. When applied to

> *The monastery philosophy of raising children cannot generate a deep intimacy with God, which alone yields a wise and moral lifestyle.*

parenting it means refraining from inhibiting a child's creative self-development. The laissez-faire parent chooses not to give authoritative guidance in spiritual or moral matters.

Charlene's dad is the pastor of a large fundamentalist church. In her teen years she rebelled, ran away from home, and got pregnant. A one-year marriage to the father of her child proved a disaster. Now at twenty-eight she is married to a successful attorney, and her career in interior design has taken off. During a quick lunch between appointments she shares some of her thoughts about raising her kids.

"Patrick and I trust our children. We want them to experiment and follow their instincts. Why not let them have their flings? After all, in spite of my dad's multitude of sermons, I sowed my wild oats. All that church attendance and Bible-reading my parents subjected me to didn't keep me from getting into trouble. My children will have the light to discover their own personal meaning without my interference. At least they are not growing up in all that pious hypocrisy."

I asked Charlene if I could share a challenge my wife and I faced in teaching our three-year-old daughter, Jenae, the meaning of the word *hot*. She nodded.

"We use a wood burning stove to heat our home. When cranked up, its surface temperature peaks at about one thousand degrees Fahrenheit. One day Mary came to me with concern, 'Dave, if Jenae plants her little palm on that stove, she will be scarred for life!'

"My masculine laissez-faire response was, 'That would teach her! She'd never touch hot stoves again.'"

I asked Charlene what kind of parent she would consider me if I allowed Jenae to learn about hot stoves through trial and error experimentation? She grimaced at the thought of Jenae's charred palm.

The laissez-faire parent forgets that the school of experience is efficient but cruel. A grotesquely scarred palm is too high a price to pay to learn the meaning of the word *hot.* The multiple deaths of teenagers is too high a cost to learn that the illicit use of drugs is wrong. Becoming the victim of AIDS or giving birth to an illegitimate baby is too high a price for a lesson in the advantages of sexual purity. The learn-by-experience, do-your-own-thing approach was popular in the sixties, but in the nineties we must wise up to its wreckage of human lives. So where do we go from here? What is an effective parental training model for the final decade of the twentieth century? How should our children learn about the "hot spots" in life?

## Learn-and-live parenting

When Mary confronted me with the danger posed by our stove, I immediately contacted a welder. He built a large, metal screen around the stove so that Jenae could not get near the searing surface. We then began an intense course in the meaning of *hot.* I took her by the hand and brought her near the stove where she could feel the heat. "Hot! Hot!" We repeated, "Hurt, Jenae! Ow! Don't touch!"

This approach depends upon our genuine love for her as our daughter, our personal conviction concerning the danger of hot stoves, and our effectiveness in teaching her those two realities. Effective training can bring her to the day when she will no longer need the screen. Jenae can mature to the point that she will decide for herself that it is foolish to get burned by insisting on planting her fist on a hot stove. She may choose to learn this lesson by getting burned. But she will be way ahead if she accepts our love and the reality of our teaching concerning the pain of burned flesh.

Today's generation needs adults who will love them enough to point out the hot spots in life, build authoritative fences to protect them from these dangers while they are immature, and invest the personal time necessary to train teenagers to make right ethical choices on their own. Our lives must demonstrate the happiness found in living wisely. We must stop coveting our teenagers' youth and fully accept our adult responsibility to teach the next generation how to live. But where do we find the correct principles for living?

**We must help kids avoid "burning their fingers."**

# Facing up to realities

Though dusty with age and far removed from the *New York Times* best-seller list, the Old Testament book of Proverbs is still the ultimate parental training manual. The Proverbs may appear to be quaint, old-fashioned relics of a bygone era or obvious trivialities everyone should know. But when mined with perseverance, they become nuggets that glisten with life's realities.

Proverbs is a gutsy book about money, sex, and power. It exposes the con-game of the drug pusher, the seduction of the prostitute, and the sarcasm of the agnostic university professor. It does not blush when talking about the intimacies of sexual love or shrink from the evolutionist's challenge concerning the creation. Its greatest gift? The revelation of God's personal philosophy of child-rearing.

God chooses neither the protectionism of the monastery nor the experimentation of the laissez-faire method. Instead, He penetrates deep inside our children's personalities and challenges them with the choices in life that bring success and those that yield disaster. He courts them to choose to love, trust, and respect Him. He advises them to be worldly-wise but to remain innocent — wise as a serpent concerning evil's allure but pure as a dove concerning involvement in sin. His top priority is an invitation. He desires to live inside their personalities and give them the power not only to know but also to make the right choice.

Will our children be able to say that their dad and mom loved them enough to teach them not just how to make a living but how to live? When our children leave the shelter of our homes, will they be sheltered by the wisdom that only God can teach?

These are not only theoretical issues for me. Mary and I are in the midst of rearing

> *Proverbs is a gutsy book about money, sex, and power.*

three sons and a daughter. Just yesterday, it seems, I waited nervously in the waiting room — back when dads were not welcome in the delivery room — while Mary gave birth to our oldest. Today he is asking me to teach him to drive. Tomorrow we'll be checking out colleges, and the next day he'll be on his own. Our parenting days are moving at the speed of light. Will we use these speeding moments to train Jonathan, Joel, Joshua, and Jenae in God's school of skillful living? Or will they be left to the school of hard knocks? Time and the personal decisions our children make will answer this question. What about *your* kids?

God teaches me from Proverbs. My family is struggling to apply the learn-and-live approach to parenting in the computer age, to learn together how to avoid sending our kids to the school of hard knocks.

This chapter is taken from *Raising Worldly-wise but Innocent Kids* (Chicago: Moody, 1990).

### Further Reading

James Dobson. *Dr. Dobson Answers Your Questions About Raising Children.* Wheaton: Tyndale, 1986.

Gary Smalley. *The Key to Your Child's Heart, Revised.* Dallas: Word, 1992.

Charles Stanley. *How to Keep Your Kids on Your Team.* Nashville: Oliver-Nelson, 1986.

David Wyrtzen. *Raising Worldly-wise but Innocent Kids.* Chicago: Moody, 1990.

# How Dad Can Build a Winning Family

*Stephen A. Bly*

## About the author

**Stephen Bly** serves as pastor of Winchester Community Church in Winchester, Idaho. He has written eleven books, including Hard Winter at Broken Arrow Crossing (Good News), How to Be a Good Dad (Moody), and the Nathan T. Riggins Western Adventure Series (Crossway). He is a frequent speaker at family conferences and Christian writers' seminars. He has also coauthored eleven books with his wife, Janet, including How to Be a Good Mom, Be Your Mate's Best Friend, and How to Be a Good Grandparent (Moody).

Joseph Walker.

Jedediah Smith.

Most history books put them in the same paragraph. Some call them early Western explorers. Some call them trappers. Others might label them Indian fighters. Their Eastern contemporaries called them reckless and foolish. They preferred the simple name *mountain men.*

They both belonged to that uncontrollable band of restless men who crossed the Mississippi toward the unexplored wilderness between 1810 and 1840. To parallel what they did in our day, you would have to put together a spaceship in your backyard and set out to explore outer space on your own.

## What made for success?

Both came West to the wilderness in their early twenties. They demonstrated toughness and leadership ability. Jedediah Smith was quickly recognized for his coolness and bravery. Bold, outspoken in his faith, he was grim, high-minded, and inflexible. His 668 beaver pelts displayed during the 1824–1825 season rank as an all-time record for any mountain man.

Looking for more beaver streams, Smith and fifteen companions headed out of the 1826 Cache Valley Rendezvous on a journey that would lead them to the Mexican land called Alta California. Smith made two such historic treks. On each one he promoted the typical mountain man way of doing things — push on, follow your hunches, blunder your way through, hang tough, drive to the end. From the Great Salt Lake, through bleak northern Arizona, and across the Mojave Desert, Smith directed his party of men. After three years and thirty-three men (twenty-six died along the way and two deserted), he had nothing to show for his efforts, not even a decent trail to California.

On the other hand, Joe Walker, who stood six feet at 200 pounds, hawk-beaked and bearded, blazed new trails in the wilds. A few years later, Walker rounded up a gang of trappers at the Green River Rendezvous and rode west to find a trail to California. Even-tempered, able to command without offending, he delighted in exploring unknown regions. When the word spread that Joe Walker commanded a crew to California, long lines of trappers volunteered. He chose forty of the best.

### Crossing the Sierras

His explorers began the trip with four horses apiece, sixty pounds of jerky per man, and all the gear needed for such a trip. He consulted local Indians along the way to chart his course across northern Nevada, along what's now called the Humbolt River, and finally to the Sierras. The first mountain crossing tried the hardiest of them, but after a rest on the large ranchos of California, they discovered a low-altitude crossing (Walker Pass) to return home.

With foresight, common sense, and a good plan, Walker, unlike Smith before him, opened up the golden lands of California. His path marked the very foundation of the famous California Trail that beckoned miners and settlers by the thousands. His pass proved the most accessible. His men served as wagon masters of countless trips. Their stories of the warm fertile California climate charmed folks for the next 150 years.

Basic skills didn't separate Smith from Walker. Both were exceptional mountain men. Desire didn't make the difference. Both wanted to carve through those mountains. Walker

> *Why does it seem that some dads achieve much more than others?*

reached his goal because he had a plan. He took the time to prepare in a proper manner.

That's why Joseph Walker succeeded, and Jedediah Smith failed.

# Caring isn't enough

There are a lot of differences between dads, too. But we've got a lot in common as well. We work hard. We enjoy our families. We care about our kids. We want to provide a world that's safe, peaceful, and beautiful for them. We hope they'll grow to be thoughtful, caring, intelligent, independent, successful children.

We care.

We really do care.

So why does it seem that some dads achieve much more than others? Some wind up with families that hum. Others find themselves bogged down with hassles and frustrations. What makes the difference?

# Have a plan

Many times it's the same thing that separated Joe Walker from Jed Smith. One blunders along, hoping all will work out. The other plans, listens, prepares, and carries out a specific action intended to accomplish a goal. There's no such thing as an absolute guarantee in this life, of course. But the odds favor the Joe Walkers.

I won't try to convince you to care about your family. I won't need to. I'll help you discover a Bible principle or two, give you some ideas on how to put them into practice, share some sad and humorous incidents, and let you decide from there what you'll do.

# Corner posts

The Old West lured many with its unlimited opportunities. It provided hardship and danger. A vast, new, wild world needed to be populated. A man could choose to run cattle, turn over the sod and farm, or dig for gold. Whichever the case, he needed to mark off the four corner posts of the property he claimed and file the proper papers at the nearest territorial courthouse. Those corner posts, or piles of rocks, delineated the boundaries of his domain. Within that boundary, he built his estate.

Building a winning family is similar. Sometimes little gets done because we've never taken time to set the boundaries. We wander aimlessly through unmarked prairies. What are the corner posts of a winning family?

### Beware of a selfish will

*First,* I assume we all want to build quality into our family life. This deserves more than just surface agreement. Subtle and selfish wills can divert the best of intentions.

Gary attends every family conference in the county. He's the first to talk about the sad decline in family life in America. In fact, it's almost a slogan with him. Gary's running for a position in the state legislature. His campaign speeches are peppered with "Strengthen Family Life" themes.

His wife Cathy is a former beauty pageant queen. She conducts an early morning aerobics class on the local television channel. Their two children attend a prestigious private school. Brad's a good tennis player who's been offered several scholarships this year. Tricia, their daughter, sings like a pro. But for now, the whole family's dedicated to one thing: getting Dad elected. As long as every member fulfills his part in this process, they're an ideal family.

But what if one of the members decides on another goal? Gary is content as long as he controls their direction. He sees his family as a necessary prop in achieving his own personal dreams.

That doesn't mean Gary doesn't love his family. He does. He's just never thought through whether he's building quality into his family life. He's too busy politicking. The truth is, any dad can fall into such a trap from time to time. We can claim great concern for our family, but the minute one of them behaves in a way that doesn't promote our pet image or ambition, we come unglued.

### Take action

*Second,* I assume we're willing to work at building a winning family. Wanting a winner of a family involves a proper attitude. Willingness to work requires self-discipline. It means pushing the old body when you'd rather just sit there in front of the television. It means not merely planning an activity but carrying it out.

Randy, Tom, Bob, and Jerry have played golf every Saturday morning for almost ten years, ever since they starred on the local college team. But Bob dropped out last September. It was a tough choice for him. He'd just lowered his handicap to three. What a time to quit. But two considerations forced his decision.

He wanted to spend more uninterrupted time with his daughters, Carrie, age eight, and Amy, age six. Also, he wanted to give his wife, Nanci, some private time to herself.

It all came about when Carrie and Amy wanted to enroll in a gymnastics class that convened in a town twenty-three miles from home. The class met on Saturday mornings. Bob could have insisted that Nanci take the girls, but that meant one more morning of hassle for her. Instead, Bob said good-bye to the foursome at Riverside Golf Course and greeted the mornings at the Sunnyside Gym. Two happy daughters giggled through lunch at a fast-food chain, while Nanci relished a whole morning to herself.

It took more than good intentions for Bob

to carry it off. The polished persimmon woods idle away in the red leather golf bag. The club championship tourney yields one less entrant. It's spring. The fairway trees are in full bloom. The warm winds smell of new-mown greens, and nerves twitch with the excitement of the crack of a hit. To invest in building a winning family cost Bob something.

## Follow biblical principles

*Third,* I assume that we're willing to recognize an authority higher than ourselves. One of the corner posts of a strong family is the Bible. As a practical guide for family matters, the Bible has proven its reliability. For thousands of years its wisdom has instructed the faithful. Today it remains the world's best-selling book. Even families who never attend church or claim direct knowledge of God base many of their actions on biblical principles. Those principles have sometimes been handed down from generation to generation until folks don't know where they originated. All they know is that they work.

Jeff's Uncle Ted took him aside on his wedding day. "Jeff," he advised, "never let the sun go down on your anger. If you and your wife argue, keep talking until you've solved it."

Jeff followed that advice. In fact, he'll tell you that's been one of the strengths of his twenty-three-year marriage. What Jeff didn't know, until just last year, was that Uncle Ted quoted the Bible (Ephesians 4:26).

Biblical principles work. They work year after year, century after century, because people don't change. Cultures change. Technology changes. Knowledge changes. But human nature is constant. For instance, the sibling rivalry of Cain and Abel (those first sons of Adam and Eve) repeats itself in millions and billions of families throughout earth's history.

Good reasons impel us to trust the Bible. Second Timothy 3:16 states, "All Scripture is inspired by God and profitable for teaching, for reproof, for correction, for training in

> *Building a winning family cost Bob.*

righteousness." The greatest people in history acted on biblical principles and urged others to do the same. We've yet to discover any man better at dealing with people than Jesus. He not only validated the entire Old Testament with His life, but He left us, through inspired writers, twenty-seven new books to search.

Perhaps the best reason to try biblical principles is because they work. I'm a rather pragmatic guy. I suppose that comes from thirty years of living and working on a farm. At every equipment show I've attended, new product salesmen astound me with their claims. The products range from chemical hardpan solvents to mechanical asparagus planters. Anything can look good displayed in a brochure or parked in a cement-floored exhibition hall. But I want to see it in action on the field. Show me how it dissolves my hardpan or plants my asparagus; then I'll tell you what I think of it.

I've been field-testing biblical principles for years. A family using biblical principles is a winning family. You can find testimonials all around you. Trust God's Word, and you will have one firmly driven stake in the boundaries of quality family living.

## Commit yourself to Jesus

*Fourth,* you've got to have a basic commitment to Jesus Christ. This marker's the simplest and the toughest at the same time. You've got to work at it. You've got to base your family life on biblical principles. But in addition, you need a personal friendship with God through His Son.

If you've already established that relationship—great! You know what I'm talking about, and you're ready to proceed. On the other hand, you may have never even considered it. You may be determined to stay as far away as

> *A family using biblical principles is a winning family.*

possible from anything sounding religious. Or you may know all about the subject but have never made a firm pledge.

Each dad needs to make his own decision to believe that Jesus is exactly who He claims to be — to trust that He has done, is doing, and will do all that He states in the Bible.

Some men object to making such a personal commitment and feel that religious beliefs fall outside of public scrutiny. They may think of religion as anti-intellectual or as something that requires dependence rather than self-sufficiency. It may seem unmasculine. I should know — I used to have all those feelings myself.

Five years after marriage I liked what was happening. I had a loving, supportive wife and two bright, healthy, handsome sons. We lived in a comfortable house in the country. I spent my days on the farm, working the land as had my father and grandfather before me. I had everything the way I wanted it. I was no neurotic.

Yet there was still something missing. In quiet moments, when I dared to be honest with myself, I wondered, *Is this all there is to life?* Was it merely to be a seventy-year cycle of planting and harvesting, of eating and sleeping, of weekdays and weekends, of getting and spending, of growing older and older?

I had no zealous friends urging me on, not even a nagging wife, and only a casual connection to church. I lived the good life, according to this world's standards, but I wanted something more. I wanted a first-class quality life, a winning life. And that seemed out of my grasp. So in a fit of introspection I suggested to my wife that we should read the Bible together because "It's been lots of good help

**A winning family comes in different sizes and shapes and shades.**

to other people. Maybe it will benefit us."

We searched through discarded books in the garage to find one and soon developed a nightly pattern of reading after we tucked the kids in bed. In those long months of study, I learned a few things. I discovered that the people in the Bible were just ordinary. Some were good, some were bad. Most could be categorized somewhere in between. But I also discerned that God constituted a real part of their lives. They acknowledged Him as alive, personal, and involved in what they did, even when they chose to ignore Him.

I knew God played no part in my life. After months of consideration, Janet and I took action. We began to attend a church and listen to what they told us. We would arrive a little late, sit in the back, and leave early. Hardly anyone knew we were there.

I soon realized that being a Christian meant more than assenting to a philosophical system. It required face-to-face confrontation with a Person who lives and loves, rules and reigns, provides for and protects all who believe in Him. I also discovered that belief in Jesus Christ was not unreasonable. It required a step of faith, but healthy evidence supported that step. The more I learned, the more convinced I became that the whole matter made sense. In fact, once I had accepted Jesus for who He was, all creation made sense. World history made sense. My family life made sense. In short, a door opened to the possibility that I could now attain the quality life that had escaped me before.

I'm still working at understanding, complying with, and enjoying this relationship with God. But the missing piece has been found.

Take time to consider your own spiritual commitment. It might need a renewal. It might need to be acknowledged for the first time. Or you could read the rest of this book and skip all that. But sooner or later, you'll be caught with one of your boundary markers down. When that happens, you'll have no clear definition of what you're trying to build.

> *Jesus Christ can be your north star, the constant guidepost to keep you on course.*

You'll still be aimless and frustrated.

"Follow the tongue" was a phrase of the Old West. When hunters, trappers, and pioneers first barged into the wastelands, no roads gave them their bearings. They simply headed West. Without road signs, maps, and friendly gas station attendants, how did they find their way? How could they make sure they rode west?

They solved that problem by reading the stars at night, locating the north star, and then pointing the tongue of their wagon due west. Next morning the stars faded from sight. All they needed to do was "follow the tongue."

That's just what Jesus Christ can do for your family. He can be your north star, the constant guidepost to keep you on course. No matter how many times you have or haven't considered Him, you must continually come back to that basic relationship with Him.

## A winning family

What does a winning family look like? That's difficult to say, because quality comes in different sizes and shapes and shades for each family. Each must find for themselves what fits best. Let me give you a glimpse of how it works for us.

Last Saturday my oldest son, Russell, and his wife, Lois, stopped by to borrow a tool. I suggested they stay for dinner. My wife, Janet, picked up on the idea and started fixing a salad; Lois chipped in to help with the dessert. I fired up the grill for the meat. Russell engaged in a lively conversation about cars with his eighteen-year-old brother, Mike.

Our youngest, Aaron, age five, pestered the big brothers until they kicked the soccer ball around with him.

We sat down to eat our simple meal. Nothing gourmet. The furnishings were webbed-patio style. The view, a neighbor's cement block wall, was less than inspiring. But the contentment was there.

We're a family who enjoys themselves. We like to be with each other. The kids treat Mom with respect and trust that Dad will have a piece of wisdom worth listening to once in a while.

A warm spring evening and a dish of homemade ice cream. No television blaring. No hostile remarks. Just six common people kicked back and enjoying life together.

Pure quality.

I'm convinced that's what family life's meant to be.

It's part of the reward of working to build a family that's a winner.

This chapter is taken from *How to Be a Good Dad* (Chicago: Moody, 1986).

## Further Reading

Stephen A. Bly. *How to Be a Good Dad.* Chicago: Moody, 1986.

Tim Hansel. *What Kids Need Most in a Dad.* Tarrytown, N.Y.: Revell, 1989.

Josh McDowell and Dick Day. *How to Be a Hero to Your Kids.* Dallas: Word, 1991.

# The right thing to do

In 1973 I found myself in the middle of the biggest political upheaval in American history. As the Watergate storm thundered around me, week after week I was subpoenaed by grand juries, summoned before congressional committees, interrogated by special prosecutors and the FBI, and all the while pilloried daily in the national press.

The real crucible came on the day I was hauled before a grand jury in the District Court Building in Washington, D. C. I was a lawyer, sworn to uphold the law – yet here I was, guarded by federal marshals as I made my way down the long, drab corridor into the jury room. As I was ushered in, I saw twenty-five of my peers seated in the jury box, most of them looking terribly bored, some asleep, one or two even reading newspapers. At the front of the room was a graying – and, I thought, leering – prosecutor.

## Trap

The questions were tough. Most had nothing to do with the Watergate case, but rather were designed to embarrass and entrap me. As an attorney, I knew exactly what my adversary, the special prosecutor, was doing. My first instinct was to evade, maybe even shade the truth a bit, and throw them off the track.

But even as I felt that lawyer's instinct for survival, another voice sounded even stronger in my mind: "There is nothing more important than telling the truth. Always tell the truth. It's the right thing to do." It was my father's voice.

My mind flashed back to the earliest days I could remember. My dad and I didn't have a lot of time together – he worked all day and went to law school at night during those tough days of the Depression. But on Sunday afternoons, my dad would take a break from his crowded schedule and sit with me on the back steps of our modest frame house just outside of Boston.

Though rugged and athletic, Dad was a gentle man who always spoke softly. I would listen, enraptured, as he described his law school classes or told me of his own boyhood experiences. Then he would invariably ask me – always in a loving, never in a demanding way – questions about school or my friends. And if he sensed I might be struggling with something, he made it clear that I could come to him anytime to discuss anything. "Just one thing," he would always add. "There is nothing more important than telling the truth. Always tell the truth."

## Faithful example

Those words and my dad's faithful example over the years stayed with me through adulthood and the White House-magnitude struggles I never could have imagined as a child. And so that day in the courthouse, I took a few deep breaths, sat up straight in my chair, and gave truthful answers. I did the same thing the forty-four other times I was called to testify under oath during Watergate – and, as it turned out, I was the only major Watergate figure not charged with perjury.

That didn't keep me out of jail, however. As I've since realized, God had His own plans for me and my time in prison. But even as I went in, I realized that at least I would be able to serve my time, pay my debt for what I had done, and do so with a clear conscience.

My father died while I was in prison – and that was one of the toughest losses of my life. But I think he experienced the same peace I did. As I was being sentenced, his question was, "Have you told the truth?"

I told him I had. He looked at me with a confident smile. "Then you'll be all right." And he was right.

**Charles W. Colson**

# Seven Kinds of Fathers

*Randy L. Carlson*

## About the author

*Randy Carlson, M.A., is the executive director of the Family Life Radio network, and his broadcast "Today's Family," cohosted with Kevin Leman, is syndicated on more than sixty stations. He is the author of* Father Memories *(Moody) and the coauthor of* Unlocking the Secrets of Your Childhood Memories *(Pocket Books).*

Human personality is made up of a complex mixture of components. Family environment, birth order, genetics, gender, and other factors play important roles in shaping our life-directing goals and the final product we call personality. There is a constant interplay between the actual father-to-child relationship, the way we remember that relationship, and the emotions we attach to those memories. Therefore, generalizing that certain types of fathering will result in specific lifestyles on the part of a child is overly simplistic.

However, my counseling experience shows that most father memories fall into groups such as the ones I will discuss below. Those categories may help you make sense out of your own memories and the life themes that you have built from them. Although each individual childhood is unique, seeing similarities between your situation and common behavioral tendencies may help you grasp the private logic that is ruling your life, governing your behavior, and interpreting your world.

Let's look at seven categories into which fathers can fall (there are others we haven't listed) so that you can get a better idea of where your father fits. Remember, he could easily fall into a combination of categories and carry some characteristics from more than one group.

# The controlling father

Greg was raised by an extremely authoritarian father, the type I call an offensive controller, someone who manipulates his environment to make others do what he wants them to do. Greg's father is a brilliant surgeon on the West Coast and a man accustomed to getting what he wants out of life and others. He always sets his sights high and over the years has expected his children to set their sights high too.

*Never, can't,* or *won't* are not in his vocabulary. When he sets his mind on something, he refuses to take no for an answer. So compliant son Greg is fearful of getting his knuckles rapped a good one if he dares to tell his father how unenthusiastic he is about pursuing a medical career. Medicine is a family tradition, and Greg knows his dad will perceive his stand as defiance.

"His work always came first," is what Greg remembers about his father. "All I ever saw in my father was his serious side. We never had fun, and everything seemed to revolve around his work, his patients, his needs. I really don't want the same for myself or my future family, but I feel like I'd be letting my father down if I don't at least give medicine a try."

Although Greg's use of the expressions "never had fun" and "everything revolved around his work" hint at overgeneralization or exaggeration on his part, the description itself indicates that Greg's father has the classic symptoms of a controller. Do you have a controller in your memories? In your present family? Check the statements that are true of you and put a plus mark by those that are true of your father. A controller reasons like this:

☐ *"It's my way or no way."*
☐ *"I'm the final authority here, and I have the final word."*
☐ *"I like to make things happen and to have them go my way."*
☐ *"Everything is set, so don't surprise me. I call the shots."*

> *"All I ever saw in my father was his serious side. We never had fun, and everything seemed to revolve around his work, his patients, his needs."*

☐ *"Life is serious and planned out. Don't rock the boat."*
☐ *"My opinion is informed and accurate — I'll talk, you listen."*

Those statements will sound familiar to an individual raised by a controlling father. A controlling father typically controls everything he touches, including you. That control can take different forms. Some controllers get right to the point and make their positions clear and unchallengeable. Others, like Greg's father, are more subtle. They will bribe, coax, manipulate through guilt, or withhold approval to insure that others behave the way they want them to.

It is true that it is healthy, desirable, and biblical for a child to be raised under the father's authority. But that use of biblically mandated authority to train the child is different from an excessive need to run the child's life. A controlling father abuses his God-given authority.

If you were raised by a controller, you were set up for unique problems. In order to maintain some control over your life you may have become a counter-controller and a rebel. Or you may have elected to maintain control by manipulating others or being overly assertive. More often, however, compliant children of controllers (especially women) become pleasers and are reluctant to take control of their own lives. They grow up to discover that they are still wrestling with some or all of the following emotions:

● *"I feel like I don't measure up to what is expected of me."*

- "I struggle with a passive-aggressive kind of anger. On the surface I appear controlled, but underneath I am angry."
- "I need to be in control of myself to feel OK."
- "I put others before myself in an unhealthy way and often refuse to express my real feelings."
- "It's hard for me to say no to others. I hate feeling like I've let others down."

If your father was a controller, you will discover one or more of the above themes in your memories. For Greg, being the son of a controller has meant a lifetime of conceding his own desires in favor of living up to his father's expectations. Through a forced smile he recalled, "I remember one day when I was about seven. I really wanted to say no to my father, but I just couldn't. I wanted to go next door and play with my friend, and at the same time my father wanted me to help him with some sort of project he was working on in the yard. It wasn't so much that I couldn't have gone next door, but I felt a pressure to do what my father expected of me."

Even though his father's request wasn't out of line, the important thing to notice is that Greg remembers not being comfortable with telling his dad he wanted to play with his friend. A general desire to please Dad is not inappropriate or unhealthy. It becomes unhealthy when the child "just can't say no" even when he could.

Greg still feels that pressure. Anytime he has a desire to do something on his own, the father he carries inside himself quickly fire hoses his great idea. Even if Greg's father never says a word, Greg anticipates his father's negative response and "hears" his father's reaction in his head. Greg has internalized his dad's messages and expectations to the point that, though no one may mention those expectations out loud, they come to mind automatically and exercise control over his decision making.

Does Greg's reluctance to say no, or his

> *For Greg, being the son of a controller has meant a lifetime of conceding his own desires in favor of living up to his father's expectations.*

feeling of constantly being under his father's thumb, sound like you? Does your dad fit the controller role? Can you hear controller themes when you tell your father memories?

# The distant father

The distant father comes in many varieties. Some distant fathers are dads who traveled frequently, worked long hours, were preoccupied with pressing problems, or were separated from their kids through divorce. Other fathers were emotionally distant and never developed deep bonds with their children. Both physical and emotional distance leave an indelible mark on a child. Most often a child experiences the absence of a father as rejection. He reasons that he or she is not worth his dad's time and attention. Children who grow up in a home with a distant father often have trouble bonding deeply with others or establishing lasting relationships.

Heather's father was around physically, but he might as well not have been as far as she was concerned. His presence did little to meet her need for a father. When she looked into his eyes nobody was home. When he came home at night, he took off his overalls in the back hall, grunted a greeting of sorts to his wife, and collapsed into his waiting Lazy Boy®. Once there, it took a crowbar or an offer of dinner to get him up. Night after night Sam lost himself in the paper or a never-ending round of TV programs. The message "stay away, please" came through to Heather loud and clear.

Heather recalls, "In all my years at home, I can't remember a single display of affection or tender moment between my parents. My father never hugged or kissed me either." A loving touch, meaningful hug, or even a peck on the cheek were absent. Heather seldom saw her father express *any* emotion. Heather came to believe the message her father was sending — *you are really not that important to me.*

Other life scripts passed from father to daughter:
- *"Work is more important than relationships."*
- *"Children are to be seen and not heard."*
- *"What I do isn't that important."*
- *"What I feel isn't that important either."*
- *"Don't wait for a man to meet your needs."*

Heather recalled that as a little girl whenever she wanted to talk to her father he told her he was busy and asked her to come back later. Heather learned quickly that "later" never happened. As a result, Heather was conditioned to believe lies about life.
- *"I need attention so badly that I'll get it any place I can."* Women in this environment tend to pick a loser for marriage. They reason that any man will do. They quickly learn that just isn't so.
- *"If I just try harder maybe I'll be accepted."* Some people will spend a lifetime trying to break through the artificial barrier of acceptance. Those of us with distant fathers pick up the AVIS complex — we try harder.
- *"I crave closeness and love, but am afraid of or uncomfortable with intimacy."* These individuals often keep their distance or back away from relationships if they grow too close for comfort.

> *When she looked into his eyes nobody was home.*

# The workaholic father

The workaholic father, like the emotionally distant father, puts work and things before people and emotions. His children grow up conditioned to think that work is the essence of life and often push themselves to unreasonable limits to achieve in order to gain the attention they need.

On the other hand, some children of workaholic fathers conclude that father *doesn't* know best. They rebel against the never-ending workload that saps all their time and energy and leaves them emotionally undernourished. "What's the use," they reason. "It's all a selfish, empty, ego-stroking escape from the responsibility to love one another. When you work all the time, there's no time to really get to know anyone or serve anyone except the business."

**The workaholic father puts work before family.**

# The encouraging father

Psychologist David Semands wrote, "The perceived 'You are's' of the parents become the inner 'I am's' of the children."[1] Children who were raised by encouraging parents have "I am's" that indicate emotional health:

- *"I am capable."*
- *"I am not perfect, but that is OK. I can learn from my mistakes."*
- *"I am a child of God, and He loves and accepts me as I am."*
- *"I am able to love and be loved by others. I love and respect myself."*
- *"It is safe to be open and vulnerable with those I am closest to."*

James Dobson, who crusades for strong families as head of the international Christian organization, Focus on the Family, was raised by an encouraging father of whom he has spoken often with the warmest affection and respect. Kevin Leman and I had the privilege of being featured for two days on Dr. Dobson's radio broadcast, covering the topic of early childhood memories. While we were on the air, Dr. Dobson told us the first memory he has of his father:

*Let me give you my first recollection of my father, with whom I had a notoriously good relationship, and you tell me what the meaning of it is. This is, I believe, the first time he ever entered into my life that I can recall. It was at the end of the day and my dad, who was a minister, had been at the church all day. He knocked on the front door instead of coming through it, and I was the one that went and opened the door for him.*

*When I opened the door, he had a smile on his face as he said, "Come with me." Then he took me around the side of the house and there was a brand new, big, blue tricycle there! It was one exciting moment. As far as surprises of my life, that one probably ranks near the top in terms of sheer delight.*[2]

That father memory oozes with love, affection, and tenderness. In Dobson's memory you

> *Father is seen as a loving, caring, giving parent eager to delight his son.*

can sense the importance of the family. Father is seen as a loving, caring, giving parent eager to delight his son. Is it any surprise that the nation's leading advocate for the family would have a father memory like that? It is consistent with how Dobson sees life.

One thing that jumps out in the memory is that he remembers taking responsibility to open the door. The adult James Dobson still takes responsibility. If a door has to be opened, he is going to open it. He's going to be willing to see what's on the other side and deal with it. Another significant phrase is Dobson's comment that his father smiled and said, "Come with me." I contend that those words characterized their relationship overall – they weren't referring just to seeing the new bike. It is also true that the adult James Dobson pictures God as a loving heavenly Father who delights in giving good gifts to his children.

Encouragement is an art. You are a fortunate person if your father memories include the theme of encouragement and loving affirmation. There is no greater legacy a father can leave with his child.

# The critical father

On the other side of the scale are the critical fathers who just have that look. You know the look I'm talking about – the kind that pierces with disapproval and rejection even if no words are spoken. You could have brought home a report card with four A's and still got the look. The message was "Why the B? This is unacceptable."

Critical fathers can sniff our imperfection from across the room. Joyce grew up with a critical father:

*I recall my first day of school. I was so excited to be out with the big kids and finally going to school myself. Mom dressed me up in a cute, fluffy pink dress, handed me a new box of crayons, and deposited me with the kindergarten teacher. I spent the day coloring pictures and playing with the other kids. One of the pictures was of a house with some trees. We were trying to color inside the lines — well I did the best I could.*

*When I got home that afternoon, I remember that my father was home early, but I don't remember why. The part of the memory I recall the clearest is the feeling of rejection after my father looked at my little paper. He looked at it and then at me without a smile or a nod of approval. And he threw my paper on the counter, saying something like, "try to be more careful with your work next time." I was crushed.*

Joyce is a creative, cautious firstborn. Although her father memory reveals an enjoyment of life, it also shows that she is captive to a fear of criticism. No matter how hard she tries she never thinks that her work is good enough. As she said, "I can't seem to keep inside those lines."

What kind of man do you think Joyce married? If you guessed "a critical Charlie type," you're right. She goes out of her way to be a pleaser, and if the boat gets rocked, she feels responsible to smooth out the waters.

"Just the other day," Joyce recalls, "I found myself trying to settle an argument between my husband and my son. Then it dawned on me that I wasn't even involved in their problem. I do that a lot."

If you were raised by a critical father, some of the emotional tones listed below probably appear in your memories. Do any of them strike a chord?
- *A fear of rejection*
- *Hurt, humiliation, despondency*
- *Trying to measure up, but not quite making it*
- *Feeling picked at or nagged*

- *Striving for perfection, yet feeling inferior*
- *Wanting to give up, but knowing you can't*

There is a better way to rear children. Contrast the behavior of the critical dads you know with God's instructions for fathers: "Don't keep on scolding or nagging your children, making them angry and resentful. Rather, bring them up with the loving discipline the Lord Himself approves, with suggestions and godly advice" (Ephesians 6:4, TLB).

# The angry father

The angry father is a one-dimensional man. He responds in anger when other emotions would be more appropriate. When he's tired, disappointed, afraid, insecure, frustrated — you name it — he gets mad. He learned, probably from his own father, that anger gets others to do what you want them to do.

If your father memories are full of anger, you may struggle with these life themes:
- *Fear of people*
- *Feeling alone a lot*
- *A sense of unpredictability and insecurity*
- *Overt anger or frozen rage (seen as depression)*
- *General anxiety*
- *Doubts about the kindness and goodness of life*

The angry father is acting in stark contrast to God's intentions. Our heavenly Father encourages us to "be quick to listen, slow to speak and slow to become angry, for man's anger does not bring about the righteous life that God desires" (James 1:19–20).

# The abusive father

The man who is emotionally, sexually, or physically abusive puts his needs before the needs of others. He sees children as objects to be used or as annoyances. Often alcohol or drug dependency is involved, and his children receive mixed messages, depending on whether their father is sober or drunk.

In adults, early father memories of abuse or neglect likewise create a mixture of messages. Research shows that most adults who were abused as children experience some or all of the following feelings or behaviors:
- *Poor self-concept*
- *Overly responsible*
- *Controlling*
- *Compulsive*
- *Obsessive*
- *People pleasers to an unhealthy extreme*
- *Perfectionistic*
- *Procrastinator*

# Encouragement

At this point in our look at fathers, some of you are weighted down and discouraged by your father memories. To those of you in that camp, here are a few points of encouragement:
- *You can be freed from father memories.*
- *Permanent change is possible – you can break the cycle.*
- *God cares about your father memories and your damaged emotions.*
- *You are not alone – many others feel as you do.*
- *You can face your felt pain and overcome it.*

In *Healing Grace* David Semands offers these suggestions concerning painful memories:

"Relive them in your emotions, but don't stop there. Relinquish them to God in forgiving and surrendering prayer. It's doubtful you can do this by yourself, so get help from a close friend, pastor our counselor."[3] Beyond that, begin today to abandon the lies that hold you captive to your memories.

This chapter is taken from *Father Memories* (Chicago: Moody, 1992).

1. David A. Semands, *Healing Grace* (Wheaton, Ill.: Victor, 1988), p. 153.
2. James Dobson as heard on "Focus on the Family" broadcast, August 1989.
3. Semands; *Healing Grace*, p. 162.

## Further Reading

Randy L. Carlson. *Father Memories*. Chicago: Moody, 1992.

Gordon Mcdonald. *The Effective Father*. Wheaton: Tyndale, 1991.

H. Norman Wright. *Always Daddy's Girl: Understanding Your Father's Impact on Who You Are*. Ventura, Calif.: Regal, 1989.

# How Mom Should Lead Her Family

*Stephen and Janet Bly*

### About the authors

*Stephen Bly serves as pastor of Winchester Community Church in Winchester, Idaho. **Janet Bly** has written four books, including* Managing Your Restless Search *(Victor) and* Friends Forever: The Art of Lifetime Relationships *(Aglow), and speaks at women's conferences and retreats as well as family and writers' seminars. The Blys have three sons and two grandchildren.*

The night of Janet's birthday Steve surprised her with an overnight stay at a beautiful southern California resort overlooking the crashing waves of the Pacific Ocean.

"Well, what did you do?" their son Aaron asked when they returned.

"We had a picnic dinner, viewed the sunset on the ocean from our balcony patio, and watched an old movie on television. Then we slept in late the next morning, had a nice breakfast, and came home," Jan reported.

"That's all?" Aaron sounded disbelieving. "Didn't you swim in the ocean? Didn't you go to the miniature golf course? Didn't you play anything?"

"Well — " Janet hesitated. "We did have a fun time."

"Yeah, it sounds really boring to me." He shrugged.

Part of his disappointment was not at our lack of activity but rather that we had not included him. At his age it's difficult for him to understand that the world does not center on him all the time.

Good moms place a high priority on privacy with dads.

If children resent that time together, it's probably because no one ever sat down to explain the family rules about married life.

## The rules of married life

One rule might be: financial problems are never, never discussed while Mom is in the first days of her monthly period. In fact, Dad should try to remove every element of added stress. Now that rule is not written down anywhere, but it is carefully guarded by the wise husband. The problem is, the kids probably don't know about this rule and so they may get caught in the crunch of wondering, "What's wrong with Mom?"

# Rules for families

For the health and happiness of the family unit, the unwritten rules ought to be explained sometime.

Here are some sample rules. You will want to add your own.

### (1) If any conflicts develop in relationships in the family, the Mom-Dad relationship takes first priority

Nick drags home, discouraged. His job is going nowhere. It's been ten long years of one draining day after another. He can't see any hope for change in the future. He obviously needs to talk.

His wife, Roxanne, puts down the dress she's hemming and eases into the den to visit with him. It's a long conversation. Years of frustration pour out.

Shellie, their daughter, bursts into the room yelling, "Mom, have you got my dress finished yet? Tony's going to be here any minute now, and I have to have that dress!"

"Oh, I'm sorry, honey, your Dad and I need to talk. I won't be able to get it done." Then Roxanne ushers her back out the door.

"But, Mom, what will I wear?" Shellie wails.

"How about the blue chambray, or else you can finish that hem yourself. But I want you to understand very clearly that the conversation your dad and I are having at the moment is extremely important."

*"What's wrong with Mom?"* .

His mother just smiles and nods. "You're right, I'm always on his side."

Shellie was sixteen years old, but she needed to understand rule 1.

### (2) In dealing with the children, Mom and Dad are always on the same side

Little Nathan was negotiating for the best deal. By last count there were fourteen presents for him under the family Christmas tree. Since that was considerably more than were there for the others, he figured out a way to keep everyone from being jealous of him on Christmas day.

"Why don't I unwrap a present or two before Christmas," he suggested to his mother. "Then it wouldn't look so, you know, unbalanced?"

It sounded quite reasonable to Nathan.

Mom relented, "Oh, I suppose one present wouldn't hurt. But wait and ask your dad."

Nathan was halfway there. When Dad tromped through the front door he was barraged with, "Daddy, Mommy thinks it would be a good idea for me to open one of my presents ahead of time, you know, since I have too many anyway. She said it was OK, but that I should ask you. You don't mind, do you?"

Nathan's dad did mind. "One of the great delights in having presents is the anticipation of opening them. Once you open one, you'll want to open another. Soon, all the good lessons, and most of the fun, are lost. I think we ought to wait until Christmas."

"But Mom said I could!" Nathan appealed.

But Mom was right behind him. "Well, Nate, I think Dad is right. You'd better wait."

"That's not fair! You always take Daddy's side," Nathan whines.

His mother just smiles and nods. "You're right, I'm always on his side."

Nathan had just been struck down, once again, by rule 2.

## (3) No child was ever damaged by seeing evidence that Mom and Dad love each other

Tommy's turbo moon rocket blaster was just about to make a successful landing on the alien planet Phlinxtorpe when he heard a strange noise. Was it the evil Spymaster returning to destroy earth? Was it another visit by the sinister Doomlaunch? Perhaps it was Princess Sweetlight trying to make it to safety.

"Nah, it's coming from the living room. Must be the TV," Tommy surmised.

Then, suddenly, the awful thought hit him. He knew what the noise was. "They're in there kissing!" He ran as fast as his legs would scurry in hopes of catching them in the act of the crime. But he was too late. Mom and Dad were sitting next to each other, hugging.

"You've been kissing in here, haven't you?" he accused.

"Oh, well, I suppose we were," his mom said. "Do you call this kissing?" She grabbed her husband and planted a kiss on his lips.

"Hey, that's enough," Tommy protested, "I could hear you clear in my room. Aren't you guys too old for that?"

"Nah." Mom smiled and kissed Dad again.

"Oh, brother." Tommy sighed. "I'm going back to Phlinxtorpe."

"Where?" his father asked.

"The planet Phlinxtorpe. Moms and dads don't kiss on Phlinxtorpe."

"It must be a very lonely place," Mom replied. Poor old Tommy. Chased away by rule 3.

**Let kids see Mom and Dad's love for each other.**

## (4) Sexual relations between Mom and Dad are private – as well as legal, moral, biblical, and enjoyable

"Mom, I've got to ask you something." Jennifer tossed down her school books as she slid into the kitchen. "Listen, we had this film at school today . . . and . . . well – do you and Dad have sex?"

Jennifer's mom almost dropped her cup of coffee.

"Oh, well, I mean – it's just that this film was, you know, a sex education film. Well, it made sex seem kind of clinical, you know, like going to the doctor, or something. Is that the way it is?"

It was a moment that Jennifer's mom knew would be arriving. She had hoped it wouldn't be quite this soon, or quite this way, but she was determined not to avoid the subject.

"Well, no, actually it's quite romantic. Did you want to talk about it?"

"Yeah."

Her mom took a deep breath. "Jennifer, do you know what actually happens when two people love each other in that way?"

"You mean, getting pregnant and all that?"

"Yes, but also, do you know what happens to the man and to the woman while they are making love?"

"Oh, sure. I guess they told us at school. But – not really. What happens?"

Jennifer's mom described the specific details as completely as she thought necessary. Then she asked, "Do you know what the Bible has to say about sex?"

"I suppose. It's kind of naughty, huh?" she questioned.

"No. The Bible says that sex is a wonderful experience given to a husband and a wife in order to produce children and to provide a deep intimacy in their love for each other. As long as people follow God's rules, it's a wonderful thing."

"Rules like, don't mess around until you get married?" said a very direct preteen.

"That's one of the most important rules.

But it wasn't given to take away your fun. God knows that when we break that rule we bring all sorts of trouble upon ourselves and others. He is saying that sex is a special gift that He has reserved for those who are married. Within that relationship it is enjoyable and deeply satisfying. Those who try sex out of the marriage commitment declare that they know more than God about human relationships. It's like a baby playing with fire. Somebody's going to get hurt."

"Mom, is sex scary?"

"Not when it's with your marriage partner. It's a relationship that grows with time. It's really – well, wait until you're married, then you'll know."

"Then you and Dad do have sex – still?"

Jennifer's mom raised her eyebrows. "Yes, we do!"

"I thought so." Jennifer reached into the cupboard for a cookie. Rule 4 was beginning to sink in.

## (5) Mom and Dad need to get away by themselves on a regular basis

Barbara happened onto the perfect part-time job. She works while the kids are in school, and, as she puts it, "I make just enough to have a house cleaner come in twice a month, pay the babysitter every week, and have enough left over for a neat date with my husband. What more could I want?"

She's one smart lady. Every Friday night, without fail, she and her husband have that date.

"But it's not fair," Kaylee sniffles. "You have Daddy all to yourself."

"Yeah, and it sure is fun," Barbara assures her.

"Well, don't you miss me?" Kaylee prompts.

"We sure do. That's why we need to get away. Just so we can remember how much we miss you! Do you understand?"

"I – I think so." Kaylee sighs.

It's tough to come to grips with rule 5.

# An appropriate word

For the Green family, Christmas 1990 was surrounded by more than the usual anticipation and excitement of the Advent season. It was the first time in four years we would all be together. It's next to impossible to gather families from Venezuela, Texas, New Jersey, and Tennessee, but by God's grace it happened!

Mom and Dad, coming directly from Caracas, were the first to arrive in Nashville. The last time I had seen Dad was in a hospital in Phoenix right after his heart attack. While flying to Phoenix, I had reviewed the events of our lives and wondered about the possibility of life without this man who had so shaped my destiny. Miraculously, within a month he was back in South America overseeing the growth of two new churches.

One by one, the families arrived. After getting reacquainted and expressing disbelief at the growth of the children (why do we always do that?), we settled into a week of rehearsing childhood memories, catching up on the details lost by the miles, discussing important events, and having precious times of prayer filled with gratitude for the Lord's sustaining grace.

## Guarded

As we sat around the fireplace and talked, I was again impressed with how carefully my father guarded his speech. Always choosing appropriate words, he seasoned conversation with insight and wisdom. I remember that as children we had sometimes sensed people-problems among the missionaries, noticed injustices, and felt the tension of living in a foreign culture among people whose customs often flew in the face of our own, yet I don't remember ever hearing a hint of criticism or seeing a telltale sign of condescension from my parents. I'm not suggesting they were perfect. Certainly they would remember failures in these areas, but as the years pass, I have increasingly appreciated their example of James 3:2 – "We all stumble in many ways. If anyone is never at fault in what he says, he is a perfect man, able to keep his whole body in check" (NIV).

**Steve Green**

### (6) Both Mom and Dad will try to give each child consistent private attention

Aaron complained loudly about his parents having their night out. It seemed they were having all the fun. Then Dad instigated Buddy Night. Now every Wednesday Aaron and his Dad spend an evening together. It's a trip to the fast-food joint, a visit to the park, a game of basketball, a couple of books to read, a project to build out in the shop, or a home video to rent. It's just Aaron and Dad, so Fridays don't seem all that lonesome anymore.

Wednesdays work well for Aaron and his Dad because that's the night that Mom directs two handbell choir rehearsals at church and Dad has the fewest meetings.

Rule 6 is working out very well.

### (7) Whenever Mom and Dad are out alone, the kids are well taken care of

Good babysitters can be difficult to find. That's why the Andersons have latched onto Vickie. She and the three Anderson kids have a great time together.

Mrs. Anderson always makes sure that there's something tasty in the cupboard for dinner, that Vickie knows where to reach them by phone, and that a neighbor is home, just in case of an emergency.

One week she had all the ingredients for chocolate chip cookies laid out and waiting for the gang to make on their own. Another time, newsprint paper and paint awaited the young artist out on the patio.

Mrs. Anderson decided she had a firm handle on rule 7 when her husband's flu forced them to cancel Friday night plans and

> *Dad instigated Buddy Night. Now every Wednesday Aaron and his Dad spend an evening together.*

all the kids cried, "Does this mean that Vickie's not coming over?"

Single parents, of course, will have to adapt their family rules to their own situation. But some principles still apply.

# Rules for single parents

### (1) Live a biblical lifestyle

Make sure your present actions meet with God's standards. No matter what the circumstances of the past, your kids need to see you now striving to do what's right in God's sight.

### (2) Demonstrate by failure what success looks like

If your singleness is a result of separation or divorce, let your kids know what you learned from your mistakes. It is shocking to hear the statistics on the number of children from broken homes who wind up in the same situation themselves. It is as if no lessons were imparted to the next generation.

### (3) Keep exhibiting good models for them to see

In-laws, neighbors, friends, and the folks in the pew ahead of you at church can all be examples. It may sometimes seem awkward for single parents to hang around happily married couples, but do it anyway. Your kids really need to see what makes it work.

### (4) Encourage your children to ask questions

They want to know about marriage, family life, and sex. They might want to know, "What went wrong?" Let them know that such subjects are not off limits. Sure, they may be painful for you to talk about, but the kids have a right to know. Remember, they are the ones paying a price for something over which they had absolutely no control. They deserve the freedom to ask questions.

# Having time alone

What's the goal of having time alone with your husband? Perhaps Jesus explained it best.

Jesus did mighty miracles. He taught us about His purpose in coming to earth. He revealed the mysteries of God's kingdom. He also schooled us in the basics of family life. In discussing the closeness of the relationship between husband and wife He quoted from Genesis.

"For this cause a man shall leave his father and mother, and shall cleave to his wife; and the two shall become one flesh" (Matthew 19:5, KJV).

"Cleave" may sound rather old-fashioned. It means to adhere to, cling to, stick fast, to be faithful.

Without special equipment a sheer rock cliff is unclimbable. You have to have handholds and footholds of some sort. You need something to cleave onto. Building a strong, healthy, vital marriage is no less difficult than climbing a sheer rock cliff without the proper equipment.

Any man who thinks he can maintain a good marriage by anything else than clutching tightly, in faithfulness, and not letting go, is due for a painful fall.

But dads have to have something to hold onto. At times, it's going to take more than a marriage certificate and a twenty-year-old pledge. He's going to need someone who will listen and encourage, plan and dream, love and embrace. Good moms make time to be with Dad — alone.

# Time to pull rank

Becoming a mother is irrevocable.

You can't throw it off. You can't hide it. You can't disguise it. You are forever, in the child's eyes, in the mind of society, and in the annals of heaven, somebody's mom.

No doubt there have been a few (brief, we

**Building a healthy marriage is as difficult as climbing a sheer cliff.**

hope) instances when you've considered ways to disenfranchise yourself from motherhood. Maybe it was during another long pouting session from your teenager or a smart-aleck retort from the younger one. Or maybe you still stagger from the baby's long crying spells. We've all had thoughts of resigning.

On the other hand, take a peek at your children's point of view. They've had their own thought of replacing mother with a more tolerant substitute. But in either case, replacement is impossible. You are, and will forever be, Mom.

There are some advantages to that state of affairs. Let's take a review of the benefits.

At least for the first twenty years of life, only God knows this child better than you do. You are in an incredible position to experience life with him.

You have the privilege to act "just like a mother." You don't need to explain why you "mother" them when you're twenty or forty or sixty or eighty. You are Mom, and you can be overprotective, overindulgent, and over-supportive, if you like.

The slightest hint of reassurance from you can inspire them to reach for heady heights.

"Mom thinks I can do it" remains an irrefutable argument. You may be the single greatest human influence their lives will ever have.

But what if you're overwhelmed?

What if everything you've read so far doesn't seem to apply to you?

Maybe your situation's too far gone, or you're new at being a mother, or you feel your own inadequacies too keenly. Wherever you are, there's a way to tell if you've got the potential for being one of the "good" ones.

# Can you be a good mom?

### (1) You have your spiritual life in focus
You've established a relationship with God through personal trust in Jesus Christ. Your spiritual commitment directly affects and influences everything you do. You know you don't have everything mastered yet, but you're willing to work on it.

### (2) You're not satisfied with just surviving
You don't want to merely tolerate a situation; you want to enjoy it and benefit from it. You're not content with accepting whatever comes your way, but you're intent to discover the meaning and purpose behind it.

### (3) You believe in ultimate accountability for your days here on earth
You consider the humans within your sphere a part of a divine purpose. You feel the glory of your uniqueness, that you could nurture little lives in a way no other person on earth could duplicate.

### (4) You believe that your own personal happiness depends to a major part on your relationship with your family,
even though you find personal pleasure from other sources too. You're committed to the fact that this is the very place God wants you to be in.

### (5) You trust that when Jesus said (in John 10:10) that He came to give us an abundant life (a life full of joy, purpose, meaning, and satisfaction), He meant to include your family.
It takes a lot of work to be a good mom. The physical load strains your body to its limits. The mental anguish and stress is almost impossible to describe at times. The spiritual battles would overwhelm you if it were not for the Lord's special grace and strength. But the bottom line still reads the same — it's all worth it.

Some folks don't understand the value of strong family relationships. They keep using the wrong measurements. They say, "Well, you work your whole life, wear yourself out, break your health, and never achieve any recognition — or even enough luxuries to spoil yourself a little. The whole thing's a waste."

Such folks are living a sad lie.

Last February we had a dinner on Janet's birthday. It was a small affair with just Russ and his wife, Lois, Mike and his fiancée, Michelle, and Aaron. Lois prepared a delicious meal of quiche, fresh fruit salad, raw vegetables and dip, huge croissants, and coconut cream and lemon meringue pie for dessert — all of Janet's favorites.

After lunch we hiked a trail along the green foothills and oak trees of southern California. Aaron led the way with singing, shouting, and exploring every rock and flower. Russ and Lois followed behind, hand in hand, quite content after three years of marriage. Mike and Michelle were next with their arms around each other, whispering secrets with little smiles, like two people who could hardly wait until that August wedding. Then along came Mom and Dad. After twenty-four years together, they still hold hands. In fact, they even steal a little smooch when no one's looking. They aren't rich or famous or powerful. They are just a man and a woman walking along a dirt road with their children — and, by God's grace, some of the most blessed people on the face of the earth.

Now if our responsibility is to put in a little extra work, a little more study, a little more prayer, a little more patience, a little more forgiveness, and a whole lot of gratitude in order to be that good dad and mom, it's worth it.

We can guarantee, it's worth it.

This chapter is taken from *How to Be a Good Mom* (Chicago: Moody, 1988).

## Further Reading

Stephen and Janet Bly. *How to Be a Good Mom.* Chicago: Moody, 1988.

Virelle Kidder. *Mothering Upstream.* Wheaton: Victor, 1990.

Grace Ketterman. *When You Feel Like Screaming: Help for Frustrated Mothers.* Wheaton: Shaw, 1988.

Patricia H. Rushford. *What Kids Need Most in a Mom.* Tarrytown, N.Y.: Revell, 1989.

# What I would give our children

I want to give our children the gift of solitude, the gift of knowing the joy of silence, the chance to be alone and not feel uncomfortable. I want to give them transportation for the inner journey and water for their desert places. I want to make them restless with diversion and disenchanted with the artificial excesses of our culture. I want to give them a desire to strip life to its essential and the courage to embrace whatever they find there.

I would teach them to be seers, to notice subtleties in nature, in people, and in relationships. I long for them to grasp the meaning of things, to hear the sermons of the seasons, the exhortations of the universe, the warnings of the wounded environment. I would teach them to listen. It would bring me joy to happen in on them one day and find them with their ears to the earth or humming the melody of the meadow or dancing to the music of the exploding symphony of spring.

Yes, I would teach them to dance! I would teach them to never so tie up their feet with the shackles of responsibility that they cannot whirl to the rhythm of the spheres. I would have them embrace the lonely, sweep children into their arms, give wings to the aged, and dance across the barriers of circumstance, buoyed by humor and imagination into the ecstasy of joy. I would teach them to dance!

## Feeling pain

I would teach our children to cry, to feel the pain that shatters the violated, to sense the emptiness of the deserted, to hear the plaintive call of the disoriented and lost, to understand the hopelessness of the powerless. I would teach them to cry – for what is locked away, for that which is broken, for those who never knew Life, for what was not realized, for the least and the last to know freedom.

## Gratitude

I would teach our children gratitude. I would have them know the gift of where they've been and who brought them to where they are. I would teach them to write each day a liturgy of praise to read to the setting sun. I would have them dwell upon the gift of what is, not wasting their energies on what could have been. I would have them know that twin of gratitude: *contentment* – contented to live and breathe, contented to love and be loved, contented to have shelter and sustenance, contented to know wonder, contented to be able to think and feel and see. To always call a halt to senseless striving, this I would teach our children.

## Integrity

I would teach our children integrity, to be truthful at any cost, to be bound by their word, to make honest judgments, even against themselves, to be just, to have pure motives. I would have them realize that they are accountable individually to God alone, and then to themselves. I would have them choose right even if it is not popular or understood, even by me.

## Prayer

I would teach our children to pray, knowing that in our relationship with God there is much to be said, and God is the one who must say it. I would have them know the difference between prayer and piety; I would make them aware that prayer often has no words but only an open, vulnerable accessibility to God's love, mercy, grace and justice. I would hope that they discover that prayer brings – and is – an awareness of our need, a knowledge without which there is no growth or becoming. I would have our children know through experience and example that there is nothing too insignificant to lay before God, yet in that openness we often find Him lifting us above what we brought to Him, making it insignificant compared to the revelation He brings to us as a result of our coming to Him. I would not have our children think of prayer as a commercial enterprise, a sort of celestial clearinghouse for distributing earth's material goods. Rather, I would have prayer teach them that what we so often think we seek is not on the list of what we need, yet God does not upbraid us for our seeking but delights in our coming to Him, even when we don't understand. Mostly, I would have our children know how synonymous true prayer is with gratitude and contentment and have them discover the marvelous outlet prayer is for communicating this delight with God.

## Soaring

Lastly, I would teach our children to soar, to rise above the common, yet find delight in the commonplace, to fly over the distracting disturbances of life, yet see from this perspective ways to attack the knotty problems that thwart people's growth and stymie their development. I would give them wings to dream and insight to see beyond the now and have those wings develop strength from much use so that others, when life becomes too weighty for them to bear, may be borne aloft as well. At last these wings, I know, will take our children high and away from our reach to places we have together dreamed of, and I will watch and cheer as they fade from my view into vistas grand and new, and I will be glad.

## Gloria Gaither

This is taken from *We Have This Moment* (Waco, Tex.: Word, 1988). Used by permission.

# The Roles Parents Talk Their Kids Into

*H. Norman Wright*

Several of the young parents arrived early for the get-together at the home of Marv and Alma Johnston. The meeting was the result of a number of couples and single dads and moms in the church expressing a desire to compare notes on parenting. Most of them felt content and comfortable with how their children, ranging in age from 5 to 11, were progressing in life. There were no serious discipline or emotional problems among these kids. Yet a number of the adults who crowded into the Johnston's family room carried vague, unspoken concerns about their role as parents.

"This is an informal meeting," Marv said after a word of prayer, "so we're going to share informally about our families. Let's take turns describing our children, our family life, and any problems we may be facing."

The group responded eagerly. As the parents spoke, the families they described seemed to reflect a cross-section of American family life. The problems they shared were mostly minor and fairly common. Still, many in the group hinted that their kids' behavior sometimes caused them to feel uncertain about their effectiveness in parenting.

## Inner wounds

A man sitting near the back of the room was the last parent to speak. "My name is Frank. Thank you for sharing so openly about your families. What I've heard here tonight is similar to what I've heard in other parent groups

> *"I was verbally abused."*

over the last few years. You know me as a parent, but you need to know something else about me which definitely relates to what we are discussing. I grew up in a dysfunctional family, and I'm still recovering from dysfunctional behavior patterns I inherited from that environment. I was abused as a child. No, I wasn't beaten, kicked, sexually molested, or locked in a closet for days. The abuse I suffered was more subtle. It didn't inflict any physical wounds or leave visible scars. Yet I have come to learn that my abuse wounded and scarred me deeply inside. You see, I was verbally abused." Several parents stifled gasps of surprise as Frank continued.

"As I listened to you describe your families, some of your stories reminded me of my home. I heard you describe children who appear to be healthy but who in reality are showing early signs of dysfunctional behavior. Thankfully, physical and sexual abuse are not a problem in this group. But if you came from a home where verbal abuse was present, that tendency will probably be perpetuated in your own family."

Frank paused for a moment, and the silence was deafening. All eyes were glued on him. No one stirred. Many of the parents felt the uncomfortable weight of his words. Finally one of the mothers broke the silence. "Will you identify for us what you heard tonight that caused your concern? Most of us shared

## About the author

**H. Norman Wright,** M.R.E., *has two honorary doctorates and is a licensed Marriage, Family, and Child Therapist. He has taught graduate school for more than twenty-five years and is the founder and director of Christian Marriage Enrichment. He has written or coauthored more than fifty books, including* Always Daddy's Girl, The Seasons of a Marriage, *and* So You're Getting Married *(Regal), as well as* The Premarital Counseling Handbook *and* When Anger Hits Home *(Moody).*

> *What you accept as normal isn't necessarily right.*

similar descriptions of our children and their behavior. Are we all on the wrong track?"

"I'm not saying that all our kids are going to end up as criminals or derelicts," Frank answered with a smile. "But the track many of us are on with our kids may not be headed toward the destination we have in mind for them. You see, the parenting track you follow is the result of your past experiences. The way you talk to your kids probably seems normal to you because that's the way you were talked to as a child. But what you accept as normal isn't necessarily right. To a large degree, the way we talk to our kids determines the role they play in the family and shapes the patterns of behavior and response they will carry into adulthood. That's why it's so important that we communicate with our children according to the guidelines given in God's Word."

## Playing a role

"What do you mean by 'roles'?" asked a single parent of two. "Are you saying that some kids learn how to act a certain way in response to how we talk to them?"

"That's right," Frank said. "For some reason a child either develops a role in the family, or a role is consciously or unconsciously assigned to him by his parents. And this role becomes the child's identity. He learns how to survive in his family and gain a sense of self-worth by performing his role. The problem is that some elements of his true identity may be blocked by the role he has assumed. We know that a child's birth order, personality, and unique make-up cause him to respond to life in a certain way. But he shouldn't be forced into that role or any other role. Balance and the ability to be flexible and experience different roles are what we are after.

"To illustrate what I mean by roles, let me play for you several segments of a cassette tape I brought along. The people you hear on the tape are parents like you and me, describing their children as we did tonight. Would you like to hear some of them?" The group of parents enthusiastically voiced their interest, so Frank slipped the cassette into the Johnstons' player and pushed START.

### Jason the Doer

The first voice on the tape was that of a woman: "I can't believe the level of responsibility that our son Jason shows at age 10. Sometimes I wonder what we would do if it weren't for him. If my husband or I overlook any detail around the house, Jason is there to catch it for us. Sometimes he's like a little parent to his younger brother and sister. I think it's great, and Jason seems to thrive on doing things for us. In fact, I've seen him get upset if one of us takes care of something he thinks he can do. Perhaps he's just a typical firstborn. I'm glad he's happy. Other parents have told me they wish their kids were like Jason."

Frank stopped the tape. "Jason's role is that of a doer. Somehow his parents have communicated to him that his worth and acceptance are based on his performance. Such children have an overly developed sense of responsibility and struggle with guilt when they don't perform well. They don't really get much satisfaction out of all they do. Even as children, they feel they can become weary, feel taken advantage of, and feel empty or neglected. That's the down side of being a doer. And when a child takes the role of a doer, he will grow up continuing in that role. Adult doers are often workaholics who must produce in order to feel worthwhile. Can any of you identify with the role of the doer?" A number of hands went up.

"In a dysfunctional home," Frank continued, "doers are rewarded and affirmed only when they perform. We all want our kids to be responsible. But some parents go too far

> *In a dysfunctional home, doers are rewarded and affirmed only when they perform.*

and actually wound their children by saying things like, 'Mommy won't give you a hug until you've picked up your toys,' or, 'If you can't sweep the porch better than that, you're no son of mine!' In a healthy home, a child with doer tendencies is accepted even when he isn't doing something productive for the family. He is encouraged to develop balance between work and play in his life."

### Liz the Enabler

Frank started the tape again. The voice of another mother came through the speakers: "My daughter, Liz, is 13. I call her the stabilizer in our family. She keeps all of us on an even keel. I guess some people might say she's a peacemaker. I've seen her take the blame for something her brother did just to avoid conflict in our home. Sometimes I wish she wouldn't do that, but I must admit I enjoy the peace and quiet. Sometimes Liz can be so insistent about something that I call her a little nag. But she does it in a pleasant way."

Frank switched off the tape. "Children like Liz tend to take on the role of an enabler. They end up feeling responsible to provide the emotional nourishment for a family. They keep everyone together and smooth out the ruffled feathers. Somehow their parents communicated ideas such as, 'God will punish you if you argue or fight,' or, 'If you kids don't get along, you're going to make Daddy and Mommy get a divorce.'

Enablers live under the fear of abandonment. When they become adults they're afraid that other family members can't stand on their own two feet, so enablers feel duty-bound to help them survive."

A young mother a few chairs away from Frank sighed audibly. "You've just described me," she said. "Could enabling behaviors and responses actually keep some of the problems alive in a family? Sometimes I make excuses for others in my family, but they just continue in their problems."

"That's a good question and a good description," Frank replied. "In their efforts to solve problems and make peace, enablers often serve only to perpetuate the offensive and harmful behavior."

### Jimmy the Loner

The next comment on the tape was from a father. "Sometimes I jokingly refer to my son as the invisible child. Jimmy moves through the house as quietly as a shadow, even when we have guests. He prefers to be alone, I guess, so perhaps he's just an introvert. Even when he comes and sits with us, he doesn't say too much. One thing I can say though: He's good and compliant, and I have yet to see him express any anger. That's a relief in light of what his older brother is like. Jimmy just kind of plods along steadily. He doesn't get much recognition at school or church, but that doesn't seem to bother him. He has a number of interests but seems to prefer being involved in these by himself."

"Invisible children like Jimmy can be called loners or lost children," Frank said as he stopped the tape. "Jimmy may appear well-behaved and compliant to his father, and who wouldn't like compliant children around? They give us some peace and quiet!" Several parents smiled and nodded. "But Jimmy is a lonely child because his parents have somehow conveyed that he's not very important. As a young child he was probably shushed when he made noise and shooed out of the room when he was a bother. His parents seemed to be happier when he wasn't around, so Jimmy adopted the loner's role. The Jimmys of the world grow up to be lost and lonely adults living in denial."

> *The Jimmys of the world grow up to be lost and lonely adults living in denial.*

### John the Star

Frank touched the START button again: "I'm so proud of John; he's such a talent in the family. He's gifted in so many areas and does most everything so well. And with him being such a stand out, we've become acquainted with so many neat people. Our life has changed a lot because of all John has accomplished. He really thrives on success and has such high standards, even though he tends to be a bit perfectionistic. Sometimes his sisters are bothered by his critical tendencies, but I think they could learn a lot about achieving from John."

Frank touched STOP. "Every parent wants his or her child to be a star or a hero, and we encourage our children to do the best they can according to their abilities. But like John's parents, some of us are so success-conscious for our kids that we push them too hard. They take on the role of the star and lose their childhood in the process. Their parents have instilled in them, 'Just making the team isn't good enough; you've got to be firststring and a league all-star,' or, 'Dance lessons cost a lot of money, so you'd better get the lead role in every recital.' Stars are so busy achieving that they seldom take time just to have fun or do nothing for a while.

"It's all right for a child to not be the star. It's important for parents to affirm them verbally and nonverbally at times for who they are. Children pushed into stardom by their parents often burn out, give up altogether, and end up dismal failures as adults."

### Amy the Joker

"You would love our daughter, Amy," the next mother on the tape said. "She's always the life of the party. She's so popular; everyone wants her around. She can be such a clown. She can make us laugh with her and at her. She's always joking and cutting up, even when she's facing a problem. Amy certainly knows how to enjoy life and help others enjoy life. Her attitude would go far toward helping other people."

"What's so bad about having a happy-go-lucky kid like Amy?" one of the parents asked as Frank stopped the tape.

"Nothing," Frank replied. "But when a joker like Amy finds it difficult to be serious at all, even when facing a problem or tragedy, she's playing a role. She has received a message from her parents that her problems and pain are to be ignored, avoided, or glossed over. Sometimes being the life of the party is a great cover-up for pain and isolation. We don't let people really know what's going on inside us. Unfortunately, some parents reinforce this behavior in their children and don't allow them to be serious. These kids learn that the only way to get attention is to be a joker.

"Are there any of you here tonight who wish others would take you more seriously and allow you to share your hurt?"

Several people raised a hand. Those sitting near them looked surprised, thinking their friends were just happy, jovial people without a real care in the world.

### Eric the Saint
"May I play one more excerpt from the tape?" Frank asked. The group nodded.

A father's voice came through the speakers: "I think our Eric may grow up to be a minister. He's the good one in the family. We have such high hopes for him. He's so responsible and obedient. We've never had any problems with him. He's also very active in his youth group at church, and he encourages us to be consistent at church. At times he's like the family's conscience. Isn't that funny? A child calling us back to what we should be doing? He seems to carry us along. I think it's good that one of

our kids is turning out that way."

"I think we all want our children to be good," Frank said as he switched off the cassette player and removed the tape. "But sometimes we hold unrealistic expectations for their behavior, and they adopt the role of the family saint trying to please us. Children playing this role often have areas in their lives which are deeply repressed or stunted. They avoid trying anything new for fear of failure." Many of the parents nodded knowingly.

### Daddy's Little Princess and Mommy's Little Man
"There are a couple of nicknames that some parents use for their children which tend to push them into playing roles," Frank continued. "Have you ever heard a child called Daddy's Little Princess or Mommy's Little Man"? A number of heads in the group nodded. "Often these nicknames are used innocently and in fun, but in some families they are not harmless. Rather they are a subtle form of verbal abuse. For example, sometimes a father will push his daughter into the role of a little princess as a substitute for his wife in some ways. He may be afraid of seeking the fulfillment of his emotional needs from his wife, so he elevates his daughter to princess status and uses her to gain emotional fulfillment. This may make his daughter feel special at first, but she is denied her childhood because of the adult demands placed upon her. And yet she may enjoy the attention she receives and begin to demand it."

# Bad and good news
One member of the group suggested that it was about time to adjourn the meeting. Marv

> *Some children avoid trying anything new for fear of failure.*

Johnston agreed, then added, "This has been a wonderful meeting, and we're very grateful to you, Frank, for sharing with us what you've learned. Some of us are aware for the first time that we may also have been the victims of verbal abuse as children and that we have been abusing our children without knowing it. But it would be a shame to leave without some positive input on what to do with what we've heard. Do you have any good news for us, Frank?"

Frank smiled and nodded. "I realize that what I have said may cause you concern for yourself and your children. A large number of you have identified with these roles. Some of you are still living these roles. Perhaps you wish you could change. The good news is that you can!

"As for your children, you want each one of them to develop into a real person with real identity and not take on a role to survive. The rest of the good news is that when you see negative tendencies occurring in your children, you can help them adjust and gain balance in their lives. One of the most significant ways to help our children become functional adults is by learning to communicate with them in a positive way. That's a big topic, but perhaps we can meet again and share some ideas. In the meantime, I suggest that you take some time to identify characteristics which might help you foster a healthy family atmosphere and positive communication with your children."

# Healthy communication

A child's development is the result of many different factors in his life. He is the product of his birth order, his neurological structure, his interactions with other family members, his biological strengths and weaknesses, and so on. But the atmosphere of the home, including verbal and nonverbal communication, plays a significant role in shaping a child's identity and behavior.

The emotional life of a child actually begins at about the sixth month of his mother's pregnancy. In his book *The Secret Life of the Unborn Child,* Thomas Verny summarizes the current data on the impressionable nature of a fetus.

First, a fetus can hear, experience, taste, and on a very simple level, even learn and feel *in utero*.

Second, what a fetus feels and perceives begins to shape his attitudes and expectations about himself. These attitudes are developed from the messages he receives from his mother.

Third, the most significant factor in the fetus' emotional development is his mother's attitude. A mother with chronic anxiety or ambivalence about being a mother can leave an emotional scar on the unborn child's personality. On the other hand, joy, elation, and anticipation can contribute significantly to the emotional development of a child.

Fourth, lest we leave out the father in this process, his feelings about his wife and unborn child are very important in determining the success of the pregnancy.[1]

Once a child is born he remains critically dependent on his parents for his emotional health and development. Consider for a moment the characteristics of a healthy or functional family. Notice how positive, nurturing communication is integral to the expression of each of these elements:

- *The climate of the home is positive. The atmosphere is basically nonjudgmental.*
- *Each member of the family is valued and accepted for who he or she is. There is regard for individual characteristics.*
- *Each person is allowed to operate within his or her proper role. A child is allowed to be*

> *The emotional life of a child actually begins at about the sixth month of his mother's pregnancy.*

*a child and an adult is an adult.*
● *Members of the family care for one another, and they verbalize their caring and affirmation.*
● *The communication process is healthy, open and direct. There are no double messages.*
● *Children are raised in such a way that they can mature and become individuals in their own right. They separate from Mom and Dad in a healthy manner.*
● *The family enjoys being together. They do not get together out of a sense of obligation.*
● *Family members can laugh together, and they enjoy life together.*
● *Family members can share their hopes, dreams, fears, and concerns with one another and still be accepted. A healthy level of intimacy exists within the home.*

What about the home in which you were raised? Do these characteristics describe your family of origin?

This chapter is taken from *The Power of Parent's Words* (Ventura, Calif.: Regal, 1987). Used by permission.

1. John Bradshaw, *Bradshaw on the Family* (Deerfield Beach, Fl.: Health Communications, 1988), adapted from the author's summary on pp. 26, 27.

---

### Further Reading

Robert Hemfelt, Frank Minirth, and Paul Meier. *Love Is a Choice.* Nashville: Nelson, 1989.

Kevin Leman and Randy Carlson. *Unlocking the Secrets of Your Childhood Memories.* Nashville: Nelson, 1989.

H. Norman Wright. *Always Daddy's Girl: Understanding Your Father's Impact on Who You Are.* Calif.: Regal, 1989.

H. Norman Wright. *The Power of Parents' Words.* Calif.: Regal, 1987.

# Capturing Those Teachable Moments

*Gloria Gaither*

When we had only one little girl, Bill and I thought we knew everything about kids. But when we had three kids, we found we had a lot fewer answers. But careful parenting is one of the clearest mandates given us in the Word of God, one that promises some of the deepest joys. How like God to accompany such an awesome charge with practical guidance in His Word and to send the Holy Spirit as our constant companion and adviser.

God's Word, the "Manufacturer's Guidebook" tells us: "Impress them [the laws and values of God] on your children. Talk about them when you sit at home and when you walk along the road, when you lie down and when you get up. Tie them as symbols on your hands and bind them on your foreheads. Write them on the doorframes of your houses and on your gates" (Deuteronomy 6:7–10).

That may sound like a lot of religion for one household. Isn't that impractical, especially at today's hectic pace? Yes. Unless we teach by *being.* We teach what we *are.* "[Parents,] love the Lord your God with all your heart and with all your soul and with all your strength" (Deuteronomy 6:5).

> ## We teach by being. We teach what we are.

### About the author

*Gloria Gaither, popular singer, recording artist, and lyricist, is a member of the Bill Gaither Trio. She has written* We Have This Moment *(Word) and* When Did I Start to Love You? *(Tyndale), as well as numerous articles. She also coauthored* Let's Make a Memory *(Word) and* Hands Across the Seasons *(Abingdon). She and her husband have three children.*

# No switching off

Children are learners; they learn everywhere. ▶

Children are learners. They learn everywhere. They learn sitting down and standing up. They learn wide awake and half asleep. They take in knowledge through their eyes, ears, noses, taste buds, and skin.

They learn while parents are teaching, and they learn when parents hope they're not teaching. Children learn from joy. They learn from pain. They learn from hot, cold, work, play, comfort, and discomfort.

Sometimes we adults associate learning with books and Bibles and devotionals. But when the books are closed and the lessons are over, children go on learning. No knobs turn off their little minds.

When I am less than the efficient, organized, calm, creative, well-groomed mother I want to be, I wish there were switches on our children's minds. But the children go on learning, watching me, seeing how I handle problems, sensing my unguarded reactions, picking up the vibes in our home.

# Teachable moments

I become painfully aware of my failures when I see some shabby action or attitude mirrored in my child. I, too, am learning. God is teaching me that all moments are teachable moments. The place to start buying up those moments is with myself.

### Alone with God

I've found it helpful to begin my day sitting alone at the feet of the Master-Teacher. There is something special about the dawn when the house is quiet and my mind is fresh. In winter I build a fire in the fireplace to warm the house and my spirit. In summer I take a cup of coffee to the yard swing, where I can listen to the earth awakening.

If I can spend the day's first moments alone with God, girding my mind with silence, feasting on the Word, listening, I am more ready to greet the day and my family. God and I have a few moments' head start.

### Finding time

The second thing I am learning is that if we are to take advantage of those teachable moments, we have to make sure there *are* moments together. Often our expectations of a "normal home life" don't match the pace of today's real world.

That doesn't mean we resign ourselves to letting the world squeeze our home life into its mold. It does mean that if we are going to let Christ remold our homes from within, we are going to have to do it *on purpose*.

There was a day when working together, eating together, taking walks, having picnics, fishing, hunting, singing, and playing table games were normal. We who grew up in a slower, less urbanized society think these things should happen in our home as a matter of course.

There is nothing wrong with our dreams. The problem is our failure to recognize that with busing, school, television, commuting, and careers these dreamt-of things are not going to "just happen." But they *must* happen if children are to be nurtured.

The warm circle of the family is still the habitat God intended for the nurture and protection of our young. The things that prey upon the Christian family today may not "huff and puff and blow our houses in," but they are far more threatening than were the big bad wolves of the prairie. And they can destroy a whole lot more than our houses.

One of the meanest bandits of the modern frontier is unrestricted television. While television has many creative, informative programs, it can also be degenerate, perverted,

bleak, and a shameful waste of eternal moments. It may be impressive to march and picket against objectionable programs, but it's a lot more effective to march across the room and switch off the set.

If enough Christian parents would discipline their families' viewing habits, the result would be evident in the ratings. Even sooner would be evident the quality of our time spent together. We will begin to see each other and hear each other and sense what each other is feeling, instead of becoming programmed, noncommunicative, afraid of silence, and terrified of human contact.

Preserving our spiritual habitat takes ingenuity and commitment to shared values. The whole family will have to learn to say no to the things that would destroy what we value most — time and energy for God and each other.

**Time for God's Word**

The third important way to shape our children for life — now and forever — is to give them the base of God's Word. Every parent has to work out the plan that best suits his or her family. But somehow, somewhere there has to be a plan for teaching the stories and words of the Bible.

Isaiah gives me an incentive: "All your sons will be taught by the Lord, and great will be your children's peace" (Isaiah 54:13). In this crazy world, God promises peace. How I want that peace for our children! If we can hide God's Word in our children's hearts, it will serve them well when time and experience bring them to a crisis. I can't count the times I have been faced with problems when something from God's Word, hidden in my heart long ago by my parents, has given me wisdom and strength.

This "hiding the Word" need not be a painful sit-down-and-shut-up-it's-time-for-worship approach. But we must refuse to turn loose unequipped and vulnerable children. Since we have no way of knowing what kind of world they'll face, we must give them the eternal

> *"All your sons will be taught by the Lord, and great will be your children's peace."*

armor of God.

The challenge is to *create* teachable moments. Relating Scripture to real life is one of the best ways, but parents must know the Word and be able to draw from its resources. Bedtime discussions about the day, friends, accomplishments, and disappointments can find meaning in one or two well-chosen verses. Walks in the woods or on the beach can bring life to verses from Psalms or Isaiah.

The breakfast table may be a good place to awaken a taste for the food of the Spirit. An early morning fishing outing with a sack breakfast can bring a special significance to the calling of the disciples, the nautical allusions Jesus used, and the feeding of the five thousand.

Working together to plant a garden can help lodge in a child's mind both the fellowship of work and the miracle of the seed. The thrill of seeing tulips bloom or tomatoes ripen can give understanding to the Lord's words about harvesting the kind of seeds we plant.

A colorful chart of the verses a child has learned, followed by a family celebration when he has accumulated twenty memorized portions, can teach that the Word of God is worth the effort.

When we reward only physical, intellectual, and social accomplishments, we teach children false values. Of course, we talk about the rewards that most people might not see — the rewards of becoming God's people as the Word becomes a part of us.

Teach a child verses that apply to his special times. Take snapshots or let him draw pictures. Then mount and date these in a scrapbook with the Bible verses to reinforce his memory.

> *How we face negative experiences teaches our children a great deal.*

Negative experiences are also a part of life, and God's Word must be woven into these times too. It is dangerous to teach children that life should always be pleasant, that God is just a miracle machine or a spiritual rabbit's foot. The Bible teaches that God is working to bring us to spiritual maturity.

How we face negative experiences teaches our children a great deal. The death of someone close, illness, disappointing grades, failure to make the team, being betrayed by a friend, loss of a pet, or an accident can be milestones to spiritual and emotional maturity.

### Special moments

With the Word and values of God woven into the fiber of our days, a fourth way to buy up teachable moments is to make some moments special. Crazy impromptu picnics, sledding parties, late summer night drives in the country, spur-of-the-moment bonfires, family basketball, volleyball, tennis, or badminton games, horseback riding or hikes, camp-outs and singing — all say to a family in a hundred ways "Of all the people in the world, I choose to spend my best moments with you. You're my very best friends."

Family traditions are important — not just Thanksgiving dinner or Christmas Eve, but other things a family can look forward to: a birthday, the get-together that always celebrates the first strawberries of the season from grandpa's garden, the popcorn-and-apples party while watching something wholesome on television, stopping for ice cream on the way home from church on Sunday night. Any celebration unique to your family implants a special memory.

Children give parents an excuse for being ourselves, an excuse to laugh and shout and

**Children value special moments.**

tumble down the hillside. One of our friends, an attorney, regrets seeing his children growing up because he'll no longer have an excuse to go sledding down the neighborhood hillside. "The neighbors will think I'm crazy!"

Perhaps that is one reason he has such special children. They have grown up knowing that of all the world, "Dad always liked us best!"

## Saying "Yes" to the best

How do we buy up those teachable moments?
* *By realizing that since all moments are teachable, we must become what we hope to teach*
* *By protecting the habitat of our homes*
* *By working the essential Word of God into the everyday nitty-gritty of life*
* *By making a life a celebration of the lordship of Christ and the value of one another*

There are no easy how-tos. When it's all

said and done, many of the choices of life are not between the good and the bad, but between the good and the best. Even good things can rob a family.

A sentence from our Sunday bulletin has been singing its way into my days. "Saying 'no' may mean that I've said 'yes' to something higher." I want to say yes — but only to the highest and the best.

*Saying no may mean that I've said yes to
    something higher.
Pleasures for a season will not buy eternity.
Joy and lasting peace and deep
    contentment are a treasure
No cheap thrills or easy rides will ever trick
    from me.
When you sense a calling to the best that is
    within you;
When you know deep in your heart you've
    found a better way —
Turn your back on all the voices that would*

*drag you downward;
Saying "no" may be the grandest "yes"
    you'll ever say!\**

This chapter appeared in the September 1978 issue of *Moody Monthly*.

### Further Reading

Gloria Gaither. *We Have This Moment*. Dallas: Word, 1988.

Tim Kimmel. *Legacy of Love: A Plan for Parenting On Purpose*. Portland: Multnomah, 1989.

Wanda B. Pelfrey. *Making the Most of Your Child's Teachable Moments*. Chicago: Moody, 1988.

# Planning Your Children's Education

*Kenneth O. Gangel*

## About the author

*Kenneth Gangel, Ph.D., is vice president of academic affairs and professor of education at Dallas Theological Seminary. His books include* The Family First *(BMH),* The Gospel and the Gay *(Nelson), and* Christian Education *(Moody). He and his wife, Elizabeth Gangel, coauthored* Building a Christian Family *(Moody). The Gangels have two children.*

We Americans like to believe we live in a child-centered society, a culture in which parents dote over their children and provide the very best for them. Yet, of the thirty-three million poor in America alone, thirteen million are children and five hundred thousand of those children have no homes. This richest nation in the world, perhaps the richest in all of history, ranks twentieth worldwide in infant survival rates, well behind most other civilized countries.[1] As one magazine put it, "In the eyes of private business, the child is seen as a raw material that needs a certain processing before it is of value."[2]

How can parents who neglect the most basic physical and emotional needs of their children be expected to plan adequately for their education? How can a society that faces annual teacher strikes in nearly every major city and that pays its entertainers millions of dollars to destroy its children's ethics — and its teachers a pittance to restore them — flaunt its efforts at universal education? How can Christian parents form a pocket of resistance in such an environment and determine that learning patterns for their family will be different?

The first step is to understand education to be more than a means to an end. In this pragmatic society parents, students, and even teachers take a strictly utilitarian view: educa- tion prepares people to make a living in a

> *How can Christian parents form a pocket of resistance in such an environment and determine that learning patterns for their family will be different?*

tough world. To be sure, it does that; but if that's all it does, we have misunderstood both biblical and historic understandings of learning. My friend Bruce Lockerbie says, "True education prepares students by inspiration. The life of the instructor should reflect the value of what he is teaching. If a teacher has no sense of his role as example, scholar, thinker, human being, or — in the case of Christian universities — follower of Jesus Christ, all he can do is transmit information."[3]

Ultimately, Christians want all education to serve the distinctive spiritual purpose outlined in 2 Corinthians 10:5: "We demolish arguments and every pretension that sets itself up against the knowledge of God, and we take captive every thought to make it obedient to Christ." Let's look at three segments of a person's educational life: preschool, elementary, secondary, and college choices.

## Preschool years

Experts tell us that by the ninth month of pregnancy the cerebral cortex is well defined and brain waves have developed patterns. Guesses at the value of extra prenatal stimulation stem primarily from an anecdotal base, but that does not stop companies from selling "prelearning tapes" and talking about "prenatal universities." One thing is sure — those one billion nerve cells available at birth quiver for action when the baby moves from its dark damp chamber into the glare of the outside world.

### Role of the family

For years, in family conferences and pastoral ministry, I have told young parents that they form in their preschool and elementary children the kind of teenagers they will live with in another ten or fifteen years. Every time you ruthlessly criticize your preschool children, showing them disrespect and rejection, they help design a self-concept that will carry them through most of their education.

Children learn in essentially three ways: *experience, modeling,* and *instruction.* All these function much better in the family than they do in the classroom.

*Experience* provides those daily teachable moments by which God allows (indeed, requires) parents to direct truth to that young child's heart.

*Modeling* speaks for itself, as children see the behavior of parents and respond accordingly. Wise parents display patterns of godly behavior such as prayer time, loving attitudes toward one another, and the general climate of love in the home. But modeling also includes whether Dad reads books or Mom can intelligently discuss world events. Patterns of education are indelibly formed by parental behavior.

*Instruction* is a more formal term, even when applied to preschoolers. Every kindergarten teacher (including both my wife and my daughter) can determine quickly which children come from homes where parents have spent time with them — talking, reading, explaining, traveling — and which children have been left alone in front of a television set. Designed adult stimulation of a preschooler's intellectual, social, emotional, and spiritual capacities sets the stage for everything that will happen later.

### The role of the external environment

Even preschool children don't spend all their time at home. They play in the neighborhood; they go to church and Sunday school; and increasingly tens of thousands of them spend

> *Patterns of education are indelibly formed by parental behavior.*

the day in some kind of care center. That external environment is so varied that few parents can have total control over the situation at all times. But since external environment plays such a crucial role in the child's development, each aspect is worthy of careful prayer and planning. With which of the children in the neighborhood will your child be allowed to play? Into whose home will he go with regularity, and what will she find and do there? What kind of church will provide a serious Bible teaching program, even at the preschool level, where precious children can learn to love God and His Word?

Perhaps most frightening of all external surroundings is the child care choice. We can argue that mothers should stay home and take care of their own preschool children, and that certainly reflects my preference. But in our society that has become increasingly difficult, and in many homes, impossible. Nearly half of all mothers have now joined the work force, and many have preschool children. Who will form their values? Who will model their behavior? In the metaphor of Psalm 127, who will shoot your arrows?

Some choices seem better than others. Grandparents or other family members would be the best choices, assuming competence and compatibility of values. Trusted friends often provide a God-sent refuge for the preschool children of single moms and dads who have to work. If you must select a day care center, ask God for wisdom beyond your own. In addition to safety, security, love, acceptance, and other central necessities, you will want to choose a place where the workers provide conversation, teach listening skills, build awareness of the world of numbers and words, and focus on social readiness. In short,

you want a child care center that will do for your children educationally what you would do if you could be at home.

### The role of prekindergarten

Let's not confuse preschool with day care. A preschool provides formal education in the year or two before kindergarten. It should not be baby-sitting or a substitute for day care. Preschool must be an educational enrichment program that moves to the next level any child ready for such an experience. It offers both learning and learning how to learn. The credentials of any preschool teachers and workers should qualify them to work with your child on a serious instructional level. Here state licensing and certification become an issue.

How do you know your child is ready for preschool? Dave and Gail Veerman suggest asking five questions:

1. *Is she bored at home?*
2. *Is he isolated from other children?*
3. *Can I give her what she needs at home?*
4. *Is he ready to be left somewhere, away from home and me?*
5. *Can I provide the same preschool experience at home?*[4]

Throughout these crucial preschool years, the main moral development in the child has to do with authority. Children learn to make value judgments, and those judgments are made by what they read, hear, and see. They have moved from fairy tales to find meaning in their own experiences and should be ready, by the time of formal schooling, to find meaning in the experiences of others as well.

# School

Every fall nearly fifty million elementary and secondary students return to school, 90 percent of them to public institutions. They are taught by more than 2.5 million teachers at an expenditure of more than $200 million a year.[5] In the midst of such an enormous enterprise, parents wonder whether they have a voice and, if so, how they can make the best choices. Essentially those choices are three, and they have been detailed in a book edited by H. Wayne House entitled *Schooling Choices* (Multnomah, 1988). Although the book is now out of print, I urge you to find a library copy and examine the arguments for and against these three options.

**Public school**

America has made a bold attempt to educate an entire population without regard for social status, race, or ability to pay. The success rate has been questioned, but no one can doubt the courage of a society that would attempt such a project. Schools do not operate in isolation; they reflect the society that makes them possible. The rebellion, crime, drugs, and anarchy common to large urban school districts reflect those very elements in the society at large. The public school campus provides a clear-cut example of the Bible's warning to Christians to be careful in the "world." What Mom and Dad encounter in a pagan office or business, their children face day by day in the halls.

Thousands of Christians teach in public schools and many of them see that as a direct service to God. The system itself, however, wants no part of forming the morality of children and young people. Its focus is almost exclusively intellectual. Former Secretary of Education T. H. Bell says,

*The first priority – taking precedence over all else that we do – is to concentrate on the attainment by every student of the highest possible level of literacy so that each student will have reached the outer limits of his or her ability to read with comprehension, write and think systematically and logically, and to speak with clarity in a manner that is articulate, precise, and reflective of an intelligent, well-educated individual. This priority should be number one, and the schools of this nation must make a fully unambiguous commitment to its attainment.[6]*

> *Never allow teachers to become a higher authority than parents.*

The facilities, equipment, academic options, and extracurricular activities are generally much more developed in public schools than in most private schools. For many Christian parents there will be no choice. The absence of alternatives will force involvement in public education. These parents must courageously make their voices heard at school board meetings, parent-teacher conferences, even athletic support groups, to speak a word of influence from a Christian point of view.

Another crucial activity for families sending their children to public school is debriefing. Never allow teachers to become a higher authority than parents. Find out what your child is learning at school, how it fits with what you want to teach him at home, and how it squares with the teaching of the Bible. In some cases you may be encouraged by "positive integration," the affirmation of biblical truth by formal education. In other cases, however, you may need to counter erroneous teaching by explaining that Scripture serves as the ultimate authority, even over the science textbook or classic literature. During the school years we parents must protect and nurture the spiritual sensitivity of our children so that their formal schooling complements the instruction they receive at home and church.

**Christian school**

As a professional educator, parent, and grandparent, my bias rests with quality Christian education at all levels. Doubtless, that sentiment comes through in this chapter; it would be dishonest to hide it. However, let me offer an important caveat. Some so-called "Christian schools" are substandard, shoddily staffed, and shamefully underequipped. Their existence, however, does not provide a blanket condemnation of Christian education any more than the barbarous environment of some urban public high schools should force us to reject all public education.

The Christian school operates on a central premise: Since there is a God, and since God has spoken in history, the most important aspect of learning for a Christian is to find out what God has said. Applying God's revelation becomes the heart of the curriculum and the burning ambition of every teacher. The Scripture provides the centerpiece of the curriculum, the bull's-eye on the educational target. The central difference between Christian and secular education involves defining truth. To the secularist, truth is relative and natural, taught basically to "good" minds. To the Christian, however, truth is absolute and supernatural and taught to minds affected by original sin.

Christian education emphasizes absolute truth based on eternal values. The two systems (public and Christian) stand in genuine disharmony; the issue of God's revelation divides Christians and non-Christians right at the beginning of all educational discussions (2 Timothy 3:14–17).

My wife and I sent our children to Christian schools for essentially five reasons:

1. *Philosophy of education*
2. *Influence of teachers*
3. *Centrality of God's Word*
4. *Friendship with Christian peers*
5. *Instruction in Christian values, morals, and ethics*

The properly functioning Christian school offers education for righteousness and truth and shows children and young people how all this fits into real life in the late twentieth century.

## Home school

Nobody really knows how many parents home school in the 1990s. One can find figures between a quarter of a million and a million

> *The central difference between Christian and secular education involves defining truth.*

students, and the popularity is on the increase. Most home schoolers are motivated by the academic deficiency of public education, the unavailability or cost of Christian education, and a genuine concern for parental voice in their children's education. New curricula, increasingly sophisticated testing procedures, and a control over the learning process all make home schooling an attractive alternative. Raymond Moore emphasizes the contact or attention differentiation between home schooling and public schooling:

*Of the 150 class minutes a day, a teacher devotes only 7 minutes in personal dialog with individual children. Unless the child is a trouble-maker, he only receives one or two responses a day. By contrast, the child in a home school receives an average 100–300 responses per day. No wonder the average home-schooled child ranks approximately at the 80th percentile on standardized tests. That's 30 percentile points above the national norm![7]*

Obviously home schooling is cost effective and, in many cases, can draw the family unit closer, enabling it to weather the storms of society. But parents must remember that home schooling is only one of three choices. Though the early Christians followed the lead of the Jews in making the home the center of education, there were no shortages of schools either in Old or New Testament times, and both Jews and Christians made use of them.

Be sure you know what home schooling cannot do as well as what it can do. Early education in numbers and language arts can be carried off effectively, but secondary education in sciences, geometry and literature provides a greater challenge. Capability of parents is the major issue. Some simply cannot handle home schooling. Their deficiencies may center not only in intellectual skills but also in their emotional and social readiness to cope with the task.

The choice is yours. You can choose the economical and readily available public system, and that may very well be God's will for you. Or His Spirit may lead you to a more creative alternative, such as a local Christian school or home schooling. We don't know what the future will hold, but for the moment Christian parents can choose freedom instead of fear and parental rather than public control. We must exercise our options to the glory of God.

# College

While schooling options at the elementary and secondary levels increase, choices for higher education are shrinking. Twenty years ago hundreds of Bible colleges, Christian liberal arts colleges, community colleges, and universities dotted the land. But because of economic pressure and a decline in the college-age population, institutions of higher education struggle to maintain enrollments, and many have closed. However, excellent schools are still available, and informed Christian parents can assist their young people in selecting wisely.

Ought Christian young people to go to college at all? Veteran college and seminary president Dave McKenna feels strongly that they should:
*Unless God calls a teen otherwise, I think he should plan on attending college. God has given each of us unique gifts and it is our responsibility to develop those talents to their fullest potential. Proper education is a part of that commitment to become all God intended us to be.*[8]

I agree, though readers could quickly accuse both Dr. McKenna and me of prejudice. Nevertheless, my intention here is to offer the information and urge you to submit to God's plan for your family.

**Types of colleges**
The American Association of Bible Colleges[9] now counts almost one hundred institutions in its membership throughout the United States and Canada. These schools come in all sizes and denominational persuasions but have certain central characteristics that set them apart from other institutions. Every Bible college student must take a Bible major (thirty hours) in addition to his other studies. He must also be practically involved in church attendance and Christian service. For many parents these are important components in producing spiritual as well as intellectual life during college years.

Expenses are relative, but Bible colleges generally make every effort to provide educational opportunities at as low a cost as possible. Scholarships and job opportunities are two important ingredients.

Christian liberal arts colleges attempt to provide a general arts and sciences curriculum with a variety of specializations. The Bible requirements vary from a full major to one or two courses. Some of these institutions have been enormously successful in garnering national attention for their academic programs and, through careful planning and curriculum updating, have maintained a cutting edge in higher education at the end of the twentieth century. Cost generally runs higher than at Bible colleges and "spiritual emphases" such as chapel attendance, Christian service, and Bible courses are often voluntary rather than mandatory. The central national organization for institutions of this type is the Christian College Coalition.[10]

Universities—large multi-school institutions providing vast career-training opportunities and academic experiences — can be public or

> **True education prepares students by inspiration.** ▶

private, secular or Christian, and are marked by their organization and academic offerings rather than philosophy or faculty. Many Christians wish to prepare for a life's work in some field that is taught only at a major university.

The community college is probably the single most important phenomenon in higher education since World War II. Huge community colleges now cover the land and provide utilitarian skill training as well as academic instruction for almost any high school graduate. Many students choose a community college because of its specific skill programs in fields such as dental hygiene, computer programming, or accounting. Others use the community college as a ladder to senior college, establishing their academic competence and then moving into the third year after graduating with an AA or AS degree. The educational quality at community colleges varies more widely than any of the other institutions, and discerning parents and students need to check the local institution with great care.

## Factors in your choice

*Size* is certainly important. A student interested in forestry has to attend a large state institution, but another student who wants to develop close relationships and participate in numerous campus leadership opportunities may decide that a small college is better. *Location* is important too. Does your child want to be close to home? Can you afford the travel costs otherwise?

Besides *cost* and *programs* offered, there are other factors. What about the type of *students* you'll find? What kind of people attend Bible colleges or Christian liberal arts colleges or universities? What kind of friends do you want during college years? Does your child want to be part of a Christian student body, or is evangelism a major goal during college years?

Don't forget the importance of *faculty*. Teachers always form the key ingredient in

**Choosing the right college is vital.**

education at any level. *Accreditation* is a must. In the 1990s no student has a good excuse for attending a nonaccredited institution. Sometimes *denominational affiliation* is important, since both parents and students want to stay close to the family's Christian heritage.

Write for catalogs of several institutions and study them carefully, asking God for wisdom in making the choice. Visit campuses. Some catalogs mislead because public relations people tend to present the institution in the very best, sometimes overglamorized, light. When you visit, be sure your child has opportunity to talk with department chairmen, admission officers, and financial aid directors.

Don't leave college choice to whimsy or chance. Pray with your young people; work closely with them in determining where they will attend and for what reason.

# A firm foundation

Parents have two wonderful opportunities for Christian education in the home. One is the example to their children of their own attitudes and actions. We all need to cry out to God to help us be the models we want to be.

The second opportunity is to give our children a lifelong foundation of the knowledge of God's principles on which to build their lives. Without this knowledge, and their putting it into action, their lives will be built on a foundation of straw. And who, with such an insecure foundation, can stand up to the storms of temptation and trials that are sure to come upon them at school and play, and in the years ahead?

Are the children getting this foundation and guidance at Sunday school and church? Thankfully, yes. But two hours a week cannot compete with twenty-five or thirty hours a week in public or private schools where God and His values are not taught. God's values have too often been replaced by a secular attitude and training that makes values relative and teaches that the distinctions made by God between right and wrong are not true.

That is why children need parents in the home to instruct them, using daily Bible reading and prayer as tools. Day by day their foundations will grow stronger and their lives made ever more secure.

### After supper

To accomplish this, the system used in our home as the children were growing up (and it continues today with the children now gone), is to have a few minutes after supper each evening for reading the Bible and for discussion and family-time prayers. While the children were young, we read them Bible stories, and the Bible itself as they grew older. There is a wealth of Bible story books available in Christian bookstores for children of all ages – from tiny tots into the school years.

But more than Bible stories are needed. The great truths of the apostle Paul and the other letters of the New Testament are also needed, as well as an understanding of the history and lessons for us today from the Old Testament.

Start early! Read the Bible together as a family every day. Include the baby, for the little ones are precious to God, and they will learn even as babies that the Bible is important to father and mother and that there is a God in heaven to whom they pray.

### Daily effort

After supper is usually the best time, when the family should be together. It is important to guard this sacred family time with God. Sometimes this takes careful planning when faced with the competition of school events, homework, television, and every other sort of complication. But it is certainly worth that daily effort to build up a solid foundation that lasts for the rest of life.

After the Bible reading comes prayer time. In our family we kneel together, and each of us participates so that the whole family can join together in each person's concerns. Here again, beginning early is important.

In addition to Bible reading and prayer, I recommend that there be some family discussion of the day's events – things that happened at school or at play, and national and world events. I recommend, too, that this family time be used to read for a few minutes from Christian biographies or secular classics, if there is time. The reading assignments at school are non-Christian and sometimes anti-Christian, so it is important to introduce the children to the lives of Christians and to other classics. If this cannot be done every night, then Sunday afternoons might be a good time for this extra reading.

Parents have an enormous responsibility and opportunity in bringing up their children in the joy and fear of the Lord. It is worthy of their time and utmost attention.

**Kenneth Taylor**

# Informal education

All during these three phases of educational life we can expose our children and young people to Sunday school classes, youth groups, camping programs, family outings, and a host of other experiences that are very educational. Though these do not take place in classrooms and no tests or grades are at stake, God holds us responsible for maximizing our opportunities and choosing educational options that glorify Him. Our monolithic society tends to pull educational choices out of parents' hands; that drift must be resisted by thinking Christians everywhere.

William McGuffey was born September 23, 1800, on the Ohio frontier. He is most famous for his *Readers,* but we should also remember him for his distinctive philosophy as a public school superintendent in the mid-nineteenth century. He once attempted to distinguish the role of teachers and parents in education by saying, "Teachers ought to know best how to do that which is required of them. Parents are, or ought to be, the better judges of what is to be done. . . . None but the natural parent can feel that natural affection which is adequate to the duties of properly educating an immortal mind."[11]

1. Jonathan Kozol, "The New Untouchables," *Newsweek,* Special Edition (Winter-Spring 1990), 49.
2. Ibid., 53.
3. Bruce Lockerbie, "The Importance of Education," in *Parents & Teenagers,* ed. Jay Kesler (Wheaton, Ill.: Victor, 1984), 655.
4. Dave and Gail Veerman, "What About Preschool?" in *Parents & Children,* ed. Jay Kesler, Ron Beers, and LaVonne Neff (Wheaton, Ill.: Victor, 1986), 304.
5. Statistics published by The National Center for Educational Statistics, December 1989, nos. 89–657.
6. David Smith, "Public School Education," in *Schooling Choices,* ed. H. Wayne House (Portland: Multnomah, 1988), 31–32.
7. Raymond S. Moore, "Can I Educate My Child At Home?" in *Parents & Children* (Wheaton, Ill: Victor, 1986), 284.
8. David L. McKenna, "Should Your Teen Go to College?" in *Parents & Teachers* (Wheaton, Ill.: Victor, 1984), 675.
9. The American Association of Bible Colleges, P.O. Box 1523, Fayetteville, AR 72702.
10. Christian College Coalition, 329 Eighth St., N.E., Washington, D.C. 20002.
11. John H. Westerhoff, III, *McGuffey and His Readers* (Nashville: Abingdon, 1978), 181–82.

## Further Reading

Gregg Harris. *The Christian Home School.* Nashville: Wolgemuth & Hyatt, 1988.

Stanley Hauerwas and John H. Westerhoff, eds. *Schooling Christians.* Grand Rapids: Eerdmans, 1992.

H. Wayne House, ed. *Schooling Choices.* Portland: Multnomah, 1988.

Ronald H. Nash. *The Closing of the American Heart: What's Really Wrong with America's Schools.* Dallas: Probe, 1990.

Cliff Schimmels. *How to Shape Your Child's Education.* Elgin, Ill.: Cook, n.d.

Cliff Schimmels. *Parents' Most-Asked Questions About Kids and Schools.* Wheaton: Victor, 1989.

# HOPE FOR BROKEN FAMILIES

# The Anti-Family Bias of Our Society

*James Dobson and Gary L. Bauer*

**66** There are exceptional women, there are exceptional men, who have other tasks to perform in addition to the task of motherhood and fatherhood, the task of providing for the home and keeping it. But it is the tasks connected with the home that are the fundamental tasks of humanity. . . . If the mother does not do her duty, there will either be no next generation, or a next generation that is worse than none at all. **99**

Theodore Roosevelt

It is hard to imagine an American political leader today articulating as clear a defense of the "profession" of parenting as Teddy Roosevelt did earlier in this century. In recent years our culture has sent hostile signals about the job of parenting even though few men and women will ever do anything more important than nurturing and raising the next generation of children.

With mothering and fathering under such fierce attack, it should not be surprising that millions of Americans have brought children into the world and then retreated from parenting. The consequences for many of our sons and daughters is devastating. In the final analysis, I fear that America's "parent deficit" will soon dwarf its "trade deficit" in significance.

## Motherhood under siege

The vanguard of the attack against mothers was led by the troops of the feminist move-

ment in the sixties and seventies. Milita[n]t feminists argued that the job of caring f[or] children was a form of oppression, slavery, [and] imprisonment. Some feminists compared th[e] mental state of homemakers to soldiers [in] World War II who had suffered severe emo[o]tional damage in combat.

### Feminist writers

In 1970, Germaine Greer wrote *The Fema[le] Eunuch,* which condemned motherhood as [a] handicap and pregnancy as an illness. Gree[r] urged women to be "deliberately promiscu[ou]ous" and to be certain not to conceive chi[l]dren. Broadening her attack against th[e] whole institution of marriage, she conclude[d] "If women are to effect a significant ameliora[tion] in their condition, it seems obvious tha[t] they must refuse to marry."[1]

The classic critique on motherhood an[d] family was Betty Friedan's *The Feminine Mys[tique.* Friedan described the family as a[n] oppressive institution. She compare[d] homemakers to "parasites" and said tha[t] sexist ideas were "burying millions of Amer[i]can women alive."[2]

### Cultural elites

Not surprisingly, this anti-mother/anti-fami[ly] rhetoric disgusted millions of America[n] women, including many who were sympathe[t]tic to some feminist goals. The rejection o[f] motherhood helped to derail the movemen[t] as a political force in the eighties. But today[,] the hostility to motherhood is no longe[r]

> *The . . . choice that must not be missed is to cherish your human connections: your relationshiups with friends and family.*

limited to the feminist fringe. Like so many other attacks on traditional institutions, this one has been embraced by the cultural elites and has become their established worldview.

The message that is being sent from the media, government, judges, Madison Avenue, and Hollywood is that parenting is a second-class occupation, best left to those who really can't do anything else.

On our most hallowed university campuses, young women are being taught that "real women" aren't just mothers and homemakers anymore. When First Lady Barbara Bush was invited in 1990 to give the commencement address at Wellesley College, hundreds of angry coeds protested. They argued that Mrs. Bush wasn't a suitable role model for young women because she had spent her life raising children rather than pursuing a career for herself. These students are supposed to be America's "best and brightest" women. What does their protest say about the value they place on caring for children or on children themselves?

### In defense of motherhood

Hopefully, they listened carefully to the First Lady's words. She courageously spoke up for family and parenting:

*The . . . choice that must not be missed is to cherish your human connections: your relationships with friends and family. For several years, you've had impressed upon you the importance to your career of dedication and hard work. This is true, but as important as your obligations as a doctor, lawyer, or business leader will be, you are a human being first*

## About the authors

*James Dobson, Ph.D., is founder and president of Focus on the Family. His many best-selling books include* Parenting Isn't for Cowards, Hide or Seek, The Strong-Willed Child, Love Must Be Tough, *and* Love for a Lifetime (Word). *He and his wife, Shirley, have two grown children.*

*Gary L. Bauer is president of The Family Research Council in Washington, D.C. and senior vice president of Focus on the Family. He served as president Reagan's Domestic Policy Advisor and as The Undersecretary of the U.S. Department of Education. He is coauthor of* Children at Risk (Word). *He and his wife, Carol, have three children.*

and those human connections – with spouses, with children, with friends – are the most important investments you will ever make.

At the end of your life, you will never regret not having passed one more test, not winning one more verdict or not closing one more deal. You will regret time not spent with a husband, a friend, a child or a parent.

This is common-sense advice, but it contradicts the anti-mothering bias that exists in our culture. Unbelievably some so-called "experts" on the family are now arguing that the maternal instinct does not even exist.

### Family experts

A few days after the New York Times ran an article about how "drugs" killed the maternal instinct and led to child abuse, they received a lengthy letter from an assistant professor of anthropology at Colorado College:

To my knowledge there is no objective substantiation of a maternal instinct in female human beings. The reasoning not only generates a mechanical fix-it mentality but also implies something specifically vulnerable and dangerous about women in this society.[3]

Can you imagine what our sons and daughters are learning in that professor's classroom? The maternal instinct does not make women "vulnerable" nor is it "dangerous." What is dangerous is the constant devaluing of the job of caring for and nurturing children.

### Politicians

Politicians and government bureaucrats often have their own warped ideas about mothering. During the 1988 campaign, Democratic presidential nominee Mike Dukakis participated in a "round table" discussion on health insurance at a Houston hospital. He turned to a woman there with her husband and three children aged ten, seven and four. "Do you work?" Dukakis asked the mother. With some emotion the woman replied, "I take care of my children. I work very hard." A chastened

Dukakis sheepishly said, "That was a dumb question."[4]

Yes it was – but it reflected the tenor of the times.

# Who deserves a break?

The Reagan Administration also revealed at times these subtle prejudices against at-home mothers. In early 1988, the Administration attempted to develop a child-care policy to counter legislation in Congress that would turn Uncle Sam into the national nanny. There was a bruising fight within the White House itself on what our approach should be. I argued for basic fairness – give every family with children under a certain age a tax credit – including stay-at-home mothers. Let them spend the money the way they see fit.

### The most important job

The fight came to a head at a meeting of White House staff and sub-Cabinet officials in the Roosevelt Room. Not surprisingly, many of the participants were women. Unfortunately, most of them favored child-care grants but only for families whose children were being cared for outside the home.

I patiently argued the case for fairness to at-home mothers, but my patience evaporated when a government bureaucrat said, "Why should some woman who is not doing anything be given a grant or tax break?"

Not doing anything? My wife was at home with our children. I saw the exhaustion in her face when I would come home for dinner. Anyone who has raised a child knows it is a tough, challenging, and often frustrating job, interrupted by moments of unsurpassed joy. Our country will rise or fall depending on whether or not the next generation will be raised with the love and attention they need. "Not doing anything?" I was incensed by the speaker's ignorance: these women are doing the most important job in the world!

As I glanced around the table I suddenly

> *Our country will rise or fall depending on whether or not the next generation will be raised with the love and attention they need.*

realized an extraordinary fact. Of the eight women in the room — none of them had children! Only a few were married. Yet here they were making child-care policy for the American family and expounding on motherhood.

The bias against stay-at-home moms even makes it to the comic pages. I recall one episode in the "Marvin" comic, which runs in many major papers including the *Washington Post*. This day, Marvin was shown asking another baby, "Molly, do you have a working mother . . . or a full-time lackey?"

The subtle messages received from the culture, particularly by our children, send a clear message about marriage and parenting. A Saturday morning TV commercial promoting a fast-food restaurant shows a group of children sharing hamburgers and french fries while they discuss what they are going to do when they become adults. One child after another, boy and girl, mentions exciting occupations. The only negative reaction is reserved for the boy who says he wants to get married!

**The anger point**

Shopping recently at a local "super mall," I saw one of those incidents that seemed to symbolize the clashing values in our culture. A child in the crowded store I was in had inadvertently stepped on the foot of a young woman shopper. The incident quickly escalated into some heated words between the young woman and the child's parents, who had three other children all apparently under the age of eight or so.

The yuppie shopper ended the exchange with an extraordinary verbal attack. "Why don't you two practice some birth control?" Several other shoppers snickered at this remark, and the couple, with their four children in tow, scurried away. The mother, in particular, looked as though a dagger had just been plunged into her heart.

What an extraordinary incident to witness. Yet it is not really that unusual except for its bluntness. Several acquaintances of ours with more than the national average of 2.3 children have shared incidents of similar hostility. Four children seems to be the anger point. Not many years ago a couple deciding by choice to have no children or only one child was vaguely perceived as being a little unusual. Today, even though the American birthrate is below replacement level, there is still an aversion to large families in some circles.

One Focus on the Family radio broadcast featured Randy and Marcia Hekman, who are parents of ten delightful children. The program focused on the joys and stresses of raising a large family. Based on the mail response, the vast majority of radio listeners that day loved the discussion.

Dr. Dobson was surprised, however, to receive at least twenty letters from people who resented the Hekmans and their large family. "No one should have the right to have that many children," they chided. Randy and Marcia said they run into similar attitudes quite frequently. Apparently some of the critics would favor a law prohibiting large families in the future. The Hekmans sometimes cry when they remember that they almost decided not to have the fifth and subsequent children.

## "Children are the problem"

This hostility toward children in society was obvious in another meeting I had at the White House with a prominent California politician. This man was known for his intellect and was considered to be a good bet for higher office down the road. After a half hour or so of talking about a variety of urban problems, he suddenly lowered his voice and said he had been playing around with a new idea for some time. He realized it would be controversial, but he wanted to run it past me confidentially. I agreed to listen with an open mind.

My visitor then suggested that major U.S. pharmaceutical companies be approached and asked to develop a contraceptive chemical that could be put in the water supply of our major cities. I was stunned! "But what about couples who want to have a child?" I inquired. "Oh that's simple," he replied. "They would go to the government, and if we felt they were suitable parents we would give them the antidote that would permit them to conceive. Children are the problem," he said. "There are just too . . . many children."

I assume he meant too many children born out of wedlock, too many children born to drug-addicted parents, too many children born with the AIDS virus. That these are tragedies and burdens to society cannot be doubted. But a return to moral common sense, a return to self-restraint and responsibility, and a rebirth of compassion, together could do much about overcoming the problems.

Apparently that idea was too radical for my guest. Faced with problems caused at least in part by government bungling and cultural drift, combined with progressive moral decay, this politician's answer was a government solution that would strike an unbelievably stupid blow at the family.

## Bias in schools

Anti-family bias even finds its way into our schools. One researcher examined ten sets of textbooks used in elementary schools throughout the country. He found there was hardly a story that celebrated motherhood or marriage as a positive goal or as a rich and meaningful way of living. Motherhood was portrayed in two or three stories positively, but these were set in the past or involved ethnic emphases that distanced the mother from contemporary American life. No story showed any woman or girl with a positive relationship to a baby or a young child.[5]

Textbook publishers understand what they must do to prevent becoming a target of protests by radical feminists. The guidelines of one major textbook publisher warn authors and illustrators to avoid material that "reinforces any sense that girls and boys may have of being categorized as a sex group." Censorship is apparently OK just so long as the right censors are in control!

## Bias in courts

Even our federal courts have sent a clearly negative message about parenting. Supreme Court Justice Harry Blackmun has written that the Court is interested in questions of marriage, family, and childhood only to the extent that they bear upon the freedom of the individual. The Justice ignores any concept of the public good or the contribution to society that individuals make through the nurture and training of the next generation or through maintaining the institution of marriage and commitment to one's spouse. Alas, Blackmun's reasoning should not be surprising when one remembers that he is the principal author of the *Roe v. Wade* decision that legalized abortion on demand.

## Bias in society

A recent Gallup poll found that only one third of parents nationwide felt that society puts a great deal of value on children while fully 20 percent felt that our society puts *little value* on children. Is it any wonder that so many women delay having children or that those who do tend to feel isolated and alone, particularly when they give up a career in order to care for their children? Our culture has made these young mothers victims of a preprogrammed guilt trip.

# World without mothers

Countless times each day a mother does what no one else can do quite as well. She wipes away a tear, whispers a word of hope, eases a child's fear. She teaches, ministers, loves, and nurtures the next generation of citizens. And she challenges and cajoles her kids to do their best and be the best. But no editorials praise these accomplishments — where is the coverage our mothers rightfully deserve?

Newspaper headlines about the disasters of drugs, suicide, and violence tell us loud and clear just how badly our young people need mothering. But it is the business pages of our newspapers that make great fanfare over the fact that "Ms. Jones is named the first female Vice President of Trendy, Cash and Now." This is the important news of the day!

There are no news stories telling us that today a child was taught what it means to be loved, an infant was hugged securely, or that the wonders of the classics were introduced to a young mind. No one seems to care that a house was made a home, or that a simple table of food was transformed into a place of community and nurturing.

In the trench wars of Washington, politicians fulminate about issues grand and small, many posturing themselves as friends of the family. But few of them understand how important the acts of love within the family really are. Few understand what a terrible fate awaits a society in which no one has time to offer those open arms that comfort a child. Even fewer take the time to stand up and praise the noble and generally thankless tasks that American mothers perform each day.

## Reversing the trend

What should we do while we wait for society to get its priorities straight? Speaking as a husband, I believe there is much that married men can do in their own homes. First of all, tell your wife you love her. Thank her for being in your home with your children. Let her

**A mother does what no one else can do so well.**

know that the choices she has made are honored by you. In short, tell her how much she matters!

A 1985 study indicates that men fall far short in this important area. A majority of women indicated they have not received adequate emotional support from their husbands. Many women complained that their husbands didn't value "mothering." Others pushed their wives back into the work force even though the women preferred to be home with their children.

But it isn't too late to restore the fine art of motherhood back to its time-honored position in our society. In spite of the current cultural hostility, lack of supporting from hus-

> *Many women complained that their husbands didn't value "mothering."*

bands, and incredible pressures inside and outside the home, women continue to affirm the importance of motherhood.

A Roper poll published in *Ladies Home Journal* in 1988 reported on a survey of women who were asked to describe the best thing about being a woman today. Sixty percent said it is "motherhood." Being a wife was in second place, and the great achievement of feminism, "Taking advantage of women's increased opportunities" came in a distant fourth.[6]

At least, today's pervasive propaganda against bearing and raising children hasn't convinced everyone!

# Flight from fatherhood

It will not be enough for us to encourage mothers, however, if we do not also restore the role of fathers in the family as well. Study after study confirms that children have the best chance of success when both parents are present. Fatherhood must be re-emphasized, not only for the sake of the family, but for the sake of men. Here too, the anti-traditional forces have promoted a philosophy that undercuts fidelity, promotes singleness, and entices men away from a commitment to hearth and home.

A man or woman faced with the temptation to cheat can find plenty of support for making an unwise decision in the popular culture. *Parade* magazine, for example, recently ran a front page story by Dr. Joyce Brothers about adultery. Brothers argues that infidelity can actually strengthen a marriage, and she cites increasing infidelity by wives as a sign of the new equality between men and women.[7]

Larger research samples leave no doubt that the levels of infidelity are much lower than those cited by Joyce Brothers. But her article and scores of others like it read by millions of people have an impact. They help tempt both women and men away from the lifetime commitments they made – usually with disastrous results. And they make faithful men and women feel out of step and behind the times.

## Wanted – fathers

David Blankenhorn of the Institute for American Values has pointed out that the phrase "good family man" has almost disappeared from our popular language. This compliment was once widely heard in our culture

*– bestowed to those deserving it, as a badge of honor. Rough translation: "He puts his family first." Ponder the three words: "good" (moral values); "family" (purposes larger than the self); and "man" (a norm of masculinity). Yet today within elite culture, the phrase sounds antiquated, almost embarrassing ... contemporary American culture simply no longer celebrates, among its various and competing norms of masculinity, a widely shared and compelling ideal of the man who puts his family first.[8]*

William Bennett put it succinctly in a 1986 speech on the family in Chicago when he asked, "Where are the fathers? . . . Generally, the mothers are there struggling. For nine out of ten children in single-parent homes, the father is the one who isn't there. One-fifth of all American children live in homes without fathers. . . . Where are the fathers? Where are the men? Wherever they are, this much is clear: too many are not with their children."[9]

## In inner cities

Nowhere is the flight from fatherhood more apparent than in the inner cities of our nation. There the full effect of the anti-family, "liberation" philosophy is painfully apparent. Much of the promise of the civil rights movement of the sixties and seventies has been destroyed by the breakup of the black family. A black child is now more than three times as likely as a white child to live in a fatherless home.

Men enticed by drugs, easy sex, and the other temptations of urban life have abandoned the responsibility of parenting and husbanding. These bad choices have been made

> *We need to restore fatherhood to its rightful place of honor.*

more likely by a culture that mocks traditional values and by government policies that many times discourage family formation.

Our current welfare system, for example, encourages the formation of "the mother-state-child family." Uncle Sam has become a marriage partner and "father" of last resort. The results are predictable – no bureaucrat, however well meaning, can substitute for a father.

### Fatherless children

Studies show that the absence of the father expresses itself in male children in two very different ways: it is linked to increased aggressiveness on one hand, and greater manifestations of effeminacy on the other. A 1987 study of violent rapists found that 60 percent of them came from single-parent homes. A Michigan State University study of adolescents who committed homicides found that 75 percent of them were from broken homes.[10] Girls without fathers fare no better. They become sexually active sooner and are more likely to have out-of-wedlock children.

But studies aren't necessary to discover what common sense tells us – intact families are better off – mothers and fathers both need to be there. Children need their parents. Too many of America's children are suffering from a "parent deficit."

Unbelievably, the truth of these statements is resolutely denied by the anti-tradition cultural army and its allies. The influence of feminism on the cultural elite is so strong that many in government and the media are unwilling to say clearly that, on the average, female-headed households are in great danger – particularly in the inner city with its many social problems.

# The penalty of permissiveness

Just blocks from my office in downtown Washington, thousands of broken families are trying valiantly to claw their way out of the ghetto. Countless women try to raise out-of-wedlock babies abandoned by the men who took their pleasure and then joined the culture of the street where a fortune in drug profits or a quick bullet in the head are very real possibilities on any given weekend.

On many inner-city street corners, gangs of taunting teenage thugs harass women and children. They are products of a society where intact families are now the exception. The glib chatter of amateur sociologists on TV talk shows, the research papers of liberal academics, the social engineering of liberal judges, and the legislating of government bureaucrats have all sown seeds that have now grown into a twisted harvest of broken lives and crushed spirits. But with all the evidence stacked against the social experiments of the past three decades, the liberal élites are still singing their siren song of "liberation."

It is possible, of course, to raise a family without a father. Countless women struggle against the odds, and many do an incredible job. But it is deceitful to suggest that on an average a single mother can do as well as an intact family. Such homes start out with the odds against them. While courage, perseverance, and faith can overcome those odds, it is preferable, for families and for the future of our nation, that our children be raised in homes with both parents.

### The battle is on

We need to restore fatherhood to its rightful place of honor. To the middle-class father we can praise his commitment to the economic well-being of his family, but we must also remind him that more than a paycheck is needed. His loving leadership and partnership with his wife in the care and nurture of children must be affirmed.

Fathers must be there to tame adolescent boys, to give a young son a sense of what it means to be a man, and to explain why honor and loyalty and fidelity are important. For daughters, a father is a source of love and comfort that can help her avoid surrendering her virtue to a fruitless search for love through premarital sex.

In the inner city, we must reinforce the place of men in the home. Welfare programs should stop replacing fathers. Tougher laws and a new seriousness about values must be pursued to remove the temptation of drugs and sex for sale in our cities. To all men a clear message must be sent: "You are needed in the home, now, standing with your wife in the important task of raising children and meeting your responsibility."

Changes in the popular culture could help too. The single man in our society is often portrayed as having the best of all worlds. Free access to numerous women, unburdened by responsibility, debts, and demands on his time. A host of lurid magazines present this enticing image of life without commitment.

But the facts tell another story. If women and children have suffered from the abandonment of men — men have also suffered from the consequences of their own flight from love and family.

Without a recommitment of fathers to the home, the cultural war over family and children will be won by those who believe that all lifestyles are equal. Those who believe that the State must be the ultimate parent will inevitably take charge of the family. Such an outcome will result in suffering for millions: men, women, and children alike. It will most certainly lead to the eventual collapse of America as a free democratic society.

We simply must stop that scenario here and now. This is where the civil war begins and where the cultural nightmare ends. From today on, we are at war!

This chapter is taken from *Children at Risk* (Waco, Tex.: Word, 1990). Used by permission.

1. Dinesh D'Souza, "The New Feminist Revolt," *Policy Review*, no. 35 (Winter 1986), p. 47.
2. Betty Friedan, *The Feminine Mystique* (New York: Norton, 1963), pp. 217–336.
3. Suzanne Fields, "When Instincts and Stereotypes Embrace," *The Washington Times*, April 17, 1990, p. F1.
4. "You Got That Right," *The Washington Times*, Sept. 21, 1988.
5. Paul C. Vitz, *Censorship: Evidence of Bias in Our Children's Textbooks* (Ann Arbor: Servant, 1986).
6. *Ladies Home Journal*, March, 1989, p. 70.
7. Dr. Joyce Brothers, "Why Wives Have Affairs," *Parade* magazine, February 18, 1990, pp. 4–7.
8. David Blankenhorn, "What Do Families Do?" Paper presented at Stanford Univ., November 1989, p. 19.
9. William J. Bennett, *Our Children and Our Country* (New York: Simon & Schuster, 1988), p. 64.
10. Nicholas Davidson, "Life Without Father," *Policy Review*, no. 51 (Winter 1990), p. 42.

## Further Reading

George Barna. *The Future of the American Family.* Chicago: Moody, 1993.

James Dobson and Gary L. Bauer. *Children at Risk: The Battle for the Hearts & Minds of Our Children.* Dallas: Word, 1990.

Anthony T. Evans. *Guiding Your Family in a Misguided World.* Colorado Springs: Focus on the Family, 1991.

Tim LaHaye. *The Battle for the Family.* Old Tappan, N.J.: Revell, 1982.

# The Pitfalls of Single Parenting

## David R. Miller

### About the author

*David R. Miller, Ph.D., is professor of psychology and counseling at Liberty University. In addition, he carries on a private family counseling practice and has written five books on family and parenting issues, including* Single Moms, Single Dads, Parent Power, *and* A Parent's Guide to Adolescents *(Accent). He and his wife have three grown children.*

Single parents, like all parents, are prone to making errors in child-rearing. The question should not be, "Why do I make mistakes?" but rather, "Why should I expect myself not to make mistakes?" Parents, like all other human beings, will fail from time to time, so they will have to find a way to correct what is done. As with parents, so it is with children and teens. There is never a time in our lives when we will be invulnerable to making mistakes in parenting.

## The overly permissive

Guilt is magnified in the custodial parent because of the day-to-day contact with the less pleasant elements of single parenting. The absent parent, usually dad, will express his guilt by trying to buy his children's happiness. When he sees the kids, he will take them out to do fun things, eat at fun restaurants, play miniature golf, and never have a boring moment. His guilt is softened by giving the children amusements, entertainment, and excursions.

The custodial parent, usually mom, does not have the time, the money, or, often, the energy to do so many fun things with the kids. Mom's guilt cannot be softened in the same manner, and so mom usually lessens her guilt by becoming overly permissive. Feeling at least partially at fault for the changes her children have had to experience, mom usually cannot muster the strength to make the difficult choices when it comes to misbehavior.

Mom may also become overly permissive as a way to earn her children's happiness. After all, she reasons, this has worked for their dad, why shouldn't it work for me? Of course, what appears to be happiness to mom may, in fact, be growing insecurity in the children. Children will react to an overly permissive parent by taking advantage of the situation and by feeling insecure and unprotected, both very negative feelings that will result in unacceptable behavior at some point.

**"I can't say no"**

Walt Matherly has been a friend of Linda's and mine for many years. We met in an undergraduate program and have kept in touch through the years. Walt is now a college professor at a large, well-known university about two hours' drive from where we live. Though a Christian, Walt and his wife separated a few years ago, and, after a fairly nasty court battle, Walt was awarded custody of their only child, Amy, now sixteen. Even though divorce has not been pursued, Walt says there is absolutely no chance of his wife's returning to him, although she does keep in close contact with Amy and has regular visitation.

The reason Walt called me was that Amy had begun — to use his words — to try and manipulate him. Walt told me how bad he felt after the separation and how that bad feeling translated into a need to "make it up" to Amy. Making it up to his daughter meant to Walt that she receive basically everything she wanted. Both Walt and his wife earned a very good living and could afford to spoil their daughter.

But the situation had degenerated to the point that Amy had literally threatened her dad with becoming pregnant unless they somehow arranged for her to have a new Mustang for her sixteenth birthday. Amy pulled no

> *He had eliminated all boundaries.*

punches, her dad reported, and simply said, "This is what I want; you guys can afford it, and I better get it!"

I was unprepared for such a confrontation between father and daughter. This level of rebellion was of such an intensity that I had had no personal experience with it, and I was at a loss in the beginning to know what to tell Walt.

We talked long and hard about what had brought his daughter to this position and decided that Amy had been taught by her father in the years since the separation that he felt guilty and was not going to establish or enforce rules for her. He had eliminated all boundaries. As Walt explained it, he just couldn't bring himself ever to tell Amy no, and now when it was getting expensive to grant her wishes, he was stuck with his history of giving in to her demands.

We didn't reach a good answer as far as I was concerned. Walt eventually decided to go ahead and buy the car, hoping and praying that she wouldn't ask for anything like this again. I felt badly for Walt *and* Amy because I am certain the issue will come up again, probably in relation to dating regulations, and Walt will be right back in trouble again. How much easier it would have been if this single father had made the hard choice years ago and taught his daughter that threats like this would not work. As the saying goes, "Pay me now, or pay me later!"

# The overly strict

After reading about Walt Matherly and his daughter Amy, you might be wondering if it is really possible to be too strict. Given the terrible results Walt experienced by being too lenient, aren't parents better off leaning more to the strict end of the discipline spectrum?

> *Strict single parents make their children feel safe and secure, though a little put upon at times.*

Generally, the answer to that question is yes, single parents *are* better off erring on the side of strictness. The challenge is to keep away from being *overly* strict and to be able to understand what *overly strict* really is!

Parents are probably being overly strict when they ask their children to do things (such as going to bed at a certain time) that nearly none of the other kids that age have to. Parents are probably being overly strict when children or teenagers seriously rebel over what the parent thought was a minor issue. And parents are probably overly strict when they begin to question whether they have made the right decision or begin to feel that they have placed too much pressure or too many regulations on the young person.

Overly strict parents reflect their own lack of security in their extra toughness with the kids. "When in doubt, toughen up" seems to be the war cry of the embattled single parent. Parents who *are* too hard on their children are telling them that (1) they don't really trust themselves as parents, (2) they don't trust the kids to know what's best for them, and (3) they don't trust God to honor His promises to look after *His* children.

Strict single parents make their children feel safe and secure, though a little put upon at times. Overly strict parents make their children feel *less* safe and secure because they convey to the children and teens that their parent thinks there is something to worry about.

Single parents must exercise their parental authority following a family breakup and let the kids know that they, the parent or parents, are still in charge and will demonstrate that reality for the kids upon demand. Single parents are encouraged to avoid superstrictness because the message communicated to the youngsters in a family is that "you may be right; there might be something to be afraid of in this family."

Single parents who can be strict and in control model a God who is in charge even when things are tough. Single parents who become too tough on their kids model a God who is less understanding and less patient with His children — something our heavenly Father never is.

# The enmeshed parent

Enmeshed single parents are overinvolved parents. *Enmeshed* differs from *overindulgency* in that enmeshed parents may not "spoil" their children or teens at all and may actually be very strict with them. Rather, *enmeshment* refers to a parent living out an aspect of his/her own life through the life of one of the children. Enmeshed parents may be lenient or strict, loving and warm, or cool and detached. But all enmeshed parents share the characteristic of being overinvolved in the life of one or more of their children.

Why would a single parent become an enmeshed parent? Given the intense loss of security involved in the dissolution of a marriage and given that mom usually is granted custody of the children, it is really not surprising to find some single mothers trying to meet their own needs in the life of a child or teen. When the marriage is lost, what remains for the parents? What is left of the "good old days" to hang on to? The obvious answer is the children.

It is the children who are always available to parents. Children normally continue to love both parents even after one leaves the home, and a single parent, even the noncustodial parent, may find himself getting his needs met through the less confused, less traumatic life being lived by the child.

Enmeshment may involve going to every

> *Enmeshment may involve going to every single junior high school football or basketball game at which your daughter is cheerleading.*

single junior high school football or basketball game at which your daughter is cheerleading. Enmeshment may be seen in the single father who lives or dies according to how his teen-aged son performs on the high school football team and talks of nothing else to friends who will listen. Enmeshment is the single mom who waits up for her daughter or son to return home from a date and asks to be told *every* detail of what happened. She is not looking for things to criticize, but rather she is asking to be fed information so that her imagination can transport her back to a more troublefree time in life.

We Christians who are enmeshed need to be reminded that we are *loaned* these children to raise *for God,* and we are never to have *our* needs met by our children. Our job, of course, is to prepare these young people for the time when they will leave home and enter the larger adult society as positive, contributing members.

Enmeshed parents try to keep the nest from becoming empty. Enmeshed parents will never be satisfied in themselves or in the life they have as long as they can have a *better* time living vicariously through their children. Enmeshment is an understandable reaction to becoming a divorced person, but it is also a reaction that must be corrected as quickly as possible for the good of the children *and* the single parent.

> *We are never to have* our *needs met by our children.*

**Take the following quiz and see if it helps you identify tendencies to becoming a stumbling block. Though not very scientific in its construction, it may help you put your finger on a problem area in your parenting practices.**

**1.** Do you feel guilty when disciplining your children?
**2.** Do you, at times, find yourself surrendering to the demands of the children rather than doing what you know to be the right thing to do?
**3.** Have you attempted to "bribe" your children into obeying?
**4.** Do you buy gifts or treats for a child after disciplining him or telling him he cannot do something?
**5.** When your teen tells you that "all the other kids get to do that," do you give in even though you are concerned about the activity?

**If you have answered yes to four or more of these questions, you may be a single parent at risk for becoming overly permissive with your children.**

# Stumbling Block Quiz

**1.** Have you recently found yourself becoming angry at some relatively minor problem with the kids at home?

**2.** Have you ever said "no" to a reasonable request from the kids even though you had no reason for refusing them?

**3.** Do you find the kids "getting on your nerves" with little things they do at home?

**4.** Have you been "toughening up" your rules recently, even though the kids are not behaving badly?

**5.** Have you said to yourself recently that "everything would be perfect if these kids would just behave"?

**1.** Do you find yourself asking your teens or children for extreme details about their lives? That is, you seem to need to know more about what they are doing than other parents you know.

**2.** Do you secretly wish your children or teens would spend less time with their friends or other activities and more time with you?

**3.** Do you feel a strong need to attend all activities in which your children or teens participate, in spite of possible requests from them that you don't need to come to everything?

**4.** Do you find yourself wondering and worrying about what you will do when your children grow up and leave home?

**5.** Do you feel an extreme sense of personal disappointment or depression when your child or teen fails to get a part in a play or isn't selected for an athletic team or some other similar experience?

**Four or more yes responses indicate a dangerous trend toward becoming overly strict and harsh with the children. Overly strict single parents are usually motivated by their own sense of incompetence as parents and believe that perfectly behaved children will make people think that they are perfect parents.**

**If you answered yes to four or more of these questions, you are either already enmeshed in the life of your child or you are about to be. It is extremely important for parents in this category to understand the truth of Psalm 127. This and other passages describe the parenting role as that of preparing children to know the Lord and to leave home ready to take their place in the world as witnesses for Him.**

## The way forward

Though God does not expect the parents who raise His children to be perfect, He does expect us to be carefully sensitive to His will spelled out in Scripture and to the leading of the Holy Spirit in areas not clearly addressed in the Bible. I believe the message is that all human parents are prone to error, imperfect people raising imperfect children, but God has an answer for each of us no matter what the problem or the unique characteristics of our children.

The Bible says that God will never leave us or forsake us (Hebrews 13:4). A contemporary way of saying this is that "God didn't bring you this far just to let you fail," and this is certainly true of parenting as well. God chose you to raise His children because He knew you could do it right.

Yes, we fail and disobey at times, and some fail totally, as is true with the neglectful parent. But we have an answer, a hope. God did *not* give us these children to raise knowing that we would fail. He gave us these children knowing that we can do a great job if we choose to obey Him, follow His principles, be sensitive to His leading, be students of the Bible, and work to reflect God to our children in our actions.

The world is full of obstacles to good parenting, but as long as parents allow the inworking of the Holy Spirit and are consumed with a desire to honor God in their responsibilities, they can skip over most of these pitfalls as if they were not even there.

This chapter is taken from *Single Moms, Single Dads: Help & Hope for the One Parent Family* (Denver: Accent Books, 1990). Used by permission of David C. Cook Publishing Company.

## Further Reading

Larry Burkett. *The Complete Financial Guide for Single Parents.* Wheaton: Victor, 1991.

Andy Bustanoby. *Single Parenting.* Grand Rapids: Zondervan, 1992.

David R. Miller. *Single Moms, Single Dads: Help & Hope for the OneParent Family.* Denver: Accent, 1990.

Virginia W. Smith. *Single Parent: Revised, Updated & Expanded.* Tarrytown, N.Y.: Revell, 1983.

Jim Smoke. *Suddenly Single.* Tarrytown, N.Y.: Revell, 1990.

# Daughters of Divorce

## H. Norman Wright

### About the author

**H. Norman Wright**, M.R.E., *has two honorary doctorates and is a licensed Marriage, Family, and Child Therapist. He has taught graduate school for more than twenty-five years and is the founder and director of Christian Marriage Enrichment. He has written or coauthored more than fifty books, including* Always Daddy's Girl, The Seasons of a Marriage, *and* So You're Getting Married *(Regal), as well as* The Premarital Counseling Handbook *and* When Anger Hits Home *(Moody).*

Several months ago I attended a wedding and was quite surprised at what I saw. I'm sure it happens more frequently than I am aware of, but it still caught me off guard. The bride was escorted down the aisle to meet the groom not by one father, but two! Her stepfather was on one side and her natural father was on the other. Both fathers kissed the bride, then sat down on either side of the girl's mother. I wondered what the bride was thinking and feeling as she clutched the arms of both fathers. Her natural father left the home when she was quite young. She had contact with him over the years but was raised by her stepfather. Her story is the story of millions of children in our country whose natural fathers have left home.

Here's another story about a daughter whose father deserted her through divorce:

*"Come into the living room, children. We have something we need to tell you." That's how our parents told us they were not going to be together anymore. After they told us they were divorcing, I sat under the table and my mind replayed again and again the words my father said. I didn't know then what it all meant, but I soon learned.*

*After Dad left, I looked through the drawers where he kept his clothes and found an old sweatshirt he left behind. I hid it in my room and kept it for years. I would cling to it when I was lonely for him.*

*My father came back to see us a few times, but his visits became less and less frequent.*

*Finally his visits stopped completely. I always wondered where he went. I wondered if he thought about us very much. I hoped that he did. But I guess I'll never know.*

What happens when a father leaves the home, and how does his departure affect his daughter? Did you experience abandonment by your father through a divorce in the home? How did it impact your life? I'm sure many of your friends or acquaintances are victims of divorce. How were their lives impacted?

When a father dies there is a sense of closure to the relationship and an opportunity to say a final good-bye. A daughter goes through a period of mourning that is rather predictable. But where is the mourning period after a divorce? A child left behind by a deserting father feels uncertain. "Is Father coming back or not?" she wonders. The child doesn't know whether the loss will be permanent or temporary. The occasional birthday card, the weekly phone call, and the weekend visits and vacations keep alive the fantasy that Father might return.

# The disruption of divorce

A couple may resolve their problems through divorce, but the problems caused by the divorce are just beginning for the children. Often a child fears that she may have brought about the divorce, causing her painful guilt. Some daughters, without the love and affirmation of their fathers, look to their mothers for extra amounts of attention, which the physically and emotionally stressed divorcee may not be able to supply. A daughter needs the guidance of adults to understand the process of divorce and to work through the adjustment.

Many family specialists feel that divorce may have a "sleeper effect" on daughters. The effect may not be evident until adolescence and young adulthood. Many daughters seem to feel derailed by divorce and anxious as they move into adolescence and adulthood. They are afraid of being betrayed by men and attribute this fear to their parents' divorce.[1]

Janet is a classic example of what can occur when parents divorce and the father leaves home. At the age of 14, several years after her parents' divorce, Janet began experiencing depression and weight loss. She didn't appear to have any desire to come out of her depression.

In time it became evident that she was filled with rage over "what her father had done." But, as with many young girls, Janet wouldn't admit her anger. When her mother tried to discuss the situation, Janet tended to support her father and told her mother not to speak negatively about him. But this only increased Janet's internal conflict since she was aware of how the divorce and her depression were affecting her mother, and Janet felt sorry for her.

Janet also struggled with guilt, feeling responsible for the divorce. Two years prior to her father's departure, Janet, a typical adolescent, became more verbal, defiant, and unresponsive at home. When her father left, she was afraid that it was her behavior that had pushed him away from the home. Janet loved her father and her mother, but loving one tended to make her feel disloyal to the other. Her inner life was a multitude of conflicts.

When there is a family breakup, the daughter often develops and believes a number of myths. In Janet's case, the myths sounded something like:

*My mother is a good person, and my father victimized her unfairly.*

*My father left because he couldn't handle my rebellious attitude. He probably also blamed Mom for the way I was.*

*My father left us because he was self-centered, caring only for what he wanted and not what we needed.*

*My mother was hurt so much through this that she can't make it without my taking care of her.*

*If I recover and am happy again, that will hurt Mother. She won't be able to handle it.*

*I have to pick one parent over the other. I can't be loving and loyal to both of them. If I show love to Dad and spend time with him, Mother will be upset.*

*My father's new girlfriend is responsible for his leaving. But I can't be angry with her either.[2]*

If a daughter is to survive abandonment by her father, these myths must be exploded and replaced by the truth. Sadly, often the other adults in the daughter's life — including her mother-are unable to move her successfully through this process.

# The fatherless daughter

A daughter who was abandoned by her father carries numerous feelings into adulthood. She may doubt her self-worth, suspicious that she failed her role in keeping the family together. She wonders what she did, or did not do, that caused the family to break up. Jean said to me in a counseling session one day, "I know of a number of families where parents didn't care for each other. But they stayed together so it wouldn't damage their kids. For those fathers, the kids were worth sticking around. But I guess I wasn't worth even that. How do you think that makes me feel about myself?"

She may carry unresolved anger over being left by her father that taints her relationships with other men. She wants a man in her life, but she is unsure about trusting him. Any violation of trust from the men she cares about is further proof that she can't trust any man. She wants to be loved, and she wants to be lovable. But anger, mistrust and fear of intimacy with men can keep her from giving herself to a man.

When an adult daughter of a divorced father approaches marriage, she may have mixed feelings about his involvement in her ceremony. Occasionally I am asked by a woman in premarital counseling how her father should participate. He abandoned her at a young age, but now wants to be involved in her life again. He even wants to walk her down the aisle. "I would much rather have my stepfather walk me down the aisle," most women tell me. "I feel closer to him than to my dad. In fact, I resent the fact that my father wants to walk back into my life now. I didn't leave him; he left me. I have no feelings for him as a father. My stepfather gave me what my father withheld from me."

Strong, negative feelings often follow an abandoned daughter into her marriage. June is a prime example. She came to me for counseling with her husband, Jim. Jim couldn't understand why his behavior bothered June so much. Whenever she tried to express her concerns to him, Jim would either turn on the TV, bury his face in the newspaper, or leave the room. Jim felt he had heard what she had to say, so why continue the discussion? But his behavior said more to her. She felt abandoned by Jim, and it wasn't until she explained her childhood relationship with her father during our session that Jim finally understood:

*When I was four months old, my father left my mother, and I never knew him. She married my stepfather three years later, and he left us when I was six. Three years later she married my second stepfather and he stayed for another three years. By the time I was 12 years old, I had been abandoned by the three most important men in my life. Even my mother left me during those years by shutting me out of her life.*

*I married you, Jim, hoping that a man would never abandon me again. When you walk out when I'm trying to talk to you, or turn on the TV or pick up the paper, a flood of terrible feelings from the past surges up inside of me. I try to talk in such a way that you'll stay and listen, but sometimes I don't succeed. I guess I'm tired of trying to make everything right, just like I tried to do as a child. I couldn't make the men stay then, and now I'm afraid that I can't keep you either.*

Does June's situation sound familiar to you? Did you grow up feeling that you had to make everything "right" in order to please your father?

## Mothers and daughters

When a father leaves home through divorce, the relationship between the surviving mother and daughter is significantly affected. A major study on this topic indicates that fatherless daughters actually spend less time alone with their mothers than other girls.[3] The daughters studied felt they received less affection from their mothers after the separation and that too much was expected of them. They understood that their mothers didn't have sufficient time for them because of work. But many of them felt emotionally trapped in the situation. They were angry at their father for abandoning them, but he wasn't available to be the target of their anger. So a daughter often felt like venting her anger on her mother, blaming her for the father's absence. At the same time, the girl felt the need to squelch her anger because Mom was all she had left, and she needed her more than ever. The pattern of daughters of divorce repressing their emotions is prevalent.

Often a mother places more responsibility on her daughter after a divorce. And some daughters take on more adult responsibilities as a means of surviving their loss. If a daughter is the eldest child or only child, she often pushes herself to assume a much more responsible role in the home. She feels the need to become an adult, filling the void created by the missing father.

One writer shared an interesting perspective on this "pseudo-maturity": "The early adoption of adult behavior thus serves two very definite functions for her. By being good and helpful, she ensures mother's continued acceptance and presence. And by being strong,

> *A daughter often felt like venting her anger on her mother, blaming her for the father's absence.*

she tries to resist identification with someone [her mother] whose low self-esteem is threatening her own."[4] Often a woman who loses her husband experiences diminishing self-esteem, appearing weak when her daughter needs to see her as strong. The daughter does not want to appear weak like her mother, so she learns the value of controlling her emotions like an adult.

When her father exits, a young daughter may also feel constrained to fill the role of adult companion for her mother as well as remaining a daughter. The girl functions as her mother's peer as well as her child. But in so doing she develops adult independence ahead of schedule and builds a defensive structure against childlike intimacy. This artificial maturity arrives much too early.[5] The girl must learn to develop and operate within a different relationship with her mother.

During a counseling session, one of my clients summarized the experiences of thousands of women when she described herself, and her relationship with her mother, in a fatherless home:

*Norm, the reason I'm here is I'm a survivor. I had to be. I know I am insecure emotionally, but I do survive. With no father since I was six, I learned to grow up fast. Perhaps I'm stronger today because of what I went through. Mom worked to keep us alive. She was tired at night and couldn't listen to all my trivia, so I learned to handle my problems myself.*

*I worked at odd jobs at age twelve and discovered I had something to offer. By seventeen I had saved enough for a car, even before I graduated from high school.*

*I have a good job now and know I'll make it financially. But when it comes to men, that's where I'm insecure. And you know what? I would much rather have a man in my life than a career. My job was more of a necessity to survive; it was not my first choice.*

## The deserted teenager

What happens when a fatherless daughter approaches her adolescent years? Are there differences between these girls and others who come from two-parent homes? Although many exceptions and variations may appear, some significant trends suggest that differences do exist.

Often fatherless daughters are more awkward or ill at ease as they approach the teen years. They lack not only the interaction with their fathers, but also an ongoing model of the father-mother relationship, a necessary reflection of male-female interaction.

E. Mavis Hetherington discovered that fatherless girls interacted with males differently than girls from two-parent homes:

*Adolescent girls who had grown up without fathers repeatedly displayed inappropriate patterns of behavior in relating to males. Girls whose fathers had died exhibited severe sexual anxiety, shyness, and discomfort around males. Girls whose fathers were absent because of divorce exhibited tension and inappropriately assertive, seductive, or sometimes promiscuous behavior with male peers and adults. . . . Girls whose fathers had died spoke significantly less with a male interviewer and were generally more silent than any other group of subjects. Girls whose parents were divorced tended to talk more with a male interviewer than with a female interviewer.[6]*

The daughter of divorce often uses the divorce to justify her distrust of men, so the young men in her life are at a disadvantage in the dating experience. She reasons that if her father is lacking, all other men must be lacking as well. Daughters whose fathers died tend to

> *The daughter of divorce often uses the divorce to justify her distrust of men, so the young men in her life are at a disadvantage in the dating experience.*

perceive husbands and fathers as having predominantly positive characteristics. But daughters who came from divorced homes tend to perceive most men as having negative characteristics.[7]

**The deserted teenager faces special problems.**

When adolescent daughters approach marriageable age, they are apt to respond to marriage prospects in one of two contrasting ways. Many fatherless daughters rush into marriage with unrealistic optimism and expectations. Often they are looking to their husbands to rescue them from past disappointments and heartache at the hands of their fathers. These fantasy-like hopes are seldom realized.

Other daughters resist marrying because of the fear of intimacy. They balk at opening themselves to men because they are afraid they will eventually drive their husbands away as they suspect they drove their fathers away. Others fear that their utopian visions for married life will disintegrate because that's what happened to their parents' marriages.

Yes, there are some negative consequences and long-term effects from being left behind by a divorcing or deserting father. Many women feel rejected by their fathers, and many were indeed rejected. Often they do not feel they can trust their emotional responses. They learned to value repression and they matured too soon. Daughters who may be afflicted the most are those who never knew their fathers and those whose fathers were outwardly indifferent before they abandoned their families.

# Hope for recovery

But the redeeming factor that helps many women through the ordeal of fatherlessness is a sensitive mother, one who works hard to defeat the negative effects of no father in the home. If her mother manifests positive and balanced coping skills, the daughter is able to learn from this modeling. These positive coping skills counter the negative effects of repression, rejection, and premature maturity. The availability of outside support systems make a difference in daughters' lives as well. Many mothers who don't remarry immediately or at all find significant, mature men who can provide some of the positive masculine modeling that their daughters lost.

But not every abandoned daughter is fortunate enough to have such a positive response to her loss. What about those who are still affected? What about you? What about your friends? Is there hope for recovery after father loss? Yes, there is![8]

This chapter is taken from *Always Daddy's Girl* (Ventura, Calif.: Regal, 1989). Used by permission.

1. Joan Libman, "No Happily Ever After in Divorce," *Los Angeles Times* (January 30, 1989), part IV, adapted from p. 8.
2. Howard Halpern, *Cutting Loose* (New York: Bantam, 1977), adapted from p. 178.
3. Elyce Walkerman, *Father Loss* (Garden City, N.Y.: Doubleday, 1984), adapted from p. 13.
4. Ibid., p. 131.
5. Ibid., adapted from p. 126–34.
6. E. Mavis Hetherington, "Girls Without Fathers," *Psychology Today* (February 1973), pp. 44–52.
7. Ibid., adapted from pp. 44–52.
8. Wakerman, *Father Loss*, adapted from chapters 2, 3, 6, 9, 10, and 12.

---

### Further Reading

Debbie Barr. *Children of Divorce: Pulling Kids Together When Their Parents Are Apart.* Grand Rapids: Zondervan, 1992.

Bob Burns and Michael J. Brissett, Jr. *The Adult Child of Divorce.* Nashville: Oliver-Nelson, n.d.

William L. Coleman. *What Children Need to Know When Parents Get Divorced.* Minneapolis: Bethany House, 1983.

Jim Conway. *Adult Children of Legal or Emotional Divorce.* Downers Grove, Ill.: InterVarsity, 1990.

# Overcoming the Pain of Abuse

*Doris Van Stone*

Those who have endured physical and sexual abuse will understand that I felt dirty, ashamed, and unworthy of human love. No matter how much I tried to be like everyone else, I knew I was different on the inside. And I thought that everyone else could see inside me.

If people could have looked inside, what would they have seen? I had been conceived out of wedlock, and my conception forced my parents into an early marriage. I was hated by my mother and abused in an orphanage and two foster homes. My mother completely rejected me. I experienced ridicule and repudiation. I was sexually molested. And I was eventually disowned by my father.

## Earliest memories

My earliest memories date back to a lonely apartment in Oakland, California, where as a child I would wait in darkness for my mother to come home. My mother gave me the responsibility of taking care of my younger sister, Marie. When Mother would arrive home, she would give Marie a hug. I was always pushed aside like an unwanted dog.

I was only six, but I knew deep pain. We often went to bed hungry. But the pain of an empty stomach was more bearable than the emotional hurt of rejection and hatred. I was never held, touched, or cuddled. I knew I was different, ugly, and a burden to my mother.

Often she would bring male companions home with her. Then she would dress my younger sister, and all of them would go out together. To make sure no one would discover that a child had been left behind alone, she would take the wall bed down, stuff me inside it, and then put it up again. There I would cry, gasping for air until I fell asleep.

Occasionally people have asked how I can remember events dating back to age six. All I can answer is that when the pain is deep, you *do* remember. My memories are still vivid.

## In the orphanage

When I was seven, my mother took Marie and me to an orphanage, dropping us off like a package at the door. She visited us just twice in seven years, bringing only a gift for Marie — none for me. Years later when my husband, Lloyd, and I visited the orphanage, I discovered to my surprise that it was only ten blocks from the apartment in which my sister and I had lived with our mother. At the time it seemed a world away.

While at the orphanage I took out my anger on the other children. I deservedly earned a bad reputation and was beaten (usually just before bedtime) every evening for seven years.

> *I knew I was different on the inside. And I thought that everyone else could see inside me.*

> *"Children, even if you forget everything else we have told you, remember – God loves you."*

But when I was thirteen, some Christian students came to tell us about Jesus Christ. As they were leaving one of them said, "Children, even if you forget everything else we have told you, remember – *God loves you.*"

Sitting on a folding chair in the parlor, I prayed for the first time in my life. I told God that if He loved me and wanted me, He could have me. On that special day I became a Christian, and I knew I was received by God. At last I had a Friend – a Friend forever.

# Breaking the silence

Little did I realize that later life for me outside the orphanage would be far worse than it was within its walls. I was shunted to four foster homes. In two, I was physically, mentally, and sexually abused. Yet the God who was with me during my closing days in the orphanage stood with me.

Sexual abuse is difficult for victims to talk about – no one wants to recall such painful events. And until recent years victims were expected to keep such secrets *secret.* But I can no longer be silent.

Almost every time I speak I am sought out by women who suffer sexual abuse. One-sixth of the female population today has been abused. As the influence of pornography and moral decay increases in our society, the rate of sexual abuse will also rise. One estimate says that one out of four baby girls born this year will be sexually abused, usually by a member of the immediate family, a relative, or a friend.

Boys are also abused, often by homosexuals who develop a craving for "younger talent,"

as it is called in the world of perversion. Some are abused in different ways by their parents or peers.

To my dismay I have learned that sexual abuse can take place in Christian homes – even in the homes of Christian leaders. This hidden sin happens behind the closed doors of some of our most respected families. It happens everywhere.

Those dark secrets are what cause the soul to become bitter, unloving, and woefully sad. They are the cause of many neuroses, and they also lead to withdrawal from society or even the contemplation of suicide.

# Sexual abuse

My sister and I left the orphanage when I was thirteen years old. We were taken to a foster home run by a woman we called "Granny." I attended junior high school, and Marie went to an elementary school nearby.

Granny began to intimidate us the day of our arrival. "If you don't mind me, you'll get *this*," she warned as she slapped my face with her bare hand, using me as an example. The blows stung, but I tried not to cry.

There was, however, something far worse than the beating I endured in Granny's home. One evening when I was sleeping, her husband came into my room, woke me, and told me to take off my clothes. Then without further explanation, he forced me to participate in sexual acts to satisfy his perverted whims and desires.

That was the first of many such experiences. *How I hated the very sight of the man!*

> *The only thing that sustained me during those painful days was the knowledge that God was with me.*

> *Apparently no one wanted
> to get involved.*

He was tall, strong, and heavyset. There was nothing I could do to stop him from violating my body. He warned me that if I ever told anyone he would kill me, and I believed him. After almost every one of those encounters, he would lock me into a closet until I stopped crying. If I cracked open the door and he was still around, he would abuse me again. One time I sobbed with such intensity and anger that I pushed my hands right through my pockets.

# Holding on to God

The only thing that sustained me during those painful days was the knowledge that God was with me. Back in the orphanage, a Christian matron by the name of Irma Freman had given me a copy of the New Testament. Each day I would read a few verses, trying to memorize them as well as I could. "Lord, You promised to be with me all the time," I would say. "All I have is You."

After about four months with Granny, Marie and I were taken to a home for girls who were wards of the state. There we had a welcome respite from the cruelty of the past few months. Unfortunately, our stay was short-lived. We were told that we would be transferred into a private home. We looked forward to this, thinking we might actually find someone who loved us. But that was not to be.

When the doorbell at the Girl's Home rang, I was stunned. There stood Granny, looking as angry as ever. "We've come to take you to a family that lives in San Francisco," she said, pointing at the social worker who was with her.

Granny, we discovered, knew our mother. We never quite understood the connection, but we were told that she was there on our mother's behalf. My sister was taken to live with a family who really wanted her. I was taken to live with a family who knew my mother.

# A living nightmare

Life in the Makin home was as bad as, if not worse than, what I experienced at Granny's. Mr. Makin was a short, stocky man with a heavy chest. He reminded me of a gorilla. Mrs. Makin looked stern with her gray hair parted down the middle. Mrs. Makin permitted me to take only one bath a month and to wash my hair every eight weeks. Over the door she kept a calendar indicating the day she would draw the water into the tub. I would have to strip in front of her, and when I was wet, she would beat me with a leather strap. I can still feel the sting.

Often I was beaten just before leaving for school, so I had to begin the five-mile walk with a bloody nose or black eye. I would use the rest room in a service station before I arrived so that I could attempt to camouflage my hurts. I'm convinced now that my teachers and other adults must have seen that I was being abused. But they pretended not to notice. If they had asked questions, they would have become responsible. Apparently no one wanted to get involved.

My hair became matted, and I developed head lice. So my hair was shaved off. To hide my embarrassment, I went to school with my head wrapped in a towel. The other children would pull it off and laugh, calling me cruel names.

Dirt encased itself around my wrists and ankles. When I walked into the classroom, I'd hear the other students say, "There's Stinky!" as they turned their backs toward me.

I looked forward to that long walk to and from school. I used the time to talk to God. Sometimes after school I would crawl into boxes in an alley or crouch behind trash cans, seeking some sort of refuge. I sought a place to pray and cry my eyes out.

The beatings I had come to expect at

Granny's were repeated at the Makins. They beat me mercilessly. Once again, I found myself running outside to hide under a step or in an alley, always looking for a place to cry.

My rollaway bed was in the hallway that led from the dining hall to the Makins' bedroom. Frequently strange men walked past my couch, shuffling their way into the bedroom. I prayed they would not touch me.

# No one listened

One day Mrs. Makin said to one of the men, "Go ahead, take her. I'll stay in the other room." The man overpowered me. He tore my clothes and forced me to participate in his sexual acts. Once again, I found myself screaming, begging, pleading that I might not have to become a part of these perversions. But no one listened to my cries. No one came to my help.

Soon other men would come to the house looking for "the little girl." The houses in San Francisco are built so close to one another that there is only room for a small alley between them. Sometimes when I heard the men coming I would run through the alley and hide under a step or run to the other side of the block. I still recall hiding one evening and overhearing the men saying to one another, "Where is she? Where could she have gone?"

I had scraped my knee as I crouched in the small crevice, waiting for the men to leave. Rotting garbage must have been near me because I vividly recall thinking that it smelled like dead rats. Amid my tears I sobbed, "If only I had a mother, this would not be happening to me!" Then a light seemed to engulf me, and I felt a sense of peace. I heard the men say, "She's not here." They left. That time God protected me.

But there were times when God did not protect me. I prayed earnestly for deliverance, calling to the Lord for help and protection, but still I was sexually abused by evil men. Once I threw a cup of hot coffee on one of my attackers but was beaten and abused

> *It is impossible to exaggerate the sense of shame and revulsion that those acts brought to my soul.*

all the more severely.

No one had to tell me that what was happening was perverted and filthy. It is impossible to exaggerate the sense of shame and revulsion that those acts brought to my soul. For a long time I would run from anyone who wanted to touch me, even if it was an innocent touch.

# No one else

God did not shield me from the violations of my body, yet I still clung to Him, believing that He would be with me. He gave me the grace to bear my trials. That's why I have never been bitter or angry with my heavenly Father. It was He who chose me to belong to Him; He led those students to the orphanage to tell me about God's love. Regardless of the heartaches I have endured on earth, I know that this present suffering cannot be compared with the glory that will be revealed in us. God has reserved a place for me in heaven, so that I may be with Him forever. Eternity is a long time. Someday I shall speak to my Savior, who stood with me when no one else did. Maybe He will tell me why I had to endure all those tears. And maybe He will point to some people and say, "Dorie, these are here because you told them about My grace and power." Just a word from my Savior will make up for the past.

I believe God is sovereign; He knew the first day of my life, and He knows the last, as well as all the days in between. Nothing can happen to me without first passing through His fingers of love. He knew that someday that dirty little girl would stand before thousands of people and tell them that God is faithful — that there is nothing in their lives too big for God to handle.

People have told me, "Dorie, you survived because you had such strong faith." That's not true. I survived because there was no one else to run to except the Lord. I had absolutely no one else. I sometimes questioned God, but I never hated Him.

# Healing

Do I have scars? Of course. But there is something beautiful about a scar. It means that you have been healed — that you are on the mend. All over the country I meet people who have been cut open emotionally, and many of them still have open wounds. Sometimes I meet people who are holding onto their bitterness; they keep reliving the painful events of the past. They are, in effect, peeling off the scabs to see whether healing has occurred — or sometimes to prove that it hasn't.

The process of healing is like major surgery. After the operation, the wound is painful and tender, but if the stitches do their job, healing occurs. Slowly the flesh begins to grow together, and the area becomes whole again. Eventually you can be hit where the scars are without feeling it.

Today I tell people, "Don't blame God for what happens to little children!" It is true that terrible things happen within the context of His permissive will and that He could prevent them. But He does not *do* the evil, and He has good reasons for allowing those things to happen.

> *I survived because there was no one else to run to except the Lord. I had absolutely no one else.*

Job did not curse God even though he lost his children, possessions, and health. His wife advised, "Curse God, and die." But he called her foolish, asking, "Shall we indeed accept good from God and not accept adversity?" (2:10). Thus Job did not sin with his lips or charge God foolishly.

Also, I have to remind my listeners, "Don't believe the psychiatrists who state that experiences of abuse will ruin you for the rest of your life and that you will never be normal." Unfortunately, many people have believed the lie that past abuse will ruin all your chances for happiness. Not so. When Christ promised that our joy would be full, I believe He meant it for all Christians, regardless of their backgrounds. He is indeed able to heal the broken-hearted. For example, I have the good fortune to be married to an understanding husband who loved me despite my abuse. He was tender and compassionate, and through his love the sexual relationship became beautiful and fulfilling. That is proof of what God is able to do.

# Somewhere to turn

My heart still breaks for the thousands of children out there who are being abused, either physically or sexually (or both), who do not know Christ as their Savior. They have to withstand the trauma alone, and they have nowhere to turn. To them God may seem cold, impersonal, and cruel. Some lash out in anger against the Almighty and against the people who have mistreated them. Even after they grow up and become integrated into society, they live alone emotionally. They never really feel as if they belong to anyone. No one helps them carry their trauma; no one makes their burden lighter. The family they marry into is often just as cruel as the one that reared them.

Christ already knows our dark secrets. We share our inmost thoughts, and He lends His listening ear. The same Christ who forgave

> *The first step in experiencing the healing of the past is to choose to deal with those dark secrets. Bring them to God.*

my sins and enabled me to come to grips with my troubled past is available to you. His death on the cross was a sacrifice for sinners so that we all can be welcomed into His family forever. We must, however, receive Him as our own. In the orphanage in Oakland I put my faith in Him and received both His companionship and the gift of eternal life. If you have not already done that, don't read any further. You have business with God.

The first step in experiencing the healing of the past is to choose to deal with those dark secrets. Bring them to God. He knows about them already, of course; indeed, He knows every detail of our history. By taking up the matter with our heavenly Father, we have the advantage of talking with someone who already knows the details if words fail us. "And in the same way the Spirit also helps our weakness; for we do not know how to pray as we should, but the Spirit Himself intercedes for us with groanings too deep for words" (Romans 8:26). The Holy Spirit takes the groanings of the soul and puts them into words. He helps us in our intercession.

Then find a friend who will believe you. Perhaps it will be someone who has also experienced abuse, though that is not necessary. There are many fine Christians who can sympathize though they themselves have never experienced the same trauma. You will need the strength of the Body of Christ in order to be healed.

This chapter is taken from *No Place to Cry* (Chicago: Moody, 1990).

---

### Further Reading

Dan B. Allender. *The Wounded Heart: Hope for Adult Victims of Childhood Sexual Abuse.* Colorado Springs: NavPress, 1990.

James Mallory, Jr., and Cindy Kubetin. *Beyond the Darkness.* Houston: Rapha, 1992.

Doris Van Stone. *No Place to Cry.* Chicago: Moody, 1990.

Sandra D. Wilson. *Released from Shame: Recovery for Adult Children of Dysfunctional Families.* Downers Grove, Ill.: InterVarsity, 1990.

# Freeing the Family from Destructive Addictions

*Bill Perkins*

Once upon a time, a young man moved into a cave in the mountains to study with a wise man. The student wanted to learn everything there was to know. The wise man supplied him with stacks of books. But before he left the cave, the wise man sprinkled a powder on the man's hand, which caused him to itch.

Every morning the wise man returned to the cave to monitor his student's progress. "Have you learned everything there is to know yet?" the wise man asked.

And every morning his student's answer was the same: "No, I haven't."

The wise man then sprinkled the itching powder on his student's hand and left.

This scenario was repeated for months. One day the wise man entered the cave, but before he could ask his question the student reached out, grabbed the bag of powder, and tossed it into a fire.

"Congratulations," the wise man said, much to the surprise of the student. "You have graduated. You know everything you need to know."

"How's that?" the student asked.

"You have learned that you don't have to wait until you've learned everything before you can do something positive," he replied. "And you have learned how to take control over your life and stop the itching."[1]

It could be that a secret addiction has created a relentless itch in your soul. You've scratched it hoping it would get better. It hasn't. Instead it demands more attention. In fact, addictions give an illusion of intimacy,

## About the author

**Bill Perkins** *is the senior pastor of South Hills Community Church in Portland, Oregon. He is the senior writer for Moody Bible Institute's "Today in the Word" monthly devotional.*

> *Addiction is not a private matter; it's a family affair.*

and this tends to displace intimacy within the family. Spouses drift apart, and parent-child relationships become superficial. When a family member suffers from an addiction, secretly or in the open, the whole family suffers. Thus, addiction is not a private matter; it's a family affair. How individuals and their family members respond to an addiction will determine whether the family ship corrects its course into a safe passage or splinters against the rocks.

If you have a secret addiction, you may have told a family member, friend, or counselor. But the itching persists, and you can't make it stop. Be encouraged. Many people like you have found freedom from their secret addictions. Let me introduce you to a few of them.

# Eating away the pain

I've seen the grace of God transform a lot of addicts. Sarah is one of them. I'll let her tell her story:

*I remember opening the front door of our tiny apartment and setting the groceries on the kitchen table. When I saw that Jack wasn't home I walked into the bedroom and collapsed on the bed. . . .*

*Everything in the apartment was tidy. At least that was one good thing about Jack. He was neat. But, honestly, I couldn't think of much else I liked about him.*

*We had only been married a few months. What a mistake! It made my stomach tighten just to think about Jack. He only cared about himself. I was sick of waiting on him.*

*Things at work were even worse. My supervisor, the head nurse at a large hospital, couldn't stand me. Instead of praising my cheerful attitude, she told me to wipe the*

*phony smile off my face. Nothing I did pleased her. Nothing! Mondays seemed to be especially hard.*

*Every day, during my lunch break, I sat at a picnic table in a park, read my Bible, and cried. I felt miserable.*

*It had been one of those terrible Mondays. I had stopped off at the grocery store on my way home from work to buy bread and milk. I knew Jack loved chocolate chip cookies, so I rounded up the ingredients I would need to make a few batches.*

*Remembering that the milk was still sitting out, I groaned, sat up, and swung my feet off the edge of the bed. Suddenly I felt a surge of energy. I walked into kitchen and put the milk and bread away. I wasn't sure when Jack would be home, so I decided to go ahead and bake the cookies for him. He would like that.*

*As I pulled the first batch out of the oven, I told myself that I would only eat two – no more, just two. After placing the second batch into the oven, I savored my treat. Actually, I was hungrier than I thought. Since I only had a sandwich for lunch, I felt that eating a few more cookies wouldn't hurt.*

*By the time Jack got home I had eaten all of both batches – except for the five I saved for him. Afterwards I felt ashamed that I couldn't control my appetite and vowed never to let it happen again.*

*"How was work?" he asked.*

*"Terrible," I said.*

*After inhaling all five of his cookies he asked me where the rest of them were.*

*"I only made one batch," I lied. "I ate a couple and gave a few to the dog," I lied again. "I saved some because I know how much you like them," I explained, not lying.*

*For the next few days the monster that had been eating at me was silent. Work went smoother, and Jack didn't waste as much time watching television. I seemed to be OK.*

*On Friday Jack and I had a horrible fight. It was about something stupid. He wanted to go skiing with a friend, but I thought it was a* waste of money. Beside, if he was going to ski, I wanted to go with him. . . .

Jack left early Saturday morning. By the middle of the afternoon I felt like I deserved a treat. After all, he had gone skiing; why shouldn't I do something special for myself? I went to the grocery store and bought a gallon of ice cream and the ingredients for some cookies. This time I spared nothing. I bought tons of nuts and the best chocolate I could find. The monster inside me pleaded for food. I could barely wait to get home and feed him.

This time I had no intention of saving any of the cookies for Jack. He certainly hadn't shared the fun of skiing with me. Once home I locked the door and shut the blinds.

After the cookies were baked I dug in. I ate three batches and most of the ice cream. Finally, the monster was satisfied. But I felt horrible. I wondered where it would end.

For several years I waged a losing battle against a beast of unimaginable power. I went on diets. I joined support groups. I begged God to take away my insatiable appetite. Nothing worked.

I repeatedly vowed never to binge again. But the monster stayed hungry. My enslavement went on for several years. Finally I sought professional help. It took awhile, but over time I began to realize that my compulsive eating was an attempt to satisfy an emotional hunger. I learned that my greatest enemy was an unwillingness to develop an intimate relationship with others, including my husband. Getting my compulsive eating under control demanded that I do something about it. The process of self-discovery was painful. For now, the monster is silent.

Sarah paid the price. She worked hard, and today her eating is under control. Her story has a happy ending.

> ## The monster inside me pleaded for food.

Eating away the pain . . .

# Desire out of control

John, a mild-mannered, personable man in his early thirties, was doing well in business. He spoke with a gentle tone and managed to maintain eye contact with others no matter what was going on around him.

Though his wife wasn't strikingly beautiful, she was attractive and supportive. John clearly loved his wife and children and had an effective ministry in his church.

But something was wrong, so John set up an appointment to see me. "I have a problem with pornography," he said. "I do fine for several weeks or maybe even a month. And then I can't resist the urge."

Rather than bringing pornographic videos into his home, John visited adult movie theaters on the other side of town. While he had discussed the problem with his wife, he hadn't been able to find freedom. He had even made himself accountable to his pastor. Nothing had worked.

For a long time he thought his problem would be solved if he moved. In desperation he uprooted his family and moved to another town. He did better for a while but then found himself enslaved again. He couldn't understand how something so horrible could have gained such control of his life.

After months of counseling, John learned that he had never identified the behavior that preceded his episodes. It seemed, as with others who have secret addictions, that certain thoughts and activities always led to a pornographic encounter. In the past he had simply tried to stop his wrong behavior. But by the time his preliminary behaviors had progressed several stages, John had gone too far to stop.

One day John realized that dealing with his uncontrolled cravings would involve more than simply saying, "I won't do it any more." He would have to identify and then stop doing the things that stirred up the cravings. And that's what he did.

# Helping till it hurts

Cara visited me because of her husband's problem with alcohol. All her attempts to help him had failed. She begged him not to drink. She threatened to leave him if he didn't stop. When he would go out of town on business she would call his hotel to see how he was doing. She felt as if he was ruining her life.

After several sessions I asked Cara if it wasn't possible that she needed to stop being so concerned with her husband. I suggested that maybe she should quit trying to force him to do something he wasn't ready to do.

> *Ultimately it's the Dragonslayer who will set you free.*

Instead, I urged her to look inside herself and see if perhaps she couldn't find some room for growth.

She was immediately defensive and offended by my suggestion that she was a part of the problem. I assured her that her husband needed to control his alcohol use, but explained that she was blaming all of her problems on him. She had allowed her life to center on one thing: rescuing her husband.

Only after Cara was willing to realize that she also had a problem could she begin to release her husband to God and start growing herself.

What exactly was Cara's secret addiction? She was a codependent. Cara had allowed her husband's behavior to affect her in such a way that she was obsessed with controlling his behavior.[2] Cara didn't begin to recover until she realized that, no matter who caused her problem, she had to accept responsibility for herself.

# The dragon within

There are other stories I could tell. I've seen strong men and women bow beneath the power of an addiction. I've wept with families destroyed by a parent's addiction. I've seen marriages devastated because of a man's sexual addiction or a woman's eating compulsions. I've counseled men and women who have emotionally starved their children because of an addiction to work.

I've related these stories because they illustrate the kinds of struggles people have with their own secret addictions. They also highlight some of the insights that need to be gained for freedom to occur, insights that will be more fully developed as we go along.

**Sex, food, or work can be as addictive as alcohol.**

Sarah described her secret addiction to food as a monster within her who demanded to be fed. I like to refer to this monster as an evil, powerful dragon. John's inner dragon roared for pornography. Cara's dragon insisted that she control and rescue her husband.

If you're battling a secret addiction, great or small, you know about the dragon within. You wonder how it grew to such dominance in your life. You know if you continue catering to its whims, you'll be destroyed.

But what can you do? You wish you could drive it away. But you can't. Nor can you kill it. The dragon is too powerful.

But that doesn't mean there's no hope or help. The power of your dragon can be broken. Ultimately it's the Dragonslayer who will set you free.

# Overcoming addiction

I define an addict as *a person who is unable to resist the repeated urge to enter into a love relationship with an object or event for the pleasure and illusion of intimacy it provides.* Addicts find nurturing through the objects or events of their preference.[3] Indeed, their lives have a single aim: the pursuit of the objects or events with which they have developed a love relationship.

● *For a sex addict it's pornographic videos or magazines, voyeurism, flirting, illicit affairs, or involvement with prostitutes.*

● *For the food addict it's certain kinds of foods, such as sweets or eating in general.*

● *For the gambler it's betting on a horse or playing the slot machines.*

● *For the spender it's the excitement of*

*excessively buying clothes, tools, electronic gadgets, and so on.*

Often our *secret* addictions begin as *hidden* addictions. In the early stages, we aren't even aware that a problem exists. "After all," we argue, "what's wrong with flipping through *Playboy* magazine once in a while?" "How can a little playful flirting with the boss be harmful?" "What's the problem with visiting the refrigerator every half hour for a snack?" Yet sex, food, work, and codependency can be as addictive as drugs or alcohol.[4]

Once we realize, or someone helps us realize, that we can no longer control our cravings, the addiction is no longer hidden to us. We are aware that a problem exists. Yet we tend to keep our addictions a secret. We're embarrassed to admit that something so "harmless" has hooked us. In fact, we may keep it a secret so long that we no longer believe it is an addiction.

Nothing is more important than discovering and dealing with your hidden and secret addictions.

Since shame is at the core of addictive behavior, it's crucial for you to counteract your negative feelings about yourself. Doing so is a choice. You can choose to say, "God unconditionally loves me, and I receive His love and love myself." Whenever you're alone, say it out loud. Say it often!

Naturally, the dragon will fight this. It wants to cut you off from the only love that will satisfy. It wants you to wallow in shame, desperately seeking love in addictive behavior.

You may know of things you do that make you unworthy of God's love. Of course! We all do wrong things. But God loves you for who you are. *He loves you!* Paul wrote that Christ died for us while we were sinners (Romans 5:8). He didn't demand a change on our part before extending His love. He loves us in spite of what we do.

There is nothing you can do to make yourself more lovable to God! You are loved just as

> *Shame is at the core of addictive behavior.*

you are. If you refuse to believe you're loved, then you're calling God a liar. You are implying that you can determine your value better than God can. Are you ready to say that? I hope not.

Saying, "God loves me and I accept His love", counteracts the voice of shame. God's love has the power to transform your life.

I recently talked with a talented woman who is a friend of mine. Since childhood she's struggled with an eating addiction. She said she never felt worthy of love. Driven to earn love, she dressed well and worked hard. Occasionally, when she felt overwhelmed with

**The spender can be addicted to shopping.**

feelings of shame, she'd binge.

I've noticed that she has a hard time accepting compliments. When I asked her why, she said, "I feel people only like me for what I do. If they knew the real me, they wouldn't accept me. Since I realize they don't know the real me, I reject their compliments."

My friend's problem was immediately thinking of the bad things she had done whenever people complimented her. She looked at the dragon instead of at the Lord. She knew her dragon didn't deserve any praise. But her friends were appreciating her, the real her. They loved her in spite of the dragon.

Overcoming her feelings of shame demands that she focus on God's unconditional love for her. She needs to see and accept herself as God does.

Accepting God's love and allowing Him to change your self-image is a free choice. You can choose to flood your mind with shameful thoughts that cloud your identity as someone God loves. Or you can say, "God loves me and I am His child." As you begin to acknowledge God's love, you will begin to see yourself as He does.

This chapter is taken from *Fatal Attractions: Overcoming Our Secret Addictions* by Bill Perkins. Copyright © 1991 by Harvest House Publishers, Eugene, Oregon 97402. Used by permission.

1. Melody Beattie, *Codependent No More* (San Francisco: Harper & Row, 1987), adapted from p. 7.
2. Ibid, p. 31.
3. Craig Nakken, *The Addictive Personality* (New York: Harper & Row, 1988), p. 7.
4. Archibald D. Hart, *Healing Life's Hidden Addictions* (Ann Arbor, Mich.: Servant, 1990), p. 3.

## Further Reading

Stephen Arterburn. *Addicted to "Love."* Ann Arbor, Mich.: Vine/Servant, 1991.

Archibald D. Hart. *Healing Life's Hidden Addictions.* Ann Arbor, Mich.: Servant, 1992.

Grant Martin. *When Good Things Become Addictions: Gaining Freedom from Our Compulsions.* Wheaton, Ill.: Victor, 1990.

Cherry Boone O'Neill and Dave O'Neill. *Living on the Border of Disorder.* Minneapolis: Bethany House, 1992.

Bill Perkins. *Fatal Attractions: Overcoming Our Secret Addictions.* Eugene, Oreg.: Harvest House, 1991.

# When Two Families Become One

*Frank Minirth and Don Hawkins*

When a stepfamily is formed, families not previously related are expected to bond together because of a marriage. Making two families into one takes more than a marriage ceremony — and more than love between the two parents.

## Mythical stepfamilies

Stepfamilies are represented by two extremes: the "Brady Bunch" type and the Cinderella type.

The "Brady Bunch" stereotype gives the impression that parents and children from two families can always resolve conflicts in a short period. In reality, stepfamilies we have counseled have a lot of intense issues to sort through — issues not easily resolved.

Real-life circumstances more often resemble Cinderella's stepfamily than those of the "Brady Bunch." There are conflicts between the stepsisters or stepbrothers — and often with a stepparent. In many instances, the promised new family beginning — the "silver carriage" — turns into a pumpkin well before midnight.

## Real-life stepfamilies

One stepfamily we counseled experienced tremendous upheaval on issues such as jealousy and discipline. Who would discipline whose children and making sure that no one overstepped bounds were major problems.

Another stepfamily we counseled was composed of a mother and her two daughters, a father and his daughter and son, and a child the two parents had together. Needless to say, there was intense competition between the children. Both sets of children accused both stepparents of favoring their biological children.

A stepparent will usually go one of two ways. He or she will favor his or her biological children (which is human nature), or he or she will try to compensate and will favor the stepchildren. One stepmother overcompensated her desire to favor her own child be becoming intensely hard on her instead. As a result, the daughter experienced a great deal of conflict and struggled with her self-concept while trying to adjust to the new family. She ended up in the hospital for treatment of depression.

Two Christian divorcees were launched in a whirlwind romance after discovering at a church "Singles Again" get-together their mutual problems of single parenting. Because they agreed on so many things regarding parenting, they assumed they agreed on other issues as well. After the wedding they were surprised to find out that what seemed to be an ideal coparenting situation revealed many unresolved differences in their relationship as husband and wife.

Although these difficulties can be very real and intense, with Christ's help, they can eventually be resolved.

## The two-family home

The joining of two families is not one that Scripture fails to address. As a matter of fact some early family conflicts involved a two-family setting: Abraham, who fathered two half-brothers, Ishmael (born of Hagar, his wife's handmaid) and Isaac (born of Sarah, his wife); Moses, who had an adopted mother and a biological mother (the latter acting as his

### About the author

*Frank Minirth, M.D., is president of the Minirth-Meier Clinic in Richardson, Texas, associate professor of pastoral ministries at Dallas Theological Seminary, and editor-in-chief of Christian Psychology for Today. His books include* How to Beat Burnout, Before Burnout *(Moody),* The Stress Factor *(Northfield), and* Love Is a Choice, We Are Driven, *and* Love Hunger *(Nelson).*

> *Stepfamilies have a lot of intense issues to sort through – issues not easily resolved.*

nurse); David, who fathered many children from eight wives, plus concubines, which made his multiple family household a place of many problems; and Eli, who fathered two older sons who turned out poorly and then had another chance at fatherhood when he was given the godly young Samuel to raise.

Today there are many books and seminars for improving Christian marriages, but these almost always apply to first marriages. They do not consider the special issues that concern second marriages, which still face problems rising from first marriages as well as the problem of bonding two families into one.

Today more second marriages, even among Christians, involve a first marriage that ended in divorce rather than in the death of a spouse. Yet individuals from those two backgrounds usually share more similar problems than do persons entering marriage for the first time. The following guidelines are for strengthening second marriages, regardless of how the previous marriages ended. These guidelines are different from those we would suggest to people entering their first marriage. This does not mean we are advocating divorce and remarriage, just that we are dealing with situations as they are.

## Guidelines for bonding two families into one

### (1) Work through the grief of ending the first marriage

Grief occurs when a marriage dies, whether it was through divorce or a spouse's death. Frequently individuals who have been involved in marital breakups experience a significant amount of grief but fail to work through it.

As *Happiness Is a Choice* (Baker, 1978) documents, there are normally five stages of grief: *denial*, when we refuse to admit we have suffered a loss; *anger turned outward*, when we blame others or even God; *anger turned inward*, when we blame ourselves and become overcome with grief, which frequently leads to depression; and *genuine grief*, when we are able to get our feelings out, look at them, experience them, and cry over them. Unless we work through the first four steps, we will be unable to experience the final step, which is *grief resolution.*

If you have failed to work through the death of your marriage, particularly if you married again a short time after the first marriage ended (within one or two years) perhaps it would be wise to sit down with a good friend and candidly ask, "At what point am I in the grief process?" Then develop a plan to work through the rest of the process until your grief is resolved.

Be aware that your children may not have come to the point of grief resolution, either. They may need to have you or some skilled counselor talk through this process with them, particularly if you have not talked with each other about your grief.

### (2) Forgive yourself
A card in a gift shop read "Podody's Nerfect." We see evidence each day that proves that every member of the human race has been affected adversely by sin. James 3:2 says, "We all stumble in many ways."

The formerly married person may have a tendency to be angry with himself or herself

for not having been a perfect marriage partner, particularly if the first marriage ended in divorce. Even if a person was widowed, he or she may practice self-blame. Two of the most common burdens of divorced individuals are bitterness toward their previous mates and bitterness toward themselves (because of anger or bitterness held toward their previous mates). In addition to forgiving their former mates, they often need to forgive themselves.

For the individual who has not done so, forgiving self must be preceded by accepting God's forgiveness, which is available to everyone who places his trust in Jesus Christ as

## *About the author*

*Don Hawkins, Th.M., is director of radio communications for Rapha in Dallas, Texas, and the host and executive producer of "Life Perspectives." He has coauthored several books, including* How to Beat Burnout, Before Burnout, *and* The One Minute Christian *(Moody), as well as* Love Hunger *(Nelson).*

> *Grief occurs when a marriage dies, whether it was through divorce or a spouse's death.*

personal Savior. Since He died on the cross to pay for mankind's sins, God offers forgiveness to those who receive Him by faith (John 1:12). For those who have received Christ, accepting God's forgiveness is based on 1 John 1:9, "If we confess our sins, he is faithful and just and will forgive us our sins and purify us from all unrighteousness." When we admit that we have failed and accept God's forgiveness, and we forgive ourselves, we have a basis on which to rebuild lives and relationships.

### (3) Forgive others

While in the process of writing *How to Beat Burnout* (Moody, 1986), we discovered a significant relationship between burnout and bitterness. Bitterness develops when anger is retained, grudges are held, and those who have wronged us — whether in big ways or in little ways — have not been forgiven.

Ephesians 4:31–32 verifies that going through life nursing bitterness and anger is not worth it: "Get rid of all bitterness, rage and anger, brawling and slander, along with every form of malice. Be kind and compassionate to one another, forgiving each other, just as in Christ God forgave you." Verse 32 stresses the positive element, the mandate to forgive, along with the example of how Christ has graciously forgiven us.

### (4) Have convictions

We're living in a world that has lost its moral moorings. Media, modern literature, and current lifestyles emphasize what some call "sexual freedom." In days when "everybody's doing it," it is essential, both for spiritual well-being and mental and emotional health, to live by your convictions. Perhaps close to half of all married couples include at least one partner who has had a sexual affair. Add to that the fact that a greater percentage of second marriages end in divorce than first marriages, and one can see the need to live by firm convictions during both the good and the bad times.

Widowed or divorced men and women face more sexual temptation as singles than individuals who have maintained one marriage. Even if previously married persons lived up to strong Christian sexual values in years past, sometimes the pull of the world and a desire for love and affection during their "single again" years lead them to lower their standards.

After they marry again, they may think they have reestablished the standard to "keep themselves only unto" their mate. They must be sure to establish their standards with firm conviction, however, not just because they love their mates (which is a good reason), but because God hates adultery and fornication. He hates it for many reasons, including the fact that it pulls individuals, families, and societies apart.

Individuals such and Joseph and Daniel in the Old Testament demonstrate the value of convictions. Those individuals were confronted with sexual and material temptations, yet they remained true to their convictions, and ultimately they prospered and were blessed. Contrast that with the consequences David experienced when he gave in to sexual temptation with Bathsheba: Bathsheba became pregnant; David had her husband killed in battle so that it could not be revealed that the baby was illegitimate; and death and violence became a way of life in David's family.

Mental health occurs when we follow the exhortation of the old hymn that says, "Dare to be a Daniel, dare to stand alone." Daniel was a man who stood for and openly practiced godly convictions even when they were declared capital offenses.

Other convictions needed to bond a stepfamily include recognizing all things as belonging to the family, not to "them" and "us." Such selfishness and greed, particularly regarding material belongings, needs to be recognized and actively thwarted. The attitude of giving of ourselves to one another totally includes material possessions. If one of "them" accidentally breaks or wears down something that previously belonged to "us," it is not reason for assigning undue blame or reacting too negatively than if one of "us" had done the same thing.

## (5) Memorize Scripture

Although there is often a great deal of instability in stepfamilies, God's Word can offer stability. If we examine verses such as Matthew 7:24, we notice that a house built on a rock is stable. Likewise, a stepfamily built on the rock of God's Word will become increasingly stable.

Memorizing Scripture can be one of the most dynamic processes that individuals can undertake to revitalize and rebuild their lives. Hebrews 11:3 says, "Through faith we understand that the worlds were framed by the word of God" (KJV). When we realize how huge the universe is, that it would take approximately a hundred thousand years to cross the Milky Way traveling at the speed of light and that Milky Way is only one of millions and millions of galaxies, it makes us marvel at how God by His word made all that. If His word could do that, then what could the Bible, His Word to us today, do in our lives?

According to Hebrews 4:12, "the word of God is living and active. Sharper than any double-edged sword, it penetrates even to dividing soul and spirit, joints and marrow; it judges the thoughts and attitudes of the heart."

To overcome any kind of problem we need, more than anything else, to maintain simple love and devotion to Christ, just as Paul states in 2 Corinthians 11:3. And one of the best ways to do that is through Scripture memorization. Remember that in stepfamilies there are many issues in the subconscious and conscious minds of all parties involved. Because of that, Scripture memorization offers hope.

We have pointed out the importance of Scripture memorization to underscore its significance in bonding a stepfamily. A stepfamily faces many stresses that threaten to tear it apart. To avoid that, it needs something strong; and nothing is stronger than the Word of God in the unconscious mind.

## (6) Design a new plan

Sometimes circumstances seem impossible, especially in new situations. In our counseling ministries, we frequently point out that whatever behavior people are engaging in, even the unintentional, constitutes a plan of behavior—plan A. Such a plan may include frequent arguments, extensive worrying, and failing to allow for difficulties caused by trying to blend two families into one.

Since plan A (both current behavior patterns and those used in the first marriage) has proved unproductive, you need to formulate and adopt an alternative. Then live and test your new plan for several weeks to see if it works better.

Specific items to include in a plan might be:
- *spending a certain amount of time alone with your spouse daily*
- *spending a certain amount of time alone with each child, preferably daily, but at least several times a week (try a fifteen- to thirty-minute period before bedtime for smaller children)*
- *regular exercise*
- *memorizing Scripture verses and spending a specific amount of time each day reading God's Word*
- *talking with a friend every day*
- *developing and agreeing upon a family contract as a basis for handling family disputes and discipline issues*

The "summit meeting" plan discussed in *Growing in Step,* by Dan Houmes and Paul Meier (Baker, 1975) gives each family member, including children (who during the between-families stage experienced greater independence and decision making than most children do), a chance to present their cases in a mature way. Someone has well said, "If we fail to plan, we plan to fail."

## (7) Spend time with your children

Frequently a parent in a stepfamily will find that time constraints make it difficult for a parent and children — biological and stepchildren — to spend significant time together. Parents will sometimes rationalize the situation by saying, "We spend *quality* time together." Our observation, however, has shown that both *quality* and *quantity* of time are important, perhaps more so in bonding a stepfamily. Certainly quality time, when the parent concentrates completely on the child and is not preoccupied with other pressures, cares, and responsibilities, is essential. However, significant amount of time must be spent together also.

Sometimes children, because of a marital break-up and the resulting feelings of depression or anger, will resist spending time with parents. Children should not be forced to spend unwanted time with a parent. Therefore, it may become necessary to look for way to motivate and encourage wanted times and activities together, ones which they will consider fun and enjoy. Camping, fishing, shopping, going out for a pizza or hamburger, or other activities that children appreciate can produce that important togetherness.

Children from broken families show more signs of stress than other children. Judith Wallerstein, executive director of the Center for the Family in Transition near San Francisco, looked at the impact of divorce on 130 middle-class children. Five years after the divorce, 37 percent were more emotionally troubled than they had been immediately after the divorce. Wallerstein also says that fear of divorce affects them later in their love lives. They "enter relationships with a high level of anxiety and have more trouble with marriage — they want a stable relationship more and are more worried about it" than children of nondivorced parents.[1]

Spending time talking with the children about the greater possibilities for a good lasting marriage among committed Christians

# At home

Being in a family should help you discover all of the following: who you are, who you want to be, who you can be, and who you ought to be. Sometimes there are powerful conflicts between these different things, but a family should be a place where powerful conflicts can safely take place.

Families are difficult places to be in, often, because it is in our families that we most fully indulge our human weaknesses. If we were our obnoxiously undiluted selves in public the way we are with family, life would be a series of broken noses. One definition of "home" is the place where you can be a complete jerk and they will still call you for dinner.

You shouldn't expect the people in your family to always understand you. Why should they? You don't often understand yourself.

**Daniel Taylor**

(even if you thought your first marriage was such) will help them reestablish hope and trust for their own lives, as well as start them on the way to developing, and looking for, qualities that build strong relationships among friends and in a marital relationship.

## (8) Allow time for yourself

If you want your children to be mentally healthy, then it is important for you to be mentally healthy, since a great deal of their mental health will be influenced by yours. Sometimes we feel that it is wrong to take time for ourselves. Frequently, individuals who are obsessive-compulsive — conscientious, dedicated, somewhat perfectionistic — feel guilty about taking time for personal fun, relaxation, hobbies, or other interests.

Both of us have a significant quantity of these obsessive-compulsive personality traits ourselves, so we say from experience that it is important to develop interests you enjoy and take time out for yourself. Whatever you enjoy — camping, softball, needlepoint, visiting friends, or browsing through antique shops — make sure you allow time for yourself.

Bonding a stepfamily is not always easy.

However, by practicing unconditional love for others, realistically appraising your position in Christ and experiencing His forgiveness, forgiving yourself, and pursuing to live one day at a time through His power, it can be done.

The bonding of two families into one can be accomplished by claiming the promise found in Philippians 4:13: "I can do everything through [Christ] who gives me strength."

This chapter is taken from *When Two Families Become One* (Chicago: Moody, 1987).

1. "Children of Divorce," *Journal of American Academy of Psychology* 24, no. 5 (September 1985).

---

## Further Reading

Tom and Adrienne Frydenger. *The Blended Family*. Tarrytown, N.Y.: Revell, 1985.

Jim Smoke. *Growing in Remarriage*. Tarrytown, N.Y.: Revell, 1990.

H. Norman Wright. *Before You Remarry: A Guide to Successful Remarriage*. Eugene, Ore.: Harvest House, 1988.

# DEVELOPING FAMILY VALUES

# Our Spiritual Family Tree

*Richard Thomas Bewes*

## About the author

*Richard Thomas Bewes, Rector of All Souls Church, Langham Place, is the author of fourteen books and a regular contributor to BBC's "Thought for the Day." He is on the British Advisory Board of Dr. Billy Graham and was chairman of Dr. Graham's "Mission '89" in London. He was made a Prebendary of St. Paul's Cathedral in 1988. For more than a decade he has been UK Chairman of African Enterprise, which specializes in Christian communication and relief work. He is listed in* Who's Who.

It was through a single sermon, preached last century by D. L. Moody, that the principle of generational continuity – transmitting a value system from family to family through the corridors of time – stamped itself indelibly upon the mindset of my own family in Britain.

## One solitary sermon

The year was 1882, and D. L. Moody, at forty-five years of age and at the height of his power, was in the middle of a whirlwind campaign through several major British cities, including Swansea, Cardiff, Plymouth, Bristol, Portsmouth, Brighton, Liverpool, and Birmingham. Tuesday evening, September 26, found the famed evangelist at the Drill hall in Plymouth-historic through its association with Sir Francis Drake and the discovery of the New World. That evening my future grandfather, then fourteen-year-old Tommy Bewes, youngest of a solicitor's twelve children, sat entranced – first with the singing of Ira D. Sankey and then with Moody's preaching.

It seems that Tommy was the only family member who attended the meeting, unable to persuade any of the others to come along. Almost certainly it would have been one of the maids in the house who finally accompanied him.

We even know what text was preached that night because Tommy wrote a memorable letter to his sister Evy that has somehow survived to this day:

*I am writing to tell you some good news which you will be glad to hear. I went to one of Moody's and Sankey's meetings on Tuesday and there I was saved. He spoke from the 9th verse of the 3rd of Genesis. It is, Where art thou? He said that that was the first question that God ever asked man in the Bible, and that it was the first question that people ought to ask themselves and he said that there were two more that he was going to speak about and they were, Where are you going? and How are you going to spend eternity? I don't think he could have chosen better ones. . . .*

One solitary sermon – and three generations later we are still feeling the effects of it. Before this momentous event, my family had not been particularly noted for any evangelical influence. We evidently came over to Britain at the time of the Norman Conquest ("Bewes" being a derivation from *Bayeux*, home of the famous tapestry in France). Today we are a large family with many evangelical connections. It was Moody's sermon that imparted the new impulse.

Thomas Bewes himself went on to study for the Christian ministry at Cambridge University. His eldest son, Cecil, my father, did likewise. He spent more than twenty years building up the growing churches of Kenya in East Africa. Four of us grandchildren entered the ordained ministry; several others were to marry evangelical clergymen; still others were to be involved in the missions and councils of Christian enterprise and service.

It would be too difficult to unravel for you the many other links and relationships that make up our family today. It is enough to say that my father once remarked, "I've just been going through my Christmas list – for family alone. How many names do you think I had on it? One hundred and two!"

But our family story is nothing unusual. In looking at this principle of spiritual continuity in the family, we are drawn inevitably to the beginning of things.

> *Your home is the laboratory to recreate you.*

## A creation principle

Festo Kivengere, the celebrated Ugandan bishop, declared during a visit to Australia, "It is in the *home* that the Spirit of God wants to do His transforming exercise – transforming you into the image of your Creator. Your home is the laboratory to recreate you." Had it been otherwise, we could have expected the Bible to have started with an erudite and exclusive philosophical argument for the existence of God. Instead, we are introduced to a garden – and to a family. The story of the Old Testament is basically the story of a family.

Interestingly the principle is established before there were any fathers or mothers as such. God's basic unit of the family takes its beginning from Genesis 2:24: "For this reason a man will leave his father and mother and be united to his wife, and they will become one flesh."

It is a creation principle; a one-man, one-woman relationship – publicly witnessed (the language of "leaving"), permanent, and monogamous (the language of "uniting" or "cleaving"). Marriage and the family predate even the Fall. They came into being before any concept of the church or the people of God had existed. Marriage and the family form God's great, original, and permanent institution. As the theologian Karl Barth observed, "To enter upon marriage is to renounce the possibility of leaving it."

Children were to be brought up to obey their parents, who in turn were to love and care for them. From the beginning parents were to provide *the* vital and initial reference point for life – and the point of contact with God. Indeed, they stand in the place of God; a child knows the laws of its parents before it knows the laws of God. Once the parental link with life is broken, disorientation results. It was so then, and it remains so today.

# A result of the Fall

If creation is the first great plank of biblical revelation, without doubt humanity's Fall, recorded in Genesis 3, is the second. It runs like a thread through every book of Scripture. Genesis 3 is arguably the most important chapter of the Bible. Without it we would have been baffled by the transformation from the innocent purity of chapter 2 to the murderous act of chapter 4 that broke up the very first family.

The Fall affects everything we say, plan, think, and do. And because the sexual drive is our second most powerful instinct (the first is survival), the effect of the Fall upon the sphere of the family is clear.

God's punishment of children for the sins of their parents, to the third and fourth generation (Exodus 20:5), is in many ways as much a natural principle as it is a spiritual one. Diseases brought on by reckless behavior are often transmitted down the line. An adoption of false values may leave future generations in poverty and deprivation. Whole societies can suffer from the sins of a single powerful dynasty.

Look at ancient Greece. With all its grandeur, it was still a degenerate society. "We keep prostitutes for pleasure," wrote Demosthenes, "we keep mistresses for the day-to-day needs of the body; we keep wives for the begetting of children and for the faithful guardianship of our homes." Later, at the time of Jesus, the Roman stoic philosopher Seneca was to remark, "Women were married to be divorced, and divorced to be married."

In a whole range of areas — money, work, politics, recreation, art, literature, and relationships — a distorted worldview is likely to be the inheritance of children and grandchildren with an unconverted ancestry. At the very heart of London the statue of Eros commemorates the achievements of the reform-

> **God has chosen to work in and through ▶ families; Jesus was born into a family in ancient Palestine.**

ing crusader, the seventh earl of Shaftesbury. He once declared, "Education without instruction in moral and spiritual principles will merely produce a race of clever devils."

Such is the power of the family to transmit its value system and its sins to successive generations that a downward spiral would be inevitable if the human race was left with only the Fall and its catastrophic results to contemplate. But there is a third major plank of God's revelation: the principle of redemption.

# A redemption principle

There is another side to the law of Exodus 20:5. According to the covenant, God would indeed visit the sins of the fathers upon the third and fourth generation, "but" — the sentence continues — He would show love "to a thousand generations of those who love me and keep my commandments." The strong implication then is that God's mercy comprehensively outweighs His judgments.

History is witness to the buoyant truth that a degenerative family line can be intercepted by the arresting — and elevating — law of redemption. We see this in the Old Testament where, despite Israel's frequent failures, the family of God raised a lone banner amid a sea of idolatry against polytheism, child sacrifice, and sexual impurity.

In the early centuries of the Christian era, Gentile Europe was the stage on which a miracle of transformation was to take place — the replacement of one set of beliefs for another. The universally accepted views of the time could not produce a satisfying interpretation of life, a credible morality, a personal faith, or an answer to death. The preaching and the living of Christ and His message first challenged

the old beliefs, then finally superseded them.

"What women these Christians have!" exclaimed Libanius, the fourth-century Greek teacher of rhetoric. Among his students had been John Chrysostom, the golden-mouthed preacher of Constantinople – whose mother, Anthusa, lost her husband at twenty, and from then on devoted her energy to the education of her son.

In family after family it was to be the same. New standards were taught – in reality they were the original standards instituted at creation, tarnished repeatedly as a result of the Fall, but then reinstated in living situations as the gospel of redemption took hold. The old, dying world had its morals, plenty of them. The stoics overflowed with morals. Then came a new generation, possessed not so much with a system of morality as with a great passion and a new love. "A believer is surely a lover," writes Søren Kierkegaard, "yea, of all lovers, the most in love!"

## The end time

The last plank of God's revealed truth is eschatological. Christian revelation holds no brief for a circular view of life. There is to be no reincarnation, no further chance in a future lifetime, no opportunity of making a fresh video. We are "destined to die once, and after that to face judgment" (Hebrews 9:27). Each lifetime then presents the individual with a unique, never-to-be-repeated opportunity. Our present lot is not the merited result of a previous existence, requiring that we face life with stoic fatalism. We can change, we can rise, we can decide – in the sure knowledge of an impending end, when we shall render to God an account of the way we conducted our lives.

The only way our actions and choices will

> *God has chosen to work in and through families.*

affect future lives upon this world will be in terms, not of a reincarnate existence for ourselves, but of people yet unborn – who will feel the reverberations of our chosen path long after we are gone. We are responsible for them. We may have a full and absorbing life, in its own way, and experience what many would call a good time. But it is impossible to pass on a great time to another generation. We can pass on only the things we have learned, the values of substance we have embraced.

Thus it is possible for a contemporary man or woman to delve back into the family archives and to thank God for grandparents and great-grandparents who, by their responsible choices, set in motion beneficial events that not even the vagaries of a fallen world can erase. God has chosen to work in and through families – until the consummation of Christ's kingdom and the ushering in of the new heaven and the new earth. That is why I, and a current generation of the Bewes family, look back with gratitude to Tuesday, September 26, 1882. And, of course, to a preacher named Moody.

### Further Reading

Dave Carder et al. *Secrets of Your Family Tree.* Chicago: Moody, 1991.

Gloria Gaither, ed. *What My Parents Did Right.* Nashville: Star Song, 1991.

Rolf Zettersten. *Train Up a Child: Imparting a Legacy of Love and Faith.* Dallas: Word, 1991.

# Family Devotions That Work

*Terry Hall*

## About the author

*Terry Hall*, Th.M., *is vice president of Media Ministries. Formerly a professor at Moody Bible Institute, he teaches Bible Panorama and Creative Teaching Seminars and has written* How to Be the Best Sunday School Teacher You Can Be *and* Finally, Family Devotions That Work *(Moody). He has three children.*

Having trouble finding time for family devotions? You're not alone. It's difficult to get the whole clan together in one place, at one time, with a relaxed attitude. And some of us don't know how to start a family worship time. Schedule a time and place to meet each week. Ask God for wisdom in applying these suggestions to your family's interests. Start small and be brief. It's better to leave children and teens wanting more than to force them to sit through a dull routine. What follows is a sample month of devotions.

## Week One: All that's fit to print

Pretend you're a newspaper editor during Old Testament days. You're to produce something that looks like a modern paper, but everything in it will be based on biblical accounts.

Select a passage you are studying at church or choose a short Bible book such as Jonah. Read it together, preferably in a version suited to your children's learning level. Let each family member choose a different part of the paper from these options:

- *headline and lead news story*
- *masthead (list of staff)*
- *other news columns*
- *"photos" (drawings, doodles, stick figures)*
- *want ads*
- *advertisements*
- *personalities in the news*
- *women's page (fashions, domestics, recipes)*

- *crossword puzzles*
- *poetry*
- *interviews*
- *maps*
- *small filler items*
- *editorials*
- *letters to the editor*
- *cartoons*
- *men's page (sports, travel, business)*

You'll need paper, pencils, and crayons for each person. As editor, you'll gather and organize the contributions. If you want to publish your creation, photocopy machines make great printing presses.

Perhaps you don't feel creative enough to handle such a project. Consider these examples from Jonah and the sample newspaper in the illustration.

- *Insert a help-wanted ad: "Prophet wanted. Must be willing to follow orders. Position requires transfer to Nineveh."*
- *Include a letter to the editor from the Mariners' Union decrying the lax port security allowing runaway prophets to use cargo ships.*
- *A "Nineveh Notes" column includes these tidbits:* "Authorities Institute Religious Services in Palace Ballroom"; "Governor Returns 5 Million Stolen Rubles to Province Coffers". *Someone could write an editorial urging Jews not to hold grievances against Ninevites since God has forgiven them.*
- *The business page might run this headline:* "Shipping Stock Plummets with News of Entire Cargo Lost at Sea."
- *On the women's page, try some ads for the new fall fashions from Nineveh like* "Sackcloth for a Simpler Lifestyle."
- *If you can doodle or draw even a little, make a Joppa Travel Agency display ad for excursion tours of Tarshish: "Special economy fare at bottom prices — if you don't mind sleeping in the cargo hold."*
- *Print an obituary of a lesser-known person, such as Jonah's father, Amittai, or the* king of Nineveh.

Interview the captain of the ship. You're not limited to people, either. Ask the fish questions: "How did you know when and where Jonah would be thrown overboard? How do you feel harboring a disobedient prophet? Did you have severe indigestion? How would you describe your Creator? What is it like to always be obedient to God?"

Discuss with your family how your news source, the Bible, differs from modern media. Read 2 Timothy 3:16–17 and ask: What does the Bible claim for itself? What is the Bible designed to do in our lives? How would our family life be different this week if we really believed these two verses? In sentence prayers, thank God for the Bible and for each other.

# Week Two: Memory music

Do you ever write songs? Relax — you don't have to know music composition to use this method. This week's suggestion is graded by age, but your children's abilities should determine the projects they take on.

### To age seven

Memorizing Scripture is easy for this age group, especially if set to simple, catchy melodies. New words can be added to familiar tunes children have learned. Visit a Christian bookstore and help your child select a tape of Scripture set to music (such as "Sing a Song of Scripture" "Kids' Praise," or "Critter Country"). Most stores have demonstration albums to preview before you buy.

### Ages eight to twelve

This age group can make up words to existing tunes, substituting one syllable per note. Sing a simple chorus or hymn, counting on your fingers the syllables in each line.

"Jesus Loves Me," for instance, has seven syllables in each of its four lines, not including

# THE  JOPPA JOURNAL

NEWS
EDITORIALS
WEATHER
GAMES
ADVERTISEMENTS
WANT ADS

**BUSINESS NEWS:**
SHIPPING STOCK PLUMMETS WITH NEWS OF ENTIRE CARGO LOST AT SEA.

**EXCLUSIVE:**
INTERVIEW WITH GREAT FISH

"What is it like to harbor a disobedient prophet?"

"How would you describe your creator?"

## EDITORIAL

At first I felt Nineveh deserved to be destroyed. But God has shown me my mistake, and now I rejoice because of their repentance.

## NINEVEH NOTES

Leaders begin worship services in palace ballroom.

**BOAT FOR SALE CHEAP**

ONLY BEEN IN 1 STORM

**RIDE THE BIG FIZH**

$

**BUY NINEVEH BONDS**

**∽OBITUARY∽**
AMITTAI, FATHER OF JONAH DIED TODAY.

**INSTANT SHADE**
BUY THEM FOR ONLY 4.6 DRACHMAS AT ASSYRIAN HOUSE PLANTS. PLANT ONE AT NIGHT HAVE COOLING SHADE THE NEXT DAY.

the chorus. Now make up new sentences with the same number of syllables. Here's an example using Jonah. Each line summarizes one chapter of the book.

*Jonah went against God's wish:*
*So he wound up in a fish!*
*Nineveh turned to the Lord:*
*But the worm got that old gourd!*

*(chorus)*
*Don't be like Jonah!*
*Don't be like Jonah!*
*Don't be like Jonah!*
*Accept God's perfect will.*

**Teenagers**
If your teen has some musical ability, he'll enjoy creating songs from Scripture, especially those suited for guitar accompaniment. He could also make up more sophisticated words to an existing hymn.

Referring to a hymnal tune, put one new syllable under each note of the hymn. You can always stretch a syllable over several notes, but don't "bunch" two or more syllables under one note.

You may also want to write the original words and put corresponding new words under them. Each child can work on separate lines, stanzas, or even the chorus. Or try grouping teens in pairs so they can work together.

Here's how Jonah 1 might look, using the tune "What a Friend We Have in Jesus":

*God did call His prophet Jonah*
*To a great and vile city.*
*Jonah ran away to Tarshish,*
*But the Lord did stir the sea!*
*Lots were cast to find the sinner,*
*And the men did fear the Lord.*
*They then threw the prophet over,*
*But a fish took him aboard!*

Even nonmusical people can write poetic rhyming verse with a regular rhythm. Sing your new song a few times, and you'll be amazed at how quickly you memorize the words and concepts.

Next, read Psalm 96 together. For two minutes, list from this psalm reasons to sing God's praise. Then prayerfully do so.

# Week Three: Anyone for a game?

An easy way to enjoy learning Bible concepts or verses is to convert a "secular" game into a "scriptural" one. Many common games, such as Parcheesi, Monopoly, or Scrabble, only need to have homemade Bible questions added. Before any player takes a move, he has to answer a question card.

The following hints may help you in designing scriptural games:

(1) The whole family should read a Bible portion together first and discuss its meaning.

(2) Choose questions from a passage suitable to your family's age levels. It's best to have about twenty new questions each time you play.

(3) Put Bible references on question cards instead of answers. When a player misses, he must look up the answer and read it aloud. He still loses his turn. But because the card is shuffled back into the playing pile, there's motivation to remember the answer.

(4) Interesting twists can be added. Try including extra statements on question cards: "Correct answer gives you three extra places," or "Wrong answer sends one of your pieces back to home base."

To create a game for younger children, paste a Bible story picture from a magazine or Sunday school paper onto stiff cardboard. Cut the picture into big pieces with gently curved lines to make a simple puzzle. Hide these pieces around the house as a basis for a treasure hunt.

Members of the family can call out "warmer" as the child approaches a hidden piece. Once pieces are found and assembled, explain the story of the picture. This makes a great review of Sunday school lessons. Thank God for the privilege of being a family and enjoying His Word together.

# Week Four:
# Guess what?

Reading Scripture can be more interesting if you ask each other questions relating to Bible facts and application. Here are some examples from Proverbs (answers are at end of chapter):

1. *Why is it wrong to be completely open-minded?*
2. *What kind of a fool is hopeless and should be avoided?*
3. *How can you recognize a slothful man? What does "slothful" mean?*
4. *What can cause family fights?*
5. *What can a person do to avoid ever being kidnapped?*
6. *Why is it foolish to get involved in get-rich-quick schemes?*
7. *How do others judge you by your friends?*
8. *Why should we never cosign for someone else's loan? What does "cosign" mean?*
9. *What is the easiest way to break up a close friendship?*
10. *How can you be sure to win every argument?*
11. *How can a fool pretend to be wise and get away with it?*
12. *What could a person do to make others be attracted to him?*
13. *How could you conquer a person who's physically stronger than you?*
14. *Why should we never rejoice when our enemy falls?*
15. *What is the only thing worse than being a fool?*
16. *What is a certain shortcut to failure in life?*

Of course, you can add humor in designing questions. Try these examples (answers are at end of chapter):

1. *Who is the shortest man in the Bible?*
2. *Who is the smallest man?*
3. *Who is the straightest man?*
4. *When was tennis played in Bible times?*
5. *What time of day was Adam created?*
6. *What did Adam and Eve do after God expelled them from Eden?*
7. *When was a rooster's crow heard by every living creature on earth?*
8. *Who was the most successful physician in the Bible?*
9. *Who is the first Irishman mentioned in Scripture?*

Questions could also be taken from a sermon or Bible study the whole family heard recently. Ask questions about missionaries you know, too, taken from one of their prayer letters.

And always ask: "What would God want me to do this week with what I have learned?" Be sure to thank Him for insights and ask His help in application.

**Answers to Proverbs questions:**
1. *4:20–27; 13:13–20; 14:6–8, 15; 15:14; 19:27*
2. *19:19; 20:19*
3. *6:6–11; 18:9; 20:4; 24:30–34: 26:13–16*
4. *26:20–21*
5. *13:8*
6. *20:21; 23:4–5; 28:20–22*
7. *13:20: 17:4; 22:24–25*
8. *17:18; 22:26–27*
9. *16:28; 17:9*
10. *15:18; 17:14*
11. *17:27–28*
12. *16:7; 19:4; 27:9–10*
13. *16:32*
14. *24:17–18*
15. *26:12; 29:20*

**16.** *5:20–23; 6:32; 28:13; 29:1*

**Answers to humorous questions:**
**1.** *Knee-high-miah (Nehemiah) or Bildad the Shoe-height (Shuhite, Job 2:11)*
**2.** *Peter, the disciple who slept on his watch (Matthew 6:40)*
**3.** *Joseph, because Pharaoh made him into a ruler (Genesis 41:42–43)*
**4.** *When Joseph served in Pharaoh's court (implied in Genesis 41:38–46)*
**5.** *A little before Eve (Genesis 2:7, 21–22)*
**6.** *They raised Cain (Genesis 3:23; 4:1)*
**7.** *In Noah's ark (Genesis 7:13–23)*
**8.** *Job, because he had the most patients (patience, James 5:11)*

**9.** *Nick O'Demus (Nicodemus, John 3:1–5)*

*This chapter is taken from Finally, Family Devotions That Work (Chicago: Moody, 1986).*

### Further Reading

Jim Berlucchi and Mark Kinzer. *Family Worship.* Ann Arbor, Mich.: Servant, 1990.

Jan Kempe. *You and God and Me Together: Exploring life, learning about our faith, and making the right moves.* Grand Rapids: Discovery House, n.d.

Carolyn Williford. *Devotions for Families That Can't Sit Still.* Wheaton: Victor, 1990.

# Learning To Set Boundaries

*John Townsend*

## About the author

*John Townsend, Ph.D., in addition to being codirector of the Minirth-Meier Clinic West, has a private practice in California. He and his wife, Barbi, have one son, Ricky.*

A young mother confided tearfully to a friend that she has been having problems with her eighteen-month-old son. "We've been so close ever since he was born, but now it seems so hard. He disobeys and disagrees with me. I miss my 'easy baby.' I guess we're entering the 'terrible twos.'"

The woman's friend responded, "Well, I can understand your frustration, but I see this stage differently. I call it the 'terrific twos.' I love to see my child's personality emerge and begin to blossom."

What a radical difference in the child-rearing perspectives of the two women! The first wishes her baby was once again compliant and cuddly and resents the stubborn willfulness of her child. The second sees the child's emerging energy as a joy. Their conversation illustrates a problem many Christians (and non-Christians) have about what a "good baby" and a "bad baby" are. Passive, obedient, cooperative babies get the white hats; those who are more self-directed and oppositional (the "strong-willed child" James Dobson talks about) get the black hats.

And yet it is this active willfulness that sets the stage for the second developmental need designed by God to be nurtured in the family: the need for separateness. Boundaries help us make responsible choices, but we need strength of will to set them. So, within biblical limits, some degree of what people commonly call "willfulness" is God-given and essential.

What makes the will so important? Simply this: our will has both a positive and a negative function: *it helps us to choose the good and refuse the bad.* Without it, we easily cave in to sin and have difficulty standing for righteousness. When it is totally undeveloped, and especially when overly compliant behavior is praised (particularly during childhood), the ability to set healthy boundaries is impaired. Dysfunctional or codependent relationships almost always result.

# Need for separateness

Many people feel they are "people persons," that they are able to bond and connect with others. Yet these same people often feel overwhelmed, anxious, and frustrated about the obligations and responsibilities their bonded relationships seem to demand. The reason for this is that bonding alone is not enough. We also need self-ownership—self-determination of what we are to do with our lives and resources. In a phrase, we need stewardship over how we use our lives (Matthew 25:14–30).

A good example of bonding without separateness is found in a Christian man in his mid-thirties I'll call Bill. He began seeing a counselor for symptoms of depression. As he explored his life and circumstances, he began to notice a pattern in his important relationships. "I'm realizing now that all my life I've been so afraid to disappoint people that I've never said no to anyone," he said. "In order not to let down my family, my wife, my boss, and my friends, I've worked later, longer, and harder than anyone I know. I even feel that God depends on me for everything too. And I'm so busy taking care of everyone else's requests for my time that I've been ignoring my own needs. No wonder I've felt burned out for years."

As time went on, Bill began to recognize the source of his problem with separateness. He had come from a family where differences of opinion were seen as rebellion and where compliance was rewarded. This injury to his will manifested itself in Bill's adult life as chronic depression.

How do mistreatments of the will lead to depression? In this way: when we don't feel free to be honest and truthful with others about our opinions and values, we set in motion the process of allowing ourselves to be controlled by the feelings and desires of others. That in turn leads to a deep sense of powerlessness and resentment, based on a feeling of helplessness. If this sense of powerlessness and resentment is not checked, one's hope of being in normal control of one's life begins to die. Depression is the result of the death of hope. Proverbs 13:12 says, "Hope deferred makes the heart sick." When we feel constantly owned and controlled by others, our heart suffers.

# Blocks to bonding

The interaction of the capacity to bond with others and yet establish boundaries is shown opposite. The value across the top, "Bonding," represents the presence or absence of deep attachments in a person's life. The value at the left of the chart, "Boundaries," represents the presence or absence of clear separateness and autonomy. The results that occur when these elements are combined are listed inside the four blocks. Let's examine each of the blocks in turn. Give some thought to which pattern, if any, applies to your life.

### Block 1

Block 1, "Intimacy," indicates that *closeness plus clear separateness produces a healthy intimacy.* In such a relationship differences of opinion and even arguments do not disturb the sense of being "rooted and grounded in love" (Ephesians 3:17).

After several weeks of intensive counseling for severe depression at a Christian psychiatric hospital program, Mary began to grasp the deep relational conflicts underlying her condition. "I've always feared that differences between me and *anybody* would cause me to be abandoned forever, whether it was my husband, my children, or even the paper boy. Working so hard to avoid conflict burned me out. Now, as a result of learning through therapy, I can 'speak the truth in love' and still feel connected to people I disagree with."

What was the epochal "truth telling" event that made all the difference for Mary? Simply that when a staff member invited her on a field trip to the beach, she declined because she wanted to do some reading. When the staff member, to whom Mary felt close, did not become angry or hurt and reject her over her choice, Mary actually wept in surprised relief! Having a relationship where differences of opinion or desire didn't result in rejection was something she'd never experienced in her family of origin.

**Block 2**
Block 2, "Fusion," indicates what happens when bonding without boundaries occurs. One or both people in a relationship are unable to be free and separate. In fused relationships, differences of opinion and normal degrees of conflict are either denied or punished. We saw an example of a fused parent-child relationship in chapter 2 in the relationship of Isaac and his mother, Sarah. Fused relationships among adults can be seen in the suffocating heat of romantic infatuation, when romantic partners do not know where one person starts and the other ends. The couple is "lost" in love for one another. Their relationship is fused, which is in large part why such relationships are usually rocky, unfruitful, and short-lived.

## Interrelationship of the Capacity to Bond and the Capacity to Set Boundaries

**BONDING**

|  | HIGH | LOW |
|---|---|---|
| **BOUNDARIES HIGH** | BLOCK 1<br><br>Intimacy | BLOCK 3<br><br>Isolation |
| **BOUNDARIES LOW** | BLOCK 2<br><br>Fusion | BLOCK 4<br><br>Chaos |

## Block 3

Block 3, "Isolation," shows what happens when boundaries exist but not bonding. An isolated individual may be very much in charge of his or her life and have a well-developed ability to say no, but at the same time not have any deep emotional relationships. People in this pattern tend to "die on the vine," withering from a lack of normal interaction and love. David's son Absalom felt isolated from his father. Absalom thought it was necessary to do drastic things to get attention, such as setting a wheat field on fire. The workaholic or loner is a modern-day example of this type.

## Block 4

Block 4, "Chaos," describes the relational capacity of a person who is injured in both attachment (bonding) and separateness (boundaries). He feels lost in relation to others and to himself. He is neither connected nor self-directed, but is in a spiritual and relational limbo.

This is the most injured category, for in it both connectedness (the basis for feeling loved) and self responsibility (the basis for self-control) are at low-functioning levels. Today we see many adolescents with these two deficits. They are unable to form deep attachments and have extreme problems in delaying gratification and being responsible for themselves. It is no wonder that drugs have become so prevalent in our culture, with their promise of helping the user to feel loved (connectedness) and to experience instant gratification (a result of having weak boundaries, which form the basis for self-control).

# Boundaries

Given that we need both attachment and freedom, how does this second ability, the ability to be separate, develop in the family?

The family was designed by God to develop our will for two purposes: (1) to protect us

> ## The word no is a boundary.

against evil, and (2) to give us the freedom to choose how we will live our lives under God. The mechanism for building our wills is called a *boundary*, that which distinguishes one person from another person. It is what sets him apart. Just as we can tell property lines of ownership by legal boundaries, in the same way spiritual and emotional boundaries exist to show us what is "mine" and what is "not mine."

Our skin is a boundary. It keeps us separate from others. It keeps bad things out (infections, dust, and germs) and good things in (our organs, muscles, and so on).

The word *no* is a boundary. When we say no, we are keeping something out, perhaps an unwanted obligation or a demand on our time or money that would be debilitating. When we use the word *no* skillfully and without fear or guilt, we help to define and protect ourselves. Using no is like developing a muscle. The skill improves with practice. The "no muscle" takes a great deal of time to mature, and it is susceptible to injury, particularly as we are growing up in our families of origin.

# Property lines

If we look at boundaries as spiritual "property lines," we can see that boundaries determine what we *are* responsible for and what we are not responsible for. God has made us responsible for those things, and only those things, that are within our boundaries. We encounter conflicts with ourselves and with others when we make one or both of the following mistakes:

● *not taking care of the things that are within our boundaries, or*

● *taking care of the things that are outside our boundaries*

Galatians 6 is a good chapter to study in connection with this point. There Paul asserts that "each one shall bear his own load" (v. 5). The Greek word for "load" means *knapsack*, or what we carry daily on our journey through life. It is the same "burden" Jesus spoke of when He said, "My yoke is easy, and my burden is light" (Matthew 11:30, KJV). This "load" comprises that responsibility we should shoulder for ourselves.

Our individual knapsacks include such items as our thoughts, attitudes, opinions, beliefs, needs, choices, feelings, values, time, possessions, money, gifts, talents, behavior, and bodies. We are to set limits around these parts of our lives and should protect them and maintain them *ourselves*. It is our responsibility to care for them.

The converse is also true. Just as we are positively to take care of the elements of our lives that are properly within our own boundaries, so we are to refrain from taking care of the things that are inside other persons' boundaries. If we fail to observe this restraint two negative results are likely to take place:

• *We will sabotage the spiritual growth of another person (Ephesians 4:15), and*
• *We will neglect our own God-given responsibilities and become poor stewards of ourselves (Matthew 25:14–30).*

The important thing about our knapsacks is that they are "divinely sewn" on our backs by God. In other words, we should not "carry" (take responsibility for) someone else's knapsack. God Himself doesn't do that. For example, He allows people to refuse His gift of salvation. Think of Jesus' words in Luke 13:34: "O Jerusalem, Jerusalem, the city that kills the prophets and stones those sent to her! How often I wanted to gather your children together, just as a hen gathers her brood under her wings, and you would not have it!"

Just as Jesus allows others to make destructive decisions for themselves, so we have to accept the reality that we aren't strong enough, nor do we have the right, to take responsibility for others. We are to love them but not to parent them (unless we are

We should not "carry" someone else's knapsack.

legally responsible for them, as in parent-child relationships). When one adult "parents" another (even when the two adults are related), codependent, dysfunctional relationships almost always follow.

In contrast to our knapsacks, Paul describes a different "load" in verse 2 of the same chapter. This Greek term is the word for *boulders*: heavy, crushing burdens that cannot be borne alone. These are the tragedies, crises, and losses that befall us and that are not our fault. As best we can, we are to help one another with these boulders. Doing so is practically the definition of brotherly love and pleases God greatly.

Thus we see that God wants us to make a clear distinction: to handle boulders differently from knapsacks. Whereas we can only love, but not take responsibility for, someone

> *The Samaritan loved the wounded man but did not take permanent responsibility for him.*

whose knapsack is giving him problems, it is entirely proper for the Body of Christ to surround the stricken, crushed member with caring and support until he or she can get back on his feet.

The story of the Good Samaritan illustrates this perfectly (Luke 10:30–37). The Samaritan, finding the injured man, didn't put him up in a hotel for the rest of his life. Instead, he provided enough funds for the man to be healed and assumed that after an appropriate time, he'd be on his way. The Samaritan loved the wounded man but did not take permanent responsibility for him. To do so would have been to deny the injured man his own identity and autonomy.

# The family and boundaries

The second great function of the family, after bonding, is to help its members take responsibility for their "loads" by setting boundaries and developing the ability to make wise and responsible choices.

How does the family provide this need?
- *By allowing family members to state their opinions*
- *By making it safe to disagree without fear of criticism, rejection, or isolation*
- *By encouraging members to think for themselves*
- *By helping members discover and train themselves to use unique gifts and abilities*
- *By allowing anger to be expressed appropriately (Ephesians 4:28)*
- *By setting limits with consequences, not*

guilt or fear
- *By respecting each other's "no" choices*
- *By allowing age-appropriate choices:*
  – *condition of a bedroom (sloppy or well-kept)*
  – *choice of relationships (within biblical guidelines)*
  – *development of Christian values*
  – *how to spend money*
  – *when to be with friends instead of family.*

The family has a tricky job: it needs to keep members intimately attached yet simultaneously separate.

# What goes wrong?

Many Christian families do not produce members who can set limits with others. What happens in these families that impairs the growth of the "no muscle," thus hindering the development of healthy boundaries?

Basically, parents who are confused about boundaries tend to produce children who are confused about boundaries. There are several source points of this confusion, some of which are given below:
- *Parents who feel abandoned when their children begin to make autonomous choices. These parents respond to autonomy in their children by conveying guilt or shame messages about their lack of love and loyalty to the family or to the parents.*
- *Parents who feel threatened by the increasing loss of control they have over their children. These parents use anger or criticism, not guilt or shame messages, to convey their unhappiness over the children's new-found separateness.*
- *Families that equate disagreement with sin.*
- *Families that are afraid of the anger of their children.*
- *Families that are hostile toward the anger of their children.*
- *Families that praise compliance in the name of togetherness over healthy independence.*

- *Families in which emotional, physical, and sexual abuse occur. These kinds of abuse cause severe damage to the children's sense of ownership of their bodies and themselves.*
- *Families in which the children feel responsible for the happiness of the parents.*
- *Families that rescue children from experiencing the consequences of their behavior.*
- *Families that are inconsistent in limit-setting with the children.*
- *Families that continue to take responsibility for the children in adulthood.*

### A problem of loneliness
Let me illustrate the first of the points listed above. Cynthia was a loving Christian wife and mother of two who could not understand why a growing, gradual sense of isolation increased in her as her children grew older. Finally, in therapy for depression, she began to realize that she was feeling abandoned by her children as they became more and more autonomous. "But why in the world would my kids' growth make me feel lonely?" she asked.

Digging deeper, she began to see that her mother had made her the center of her life. If Cynthia was around to support her, Mom was happy. But if Cynthia wanted to spend time away from home with friends, Mom became sad and depressed.

When Cynthia married and moved out of state, her mother began isolating herself, developing physical problems, and making sure that all letters and phone conversations to Cynthia were directed toward how empty life was without her. Those messages were like a knife in Cynthia's heart, full of guilt and

shame messages about what a neglectful daughter she was.

Cynthia's mother felt abandoned because she made Cynthia responsible to take care of her loneliness instead of developing her own adult friendships. As a result, Cynthia was conflicted about her own autonomy. Her boundaries were fuzzy. This pattern was repeated in Cynthia's own family when she married and had children. She felt the same feelings toward her own children that her mother had felt toward her. That is why she came into counseling as her children matured. There was a difference, however. Cynthia wanted the family pattern stopped in her generation and worked hard to allow her kids age-appropriate freedom without feeling responsible for her loneliness. She wanted to halt the cycle of transmission so that godly patterns might be sent down the line instead of ungodly ones.

As we can see, where the family makes the child (1) responsible for what is not his, or (2) not responsible for what is his, boundary injuries ensue. Note that we say boundary "injuries" and not simply "confusions." Errors in this area do a grievous injury to a developing human being.

## What is the result?
When a family has not provided clear "ownership" guidelines to its children, the children learn to say yes to what is not theirs (yes to the bad) and no to what is theirs (no to the good). Although some families produce children with one or the other patterns, many more families produce children who live out both extremes.

"There's just no hope for me," Phyllis said bitterly in her therapist's office. An attractive woman in her late forties, she was grieving the demise of her third marriage. "I always end up with the same type of man: charming, flashy, and totally irresponsible. Am I a magnet for these losers?"

> *"But why in the world would my kids' growth make me feel lonely?" she asked.*

Phyllis's latest failure had come about when she found that her husband of three years was having an affair (in addition to being chronically unable to hold down a job for more than a few months). She had been the stable breadwinner in all three marriages. Was she a magnet?

In a way, yes. Both of Phyllis's parents had been alcoholics, loving in their intentions but consistently inconsistent in following up on their promises. Phyllis had painful memories of being left at school without a ride, of meals she had to make herself, and of promises of gifts that never materialized and special events that never occurred.

Yet Phyllis had never learned that this pattern was not her fault, but her parents'. In one session she remarked, "I figured they didn't follow through because I wasn't good enough, so I became better than good. . . . I became the most responsible little girl in the world."

Then the responsible little girl entered adulthood. Typically, when these types of conflicts are not noticed and worked through, there is a repetition of the pattern in the next generation, and that is what happened in Phyllis's case. She married men like her parents, who "talked their talk" but didn't "walk their walk."

Why? She put it together one day: "I've been trying to *fix* these men with my love, the way I *couldn't* fix Mom and Dad." She had developed a hallmark symptom of codependent relationships: the need to "fix" other adults.

Phyllis is an example of someone who had been trained by her environment to allow irresponsible people into her life, thinking their irresponsibility was hers to repair. Put in our boundary discussion terms, she had learned to say yes to the bad.

It's sad. Think of all the mature, reliable, consistent men who had possibly been interested in Phyllis but in whom she was not interested. There was nothing to fix in their lives! Phyllis was not only saying yes to the bad, she was also saying no to the good.

# Boundary problems

The table opposite illustrates the types of boundary problems individuals contend with, both in relation to themselves and to others. Perhaps you'll see yourself, elements of yourself, or your loved ones here.

### Block 1

Block 1 represents the person who can't say no to others because of guilt, fear, or an excessive desire to please. This person gives up stewardship of his life to the control of others' wishes, needs, and demands. Though he is active in helping others, the inability he has in setting limits for himself often causes him intense confusion, anxiety, and frustration because of a lack of direction. Bill, cited earlier as a workaholic who didn't want to disappoint anyone, fits into this category. In contrast, God warns us against "seeking the favor of men" too much (Galatians 1:10) but rather urges us to seek to please Him as the number one priority in our lives.

### Block 2

Block 2 refers to the individual who does not respond to others' boulders, the "excessive loads" of Galatians 6:2. He does not say yes to valid needs of others. His behavior is in direct contrast to the pattern exhorted in Proverbs 3:27: "Do not withhold good from those to whom it is due, when it is in your power [note the condition here] to do it."

The neglect of caring that is characteristic of persons in this category is usually due to one of two causes:
- *a critical spirit toward others' needs (Pharisaism)*
- *a self-absorption in one's own desires and needs to the point of excluding others (narcissism)*

It is important here not to confuse self-absorption with a God-given sense of taking

## Boundary Problems

| | CAN'T SAY | CAN'T HEAR |
|---|---|---|
| "No" | **BLOCK 1**<br><br>Feels guilty and/or controlled by others | **BLOCK 3**<br><br>Wants others to take responsibilty for him |
| "Yes" | **BLOCK 2**<br><br>Self-absorbed; doesn't respond to others' needs | **BLOCK 4**<br><br>Can't receive caring from others |

care of one's own needs first so that one is then able to love others.

Whereas blocks 1 and 4 have to do with the codependent person, Blocks 2 and 3 have to do with the dependent person, the one who takes little responsibility for his own life but instead seeks to make others bear the load. Dependent people tend to gravitate toward codependents, because a codependent's lack of proper boundaries is likely to cause him to neglect himself and "rescue" the dependent individual. That is what had happened to Bill. He had a dependent mother, wife, and boss, and he could not care for all of them and himself too. The result was depression and burnout. Phyllis illustrated the other half of the equation. She consistently found dependent types to marry so that she, in her codependence, could rescue them.

### Block 3
Whereas Block 1 refers to the person who can't *say* no, Block 3 refers to the person who can't *hear* no. People with this boundary problem tend to project responsibility for their lives onto others and either through manipulation or demand get others to carry the load God intended for them alone. These people generally have not had consistent limits set for them by their families and so tend to exploit others to get their needs met, thus violating the boundaries of others. They have extreme difficulty in taking ownership for their actions, indeed for their whole lives.

Roger grew up in a well-to-do family where all normal responsibilities had been taken care of by his parents or the hired help. He had never held a summer job, nor had he been held accountable to make good grades in school. After a few months of marriage, his wife was

> *She consistently found dependent types to marry so that she, in her codependence, could rescue them.*

amazed to find that he had run up thousands of dollars of credit card purchases and was writing bad checks. When she angrily confronted him over it, he said resentfully, "Don't worry, someone will take care of it."

That someone had always been his parents, who, because of their own boundary conflicts, had acted as Roger's financial safety net. They took responsibility for things inside Roger's boundary. He had always assumed that someone would absorb the consequences of his actions, but that someone was never himself. Now Roger's inability to delay gratification was causing him to violate his wife's financial boundaries. He couldn't hear "no" from her regarding his excesses.

God sees a situation like this quite differently from the way Roger did. He has ordained a law of the universe we informally call the "law of sowing and reaping." Responsibility brings success; irresponsibility brings failure. As Paul wrote in 2 Thessalonians 3:10b, "If anyone will not work, neither let him eat." An empty stomach would quickly help teach Roger to respect his wife's boundaries more!

### Block 4

Block 4 refers to the person who denies God-given needs because of guilt, a desire to please others (Colossians 3:22–23), or a fear of emotional abandonment. This is a matter of setting boundaries where none should be. The person believes it's not OK to have needs, whereas in actuality no such barrier or boundary exists. People who have difficulty in being direct with others about their needs for comfort, support, encouragement, and caring fall into this category.

People in Block 4 usually fall into two groups:
● *those who are afraid of, or feel guilty about, asking for what they need (in contrast to Jesus' encouragement in Luke 1:8 to "ask," "seek," and "knock"), and/or*
● *those who are unaware that they have emotional, spiritual, or relational needs (in*

*contrast to Jesus' blessing in Matthew 5:6 on those who "hunger and thirst for righteousness, for they shall be satisfied")*

The people who fall simultaneously into Blocks 1 and 4 are codependent. They take responsibility for others' needs but neglect their own.

# Obstacles to ownership

The heart of the problem of ownership is *responsibility*, determining what is and is not mine. It is failing to take appropriate ownership within appropriate boundaries. Part of what hinders us from doing so is a reliance on myths about God, others, and ourselves:

### Boundary confusion about God
● *God should always say yes to me ("Genie in a lamp").*
● *God is responsible to keep me from suffering loss, whether or not I take responsibility for my life.*
● *God expects me to love Him and others without being responsible for my own legitimate, God-given needs.*

### Boundary confusion about others
● *If I say no to others, I'm being selfish.*
● *I am indispensable to the needs of others.*
● *My happiness is the responsibility of someone else in my life.*

### Boundary confusion about ourselves
● *If I am needy, I am bad.*
● *If I love, I should be loved in return.*
● *My life is not my responsibility.*

Fundamental to these myths is a confusion about the relationship of love and limits. Many families operate on the unspoken assumption that love and limits are antagonistic. One wife told her husband tearfully, "You never provide enough money for us to have traveling vacations. If you really loved me and the family, you'd do something about it." Yet at this point in their married life, the husband was

> *Many families operate on the unspoken assumption that love and limits are antagonistic.*

trying to work their way out of severe debt problems, and it was tough going.

Why did the wife fail to see that? Because she interpreted her husband's appropriate limits (i.e., "No fancy vacations until we're out of debt") as an absence of love, whereas in reality it was healthy responsibility. Strange though it may seem, often people with firm (healthy) boundaries are characterized by people around them with unhealthy boundaries as being selfish, uncaring, or unloving. Instances of this are not uncommon. Their frequency indicates how far we as a society have strayed from God's healthy design.

People who have good boundaries tend to be the most loving people in the world. Why? Because they don't give from obligation or fear, but as "cheerful giver[s]" (2 Corinthians 9:7). Loving people are to have firm boundaries, and firm people are to love. That is growth into the image of God.

This chapter is taken from *Secrets of Your Family Tree* (Chicago: Moody, 1991).

## Further Reading

Foster Cline and Jim Fay. *Parenting with Love and Logic.* Colorado Springs: NavPress, 1990.

Henry Cloud and John Townsend. *Boundaries: Gaining Control of Your Life.* Grand Rapids: Zondervan, 1992.

James Dobson. *Dare to Discipline, Revised.* Wheaton: Tyndale, 1991.

James Dobson. *Parenting Isn't for Cowards.* Waco, Tex.: Word, 1987.

# Television's Impact on Your Kids

*Coleen Cook*

I reach for the knob on the nursery door, and it opens to a semi-darkened room where my two year old lies sleeping in his crib. "Good morning, son." He stirs at the sound of my voice. Struggling to his feet, with eyes full of sleep, he reaches to me with outstretched hands. As I lift him from the crib to hold him in my arms, he mumbles his first audible words of the day: "Big Bird."

It is the first thought on his mind. Not me, not even toast or Cheerios, but the giant yellow canary of "Sesame Street." We hurry down the stairs and into the dining room, where he points to the darkened TV set, crying again for Big Bird. A mere flick of the switch pacifies him into mesmerized silence. Gone are the nagging cries for cereal, the demands for juice — in fact, I can ask several times about what he wants to eat, but he is now so engrossed that my inquiries about breakfast bounce back to me without answer, like echoes from an empty canyon. It will be this way for the next hour. Or the hour after that or the hour after that, if I permit it.

## What can it hurt?

It is the ultimate temptation for the parents of young children to plop them in front of the tube, where they are physically safe, quiet, and out of our way. Every moment spent there buys us a precious moment of uninterrupted peace — a rare commodity for a busy mom or dad. It is an easy habit to cultivate — and what can it hurt, we argue?

**Lack of life experience**

However, kids are even more vulnerable to the fantasized version of life presented on the screen than are adults. Children, especially young children, don't view television the same way that adults do because children have very little in terms of life experience to bring to viewing.

Preschoolers lack a fully developed frame of reference with which to evaluate what they see. They are less able to call up other mental information or values to balance out the impressions that TV leaves. Toddlers and preschoolers, especially, absorb and store TV imagery like a sponge, with little or no capacity to interpret what they see beyond its face value. As one critic points out: "Very young children are unable to distinguish fantasy from reality on the television screen. They do not know what is fact and what is opinion. They do not understand the basis of many of the events that occur. They are exposed to the whole world — as seen through the eyes of a TV screen — before they have developed the ability to understand and to cope with the larger society."[1]

A young child will be frightened by a monster movie, for example, not only because it leaves a lasting mental residue to haunt him again and again but because he cannot men-

> *A mere flick of the switch pacifies him into mesmerized silence.*

tally distinguish between reality or make-believe by himself.

The powerful effect of some of these artificial memories is vividly illustrated by a phenomenon some fire fighters call the "Darth Vader Syndrome." Increasingly, masked fire fighters are noticing that many small children caught in burning homes are running from, hiding from, or furiously fighting and resisting rescuers instead of cooperating with them in the middle of life-threatening situations.

Subsequent interviews with small survivors pinpoint the problem. "I thought you were a spaceman," or, "I thought you were Darth Vader," they confess. The gas masks and protective helmets worn by fire fighters are

> *A young child . . . cannot mentally distinguish between reality or make-believe by himself.*

reminiscent of images of TV monsters or villains deeply embedded in the child's subconscious. Fire officials say the tragic juxtaposition of imagery may be costing some children and fire fighters their lives in the critical moments of rescue.[2] This problem also vividly illustrates the powerful effects that TV imagery can leave on children.

**Kids are vulnerable to the fantasized version of life presented on the screen.**

## About the author

*Coleen Cook has been a television news anchor, producer, talk show host, and reporter. Now a free-lance writer, she and her family live in Louisiana. She is author of* All That Glitters *(Moody).*

### Adults before they are ready

In what other ways are children being shaped by television? One dilemma TV presents for children is that it is turning them into adults before they are ready. Children now carry many adult images in their minds that they consider to be both reliable depictions of reality and something to model.

There is a lively debate over the quality of children's programming, and parents should be concerned about it. However, regardless of the rhetoric over more and better children's programs, some surveys suggest that kids watch adult TV programs more often than they watch children's programs[3] and that many children prefer adult programming over kiddie shows. For example, the program

"Dallas," along with several other prime time adult programs, ranked among the most popular programs in all age groups, including ages two to eleven.[4] That isn't surprising, since it is hard for adults to insulate children from what they watch. Too few parents consider carefully enough the potential impact of adult programming on children or seem willing to modify their own viewing habits for the sake of their kids.

### Uncontrollable pace of learning

Consequently, childhood as it once was no longer exists, points out communications professor Joshua Meyrowitz. Why? Because human development is based on more than just a series of biological stages. It is based as well on patterns of access to social knowledge. It used to be, according to Meyrowitz, that kids learned the "secrets" of adulthood slowly and in stages. They could be shielded from material they were too immature to handle. There were things appropriate for the sixth grader that parents would keep hidden from the first grader or the toddler. But no longer, writes Meyrowitz, because today "a secret revelation machine" is now a part of the living room.

Communication through print allows for a great deal of control over their social information to which children have access. Reading and writing involve a complex code of symbols that must be memorized and practiced. Children must read simple books before they can read adult books.

On TV, however, there is no complex code to exclude young viewers. . . . Even two-year-old children, unable to read or write their own names, find television accessible and absorbing.[5]

The ability to read and the level of skill are no longer buffers for social information revealed to children. "Television undermines behavioral distinctions," he observes, "because it encompasses both children and adults in a single informational sphere or environ-

> *Too few parents . . . seem willing to modify their own viewing habits for the sake of their kids.*

ment."[6] Since we can't censor our children's viewing without censoring our own, Meyrowitz points out that television takes our children across the globe even before we give them permission to cross the street.[7]

Television transported both parents and children to the Persian Gulf War, despite the fact that few children could put what television showed them into meaningful context. One eight-year-old boy who watched coverage from the Persian Gulf expressed his feelings about what he saw this way: "I feel scared that they might blow up my block and — boom! — My mom and everybody would be gone and then there would be just me."[8] This child had difficulty conceptualizing the vast distance between Arabia and America and putting it into a meaningful perspective.

Glen Sparks, a Purdue University communications professor who has extensively researched the emotional effects of visual imagery on children, says such a response is typical for a child of eight. He says kids ages six to twelve are especially vulnerable in less obvious ways, not only to fantasy violence and horror movies but also to news coverage of real disasters and wars.[9] After seeing TV reports of collapsed bridges in San Francisco during the major earthquake of 1989, my own six-year-old son became repeatedly panicky each time we drove across the Mississippi River bridge at home in New Orleans.

### Coping emotionally

Children in the six- to twelve-year-old age range, says Sparks, are old enough to distinguish news events from "pretend" but lack the emotional maturity to mentally cope with either. Many are deeply troubled by what they see but are sometimes afraid to express their feelings, especially if they are ridiculed by adults. Sparks says many unsuspecting parents expose young children through television to images of war and disaster that they still need protection from until they have a chance to catch up emotionally.[10]

Author Neil Postman declares that "television all by itself may bring an end to childhood."[11] Increasingly, in homes where both parents work, the latchkey child who comes home to an empty house now has unlimited access to whatever TV serves up.

Experts warn that children of divorce are especially vulnerable to the effects of TV distortion, because it can become a frequent and welcome escape from the pain of losing a parent. In such cases where divorce results in a latchkey situation, the combination is not a healthy one.

Psychiatrist David Elkind also warns that TV is a major vehicle for thrusting premature adulthood on teens: "Teenagers are now expected to confront life's challenges with the maturity once expected only of the middle-aged, without any time for preparation."[12]

## Behavior modeling

A second way television changes children is through the behavior it models. Perhaps nowhere is the power of artificial imagery more obvious than in a child's behavior. We know that children copy and emulate what they see modeled before them. It does not take a mental giant to figure out that much of what children now copy and act out is from television. Characters and scenes pressed a thousand times into the memory bank can replace and stifle a child's own creative thought patterns. Someone else's view of life becomes a subliminal part of his psyche.

### In the home

Children also copy what they see modeled in

the home. We sometimes joke about the danger of children becoming like their parents. It is certainly true that parents exert tremendous power over their children, if the child has ample opportunity to observe and imitate parental behavior. We know that they often clone us in ways that we would rather they miss, picking up traits and habits that we wish they wouldn't notice. We have a tremendous opportunity to influence our children's behavior and beliefs through our own conduct, unless of course, they spend more time gazing at another role model. Are parents unwittingly allowing TV to usurp their authority as chief role models?

Many children now spend more time with fantasy television characters than they do interacting with their parents. The important job of modeling behavior is now shared with or, in some cases, delegated to television. TV is increasingly the major competitor with parental influence. The risk in this is that children will be more influenced by the unrealistic view of life offered by TV than with the real-life experience they encounter in the family sphere.

Home is the boot-camp of life — the place where children need to learn about good and to be protected from evil. However, when TV becomes the mediator between parents and children, it sometimes reverses the process. When our children are watching the tube, they are often learning the opposite of what we as parents may wish. Current trends in programs and commercials that portray kids as free-wheeling, savvy, independent spirits in control of their own little spheres have strong appeal to immature minds. Communications professor Jay Rosen of New York University notes that because TV sells consumption as a way to happiness, "TV [tries] to sell children on a way of life . . . their parents may not want for them. . . . One way is to present [images of] kids who are independent, who have nothing to learn from their parents, because then children have a right to consume the way they

want to consume and parents have no basis on which to say no."[13]

TV sets up a conflict in the home between the view of the world that parents may wish their children to have on a variety of matters and the phony world that television presents so convincingly. Observes Alvin Poussaint, psychiatrist and consultant for "The Cosby Show," TV parents "are overly permissive, always understanding; they never get very angry. There are no boundaries or limits set."[14] What effect do such images of parental perfection have on real relationships between kids and parents?

The problem may be particularly critical in the first five years of life, which are especially strategic. Experts tell us that that is when the core of a child's personality is formed. Yet since that is the time when children are the most demanding, it is also the most tempting time to use the TV as a baby-sitter. Since both of my children were in this age category while I wrote this, I know firsthand how tempting it can be to let the TV do the baby-sitting!

Nielsen figures show that children ages two to five now watch TV an average of about twenty-eight hours a week.[15] Remember, that's only an average. That means that those most vulnerable to television are spending a significant amount of time in the most critical developmental phase of their life, learning "reality" from a medium that has a serious problem presenting it. Subtly the personalities of our children are being refashioned to some degree in whatever images TV provides.

### In the world

What are some of the most damaging messages that I see children getting? That aggression is the way to become powerful and significant; that violence and crime are the norm, not the exception; that the world is an immoral, dishonest, unethical place and if you can't lick 'em, you might as well join 'em; that it is hopeless to try to change society; that

> *The modern home is now boring compared to the home of a hundred years ago.*

It is important to interest kids at home.

materialism brings contentment; that casual sex satisfies and is guilt-free; that drinking is a solution to problems; that women are second-class citizens; that kids are smarter than adults; that life should be fun all the time; that if information isn't entertaining, it's not worth knowing. Are we coming to grips with the long-term impact of these kinds of messages on kids?

The problem is not confined to the under-twelve crowd. What impressions do teenagers embrace from a steady diet of unreality? Researchers who studied TV's effect on the ethnic attitudes of more than a thousand New York City high school students found that many teens regard TV as both a learning tool and an accurate reflection of the real world. One in four agreed that "TV shows what life is really like" and that "people on TV are like real life," and 40 percent agreed that they learned a lot from the tube. The research also showed that blacks (who watch significantly more TV than whites) were the group most likely to see television as a reflection of real life.[16]

### In business
Columnist Herbert London played clips of "Dallas," "Dynasty," and some other evening soaps with big business themes to a group of teens and then asked them to what lengths they would go to save a failing enterprise. Most told him they would do anything short of harming a family member to stay afloat. When asked if they would engage in immoral behavior to stay on top, as do the characters in the shows, not one teenager said no. When they were asked if they thought the behavior of businessmen on such shows was typical of American businessmen, most of the students said yes. However, when London asked if the teens actually knew any businessmen personally who behaved like J.R., most admitted they did not.[17]

## Parental control
Although surveys suggest that Americans think parents should control their children's TV selections, two-thirds of those asked admit that not enough parental guidance is being applied.[18] I think there are a variety of reasons for this. As I mentioned previously, it is hard to restrict children's viewing without restricting your own, and TV is too tempting a babysitter for the busy, overstressed parent of today. Peer pressure from other children that breaks down the resistance of parents to some shows is another factor. Still another, less obvious, reason TV is hard to regulate is that the modern home, in many ways, is now

boring compared to the home of a hundred years ago. Observes pastor and author Kevin Perrotta: "Home is less a center of activity than formerly. In many ways, it is a less interesting place to be."[19]

In many neighborhoods the open fields and wooded areas where I spent hours playing as a child have given way to the narrow streets and postage-stamp yards of subdivisions. Because many children are in day-care, subdivision streets and playgrounds are now ghost towns for the few children who remain home in the daytime. Today, it is harder in some ways to amuse and stimulate children at home, which also may be why many parents send children to preschool at a younger age.

I have talked with some Christian parents who exhibit concern about sending small children away at a young age for a few hours a day. Yet some of those same Christian mothers I know who distrust preschool will keep their children confined inside the home and in front of the TV set for hours on end. Some never realize that their children, especially the younger preschooler, can be mentally more detached and further from parental influence when they are watching TV at home than if they were at a school miles away.

Even the more wholesome programs present unrealistic expectations of life convincingly. Quickly resolving plots, instant gratification, and simplistic solutions foster an unnatural, unbalanced view of how the world really is. Someday our children will have to learn the difference between the two — and it will be painful. Warns one researcher, the terrible "toos" now inflict children of all ages — too many expectations, too many media images of perfection and achievement, too many fears, and too much guilt from too many shoulds. The result, according to Joseph Procaccini of Loyola College in Baltimore, is a growing number of children burned out from too many unrealistic expectations of life. He claims that what begins as lethargic and irritable behavior and progresses to mental exhaustion and forgetfulness can end up in anger or paranoia, or, in extreme cases, a dropout attitude or suicide threat. Procaccini blames "constant images of perfection and impossible achievement" in the mass media as a major factor in child burnout.[20]

# Religious systems

Since Christianity fares poorly on TV, and children watch people on TV resolve problems day after day without bringing religious or moral belief systems into play, it doesn't surprise me that the increasing number of children and teens I know seem to feel that religious experience is confined to whatever happens on Sunday morning and has no bearing on behavior the rest of the week.

Unfortunately, Eastern religious concepts lend themselves well to the TV theater, and some children's programs are riddled with them. Children now learn the dualistic concept of evil equally matched against good, which is Eastern, instead of the concept of the sovereign God of Christianity who has evil on a leash. Cartoons preach the human ability to possess "superpowers" and to become "masters of the universe." Many of these fantasy concepts reflect Eastern religious philosophies, but Christian parents, many of whom have a hazy understanding of their own theological beliefs, much less those of Eastern religions, are unaware of the implications. Impressionable children can now go "ghost busting" on a program that encourages them to exert power over the occult in a cute and humorous context. Yet many parents are oblivious to the messages in these disarmingly "cute" programs, and consequently some make no attempt to refute or shield children from such ideas in the most formative years of their lives.

Years ago Walt Whitman wrote:

*There was a child went forth every day and the first object he look'd upon,*

*that object he became*
*and that object became a part of him for the day*
*or a certain part of the day*
*or for many years or stretching cycles of years.*[21]

A generation later, while real life passes by, the adults of tomorrow sit watching, passive and unprotected, as strange and mixed messages pour into the living room. The result could be mass behavior modification to an unprecedented degree.

When I was growing up, we used to sing a little song in Sunday school that went something like this:

*Be careful little eyes what you see*
*Be careful little eyes what you see*
*For the Father up above is looking down in love*
*So be careful little eyes what you see.*

Perhaps there was far more urgency in that simple little verse than most of us could ever have imagined.

This chapter was taken from *All That Glitters: A News-Person Explores the World of Television* (Chicago: Moody, 1992).

1. Patricia Skalka, "Take Control of Your TV," *Friendly Exchange*, Spring 1983, p. 26.
2. Lee Dalton, "The Monster in the Mask," *Friendly Exchange*, May 1986, p. 46.
3. Joanmarie Kalter, "How TV Is Shaking Up the American Family," *TV Guide*, July 23, 1988, p. 5. Reprinted with permission from *TV Guide Magazine*. Copyright © 1988 by New America Publications Inc., Radnor, Pennsylvania.
4. Joshua Meyrowitz, "Where Have All the Children Gone?" *Newsweek*, August 30, 1982, p. 13.
5. Ibid.
6. Ibid.
7. Joshua Meyrowitz, "Is TV Keeping Us Too Well-Informed?" *TV Guide*, January 9, 1988, p. 5.
8. Glen Sparks, interview on WWL Radio, New Orleans, Louisiana, February 11, 1991.
9. Ibid.
10. Ibid.
11. Neil Postman in *Teaching as a Conserving Activity*, quoted by Jim Trelease in *The Read Aloud Handbook* (New York: Penguin, 1982), p. 99.
12. David Elkind, "Teens in Crisis: All Grown Up and No Place to Go," *Focus on the Family*, April 1985, p. 2.
13. Kalter, "How TV Is," p. 11.
14. Ibid.
15. *The Nielsen Report*, 1990, p. 8.
16. S. Robert and Lynda S. Lichter, "Does TV Shape Ethnic Images?" *Media and Values*, Spring 1988, p. 6.
17. "What Is the Impact of Violent and Sexually Explicit TV on America's Children?" *Concerned Women*, May 1990, p. 20.
18. *America's Watching, The Television Information Office/Roper Report*, 1987, pp. 12–13.
19. Kevin Perrotta, "Watching While Life Goes By," *Christianity Today*, April 18, 1980, p. 17. Adapted from *Taming the TV Habit* (Ann Arbor, Mich.: Servant, 1982). Copyright © 1982 by Kevin Perrotta. Used by permission.
20. Joseph Procaccini, quoted by Mary Maushard, "Kids Suffer Burnout, Researcher Warns," *The Baltimore Times Sun*, reprinted in *The Times Picayune*, October 15, 1990, p. D-8.
21. Walt Whitman, in Edward E. Ford and Steven Englund, *For the Love of Children* (Garden City, N.Y.: Anchor Press/Doubleday, 1977), p. 3.

### Further Reading

Coleen Cook. *All That Glitters: A News-Person Explores the World of Television*. Chicago: Moody, 1992.

Ben Logan. *Television Awareness: The Viewer's Guide for Family and Community*. Nashville: Abingdon, 1979.

Malcom Muggeridge. *Christ and the Media*. Grand Rapids: Eerdmans, 1977.

Phil Phillips. *52 Things for Your Kids to Do Instead of Watching TV*. Nashville: Nelson, 1992.

Quentin J. Shultze. *Redeeming Television: How TV Changes Christians – How Christians Can Change TV*. Downers Grove, Ill.: InterVarsity, 1992

# Hope for the Cluttered Home

*Elva Anson*

Imagine entering your home and facing utter chaos. You see a kitchen counter covered with dirty dishes. Jelly, butter, and bread have been left out. Several jagged blotches of dirt cling to something sticky spilled on the tile. Mail and magazines litter the coffee and end tables. School books clutter the kitchen table. Newspapers lie rumpled and scattered on the carpet. Throw pillows have been thrown into the middle of the floor to join three pairs of shoes and a pair of bedroom slippers. Coats hang from door knobs and on the backs of chairs. Everywhere you look things are in disarray. What a mess!

Actually I am describing what happens at my home sometimes, and maybe this scene is familiar to you as well. How do you react? If you are like me, it is unlikely that you immediately go into action in an effort to put things in order. You are more likely to find a chair or couch on which to slump and allow waves of helplessness and despair to roll over you as the disorder immobilizes you for a while.

Children often react with the same feelings. They do not have the experience or skill to estimate the size of tasks. Children's size and underdeveloped coordination and strength combine to make them throw up their hands and say, "I can't do it."

## Simplify

If you want to make work easy enough for children to handle, you must simplify. Some-

one once said, "To simplify is man's most complicated task." So how do you simplify?

**Bedrooms**

Start in your child's bedroom. Sit on the floor in the middle of the room and carefully check it for easy care and simplicity. If you sit on the floor, you will have a better perspective of your child's view of the room.

Ask some tough questions. Is the room easy to pick up and clean? If not, what makes it difficult? How can you remove the obstacles? Is the room bulging with toys, furniture, and clothes? Can your child reach the rod or drawer where her clothes belong? Does she have too many clothes? Do you have out-of-season clothes among seasonal clothing? Do shoes, boots, and pajamas have a place? What about dirty clothes? Is there a box, basket, or hamper for them in the room? Is there adequate storage for folded clean clothes, books, toys, games?

Does the room have a place for trash, a place to write on, a bulletin board, a clutter drawer or shelf? Is the bed easy to make or difficult to make? Is it too close to the wall? Does it have too many ruffles, pillows, or stuffed toys? Are the blankets easy to pull up? How can you change it so that it could be easy to make? Teach your children to streamline their bedrooms. Look at the tops of dressers and desks. Can the things that sit there be kept in drawers or on closet shelves? Eliminate permanent clutter. Keep knickknacks to a minimum.

> *Everywhere you look
> things are in disarray.*

Get rid of toy boxes. They hold far too many toys, and children often dump them to find one small treasure. Have your children store their toys in small bags or containers. Build shelves into children's closets to help them organize their belongings. Everything must have a place so that it can be put there when not in use. If your child has more things than space to store them, they will spill over into the room. Asking your child to clean such a room is asking for the impossible.

Go through the room with three boxes — one for things to store, one for things to give away, one for things to throw away. If your children are under six, you can do this organization yourself. If they are older, they need to be included so that they can understand what needs to be done to make the room easy to take care of. You need to respect their property and not violate their rights by throwing away their things without their knowledge or permission.

Children go through ages where they want to collect things such as stamps, coins, models, puzzles, postcards, and so on. When that happens, help them find ways to store or exhibit these treasures with minimal care. Models, for example, can be hung by thread or fish string from the ceiling. Stamps can be kept in stamp books, coins in coin books. If they collect butterflies or salt-and-pepper shakers, suggest that they store most of them in an appropriate box and display a few at a time.

If your children have too many toys or clothes, devise a rotation system so that all of them are not available all of the time. They can be rotated from a top closet shelf or from a garage, attic, or other storage space. You might give grandparents excess toys for your children to play with when they visit them.

### About the author

*Elva Anson, M.A., is a licensed marriage, family, and child therapist in private practice in Fair Oaks, California. She wrote* How to Get Kids to Help at Home *(Moody) and coauthored* The Complete Book of Home Management *(Moody). She and her husband, Everett, have three grown children.*

Make favorite toys available to the children. Do not put them with toys to be rotated.

Keep in mind that what you do not have, you do not have to take care of. Less is best. Excess of anything creates problems, so get rid of the excess. Go through your entire home with this thought in mind. Do not keep what you do not use. If you streamline your home, you will find it easy for everyone to maintain.

Make an inspection tour of your home. View each room with a critical eye. To get a child's point of view kneel on the floor and try to see the room from their vantage point. What do you do in the room? What are the trouble spots? How easy is the room to maintain? What can you do to improve its function and decrease the work it takes to maintain it? What can you expect your child to do without too much effort and without feeling overwhelmed?

---

> *Get rid of the excess.*

## Bathrooms and kitchen

Give special attention to the bathrooms and the kitchen. Assign each child a towel bar that she can reach. Attach snaps or Velcro to towels to keep them from falling on the floor. Make a net bag to hold bath toys. Hang it over the tub where the toys can drip dry. Hang a shoe bag on the back of the bathroom door to store shavers, hair rollers, combs, brushes, and other supplies. Have hooks on the door for hanging clothes. Give teenagers a small bucket or basket to use as a makeup tote. A bucket with shampoo, rinse, and razors can go to the shower with them. They can also use it to wash underwear or hose. Provide step stools so that small children can reach bathroom or kitchen sinks.

If you simplify the kitchen, children will find what they need more quickly. Store tools you use every day in easily accessible places. Get rid of those you seldom use, or store them on a high shelf where you can retrieve them on special occasions. Be sure children can reach silverware and dishes when they have been asked to set the table.

Once or twice a year go through your home ruthlessly and evaluate what you have. Keep and care for only the things you value and use often. These things must pay their way. Anything else should be discarded or stored. You won't have to clean them, put them away, wind them, dust them, feed them, count them, paint them. That means a smaller work load to divide among the family so the work you do have to do will be easier.

## Get rid of clutter

What clutters your home? For a week have everyone keep track of what is cluttering. Then brainstorm ways to take care of those things.

## Containers, baskets and racks

Here are some possibilities. Put a large container near the front or back door to store balls, bats, skates, tennis rackets and balls, and other play equipment. The container can be a painted chest, a window seat, or a large trunk. Use your imagination. It can stand in the entrance hall, a coat closet, the washroom, or whatever fits for your family. Placing it near a door to the outside will make it easier for family members to remember to put away equipment they used. An unused thirty-gallon garbage can with a lid can store play equipment outside, beside the back door. To keep bicycles and tricycles in their places, paint lines on the garage or patio floor to show where each piece of equipment belongs.

Baskets or magazine racks in the living or family room can store current magazines and newspapers. Provide a basket for mail, too. Old newspapers should have a place in the garage or storage shed until they can be taken to a recycling center. That should be done at least once a month. If you must keep magazines, store them upright in a box. Store a year's issues and label the box. Rolled up newspapers or magazines can also go in attractive wine racks.

Attach a small shoe bag to a coat closet door to store gloves, cloth hats, the dog leash, scarves. Or you can put hooks up for each person and nail a wicker basket above or below the hook to store billfolds, change, or gloves. Attach a mug rack to hang purses and sweaters.

## Clutter space

Provide a clutter space in each bedroom and perhaps in the coat closet and kitchen. This can be a drawer or a shelf designated for clutter. The clutter drawer or shelf must receive top priority once a week for cleaning and sorting. That leaves it empty for the next busy week's clutter.

You will find that each one uses his or her clutter space differently. Janeé had a dresser drawer that she kept fairly well cleared from

# Special memories

The very happiest days of my growing years occurred when I was between ten and thirteen years of age. My dad and I would rise very early before the sun came up on a wintry morning. We'd put on our hunting clothes and heavy boots and drive twenty miles. After parking the car and climbing over a fence, we entered a wooded area where we would slip down to the creek bed and follow the winding stream several miles back into the forest.

Then my dad would hide me under a fallen tree which made a little room with its branches. He would find a similar shelter for himself around a bend in the creek. My dad and I were then ready to watch as the breathtaking panorama of the morning unfolded and spoke so eloquently of the God who made all things.

### Setting the tone

Most important was what occurred out there in the forest between my dad and me. The intense love and affection generated on those mornings set the tone for a lifetime of friendship. There was a closeness and a oneness that made me want to be like that man – that made me choose his values as my values, his dreams as my dreams, his God as my God.

My mother was a godly woman, deeply devoted to her husband, and wise when it came to raising her kids. I remember her test of my independence when I was seventeen. My folks were going on a two-week car trip and leaving me behind with the family car and permission to invite my (male) friends to spend the fourteen nights at our home. I remember being surprised by this move and the obvious risk my parents were taking. I wondered if they were wise to give me that much latitude.

I behaved responsibly while my folks were gone, but I always wanted to know why my mother took that risk. After I was grown and married, I asked her. She smiled and replied, "Because I knew in approximately one year you would be leaving for college where you would have complete freedom with no one to tell you how to behave. And I wanted to expose you to that independence while you were still under my influence." My mother exemplified two important child-rearing principles: she knew how to hold me with an open hand, and she knew how to hold me close and then let me go.

**James Dobson**

week to week. Carla, a born organizer, filled her clutter drawer with boxes of various sizes. She even organized her clutter. Eric had a large clutter box on a closet shelf. He had to be reminded frequently that his clutter box was overflowing and in need of sorting and putting away.

Treasure boxes and bulletin boards can solve clutter problems. Let children choose prize possessions that can go into treasure boxes. They can display awards, birthday cards, and papers from school on bulletin boards in their bedrooms.

To handle the high intake of children's papers, provide a box or dishpan for each child. When the dishpan or box has reached its limit, encourage the child to go through the papers and select a few to put in her treasure chest. She can discard the rest to make room for more.

Some children do well with cloth or heavy paper shopping bags with handles. Everything to be carried to and from school goes into these bags. Children put assignments, homework, books, and lunch money into the bag. Nothing to be used in school goes anywhere but in the bag. When the child is at home she hangs her school bag on a hook provided for it in a convenient place.

Clutter is inevitable in a busy family, but it does not have to be an obstacle to making work easy. Let your family brainstorm other ways to tame clutter. You will be surprised at how creative you can be and how easily you can get clutter under control.

# Teach principles

Prevent work whenever possible. Teach your family to eat at the table and never on foot. If you confine eating to the kitchen, it will save hours of clean up.

Put things away, not down. Many things, including paper, do not have to be touched as many times as we touch them. By teaching yourself to put a piece of paper or any other item where it belongs the first time you touch it, you save a lot of work.

Use inexpensive paper plates occasionally to give everyone a break in cleaning up after a meal. Teach everyone to clean up after himself as he works. Cleaning fresh spills takes little effort, but washing off dried, hardened food or other spills requires a great deal of work, and spills sometimes attract ants. Use spoon holders at the preparation and cooking centers of your kitchen.

Make drippings in your broiler pan easier to remove by putting a little water in the bottom of the pan. Keep the sifter in a plastic bag to catch surplus flour. Wipe off the rims of bottles, dishes, and pans to prevent food from drying on them. Measure dry ingredients before liquids so that you will not have to wash measuring spoons or cups twice.

Eliminate ironing by buying no-iron clothing and linens. Fold and hang clothes immediately after the dryer shuts off. Buy home furnishings that have easy-care features. A self-cleaning oven and a self-defrosting refrigerator will save you hours of work.

Sometimes you can double up. You can double a recipe and prepare two casseroles, freezing one and serving one. Set the table from the dishwasher. Never go from one part of your home to another with empty hands, especially if you have a two-story house. Make sandwiches for the week and freeze them.

Begin thinking in terms of eliminating work. How can you save time and steps? Keeping plastic bags beside the back door, for example, can prevent mud tracks. Slip the bag over your boots or garden shoes when you need to make a quick trip indoors.

Schedule regular pick-up times every day. You can pick up before going to bed, before leaving your home in the morning, before or after dinner — whatever works best for your family. If you put things where they belong, your home will look clean. Learning to pick up after ourselves keeps work manageable and easy to do.

> *Put things away, not down.*

# Organizational skills

If children have learned something about organization and routine from the time they were babies, those skills will help them manage themselves and their work. Some people have a natural preference for structure and organization. Others prefer spontaneity. Nevertheless, basic organizational skills benefit everyone.

### Understanding about time
Begin when children are young by making clocks out of paper plates and construction-paper hands that indicate pick-up time, bedtime, time to go to school, and perhaps mealtimes. Use timers to give children a sense of time. As soon as children can tell time, give them an alarm clock and make them responsible for getting themselves up in the morning.

### Weather reports
Put a large thermometer where everyone can check it to decide how to dress for the day. Posting a weather report on the bulletin board each morning would give added information. Just clip it out of the morning newspaper.

### Day to day materials
Invest in a carrier tray for cleaning supplies. Fill it with glass cleaner, rags, paper towels, dust spray cleanser — whatever you need for cleaning. Having supplies easily transportable cuts down on cleaning time and effort. If you have a very young child, be sure to store the carrier in a place toddlers cannot reach.

Supply your children with organizational material, such as calendars, budget and address books, file folders, pencils, transparent tape, paper clips, and so on. Teach them to store these supplies where they can find and use them. Help them write important dates — including birthdays — on their calendars. Buy birthday gifts as you find them, and store them on a shelf or box set aside for the purpose until the big day arrives.

Teach your children to organize their shelves and drawers so that each thing they own has its own place. You can even trace around larger items or containers to show where they belong.

### Use of colors
Use colors to make organization easy for your child. If she is a preschooler, organizing her things in this way will be a natural way to teach her colors. You can think of multiple ways to organize with color. You will find a variety of items available in colors: stickers, index cards, adhesive tape, thread, ribbon, clothing, linens, bedding, marking pens, file tabs, and much more.

Each member of the family can choose a color to identify his or her possessions. Mark children's rain boots, lunch pails, and school bags with a dab of quick-drying enamel paint or colored tape. You can buy a set of small bottles of paint in a variety of colors. Color code messages on the family calendar so everyone can see at a glance whose event is written there. Socks can be marked with thread sewed into the heel or toe. Toothbrushes, plastic drinking glasses, hair brushes, and combs can all be color coded. Colored towels, washcloths, and sheets can keep the household organized. Blue linen belongs to Carla, red to Janeé, and green to Eric. If you prefer matching linens to the color of the bathroom, sew patches of colored tape to the towels and washcloths to identify who uses them. Each person can store his towels and washcloths in his own closets.

You can use color any way you like to teach organizational skills to your children. What works for me and my family might not work for you. Experiment until you find ideas that make work easier for you and your family.

## Message center

Every home also needs an effective message center. How you create your message center will depend on the structure of your home. What walls are available for bulletin board material? Are there shelves or cupboards that can accommodate telephone books or other material? Can the telephone be the focal point? If your message center has been set up well, it will enable your children to learn some fundamental organizational skills.

Items in your message center should include the telephone, a telephone message book, a list of personal telephone numbers put together by the family, a commercial telephone book, the family calendar, the shopping list and dinner menu for the week, the chore chart, emergency instructions, a pencil can full of sharpened pencils, a small desk supply jar, and perhaps a repair list.

Our family calendar hangs on the wall above the telephone. We use the side of the cupboard to hold a list of emergency numbers and other important numbers. On the kitchen counter we keep our telephone message book, the ongoing shopping list, a decorated can full of sharpened pencils and a large see-through plastic container filled with other office supplies we often use. We store the city telephone book, church directory, and frequently called numbers in a cupboard under the telephone. The children write the names of their friends in this family-made collection of often-used numbers. That teaches them the importance of having such numbers at one's fingertips, and it saves us a lot of time when we need to contact one of their friends or their families.

A few steps away is a larger cupboard. We covered the side of that cupboard with corkboard to create a family bulletin board. Here we post our chore charts, the weekly dinner menu, and important schedules and information, such as our couples' group prayer chain sequence.

A large family calendar with plenty of writing space will keep everyone in touch with everyone else's activities. Encourage all members of the family to write down dates and appointments. Stores sell stickers of important events that young children can glue to the calendar to remind them of birthdays or other special occasions. Sunday, for example, could have a tiny church stuck to its space.

## Planning meals

Taking time to plan and post a menu has many advantages. Children can see at a glance if it is appropriate to ask someone to stay for dinner. Whoever arrives home first can begin the meal. Shopping is simplified if you know what you are going to serve. Best of all, you do not have to struggle every day with the problem of what to have for dinner. You plan that once a week.

I simplified the task of planning meals by listing some easy-to-fix meals, complete with salad, vegetable, and main dish, in a spiral notebook. I numbered the meals as I listed them. To my surprise, I ended up with more than a hundred different simple meals. Now all I have to do each week is to thumb through the notebook and write the number of the meal on the menu that I post. It is a task older children enjoy doing as well. If someone wants to know what we are having for dinner, they find the number in the notebook.

I use the book to prepare my shopping list so that we have all the ingredients on hand. I find that this method really takes the work out of meal planning. It also enables children to experience in a practical way the value of organizational skills.

## Telephone messages

The telephone message book, another simple idea, has saved our family a great deal of time. Every morning I record the day's date in this spiral notebook. Anyone who takes a call records the name of the caller, his telephone number, and who the call is for. We write down any other information given by

| *Get more done in less time.* |
| --- |

the caller, too. We also record outgoing calls, which gives us an excellent record of who we have called and what information we have collected. When anyone returns home, the first thing he does is check the book to see if there were any calls for him while he was gone.

No longer do we have bits and pieces of paper with telephone numbers and notes scribbled on them. We use the message book to check on long distance calls, to look up information we have forgotten, to verify the date of a call, and so on. You can add to the usefulness of the book by buying a notebook with pockets in it. Warranties, important current information, and other bits of paper that you cannot throw away can be tucked into these pockets for future reference.

If you can use and teach some simple basic organizational skills, even your spontaneous, unorganized family members will get more done in less time and have more time to do what they want to do. If you struggle with structure and organization, look for one trouble spot you might try to improve. Give yourself lots of encouragement for any small amount of success. The payoff will be worth any effort you are willing to make.

### Helping children to succeed
Think about your child's size and ability when you provide him with cleaning tools. Children should not be expected to use heavy hard-to-manage vacuum cleaners. If they vacuum, provide a lightweight, easy-to-use machine. Be sure it has a storage space and will be put there when it is not being used.

Small children should have small brooms, sponges, and pails so that they do not feel overwhelmed by the tools they must use. Always teach children how to use equipment they have not used before. Do not forget to

**Let the kids help tidy and organize.**

teach them safety rules and caution them about the danger of using toxic cleaners.

Sponges should fit children's hands. Color code sponges to be used on floors or cut off the corners to identify them. A soft-bristle, one-inch-wide paint brush is good for dusting. Cloth diapers make excellent dust rags.

If you evaluate each task and the equipment needed to do it on the basis of your child's ability you will help make it easy for him to succeed. Children thrive on success.

Making work easy will go a long way toward creating an environment in which children will want to help. And that will be good for everyone.

This chapter is taken from *How to Get Kids to Help at Home* (Chicago: Moody, 1989).

## Further Reading

Elva Anson. *How to Get Kids to Help at Home.* Chicago: Moody, 1989.

Carol Van Klompenburg and Joyce Ellis. *When the Kids Are Home From School.* Minneapolis: Bethany House, 1991.

**What shall it profit men or women if they gain the whole world but lose their own families?**

With a 50 percent divorce rate and more and more two-wage-earner households, the home as we have known it in the past, indeed, as God established it, is truly an endangered species.

Marriage and the family were not quaint ideas cooked up by society. The family was ordained of God before He established any other institution, even before He established the church.

**I want to suggest ten commandments for a solid, happy, God-honoring home:**
1. Establish God's chain of command. The Bible teaches that, for the Christian, Jesus Christ is to head the home, with the wife under the authority of a Christlike husband and the children responsible to their parents.
2. Obey the commandment that you love one another.
3. Show acceptance and appreciation for each family member.
4. Family members should respect God's authority over them and the authority God has delegated down the chain of command.
5. It is important to have training and discipline in the home – and not just for the family dog!
6. Enjoy one another and take the time to enjoy family life together. Quality time is no substitute for quantity time. Quantity time *is* quality time.
7. Do not commit adultery. Adultery destroys a marriage and is a sin against God and against your mate.

# Ten Commandments for the home

*Save your people and bless your inheritance.*
*(Psalm 28:9)*

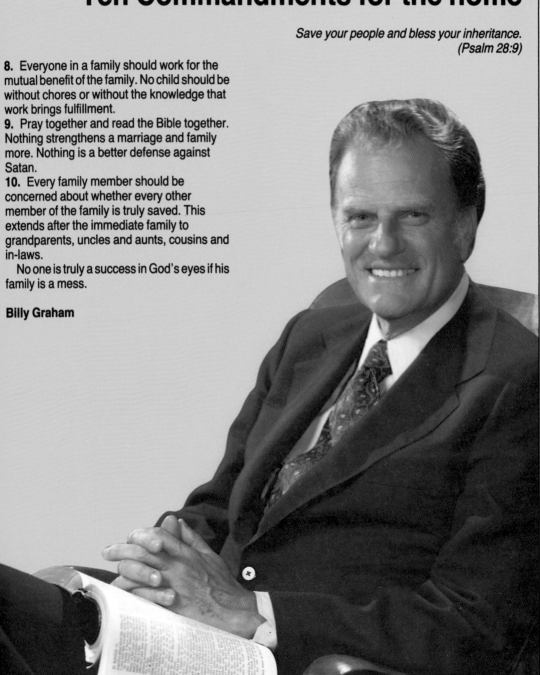

**8.** Everyone in a family should work for the mutual benefit of the family. No child should be without chores or without the knowledge that work brings fulfillment.

**9.** Pray together and read the Bible together. Nothing strengthens a marriage and family more. Nothing is a better defense against Satan.

**10.** Every family member should be concerned about whether every other member of the family is truly saved. This extends after the immediate family to grandparents, uncles and aunts, cousins and in-laws.

No one is truly a success in God's eyes if his family is a mess.

**Billy Graham**

# How Our Family Discovered the World

*Tim Hansel with Vicki Hesterman*

Our sons, Zac, seventeen, and Josh, fourteen, had been working alongside my wife Pam under the hot Ecuadorean sun, laying cement blocks, using mud as mortar. A dozen skinny dogs wandered in and out of our building site, barking in Spanish. What would come to be known as "The Hansel Wall" was already several blocks high by the time I joined my family.

## Novice at work

I was eager to lay my first block. I carefully tucked the mud around all the corners and was verifiably proud — only to notice one of my disabled friends, who was sitting in his wheelchair directly across from me, pointing at my brick and saying loudly, "Malo! Malo!"

I knew enough Spanish to realize he was telling me that my first attempt was "Bad! Bad!" A careful look revealed the problem — I had put the block in backward.

Such was my auspicious beginning as a short-term missionary.

Zac, my oldest son, couldn't resist laughing. We all laughed. Laughter is a very important commodity in our family — especially in new situations.

Last summer my family set out to take some risks, to love and to serve. In a place far removed from our comfortable southern California existence, we discovered another, bigger world. In the process, my sons also discovered some of the deeper values of life.

## Serving the poor

We had the privilege of going to Ecuador with World Servants, a short-term missions agency that serves the poor and disabled. The Hansel family experienced Christ in new ways — felt His servant's heart for the needs of the world — by actually working alongside each other, praying with each other, laughing with each other, sweating with each other, and learning much with and through each other. The key is that we did it together — mom, dad, sons. It changed our lives.

One of our tasks was to build a school in Quito, one of the largest cities in Ecuador, located high in the Andes Mountains. We worked in Canteras, one of the city's poorest areas. This small barrio of a thousand people — eight hundred of them under the age of ten — is crammed into the equivalent of a city block. The buildings are all makeshift; big stones help hold the tin roofs down.

Men leave early in the morning to work construction and do not return until late at night. Women cook food and make crafts to sell in the marketplace. Until World Servants came, there was no school. I was shocked when I realized that the entire community gets its water (contaminated) from one small spigot.

It was the first time my boys had ever seen such poverty. For a time, Josh, our fourteen-year-old, was nearly paralyzed by it. Zac had a different reaction. He said he felt a great sadness, but he also sensed their dignity and simple joy in the midst of their suffering.

Amidst their extreme poverty, the people were beautiful! Their toothless smiles were contagious and encouraging. It was humbling.

An old proverb says, "I heard and I forgot, I saw and I remembered, I did and I understood." I have devoted most of my life to experiential education, and yet in some ways I forgot to fully use those truths in my own home to help my kids discover the deeper values of life.

I have written about servant leadership, talked about it, and tried to model it, but it is difficult for my boys to see servant values in Southern California. It's a struggle many parents in the United States contend with. Our children hear us talk about it, but words are slippery. The most important things we can give our kids are our time, our lives, and our values — and values are *caught* much more than they are *taught*.

When we were invited to join the two-week mission trip to Ecuador, I realized this might be a special opportunity for our family to grow together. It offered short-term missions opportunities to people — including families — that can set the stage for longer term missions.

Because Pam is on the staff at a local university and our boys are both in high school, we were able to take the summer trip together.

Of course, we faced the natural obstacles — time, commitment, money — but I knew this could be the best chance I would ever have to help my kids see firsthand how the rest of the world lives.

## Setting off

We flew out of Miami on a Monday afternoon in early August. We each took two bags crammed full of soap bubble bottles, Spanish Bibles, crayons, construction paper, and other

## *About the author*

**Tim Hansel** *founded Summit Expedition, a year-round wilderness program. He is currently vice president of Communication resources for World Servants. His several books include* Real Heros Eat Hamburgers, Real Heros Wear Jeans, *and* Through the Wilderness of Loneliness *(Cook), as well as* Holy Sweat *(Word) and* What Kids Need Most in a Dad *(Revell).*

goodies for the Ecuadorean children. We also stuffed in our clothes. The bags were so full that five of them ripped before we got to Quito.

Our group of eighty ranged in age from four to seventy-one. Fifty of us were families — one family represented three generations. The rest were high school and college students from Grace Fellowship Church, Baltimore.

We were white, black, Asian, Hispanic, athletic, not-so-athletic, lean, not-so-lean, male,

> *Last summer my family set out to take some risks.*

female, teenager, businessman, pastor, lay person — every variety of ordinary person God uses to change the world.

We stayed in dormitories in Campimento Nueva Vida, a camp for the disabled near La Merced, a small mountain town an hour and a half from Quito. Our accommodations were basic — two little rooms and a bathroom for each family. The toilets had no seats, and our kids slept on the floor because their beds were so saggy.

The people were glad to see us and made us feel welcomed. Most of the women of the town washed their clothes in little rivers and irrigation ditches. They would wave as we passed. It took them all day to wash their clothes, and when they hung them out to dry, they looked like a rainbow of reds, purples, yellows, and greens.

## Work begins

Each morning, the teens and college students would board the bus for the ride to Canteras, the Quito barrio where they were building the school. Those of us who came as families stayed in the camp at La Merced, where we built a workshop for the disabled — the site of the fabled "Hansel Wall."

During the next two weeks, we discovered how much fun it is to serve. We worked hard with brick and mortar, sweating and singing. There was much prayer and fellowship, and we made close friends with both Ecuadoreans and other Americans. All of us served in some way — carrying bricks or teaching Bible school, building buildings or nurturing young souls. We had no luxuries, but the time flew by. In our toil we experienced deep joy. There are too many stories to relate here, but I'll give you just a few.

## A learning experience

Kathleen Smith and her eighteen-year-old daughter Linda, had prayed together before the trip that Christ would actually meet Linda there in a special way and prepare her spiritually for entering college in the fall. On their last evening in Quito, Linda tearfully told her mom, "Jesus answered my prayers, Mom. I met Him in a wheelchair and in a baby's broken, calloused feet."

Tim and Janet Gibson brought their sons Nathan, eight, and Andrew, five. "Nathan is normally shy, but he got so caught up with the rest of the families in VBS that he figured out ways to share his faith," says Tim. "Andrew carried cement blocks to the building site until he got tired. Then we'd find him playing in the sand with Ecuadorean children, breaking all the barriers of language and culture."

All six members of the Prince family came to Ecuador. An "Ecuador Jar" kept in the middle of their family room for months helped pay their way. A part of what each family member earned — even birthday money — went into the jar.

Steve Vargas, a brilliant young doctor who was volunteering his time, told me about being asked by a young Ecuadorean teenager, "Why are you doing this?"

Steve said simply, "Because we love God, and God calls us to pass that love on to others. We have a heart transplant — His heart has become our heart." The teen was so impressed that he joined the crew for the rest of the week.

We went to learn, and we did. At our group devotions each evening, Tim Gibson, the trip leader, asked, "What did you learn today?" Kids from the youngest to the oldest made their reports:

"I learned how to make bricks."

"I learned how to sing 'Jesus Loves Me' in Spanish."

"I learned that what I wear doesn't matter and that music transcends language."

"I learned that it's OK to get your hands dirty for Jesus' sake."

Too soon our two weeks of service were over and it was time to return to our regular lives. After our final worship service on Saturday night, the kids all wanted to say good-bye to their new friends, so we were all up until well after midnight to pack. Then we got up at 3:15 Sunday morning to catch the bus to the Quito airport.

## Changes all round

The next day, the Hansels were home in California, back to our comfortable beds, running water, and busy, normal lives – but we were different. Our family had gone to Ecuador to discover the world, perhaps to change it. Yet it was we who came back changed. The evidence was everywhere.

Take Josh. He's normally a little shy about his faith. But he prayed one morning during our devotional time – and prayed and prayed. It came from the deepest place in his heart. Later he said, with a huge smile, "You know, I think I prayed longer than anyone else this

morning." That was new for a kid whose previous prayers were limited to a few words.

The following weekend, Josh told us he was working real hard to get one of his friends to join him for a church picnic. "Dad, I really want him to meet Jesus," he said.

My oldest son, Zac, is seeing the world in whole new ways too. His relationship with Christ is different and deeper – reflected in his eagerness to reach out to his friends, to pray, to study, to serve. Now he describes a missionary in this way: a person who at any time or place is willing to get outside of himself and serve others in need. These may seem like little things to some parents, but they were a part of a big step in my son's journey with Christ.

## Sharing the experience

On Sunday afternoon about a month after we returned home, we sat down as a family to

**The Hansel family help build a school in Quito.**

discuss the experience. I wanted my boys to describe what they had seen and done and learned. I knew from our twenty years in Summit Adventure ministries that experience alone isn't enough – people have to translate it into terms real for them. Being typical teens – with friends to see and things to do – they were reluctant to take the time at first, but the more they talked, the more they opened up.

Zac brought up the village woman who had built her home from spare car parts and propped it against one of the quarry walls. She had amazed us all. "Dad, even in the midst of all their poverty, they had dignity. I mean, they didn't just lie there begging. They worked hard to change their situation – and they are some of the most ingenious people I've ever seen. They could fix anything and use anything."

Zac said what really made him sad was that when we returned to the United States he saw people who had everything – more than enough – but were still apathetic and unhappy. "Maybe," he wondered aloud, "we have more to learn from the people in Ecuador than they do from us."

Josh seemed to be thinking along the same lines. "I realized that disabled people are just like anyone else," he said. "And I realized that we don't need everything in life to make us happy. Maybe TVs and all our things can be distractions."

The trip taught Pam and me that it was important to let our boys be real – to be different from each other, to grow in their own fashion, and to solve their own problems. We tried to let this happen naturally in Ecuador.

"I enjoyed seeing the boys make new friends and develop new skills – without my prodding," Pam says. "They still worked very hard, even when we weren't there. They're growing up – and God is going to use them in very special ways."

When we first arrived in Ecuador, there were *people*. When we left, there were *persons* – individuals, with names, unique stories, and a contagious love of the same Lord that we serve. Boundaries of all kinds had begun to melt. There were no more Ecuadoreans or North Americans, just children of God.

We learned again, as a family, that we're called to serve, and to work *with* people, not just *for* them.

We were reminded again that people with disabilities and people the world calls poor have much to teach us.

We didn't learn a lot of fancy theology, but we learned a lot about the real stuff of the gospel.

We learned that eighty people can make a difference – that even one person, through Christ, can make a difference.

We learned that Christ actually does live within us and expresses Himself and His incredible love through us – and that it is this Christ within us who is the hope of glory (Colossians 1:27).

*A similar version of this story appeared in the January/February 1992 issue of Christian Parenting Today.*

---

### Short-term Missions Resources

Caleb Project, 1605 East Elizabeth Street, Pasadena, CA 91104

International Teams, P.O. Box 203, Prospect Heights, IL 60070

World Servants, 8233 Gator Lane #6, West Palm Beach, FL 33411

Wycliffe Bible Translators, P.O. Box P-77, Huntington Beach, CA 92648

# In love with life

If I were to pick out a verse that best describes the way my parents raised us, it would be Deuteronomy 11:18–19: "Fix these words of mine in your hearts and minds. . . . Teach them to your children, talking about them when you sit at home and when you walk along the road, when you lie down and when you get up." That passage underscores the fact that every family function can and should be sacred.

Color and excitement characterized many of our lessons about God. When we'd go camping on the beach, nighttime stories around the fire included not only the real-life escapades of my father hunting bear and trading with the Indians, but the real-life adventures of Noah, David, and Moses. Dad would talk about the days when he sailed clipper ships and explored the Upper Yukon, but he'd also talk about Moses, brave and trusting, exploring the wilderness of the desert beyond Egypt. Wherever he led us in his stories, we knew that the people he loved were real, were adventurers, and were in love with life.

### Learning respect

It was one thing to learn about God's creation by listening to stories or reading the Bible, but that creation came to life on each family outing. While horseback riding through the woods with my family, I learned at an early age the difference between oaks, maples, poplars, and elms. Along the trail, Daddy would point out the tracks of different animals. We learned to respect and not disturb the anthills and spiderwebs, and we also learned to leave the most delicate blossom untouched for the next passerby to enjoy.

My mother carried the "every family function is sacred" theme into the home. She made certain that we handled our knives and forks properly and learned good table manners. We were taught the proper way to pass platters and knives. It was important to answer the phone politely and to greet guests cordially.

**Joni Eareckson Tada**

# Family Financial Planning

*Larry Burkett*

Communication is vital to family financial planning. To enhance that communication, here are some questions for both husband and wife. I suggest you do them separately. Write every answer as if your spouse were asking the question. Then, when you won't be interrupted, evaluate these together. Begin your evaluation by praying about your time together, opening your hearts to the Holy Spirit.

The questions are intended to enrich the discussions of mature, communicating Christian couples. They are not intended to become an additional source of friction for couples totally void of communication. Use them as tools of love, not ammunition for war.

## A. Personal goals

To be answered as if your husband or wife were asking:

1. What are your personal goals in life?

2. What personal goals have you set for this coming year?

3. How can I help you achieve your goals?

4. What can I do to help or improve our financial situation?

5. Do you feel there is a proper balance between my outside activity and my time at home?

6. Would you like me to do more things around the house, such as cleaning and decorating?

7. In regard to my activities outside the home, what would you consider as priorities?

8. Do you feel I need to improve in any area, such as my appearance, manners, attitudes?

## B. Marriage goals

1. Do you believe our marriage is maturing and we are coming closer together?

2. Do you feel we clearly communicate?

3. Do you feel that I am sensitive to your personal needs?

4. What would you like me to say or do the next time you seem to be angry with me or you are not speaking to me?

5. The next time you are late in getting ready to go some place, what would you like me to say or do?

6. What would you like me to say or do the next time you seem to be getting impatient with something or someone?

7. What would you like me to say or do if you begin to criticize someone?

8. Do you feel I need to improve in getting ready on time or getting to meetings on time?

9. Do you feel we should go out together more often?

10. Do I make cutting remarks about you or criticize you in front of other people?
_____

11. What should I do in public to encourage you?
_____

12. Do I respond to your suggestions and ideas as if I had already thought of them instead of thanking you and encouraging you to contribute more? _____

13. Do I tell you enough about what I do every day? _____

14. What little acts of love do I do for you?
_____

15. What most often causes you to get angry with me? _____

16. Do I convey my admiration and respect often enough? _____

17. Do we "play act" a happy marriage in front of other people? _____

18. What do you think 1 Corinthians 7:3–7 means? _____

19. Do you feel we need to see a marriage counselor? _____

20. What are the responsibilities of a "help-mate"? _____

21. Do we give each other the same attention we did before we had children?
_____

## C. Family goals

1. What are our family goals? _____

2. Are we achieving our family goals?
_____

3. a. (Wife) What can I do to help you fulfill your responsibilities as spiritual leader of our family? _____

### *About the author*

*Larry Burkett, having degrees in marketing and finance, is the founder and president of Christian Financial Concepts, Inc. A former manager in the space program at Cape Canaveral, his daily radio broadcasts are heard on more than one thousand outlets throughout the world. Among his best-selling books are* Debt-Free Living, Your Finances in Changing Times, *and* The Coming Economic Earthquake *(Moody), as well as* Business by the Book *(Nelson),* Preparing for Retirement *(Moody) and* Investing for the Future *(Victor). He and his wife, Judy, have four children and seven grandchildren.*

b. (Husband) How can I better fulfill my responsibilities as spiritual leader? _____

4. Do you feel we are meeting the spiritual needs of our family? _____

5. What kinds of family devotions should we have? _____

6. List the responsibilities stated for the husband and wife in the following passages:
1 Peter 3:1–2 _____

Colossians 3:18–19 _____

1 Timothy 2:11–15 _____

1 Corinthians 11:3 _____
_____

Ephesians 5:17–33 _____

7. Do you feel we have a consistent prayer life together? _____
_____

8. Do you feel we are adequately involved in our local church? _____
_____

9. Do you feel we are meeting the physical needs of our family? _____
_____

10. Should we improve our eating habits? _____
_____

11. Should we get more exercise? _____
_____

12. Do we make good use of our time? For example, do we watch too much television? Should we have more hobbies? Read more?
_____

13. How and when shall we discipline our children? What do you think is the biblical viewpoint of discipline? _____
_____

14. On a sheet of paper, list the responsibilities of parents and their children in the following passages:
Colossians 3:20–21 _____
_____

Hebrews 12:5–11 _____
_____

Proverbs 3:11–12 _____
_____

Ephesians 6:4 _____
_____

15. What kind of instruction and training should we be giving our children in the home?
_____

# D. Financial goals

1. Do you think I handle money properly?
_____

2. How could I better manage our money?
_____

3. Do you think I am:
Too frugal? Too extravagant? About right? Why? _____
_____
_____

4. Do you think I accept financial responsibilities well? _____
_____

5. Do you think we communicate financial goals well? _____
_____

6. What is your immediate financial goal?
_____

7. What is your primary goal for this year?
_____

8. What is your plan for our children's education? _____
_____

9. What is your retirement goal? _____
_____

10. What do you think about tithing? Is tithing necessary? _____
_____

How much? _____
_____

Where should it go? _____
_____

11. How do you feel about giving in general?
_____

12. Do you like the way we live? _____
_____

13. What changes would you like to see?
_____

# The family budget

Why is a budget necessary?
• To help those who are not living within their means to do so.
• To help those with a potential surplus to fix their level of expenses.
• To help establish a reasonable level of living for those who want to do so.

The initial tendency is to create an unrealistic budget, one that makes no provision for variables like clothes, dentists, doctors, or entertainment. To do so will only frustrate your efforts, cause your budget to fail, and cause you and your spouse to lose confidence in budgeting.

The next tendency is to create a budget — and then stop! There is no magic in a budget; it is only a written expression of what you must do to be a good steward. Action is required to make it work, and you may need to make sacrifices to live within your budget.

Two budgets are actually necessary. The first determines your present status. The second determines your goals (a budget based on spendable income). If you are really serious about being the best steward possible, then a budget is necessary. But no amount of *intention* is effective without action.

In making and using a budget, there are several logical steps, each requiring individual effort.

### Step 1 – List expenditures in the home on a monthly basis.

*Fixed Expenses*
- Tithe
- Federal income taxes (if taxes are deducted, ignore this item)
- State income taxes (if taxes are deducted, ignore this item)
- Federal Social Security taxes (if taxes are deducted, ignore this item)
- Housing expense (payment/rent)
- Residence taxes
- Residence insurance
- Other

*Variable Expenses*
- Food
- Outstanding debts
- Utilities
- Insurance (life, health, auto)
- Entertainment, recreation
- Clothing allowance
- Medical-dental
- Savings
- Miscellaneous

NOTE: In order to accurately determine variable expenses, it is suggested that both husband and wife keep an expense diary for thirty days. List every expenditure, even small purchases.

### Step 2 – List available income per month.

NOTE: If you operate on a non-fixed monthly income, use a yearly average divided into months.
- Salary
- Rents
- Notes
- Interest
- Dividends
- Income tax refund
- Other

### Step 3 – Compare income vs. expenses.

If total income exceeds total expenses, you have only to implement a method of budget control in your home. If, however, expenses exceed income (or more stringent controls in spending are desired), additional steps are necessary. In that case, you need an analysis of each budget area to reduce expenses. These areas are outlined below.

# Budget problems analysis

### Bookkeeping errors

In order to maintain an orderly budget, it is necessary to keep records. This includes both the previously established home budget and adequate bank records. Many people fail to exercise any control over checking accounts and seldom or never balance their records. It is *impossible* to balance a home budget without balancing your checking account. Go to your bank account manager and ask for help if you cannot balance your records. Some helpful hints for this area are:

1. Use a ledger type checkbook (as opposed to a stub type).
2. List all check numbers before writing the *first* check.
3. Record *every* check in the ledger immediately, in detail.
4. Have one person keep the ledger and checkbook.
5. Balance the ledger *every* month.

### Hidden debts

These include bills that may not come due on a monthly basis. Nevertheless your budget must provide for reduction of those items; failure to do so will only frustrate your efforts to be a good steward.

Some debts of this type might include:
1. Audio and video cassettes, compact disks, books, magazines.
2. Retail outlet stores credit.
3. Family, friends.
4. Doctor, dentist.
5. Taxes.
6. Yearly insurance premiums.

### Impulse items

Impulse buying is common to most of us. Unfortunately, credit cards have provided the means to buy beyond the ability to repay (to the sacrifice of other needs).

A list of impulse purchases can range from homes, cars, and expensive trips, to tools and entertainment items. The value is not the issue; its necessity is. Consider every purchase in light of your budgeted items and avoid buying anything on impulse.

Some hints to reduce impulse buying:
1. Use a delayed-purchase plan. (Buy nothing that is outside your budget unless you wait for thirty days.)
2. During those thirty days, determine to find at least two items similar to the one you want to purchase to compare prices.
3. Allow only one new purchase at a time that is not part of your planned budget.

4. *Never* use credit cards on impulse.
5. Stay out of the stores.

### Gifts

These items can jeopardize a budget quickly. It is unfortunate that in our society we tend to place more emphasis on the gift than the giver, and too many times busy parents substitute expensive gifts for personal involvement with their children.

Begin to seek alternatives for costly gifts both within the family and with friends. Regardless of your financial status, determine to bring this area under control. The following are some hints.
1. Keep an event calendar and plan ahead.
2. Initiate some *family* crafts and make the gifts you need. For example: wall plaques, knickknacks, purses, or string art. Not only do these make good gifts, but they reflect effort and love.
3. Draw family names for selected gifts rather than each family member giving to everyone.
4. Do not buy gifts on credit.
5. Help your children *earn* money for gifts.
6. Send cards on special birthdays and anniversaries.

# Budget busters

"Budget busters" are the large potential problem areas that can ruin a budget. Failure to control even one of these problems can result in financial disaster. This area is evaluated by *typical* budget percentages for a $12,000–$30,000 income. Naturally, these percentages are not absolute and will vary with income and geographical location. The percentages listed total 100 percent. Remember, if your expenditures exceed the percentage allowed in one area, you must reduce another.

### Housing *(38 percent of net income)*
Typically, this is one of the largest home

budget problems. Many families buy a home they can't afford, motivated by peer pressure or some other pressure. It is not necessary for everyone to own a home. The decision to buy or rent should be based on needs and financial ability rather than internal or external pressure.

**Food** *(12 percent of net income)*
Many families buy too much food. Others buy too little. Typically, the average American family buys the wrong type of food. The reduction of a family's food bill requires quantity and quality planning.

One of the best ways to plan food purchases is to decide on your daily menu *first*. Once you have established what your family is to eat, then select the various ingredients. Few homemakers take the time and effort to actually write out daily menus, but once the habit is developed, its benefits are obvious. Grocery shopping ceases to be a hunt-and-find weekly expedition; it becomes another step in financial planning.

**Automobiles** *(15 percent of net income)*
The advertising media refer to us as "consumers," but that's not always the best description. I believe that P. T. Barnum had a more apt word — suckers. Often we are unwise in our decision making when it comes to our machines — especially cars.

Many families will buy new cars they cannot afford and trade them long before their utility is depleted. Those who buy a new car, keep it for less than four years, and then trade it for a new model have wasted the maximum amount of money. Some people, such as salespeople who drive a great deal, need new cars frequently; most of us do not. We trade cars because we *want* to — not because we *have* to. Many factors enter here such as ego, esteem, and maturity. But few Christians seek God's will for the purchase of cars, so they suffer later because of the financial strains placed on home finances.

**Debts** *(5 percent of net income)*
It would be great if most budgets included 5 percent debts or less. Unfortunately, the norm in American families is far in excess of this amount. As previously discussed, credit cards, bank loans, and installment credit have made it possible for families to go deeply into debt. What things can you do once this situation exists?
● Destroy *all* of your credit cards as a first step.
● Establish a payment schedule that includes all creditors.
● Contact all creditors, honestly relate your problems, and arrange an equitable repayment plan.
● Buy on a cash basis and sacrifice your wants and desires until you are *current*.

**Insurance** *(5 percent of net income, assuming you have some employee's insurance)*
It is unfortunate to see so many families misled in this area. Few people understand how much is needed or what kind is necessary. Who would be foolish enough to buy a Rolls Royce when he or she could afford only a Chevrolet? Yet many purchase high-cost insurance even though their needs dictate otherwise.

Insurance should be used as supplementary *provision* for the family, not protection or profit. An insurance plan is not designed for saving money or for retirement. Ask anyone who assumed it was; the ultimate result was disillusionment and disappointment.

Do not allow someone else to decide what and how much you need. Select insurance based on God's plan for *your* life.

In our society, insurance can be used as an inexpensive vehicle to provide future family income and thus release funds today for family use and the Lord's work. In excess, this same insurance can put a family in debt, steal the Lord's money, and transfer dependence to the world.

One of your best insurance assets is to have a trustworthy agent in charge of your program. A good insurance agent is usually one who can select from several different companies to provide you with the best possible buy and who will create a brief, uncomplicated plan to analyze your exact needs.

Christians must learn to be prudent and creative in the area of insurance just as in any other purchase. A prudent application of insurance can help avoid calamitous financial debt by *reasonable* purchases.

*Adequate life insurance.* Considering the low cost of death provision, a Christian should evaluate life insurance, especially where there are minor children involved. Proper provision for the family involves carrying sufficient insurance to remove the burden from others if possible. That does not mean that God dies with you and, therefore, every contingency must be covered.

The discussion often arises about term insurance versus permanent or "whole life" insurance. Generally, unless insurance premiums can be tax deductible, term insurance is far less costly. The principle to observe is to purchase insurance for *provision,* not *investment.* Insurance cash reserves typically yield less than interest-bearing accounts. Therefore, purchase what is required at the least cost.

Term insurance is now available that extends to 65 or 70 years of age and will probably be extended further but, as age advances, the need for insurance normally diminishes. If whole life policies are in existence, a thorough analysis should be made by a qualified insurance agent to determine whether the policies should remain in force or be converted. Particular attention should be given to at least borrowing the cash reserve of the policy and reinvesting in a secure, higher interest program.

*Major medical insurance.* Except for the chronically ill with pre-existing coverage, hospitalization insurance is generally a poor expenditure. (The exception to this would be "group" insurance policies. These normally provide inexpensive, broad-range medical coverage.) However, major medical insurance that will pay most costs involved in serious illnesses is relatively inexpensive. For example, insurance paying 80 percent of medical expenses, for a family of 5, costs less than $800 per year.

## Recreation-entertainment *(5 percent of net income)*

We are a recreation-oriented country. That is not necessarily bad if put in the proper perspective. But those who are in debt cannot use their creditor's money to entertain themselves. The normal tendency is to escape problems, if only for a short while — even if the problems then become more acute. Christians must resist that urge and control recreation and entertainment expenses while in debt.

What a terrible witness it is for Christians who are already in financial bondage to indulge themselves at the expense of others. God knows we need rest and relaxation, and He will often provide it from unexpected sources once our *attitude* is correct. Every believer, whether in debt or not, should seek to reduce entertainment expenses. That can usually be done without sacrificing quality family time.

## Clothing *(5 percent of net income)*

Many families in debt sacrifice this area in their budget because of excesses in other areas. And yet, with prudent planning and buying, your family can be clothed neatly without great expense. This requires effort on your part in terms of:

1. Saving enough money to buy without using credit.
2. Educating family members on care of clothing.
3. Applying discipline with children to enforce these habits.
4. Developing skills in making and mending clothing.

Learn to be utilizers of our resources rather than consumers. How many families have closets full of clothes they no longer wear because they are "out of style"?

Many families with large surplus incomes spend excessively in the area of clothes. Assess whether it really matters that you have all of the latest styles. Do your purchases reflect good utility rather than ego? Do you buy clothes to satisfy a need or a desire?

**Medical-dental expenses** *(5 percent of net income)*
Anticipate these expenses in your budget and set aside funds regularly; failure to do so will wreck your plans and lead to indebtedness. Do not sacrifice family health due to lack of planning but, at the same time, do not use doctors excessively. Proper prevention is much cheaper than correction. You can avoid many dental bills by teaching children to eat the right foods and clean their teeth properly. Your dentist will supply all the information you need on this subject. Many doctor bills can be avoided in the same way. Take proper care of your body through diet, rest, and exercise, and it will respond with good health. Abuse your body and you must ultimately pay through illnesses and malfunctions. This is not to say that all illnesses or problems are caused by neglect, but a great many are.

Do not hesitate to question doctors and dentists in advance about costs. Also, educate yourself enough to discern when you are getting good value for your money. Most ethical professionals will not take offense at your questions. If they do, that may be a hint to change services.

Shop around for prescriptions. You will be amazed to discover the wide variance in prices from one store to the next. Ask about generic drugs. These are usually much less expensive and are just as effective.

**Savings** *(5 percent of net income)*
It is important that some savings be estab-

> *One of the most important factors in home expenses is you.*

lished in the budget. Otherwise, the use of credit becomes a lifelong necessity and debt a way of life. Your savings will allow you to purchase items for cash and shop for the best buys, irrespective of the store.

**Miscellaneous** *(5 percent of net income)*
This can include a myriad of items. Some of the expenses occur monthly whereas others occur on an as-needed basis (such as appliances).

One of the most important factors in home expenses is you. If you can perform routine maintenance and repair, considerable expenses can be avoided. Many people rationalize not doing those things on the basis that their time is too valuable. That is nonsense. If every hour of the day is tied up in the pursuit of money, then you're in bondage. A part of care and maintenance around the home relates to family life, particularly the training of children. When they see Mom and Dad willing to do some physical labor to help around the home, they will learn good habits. But if you refuse to get involved, why should they? Where will they ever learn the skills of self-sufficiency?

Some men avoid working on home projects because they say they lack the necessary skills. Well, those skills are *learned,* not *gifted.* There are many good books that detail every area of home maintenance. In the future many of those skills will be necessities rather than choices.

# Summary

At this point, you have the necessary tools to establish your own budget. Only one additional ingredient is necessary – desire. No budget will implement itself; it requires effort and good family *communication.*

Living on a budget is not only prudent, but it can be fun. As you have successes in various areas, share them with others. Challenge your children as well. Establish budget goals for them and rewards for achievement.

The following is a summarized list of the financial principles applicable to home financial planning. Study these and apply them. Then share God's blessings with others around you.

## 1. Principles dealing with home finances

a. Use a written plan.
b. Provide for the Lord's work first.
c. Excel at your tasks.
d. Limit credit.
e. Think before buying:
  - Is it necessary?
  - Does it reflect your Christian ethic?
  - Is it the best buy?
  - Is it an impulse item?
  - Does it add to or detract from the family?
  - Is it a highly depreciable item?
  - Does it require costly upkeep?
f. Practice saving money regularly.
g. Set your own goals – with your family.
h. Get out of debt.
i. Limit business involvement.
j. Avoid indulgences, lavishness.
k. Seek good Christian counsel.
l. Stick to your plans.

## 2. Purpose of a budget

a. To define income vs. expense
b. To detect problem areas
c. To provide a written plan
d. To aid in follow-up
e. To schedule money in and out of the home

## 3. What a budget will do

a. Help you visualize your goals
b. Provide a written point of reference for husband and wife
c. Help family communications

d. Provide a written reminder
e. Reflect your habits

## 4. What a budget will not do

a. Solve your immediate problems
b. Make you use it
c. Take the place of action

## 5. How to:

a. Calculate actual expenses.
  - Use a thirty-day expense diary (notebook).
  - Use a checking account ledger.
  - Use a creditor ledger showing each debt due.
b. Make out a family budget.
  - Define actual expenditures (present budget).
  - Define proposed expenditures (future budget).
  - Calculate income.
  - Calculate fixed expenses.
  - Calculate variable expenses.
c. Use a budget.
  - Post it in the open.
  - Set an achievable goal.
  - Keep it up-to-date.
  - Establish a set time and day to review it.

This chapter is taken from *Your Finances in Changing Times* (Chicago: Moody, 1975, 1982).

---

### Further Reading

Ron and Judy Blue. *A Woman's Guide to Financial Peace of Mind.* Colorado Springs: Focus on the Family, 1991.

Larry Burkett. *The Complete Financial Guide for Young Couples.* Wheaton: Victor, 1989.

Larry Burkett. *Debt-Free Living.* Chicago: Moody, 1989.

# Teaching Your Children About Sex

## Steve Farrar

The policy is easy to remember: *Get to your kids before their peers do!* That's it. The question is, At what age will their peers begin to bring up the issue?

I like the point Connie Marshner makes in her book, *Decent Exposure: How to Teach Your Kids About Sex.* Connie writes, "if your child is ten years old and there has been no communication between the two of you about reproduction, sexuality, or male female differences, there is no time to waste."[1]

Connie is exactly right; there is no time to waste. If your child is ten years old and doesn't know the scoop yet, get on the stick! If your child is ten, let me assure you that he knows more than you think he knows. He has already gotten the information. The only question is, From whom did he get it and how accurate is it?

Let's reiterate the policy: *Get to your kids before their peers do!* That means if you're going to err, err on the side of introducing the subject too early rather than too late. Remember, dads, *we* are to be the instructors of our children, not some kid on a playground. That means we must be tuned in to our kids. We must be alert for the subtle signals they send out that indicate big questions in their mind. Your wife can be a big help here. As June Cleaver used to say, "Ward, I'm worried about the Beaver."

It may be that you are in tune, but not getting any signals. That's OK. Maybe it hasn't crossed his mind yet. In my opinion, however, as a boy approaches the age of seven, a father should begin to think about an opportune

> ## Get to your kids before their peers do!

time to speak with his son about sex. Your son may not be thinking about it, but I guarantee you that at least one of his friends is. The same approximate guideline can be used for mothers and daughters. Please understand that this is simply a guideline. It doesn't come from inerrant Scripture; it's only a suggestion.

In some cases, it may need to happen sooner; in others, a little later. If you ask the Holy Spirit to give you wisdom as to the best time for your child, He will give it to you. Don't feel pressured. Just be sensitive to your child and to the Lord. He'll let you know when it's time.

One of his closest friends said that Winston Churchill spent a good part of his life rehearsing impromptu speeches. One day his valet, having drawn his master's bath shortly before, heard Churchill's voice booming out from the bathroom. The valet stuck his head in to find out if anything was needed. Churchill, immersed in the bathtub, said, "I was not speaking to you, Norman, I was addressing the House of Commons."[2]

When a man sits down to talk with his son, he should follow Churchill's example. You want to be impromptu, but you also want to be prepared. Let me offer eight suggestions that will give you guidelines as you prepare your impromptu session on sex and also for the continuing discussions thereafter.

## Small questions

I heard about a little boy who approached his father after dinner and asked, "Daddy, where did I come from?" The father nearly choked with surprise but managed to gather himself. Since they were alone in the den, he thought this would be as good a time as any, so he commenced to tell the boy about the sperm, the egg, and all of the pertinent information. After about five minutes, he looked at his son's blank stare and asked, "Son, is this making any sense?" The boy replied, "I guess so, Dad, but Tommy came from Cleveland. Where do we come from?"

Make sure you understand the question before you commence with an answer.

## Big questions

The other night as I was watching the news and John was reading a book, he overheard the newscaster's story and said, "Dad, what is AIDS anyway?" That's what you call a big question. It got a big answer. Up to that point in his life, John did not know about homosexuality. After our discussion, he did know about it. And he was shocked.

When I told him there were men who had sex with other men, he could not believe his ears. I was sorry he had to hear about it at all. But I wanted him to hear it from me and not someone else.

## Frank questions

Several weeks ago, John came running upstairs and said, "Dad, I've got to ask you a question."

I said, "OK, shoot."

He said, "It's private."

I said, "OK," dropped what I was doing, and John shut the door.

He said, "Dad, if a couple gets married, and then gets divorced, and then later they decide that it was a mistake to get a divorce and they

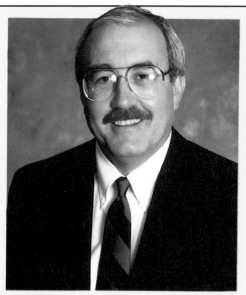

### About the author

*Steve Farrar holds an earned doctorate from Dallas Theological Seminary and is president of Strategic Living. A popular speaker and author of* Point Man: How a Man Can Lead a Family *(Multnomah), he and his wife, Mary, also speak at many Family Life Marriage Conferences across the United States. They have three children.*

get married again, would they have sex again?"

I have no idea where that question came from. But it was something John was trying to figure out. He asked me a frank question, and I gave him a frank answer. I said, "Yes." He thought for a second, and said, "OK, thanks, Dad," and went back downstairs to play with his Legos.®

Regardless of how well you think you are explaining everything, a boy of that age has not put all the pieces together. It's sort of like playing with Legos. You can give your kids all of the pieces and explain each piece as carefully as possible, but it will take a child several years to be able to coordinate all of those pieces.

John wanted to know if a divorced couple who got remarried would want to have sex again. You and I know the obvious answer. He didn't. Like any young boy, he's still putting the pieces together.

It's like what a friend of mine told several of us a while back. He has three children and was explaining the facts of life to his seven-year-old son. When he told his son that babies came from sexual intercourse and proceeded to explain what that was, his boy got an astonished expression on his face and said, "You mean that you and Mom have done that three times?"

## Be casual and natural

The reason for this is simple: If you're tense and nervous about discussing it, you're going to make your children tense and nervous. The fact of the matter is that there is nothing to be tense about.

You want to create an environment for your children that makes them feel that the most natural thing in the world is to ask Dad and Mom their questions about sex. So be casual and natural. Be relaxed. Even if you're tense on the inside and you have to chew two or three packs of Tums afterwards, don't let on that you're tense. Be cool. Chill out. Defrost, if necessary. Whatever you do, create an atmosphere where they feel comfortable in coming to you. If you don't, they will go to someone else. And that, my friend, is something to get tense and nervous about.

## Teachable moments

You never know when a teachable moment is going to show up. When one does, make sure you teach. A teachable moment is a special time or circumstance that ignites an unusual teachability in your child. Take full advantage of these times. They are gifts from God.

Josh McDowell relates a teachable moment that happened with his kids. His wife was

> *"Give me the children until they are seven and anyone may have them afterwards."*

unable to pick him up at the airport, so his secretary came to get him with his two oldest children. As they were driving home, his kids got in an argument. "F—— you!" said his son to his sister.

What would you do in that situation? Listen to how McDowell turned that into a teachable moment:

*Sean obviously didn't know what the word meant. If I had jumped on him and told him how dirty the word was, he would have learned not only that the word was bad, but he would also have a negative impression about the sex act itself when he learned what it was.*

*So instead I said, "Son, where did you learn that word?"*

*"On the school bus," he answered.*

*"Do you know what it means?" I asked.*

*"No."*

*"Can I explain it to you, then?"*

*"Yeah!" he answered. "What is it?" He was dying to know.*

*And for the next forty minutes, I had a fabulous opportunity to teach my son and daughter about the sanctity, the beauty, and the purpose of sex. It was an opportunity for which I was extremely grateful, an experience I'll never forget – nor I suspect will they.[3]*

Note that Josh created a teachable moment out of what might have been an explosive one instead. He had the wisdom in that situation not to react but to teach.

St. Francis Xavier once said, "Give me the children until they are seven and anyone may have them afterwards." That's true if you'll capture the teachable moments.

# Use the right terms

Sometimes this is tough to do. It's not that you will be embarrassed for using the right terms but that your kids will embarrass you when they know the right terms. Some friends of ours are very good parents and have been careful to use the right terminology with their children.

One day while grocery shopping, the mother walked thirty or forty feet away from the cart, past the crowds of people, looking for a specific item. Suddenly her little three-year-old, sitting in the cart, yelled out with great excitement, "Hey, Mom, look! I've got an erection!"

Sometimes it's tough when your kids know the right terms. But the thing about kids is that they can embarrass you even when they don't know the right terms. So go ahead and tell them the right terms. You may have to change grocery stores, but that's OK.

# Consider the child's age

We have already touched on this issue, but to underscore our previous remarks, remember that you are going to give a five-year-old a different answer to the same question that you give a nine-year-old.

# Straight answers

Let them know that they can ask you anything and get a straight answer. This is the cardinal doctrine of parental sex education. If you establish this, it doesn't matter what they hear somewhere else, for they will come to you for clarification. At certain points you may have to swallow hard before you answer, but whatever you do, don't skirt the issue. Deal with it head on. This kind of honest dialogue will be the greatest investment you will ever make. It will pay dividends in your relationship for the rest of your lives.

From time to time, I'll be in a conversation with a group of men, and this subject will come up. Inevitably, men express their frustration about knowing exactly what to say to their sons. They know they should say something, but they are not sure how to go about it. They didn't hear it from their dads growing up and therefore don't have a model to work from. But if you are clued in to the eight principles above, you will create an environment for your children where it is natural for them to talk with you about sex.

This chapter is taken from *Point Man: How a Man Can Lead a Family* (Portland: Multnomah, 1990). Used by permission.

1. Connie Marshner, *Decent Exposure: How to Teach Your Kids About Sex* (Nashville: Wolgemuth & Hyatt, 1988), p. 179.
2. John Gardner, *On Leadership* (New York: Free Press, 1990), p. 51.
3. Josh McDowell, *How to Help Your Child Say No to Sexual Pressure* (Waco, Tex.: Word, 1987), p. 99.

## Further Reading

James Dobson. *Preparing for Adolescence, Revised.* Edited by Kathie Mills. Ventura, Calif.: Regal, 1989.

Mary Kehle. *You're Nearly There: Christian Sex Education for Preteens.* Wheaton: Shaw, 1973.

Grace H. Ketterman. *How to Teach Your Child About Sex.* Tarrytown, N.Y.: Revell, n.d.

Josh Mcdowell and Norm Wakefield. *The Dad Difference: Creating an Environment for Your Child's Sexual Wholeness.* San Bernardino: Here's Life, 1989.

Greg Speck. *Sex: It's Worth Waiting For.* Chicago: Moody, 1989.

# Teaching Your Children About Marriage

*Selwyn Hughes*

Preparing children for marriage is one of the priority tasks of parenthood, particularly when the parents are committed disciples of the Lord Jesus Christ. This does not mean we ought to pressure our children toward marriage, but we ought, as best we are able, teach our offspring the biblical issues underlying this sacred institution.

But how do we parents go about this? What do we do and what do we say to help prepare them for what, next to conversion, without doubt is the most important decision any person can make? I want to focus not so much on modeling, important though that is, but on how to *teach* children the biblical principles of marriage.

I am the father of two children, David and John, both now in their thirties and each with two children of his own. My wife Enid died in 1986 and thus ended what was a good and happy marriage. Although I believe I modeled a good and godly marriage to my children, I did not spend as much time as I ought in the direct teaching of biblical principles. I am somewhat saddened that I did not initiate for them a long-term teaching program about marriage in their early developmental years. If I could have my time as a parent all over again, here are the steps I would take.

## A biblical definition

First, I would concentrate on developing a clear biblical definition of marriage. Children hear from their peers, or from television, definitions of marriage that can have a negative influence. Comedians will talk about marriage as "Nature's way of preventing us from fighting with strangers" or "The world's most expensive way of finding out our faults." We laugh, but we must be alert to the harm they can do unless countered by a biblical alternative.

In truth, marriage is the refining process God uses to make us into the kind of people He wants us to be. A Christian marriage involves three persons: the bride, the bridegroom, and God. Genesis 2:24 says, "For this reason a man will leave his father and mother and be united to his wife, and they will become one flesh."

From that biblical statement and its context, I would settle for this as a biblically based definition: *Marriage is an exclusive union between one man and one woman, publicly acknowledged, permanently sealed, and physically consummated.* This is not the definition I would give my children, but I would keep it very much in mind, for it is based on the most powerful and most comprehensive statement on marriage found anywhere in Scripture. It presents four clear principles:

*First, marriage is built into creation.*
*Second, marriage is intended to take place between one man and one woman.*
*Third, marriage involves a leaving of one's parents.*
*Fourth, marriage is a deep spiritual and physical commitment.*

# Applying principles

How does one apply these important principles to the minds of growing children? Clearly, because God established marriage at creation, it has a permanent and not a temporary validity. In other words, it is something God established for all people, in all parts of the world, for all time.

I would watch for television programs or documentaries that portrayed a wedding, particularly a wedding in another culture, and make the point that the child is witnessing the result of what God set in motion millenniums ago.

But the universality of marriage is one thing, its purpose another. When an intriguing question is asked, something happens in the mind that sustains interest. For instance, "How many marriages do you think have taken place since the world's first wedding in the Garden of Eden?" What do you think God had in mind when He planned for people to be married? What do you suppose would happen if God had not established marriage?"

Take advantage of the curiosity aroused to plant in your child's mind some of God's purposes for marriage – the procreation of the human race, the raising of children in a close and loving relationship, the importance of a family unit and its influence on society, and how the intimacy of marriage reflects the relationship between Christ and His church. It is in this way that I would hope to lay down in my child's mind the idea of a loving God who has at His heart the highest interests of His creation.

The Genesis model gives us the criteria for evaluating every relationship that describes itself as a marriage. Polygamy (many wives) and polyandry (many husbands) are out, because they are a violation of the one woman—one man principle. God tolerated those conditions in Old Testament times, but He most certainly did not intend it to be that way. That would need explaining to a child.

## About the author

*Selwyn Hughes is the founder of Crusade for World Revival and author of the widely read Bible reading notes,* Every Day with Jesus. *He has also written* How to Live the Christian Life *(HarperCollins). A Welshman, he was trained in theology in Bristol, England, and later attended counselor training courses in the United States. He was a pastor for eighteen years before founding CWR and has traveled in many countries presenting seminars on the Christian life. He is an executive director of CWR, responsible for the counselor training program at Waverley Abbey House.*

*Marriage is an exclusive union between one man and one woman, publicly acknowledged, permanently sealed, and physically consummated.*

> *No provision is given for divorce in the Genesis model.*

To teach this principle of one man—one woman, I would watch for news reports where it was violated. I would explain from Scripture that polygamous, homosexual, and lesbian relationships are a violation of God's order.

A new section of society is established whenever a man and woman get married. A man leaves his father and mother and is joined to his wife, creating a brand new family unit. Clearly, then, marriage is not to be done in secret but before the whole community. Marriage is a social event and has to do with the larger human family (not just the couple concerned).

## Family weddings

Take advantage of every family wedding to explain how most of what happens is rooted in Scripture. I would ask my child, "Would you like to know why ushers seat the family and friends of the bride and groom on opposite sides of the church? Because it provides a covenant setting such as we see in Genesis 15:10–17." I would ask, "Would you like to know why the groom enters first? He is signifying that he is the covenant initiator" (Genesis 2:24).

Other questions that might arouse a child's curiosity are these: Why does the father walk with the bride down the aisle? Because he has responsibility for his daughter until the time she is married (Deuteronomy 22:13–21). What is the significance of the white wedding dress? It is symbolic of the purity of heart and life for which the husband is responsible in the life of his wife (Ephesians 5:25–28). At some time during the teaching of this principle I would take out my own wedding photographs and reflect as a family on the day and the won-

**Marriage is to be done publicly.**

der of all that came out of it — not the least of which are the children.

## Union for life

Scripture says that a man is "united to his wife, and they become one flesh" (Genesis 2:24). This suggests a union that is not just close, but one that also lasts for a lifetime. No provision is given for divorce in the Genesis model. Whatever reasons might be advanced for its justification, it was not part of God's original intention.

A friend of mine taught his children the principle of bonding by gluing two pieces of wood together and later inviting his children to try to take the two pieces apart. Of course, when they wrenched the pieces apart, the wood was completely splintered. He said, "That is what it is like to have a broken marriage." A little

> *The Bible opens and ends with a wedding.*

dramatic perhaps, but his children told me years later that they saw divorce as the most heinous thing that could happen to them.

Marriage is the closest relationship one can experience, because it involves the union of spirit, soul, and body. Assuming that my children were an appropriate age, I would explain the significance of the sexual union and how God has arranged for babies to be made in the atmosphere of love.

## Roles

I would say something too about the roles God has designed for every member of the family: the father, a loving leader; the wife, a creative responder; the child, a willing and obedient learner (Ephesians 5:22–6:1). I would explain that when these roles are kept out of love for Christ, the family unit grows in strength and power. Should the children of that marriage go on to be parents themselves, those marriages would be the better for it.

Communication is crucial. Relationships develop and grow only as people talk out their problems. I would share the principles of conflict resolution my wife and I applied whenever we had a strong difference of opinion. I saw my role as the constant initiator, the one to gently press for a satisfactory end to conflicts. A husband, says the Scriptures, is to love his wife as Christ loves the church (Ephesians 5:25).

## The unmarried

I would not forget to make the point that some people never get married. Some have no natural desire for such a relationship, some are unable to marry due to illness or physical disability, and some quite simply never fall in love. Regardless, clear biblical teaching on the important aspects of marriage ought to be a part of every child's spiritual education in the home.

We ought to delight in marriage as God delights in it. The Bible opens and ends with a wedding. And the very first miracle Christ wrought was to save a wedding from embarrassment. Anything we do to help prepare our children for this great experience will have a positive effect on their future, but to prepare them by helping them understand the principles of Scripture will bring not just temporal but eternal rewards.

### Further Reading

James Dobson. *Dr. Dobson Answers Your Questions About Marriage and Sexuality.* Wheaton: Tyndale, 1986.

Kevin Leman. *Were You Born for Each Other? Finding, Catching, and Keeping the Love of Your Life.* New York: Delacorte, 1991.

Josh McDowell. *The Secret of Loving.* San Bernardino: Here's Life, 1985.

H. Norman Wright and Marv Immon. *Preparing Youth for Dating, Courtship and Marriage.* Eugene, Ore.: Harvest House, n.d.

# CHILDREN AS PEOPLE

# Connecting With Your Kids' Distinct Personalities

*Jim Brawner*

Years ago on a trip to the zoo in Little Rock, Arkansas, our family discovered anew what unique "animals" make up the Brawner menagerie.

Lionhearted as usual, our son Travis had the entire day planned. "First we're gonna see the lions and the tigers, and then we've gotta see the poisonous snake exhibit. That's my favorite!" Simply seeing *some* animals during a nice day at the zoo was not his goal – seeing *all* the animals was. And he was going to direct *our* movements as well.

By contrast, my wife Jill and I viewed the day as a chance to take in as many exhibits as possible. The fun-loving part of us wanted to be sure to see the monkeys and gorillas.

Jason, who's usually the "whatever makes everyone happy" member of our family, preferred to spend the whole day at the petting pavilion. He would rather make friends with just a few animals than see five hundred animals in one afternoon.

Suzette, who's also a people person, views a trip to the zoo – or anywhere else – as a time to be with the family. She majored on the relational aspects of our outing.

As you can see, there is an incredible variety of personalities in *family* zoos. And it is important to allow each individual the freedom to roam beyond his preconceived category.

Zoos once consisted of concrete buildings made up of long hallways, with cages having heavy steel bars on each side. In modern zoos, however, there are few pigeonholes. In some, animals roam in natural environments as visitors ride through their domain in their own cars or "cages" cleverly disguised as safari jeeps on rails.

The family zoo has undergone some dramatic changes in the past thirty years as well. Some trends haven't been positive. But one positive change is the realization that not all children neatly fit into one category.

Jill, Jason, and Travis have three different types of personalities. It's amazing that the same parents in the same environment can produce such variety.

## The Master's menagerie

During the time of the early Christian church, the apostle Paul was aware that there was great diversity in the Master's menagerie. He wrote of them as various parts of the Body of Christ. He affirmed diversity as being a key element for a healthy whole:

*Now the body is not made up of one part but of many. If the foot should say, "Because I am not a hand, I do not belong to the body," it would not for that reason cease to be part of the body. . . . But in fact God has arranged the parts in the body, every one of them, just as he wanted them to be. . . .*

*The eye cannot say to the hand, "I don't need you!" And the head cannot say to the feet, "I don't need you!" On the contrary, those parts of the body that seem to be weaker are indispensable. . . . If one part suffers, every part suffers with it; if one part is honored, every part rejoices with it.* (1 Corinthians 12:14–26)

> *Just as diversity in the Body of Christ is desirable and God-given, so also is diversity in families.*

This passage forever breaks the cookie-cutter concept of Christianity. There are many types of personalities in the Body of Christ. And each one is an important, indispensable individual. Pastor and speaker Jimmy Johnson writes,

*We have confused holiness with certain temperament or personality traits. Each church has its own standards for a "holy personality." In my denomination, it's the quiet, submissive, morning person who is "holy."*

*I'm convinced that 90 percent of the problems in churches . . . is not "sin," but trying to force others to conform to our definition of "spiritual" temperaments.*[1]

The passage also breaks forever the concept of cookie-cutter parenting. Just as diversity in the Body of Christ is desirable and God-given, so also is diversity in families. Given the wonderful variety of children in our families, it would be ludicrous to raise them all the same way. Yet that's what many parents try to do.

Psychologists cannot agree on how many types of personalities roam this planet. In fact, they can't even agree on how to classify these very different people. Or even what the categories are. For our purposes we're going to define personality as *an individual's characteristic pattern of behavior and thought.*

Each of those words is important. We are unique individuals. There has never been, nor will there ever be, another person who is genetically identical. (Even identical twins have unique fingerprints.) Add to these hereditary differences a variety of experiences, and you have infinitely unique individuals.

### About the author

*Jim Brawner, M.Ed., a U.S. national swimming official, is director of Kanakuk Kamp, a Christian sports camp in the Ozarks of Missouri. He is the author of* Connections: Using Personality Types to Draw Parents & Kids Closer (Moody) *and the father of three children.*

Each person has an individual character. That doesn't mean that he will always act in character, but there is an overall, general pattern for most people's behavior and thought.

Personality, then, is not who we are, but how we act (and react) in most situations.

Family harmony — and strife — occur when these very different kinds of personalities begin rubbing against each other. Sparks can fly, as any parent knows.

Before we begin talking about various types of personalities, I strongly suggest that you take time right now to have each member of your family fill out one of the following surveys.[2] You may want to photocopy more surveys so that there are enough for all the members of your family.

After you have filled in the adult or child survey, plot the results on the graph. Take the number of words or sentences you circled and make a bar chart in each category. For example, if you circled three words for list L, make a dot on the L scale three points high (see left-hand values). Then connect the dots between the four scales to make a graph. (Again, don't skip this step; if you have not taken the test, stop and do so now.)

As we describe various personality types, keep in mind that no type is right or wrong, better or worse. They're just different. The categories simply describe the characteristic ways we think and respond to situations.

Also, be aware that no one is a 100 percent purebred. We are all various mixes of personality types.

# Four personality types

Let's take a sneak preview of the four types of personality we'll be using: the Lion, the Otter, the Golden Retriever, and the Beaver. (But let me urge you to take the test first before reading the following material, otherwise you'll be prejudiced from reading the material below.) To illustrate the four personality types, consider this amusing anecdote.

If all four personality types fell off the Empire State Building, they would all experience the same event. But because of their unique personalities, they would have four unique reactions.

The Lion would say, "We're all as good as dead!" (Lions want to get to the bottom line — literally in this case!)

The Beaver would calculate, "We'll all be dead in thirty seconds." (Beavers like precision and planning.)

The Golden Retriever wouldn't say anything but would be looking for a paw to hold. (Togetherness and relationships are more important than outcomes to Retrievers.)

And the Otter would observe, "So far, so good!" (Otters are eternal optimists!)

---

### Personality Survey for Adults

Choose those words or phrases that describe you.

| List L | List O |
|---|---|
| Assertive | Fun-loving |
| Competitive | Motivator |
| Decisive | Avoids details |
| Adventurous | Optimistic |
| Goal driven | Enjoys change |

| List R | List B |
|---|---|
| Loyal | Orderly |
| Deep relationships | Predictable |
| Avoids conflict | Precise, factual |
| Adaptable | Discerning, analytical |
| Dislikes change | Persistent |

Total the number of words circled in each list:

L: _____  O: _____  R: _____  B: _____

---

There are other valid ways of looking at and organizing our behavior. But I've found the system used here — based on the Lion-Otter-Golden Retriever-Beaver criteria — to be the best, especially in terms of reliability, comprehensiveness, and ease of understanding.

It was developed by my friend John Trent, based partially on the Personal Profile System (DiSC), by Performax.[3] Trent examined that test, plus thirty others, in an attempt to formulate a user-friendly yet highly reliable personality assessment tool. He and his partner Gary Smalley have done an outstanding job in developing the tool, and I am grateful to them for their input.

> *No type is right or wrong, better or worse. They're just different.*

## Personality Survey for Children

Choose the sentences that are most like you.

**List L**

I like being the leader.
I say what I think.
I don't like a lot of rules.
I hate to lose games.
I'm not often scared.

**List O**

I'm funny and playful.
Others like my ideas.
My room is often messy.
I know lots of people.
I like to talk to people.

**List R**

I have a few close friends.
I'm loyal to my friends.
I want to please others.
I'm kind to others.
I don't like big changes.

**List B**

I like to do things right.
My room is often neat.
I often hide my feelings.
I'm not good enough.
I do well at school.

Write below the number of sentences you circled in each list:

L: _____   O: _____   R: _____   B: _____

## Summary Graph of Results

— L — O — R — B —

5
4
3
2
1
0

Name _____   When taken_____

# Interpreting the results

Now let's interpret the survey you and your family members filled out. Your test will probably have words circled in each of the categories. Most who take this personality test find that they score high on one or two categories and low on one or two categories. And in most cases there is one type that is more dominant than the others.

The most important chart is the bar chart where you plotted the strength of each trait. It graphically reveals the fact that none of us is purely any one type – we're all blends of the four traits. Nevertheless, you'll probably have one or two scales that are higher than the others.

As you look over your results, keep in mind that our goal is not neatly to classify – as the older zoos did – but to gain a general under-standing of ourselves and the other personalities that make up our unique family zoo.

The principles will help you understand how you relate to others and how others relate to you. And by knowing this, you'll be better able to understand your family and better motivate your children.

## L is for Lion

As we picture the king of the jungle in our minds, we see one who boldly takes charge and is assertive and determined. Those with pure Lion personalities are goal driven and enjoy difficult challenges. They climb Mount Everest "because it is there" – and are always looking for a goal to achieve.

Our second-born, Travis, is the Lion of our family. You can usually spot a strong Lion without a personality test. He or she has a strong opinion on every subject.

If the neighborhood children are playing school, the Lion is the principal. If the children are playing backyard baseball, he appoints himself the captain.

We parents are also a combination of personality types. So as we discuss the various animals, be aware that your personality mix also plays a large role in the makeup of your menagerie. For instance, if both child and parent are Lions, there is a tendency to come at each other with fangs bared. In fact, Lions actually gain energy from confrontations — whereas Golden Retrievers run for cover.

### O is for Otter

Those who score high on the O category are extremely verbal and group-oriented. The Otter personality, like its furry counterpart, is fun-loving, energetic and impulsive. They're great talkers and motivators but hate details and are often shortsighted.

Our third-born, Jill — and her dad — are Otters. (I'm sort of half Otter and half Golden Retriever.) You can easily spot an Otter's room. The bed — if made at all — is just thrown together. The floor is cluttered with half-finished puzzles, partially colored pictures, and two-thirds of a LEGO project. Otters love starting things but often get distracted by new opportunities before the original project is completed.

One important — and possibly lifesaving — bit of advice: Never, never, never open an Otter's closet. Jill's idea of cleaning her room is to stuff everything into her closet. You open her closet door at your own risk!

A parent who is purebred Otter will have a good time with his or her children but will run into problems if that trait is allowed to run wild.

### R is for Retriever

Golden Retrievers are the most loyal. They're tolerant, sympathetic and easygoing. They're "man's best friend" because they're motivated by relationships and the approval of others. However, they're extremely eager to

> *"What personality type was Jesus?" The answer is simple: "All of the above."*

please, so decision making is difficult, since they don't want to offend anyone.

Our firstborn, Jason, is our Golden Retriever. (Remember, he was the one who often answers, "Whatever makes everyone else happy.")

Retrievers' walls are covered with pictures of their friends and posters of their heros. Retrievers are almost the purest form of "people people."

Unless they have some Lion blood, Retrievers can be pushovers as parents. They tend to cave in to children's demands because they want so badly to keep everyone happy.

My wife, Suzette, is a strong Retriever, but she is a balanced blend of Lion, Otter, and Beaver. That allows her to be a peacemaker for our family zoo.

### B is for Beaver

Unlike the let's-have-a-good-time Otter, Beavers work slowly and methodically, with great attention to detail. "Quality is job one" to the industrious Beaver.

Their beds have hospital corners, their closets are arranged in alphabetical order (blouses to vests), and if they're old enough to write, there is sure to be a "to do" list prominently displayed. They are highly analytical, which can be both a strength and a weakness, depending on the situation.

Beavers have something in common with Lions. Both types can be the most insensitive of the parenting animals when pushed to an extreme. A Beaver parent can be too demanding and harsh, literally destroying the self-esteem of his or her offspring. A Beaver's children may attempt to escape the overly rigid atmosphere with drugs, alcohol, or compulsive behavior such as anorexia or bulimia.

Similarly, Lion parents, if untempered, can blast their children's self-concept to dust.

## Bible animals

I'm often asked after a presentation of these four personality types, "What personalty type was Jesus?" The answer is simple: "All of the above." He had the most amazing personality ever, as we noted earlier.

For instance, we see the Lion side of Christ when He roared into the Temple and sent the moneychangers scurrying out of His Father's house (Matthew 21:12–16). He obviously was an Otter who was invited to parties (John 2:2–11) and told entertaining yet convicting parables (Matthew 13:1–52). His Retriever side is seen in His compassion for the crowds and His tears at the tomb of his friend Lazarus (John 11:1–44). Finally, His Beaver side is seen in His careful organization at the feeding of the five thousand: He divided the crowd into groups for distribution and even organized an efficient cleanup committee (Matthew 14:13–21).

Jesus was able to respond appropriately to each type of audience and situation. Just as He was fully God and fully man, He was the perfect blend of positive Lion, Otter, Retriever, and Beaver qualities.

"Jesus had the only perfect personality! And that is why all of us are needed to accurately reflect (the body of) Jesus. The strengths of my temperament will offset your weaknesses. Where I am weak, others are strong."[4]

The purpose of examining the four personality types is not so that we can justify our imperfect behavior. "Hey, I'm a Lion; I can't help it if I prowl around growling and snarling at people!" Rather, we want to discover our areas of weakness so that we can allow Christ to mold us closer and closer to His image.

I've noticed that as people allow Christ to work in their lives, they begin to become more balanced in their personalities — closer to the

# History day

One of the special times I remember as a child was our yearly "History Day." Even though my father was from England, he very much felt that we should understand American history. We children were allowed to suggest places we would like to go, and then my father would plan an itinerary and surprise us on that day. Because we never had a car, our journey started with a bus ride to the depot and then a train trip to Boston. We then took the subway or walked to each different spot. My father had always studied up on the places we visited so that, even if there were no guides, he could fill us in on the historical background. Bunker Hill Monument was just a picture of an obelisk until we all climbed the stairs to the top. Faneuil Hall didn't sound like a marketplace until we saw the sides of beef hanging on hooks in the open square. Paul Revere was just a name in a history book until we saw his birthplace and traced the ride he took to warn that the British were coming.

**Imagining**

Recent surveys show that young Americans are woefully ignorant of American history even though it is taught in school. One major reason is that history out of a book has little meaning, but take a child to see the replica of the *Mayflower* and he will begin to imagine what those months cramped in that little space must have been like! Wherever you live, there is some history nearby that costs little or nothing to visit. As with any meaningful experience, this kind of special day takes time and effort on the part of a parent, but the benefits could stimulate in your child a real love of American history.

**Florence Chapman Littauer**

ideal balanced pattern that He would desire.

The book of 2 Peter reminds us of God's desire for us to be balanced. Try to pick out the family animal types in this section of Scripture:

*His divine power has given us everything we need for life and godliness through our knowledge of him who called us by his own glory and goodness. Through these he has given us his very great and precious promises, so that through them you may participate in the divine nature and escape the corruption in the world caused by evil desires.*

*For this very reason, make every effort to add to your faith goodness; and to goodness, knowledge; and to knowledge, self-control; and to self-control, perseverance; and to perseverance, godliness; and to godliness, brotherly kindness; and to brotherly kindness, love. For if you possess these qualities in increasing measure, they will keep you from being ineffective and unproductive. (2 Peter 1:3–8)*

Did you notice some of our animals in those verses? Lions excel in *perseverance*. Golden Retrievers pulsate with *brotherly kindness* and *love*. Beavers are unsurpassed when it comes to *self-control*.

But we certainly can't allow ourselves to rationalize, "I'm an Otter, so I shouldn't be expected to show self-control." God's plan is that we develop in all areas through our interaction with Him and His children. God can use trials and tribulations to moderate some of our too-strong personality traits.

For instance, when I took a personality test ten years ago, I scored as a very high Otter and a very low Lion. I thought, *Lord, help! Here I am going to be a principal and school administrator, and I'm not much of a Lion. I'm in trouble!*

So I've worked on that area. Through various life experiences and specific practice in this area, God has helped develop my Lion scale to where today I can hold my ground when the situation demands it.

So don't think that your current score will

> ## It's a lifelong process.

be your profile forever; remember that personality tests are simply a freeze frame or snapshot of one's behavior pattern at that particular point in time. God has designed us to continue growing and changing to be more balanced. It's a lifelong process, and your score will change to reflect your personal growth as the years roll by.

# Adapting our interaction

Because Christ has the perfect blend of temperaments, He can relate to each of us right where we are in that lifelong process.

He did so with the disciples: to Otterish/ impulsive Peter, Christ was direct and to the point (showing the Lion trait) when He upbraided him over a suggestion that wouldn't fit with God's plan: "Get behind Me, Satan! You are a stumbling-block to Me; for you are not setting your mind on God's interests, but man's" (Matthew 16:23, NASB). How's that for being to the point?

Of course, the classic Lionhearted act on Jesus' part was the clearing of the money-changers from the Temple (Matthew 21:12–16). He didn't lack for bold resolve when action was called for.

When the Beaver-like Pharisees wanted the woman caught in adultery stoned ("In the Law Moses commanded us to stone such women"), Jesus bared His Lion teeth and calmly said, "If any one of you is without sin, let him be the first to throw a stone at her" (John 8:3–11).

Jesus showed His Otter side when He went fishing (and even walking on the water) with Peter the Otter (Luke 5:1–11; Matthew 14:22–36).

In the case of John the Retriever, He put His arm around the beloved disciple at the Last Supper (John 13:23–25).

Similarly, Christ delegated the Passover

details to Peter and John, who must have had the organizational skills of the Beaver. And He often organized large events very well in Beaver-like fashion, as during the feeding of the five thousand. He adapted His interactions with others according to the needs of each individual situation.

In the same way, we parents need to respond to our children in an appropriate way based on their individual temperaments. Like the modern zoo, we must not cage them with our expectations but give them the freedom to become the unique individuals that God created them to be.

Now that we've had a brief orientation to the four-animal system of personality traits, and you've had a chance to see where you and your kids score on the various scales, you will have new insight into the behavior of your spouse, your kids, your parents, co-workers, and a host of other people in your life — not the least of which is you!

This chapter is taken from *Connections: Using Personality Types to Draw Parents & Kids Closer* (Chicago: Moody, 1991).

1. Jimmy Johnson and James Watkins, *Perfect Love* (Indianapolis: Wesley, 1987), 50.
2. The personality survey for adults and the four-animal concept in general are adapted from Gary Smalley and John Trent, *The Two Sides of Love* (Pomona, Calif.: Focus on the Family, 1990).
3. Another view of the Performax system (especially the biblical aspect) is found in (both book and workbook) *Understanding How Others Misunderstand You* (Chicago: Moody, 1990), by Ken Voges and Ron Braund.
4. Johnson and Watkins, *Perfect Love,* 52.

## Further Reading

Jim Brawner. *Connections: Using Personality Types to Draw Parents & Kids Closer.* Chicago: Moody, 1991.

Kevin Leman. *Parenthood Without Hassles – Well, Almost!* Eugene, Ore.: Harvest House, n.d.

Gary Smalley and John Trent. *The Two Sides of Love.* Colorado Springs: Focus on the Family, 1990.

Ken Voges and Ron Braund. *Understanding How Others Misunderstand You* (book and workbook). Chicago: Moody, 1991.

# How To Lead a Child to Christ

*Daniel H. Smith*

## Don'ts

### Don't "play God"

We can pressure, force, or coerce a response from children and presumptuously move into an area that is the sole prerogative of the Holy Spirit. We may also play God by jumping too quickly to conclusions and evaluating opinions about children and their situation without properly listening or discerning.

### Don't get locked into a prefabricated approach

Children's needs will be as varied as their faces, and we must always be concerned about the individuals — where they are in gaining knowledge of the truth as well as their readiness to respond to the convicting work of the Spirit. Children will have misunderstandings and misconceptions, and it may take a great deal of patience and some skill to discern their problems and minister to them. The wise evangelist will keep in mind the necessary information that must be conveyed in an adequate presentation of the gospel.

### Don't merely ask leading questions

Leading questions are questions that imply a desired answer and usually require only a "yes or no" response. Illustrations of leading questions include: "You all know that you are sinners going to hell, don't you? You know that Christ died for your sins, don't you? You know that by trusting Christ you will be saved from hell and on your way to heaven, don't you? You want to let Jesus come into your heart right now, don't you?" If an adult cannot lead a child or group of children to a series of yes responses with his personal influence and tone of voice then he is not very skilled at working with children. But one's leading children into a series of yes responses does not mean that they have been saved. Leading questions characterize quick and shoddy work in evangelism.

### Don't confuse the child with too many illustrations, Scripture verses, or concepts

The attention span of a child and his or her simple pattern of thinking can be complicated by a profusion of ideas or Scripture. If you throw terms like *believe*, *trust*, *faith*, and *receive* at a child in one statement, you may generate perplexity. To jump from Revelation to Genesis and back again in a series of quotations may work against the child's understanding.

### Don't expect "standard" terminology

Believers are familiar with and love certain expressions and terms. However, children may surprise us by sincerely using unconventional terminology. I remember one young person who, upon hearing the gospel for the first time, responded, "Wow, dis Jesus Christ stuff!" This was repeated three times before I could recover from my shock about such non-traditional language! Actually there was a deep and genuine response in this individual that became apparent in his growing interest in the gospel and eventual confession of Christ as Savior. Even in describing what has happened in their lives, many new believers will use nontraditional language. We need to be prepared to deal with them not only in traditional ways.

### Don't always get the child unsaved first
This awkward statement is designed to counter the thinking that when a child expresses an interest in Christ it is assumed that the child is unsaved. Or we may assume that we must always make the child aware of his or her guilt and lost condition. Experienced adults find that a significant percentage of children who respond to a personal invitation are already believers. They may need help in assurance of salvation or dealing with sin in their lives. As noted previously, we can become part of the problem rather than a part of the solution if we unwittingly "recycle a profession" rather than intelligently ascertain where the child is spiritually.

### Don't overemphasize fear
Fear or any other strong emotion wrongly used can cause us to run ahead of the Holy Spirit and precipitate a false profession. A certain amount of emotion is normal and healthy in response to the gospel, but we can overdo playing upon emotion to the detriment of the child.

### Don't create false issues
False issues include matters such as raising the hand, kneeling, coming forward, talking to an adult, and any number of things that might be imposed upon a child arbitrarily. We know that none of these are necessary for salvation, but we can unwittingly make these issues important in the mind of a child and either frustrate or precipitate some type of shallow response. We must never forget that salvation is of the Lord.

## About the author

*Daniel H. Smith, Ed.D., president of Emmaus Bible College, has been teacher, administrator, and counselor and has ministered at camps and conferences. He is author of* How to Lead a Child to Christ *(Moody). He has three children and two grandchildren.*

### Don't fail to give the opportunity to settle the issue of salvation now
Skillful salesmen point out that one weaknesses in many evangelistic efforts is that we fail to "close the deal." Since we are reluctant to force a profession, we may err on the other side and not make the urgency of the response clear. The message of the gospel is an urgent one, and we must not leave the issue of the child's personal response indefinite.

### Don't insist that the child get saved now
This is the other side of the coin. We may insist to the point that we do not let the work of the Holy Spirit come to maturity. Many testify to having been pushed into a false profession by overeager evangelists.

> *Let the Word of God tell the child he is saved.*

## Don't fabricate a prayer

At this point some readers may take issue with me. It seems common among evangelicals to lead children to "pray the sinners prayer." I am personally convinced that if the work of the Holy Spirit has come to maturity and the child has been adequately and carefully instructed, there is no need to fabricate a prayer. We may need to tell the child that he or she needs to speak to the Lord Jesus to tell Him of his or her need and desire for salvation. But it seems quite apparent that if one cannot express to the Savior the natural desire for Him and His salvation, we must doubt if the work of the Holy Spirit is complete. God does not shut off the thinking processes of the child in the crucial issue of conviction and salvation. Rather, He would say now as He did long ago, "Come now, and let us reason together" (Isaiah 1:18).

## Don't tell the child he or she is saved — let the Word of God do it

Those who have been with a child who is genuinely exercised about salvation and have heard those beautiful childlike cries to the Lord for salvation know what a great temptation it is to say, "Wonderful, now you are saved!" Even if the child prays in your presence and intelligently and sincerely invites Jesus Christ to be his or her Savior, please don't lay the foundation of assurance of salvation in your words. Rather, turn the attention of the child right back to the passage of Scripture that you were using to point him to Christ, and let that speak to him and give him the first foundation for his assurance of salvation. You may have heard the expression "The blood secures: the Word assures." We may encourage and instruct as we lay the foundation for assurance. But let the Word of God tell the child he is saved.

## Don't think your job is over when a profession is made

In one sense, follow-up work is outside the scope of this discussion. But to do evangelistic work without efforts of follow-up borders on the unethical. Though all individuals who come to Christ need follow-up ministries, it is a particularly urgent matter with children. We should carefully and prayerfully develop ways to follow up and support those efforts with intercessory prayer as the apostle Paul and others did.

# Do's

At this point let us turn to the positive ingredients of leading children to Christ. You will note my attempt to avoid a mechanical prefabricated method.

## Do be available and accessible

Some adults have worked with children for years and have never had the privilege of dealing face-to-face with a child who has expressed an interest in becoming saved. Sunday school teachers who rush into class late, then gather up their books and dash away as soon as the closing bell rings, will rarely have such a privilege. Camp counselors who spend virtually all their time either hobnobbing with fellow counselors or fighting with energetic campers will rarely have such a privilege. In fact, one of the advantages in using visual aids in teaching children is that it gives a few minutes to naturally hang around after class to pick up the pieces and gather up the materials. This is available and accessible time for children to approach. We need to consciously cultivate our skills of availability.

It is a rare and desperate child who will approach adults who are rushing preoccupied through life. For the most part, it will take a good bit of courage for a child to approach an adult to ask for further discussion or help with their spiritual concerns. Genuine love and acceptance, relaxed and friendly contacts,

**Turn the attention of a child to
Scripture to point him to Christ.**

and patience and physical accessibility will result in opportunities to minister to children. Many of us need to discipline ourselves to take time to display the attitudes of availability.

## Do facilitate the conviction of the Spirit

In John 16:7–11 the unique work of the Holy Spirit is described. He will convict the unsaved of sin, righteousness, and judgment. Fortunately, Jesus described these three dimensions of conviction to us.

First, the Lord Jesus described the conviction of sin. Note Jesus did not say "sins." The Spirit has always convicted people of sins. The unique work of the Spirit now is to convict individuals specifically of the sin of unbelief, the ultimately condemning sin. As the Lord told Nicodemus, "whoever does not believe stands condemned already because he has not believed in the name of God's one and only Son" (John 3:18). In the light of the finished work of Christ, the cardinal sin is the sin of unbelief. We must make sure that our ministry of the gospel emphasizes the issue of unbelief and the command of the gospel that requires the obedience of faith in Christ.

Second, the Lord Jesus described the conviction of righteousness. Jesus did not say *un*righteousness. Again we must note that the work of the Holy Spirit through all history has been that of convicting men and women of unrighteousness. Our Lord taught His disciples – and us – that the unique work of the Spirit in this age is to convict the world of righteousness: "in regard to righteousness, because I am going to the Father, where you can see me no longer" (John 16:10). Only the righteousness of God qualifies one for the presence of God. The Lord Jesus inherently possessed that righteousness and thus was qualified to be received back to the throne in heaven. The Holy Spirit makes people aware that without the righteousness of Christ they will never follow Christ to heaven.

Scripture describes two kinds of righteousness. The first is a righteousness derived from obedience to the law (Philippians 3:9). Human righteousness, however experienced and developed, will never qualify us for heaven. The gospel message is a message that reveals God's righteousness (Romans 3:21–28) as a different *kind* of righteousness. This kind or quality of righteousness alone qualifies one for heaven. It is not generated by human effort but is received by faith when one receives Christ as Savior. In salvation Christ is made unto us righteousness (1 Corinthians 1:30). This righteousness is offered to all in the Person of Christ but is upon all those who believe (Romans 3:22). We need to make sure that our presentation of the gospel gives the Spirit the equipment to work with in bringing that conviction.

Third, the Lord Jesus described the conviction of judgment. Although many properly fear a judgment to come, the Lord Jesus taught that the unique work of conviction by the Spirit emphasized a judgment already passed: "The prince of this world now stands condemned" (John 16:11). The judgment of Satan and his host became a reality in the death and resurrection of Christ (Colossians 2:14–15). The idea that good and evil are struggling in the world and we are eagerly waiting to see which side wins is a false notion derived from pagan philosophy and religion. We already know who is victor. Christ has triumphed over the host of evil, and He is already the victorious one. We merely wait for the fulfillment and manifestation of that victory. Satan is already a condemned foe, and his cause is already lost.

It is futile to hold out against the claims of Christ, for the issue is already settled. Nothing is to be gained, but everything is to be lost by remaining in unbelief.

The gospel should be presented to children as well as all others in light of the necessary work of the Spirit in conviction. As spokesmen for God, we should desire that our efforts will enhance the work of the Spirit and in no way replace or preempt that necessary work. We have the glorious confidence that God will faithfully do His work, for He "wants all men to be saved and to come to a knowledge of the truth" (1 Timothy 2:4).

### Do draw out the child

We can develop skill in finding out what a child understands or misunderstands in regard to the gospel and ascertain his readiness to receive Christ. Rather than a series of leading questions, ask the child to explain the way of salvation. Pose a situation in which a friend asks how one can know how to get to heaven. Listen to the child's answer discerningly, for in such a response you will be able to detect what the child does or does not understand about salvation.

### Do correct incorrect or inadequate understanding

If you take time to listen to a child and draw him out, you will probably be amazed at the inadequate or incorrect elements of his concept of biblical truth. Remember, an important way to look at personal evangelism is to see it as a specialized form of one-on-one teaching. We can systematically explore areas of truth and understanding that are a part of the message. Of course, this requires us to be thoroughly grounded in the doctrines of salvation. And it should be noted that I am not implying that the child must become a theologian before he or she can trust Christ. But it is important to view personal evangelism as refined and specialized teaching of biblical truth.

### Do stress the urgency of salvation

This can be done without manipulation. We need to make children aware of the urgency of salvation. In fact, it is to believers that the apostle Paul says, "now is the day of salvation" (2 Corinthians 6:2). The specific personal response of faith in Christ is God's one condition for salvation. We must make this crystal clear to children and remind them that we do not have the promise of tomorrow.

### Do stick to the basic issues

We must learn the lesson that is so vividly conveyed by the Lord Jesus in His conversation with the woman of Samaria in John 4. He appropriately responded to her questions that potentially sidetracked His train of thought. But He was careful to press the essential issue of her personal need and His ability to provide for all of her needs in His saving grace. Though adults may sometimes intentionally sidetrack an evangelist to avoid pressure, children may also unwittingly divert an adult with all sorts of questions and issues that pop into their minds. It is our responsibility to be disciplined to keep the conversation on track.

### Do use the Bible

If at all possible, open the Bible, look at it, read from it, have the child read a portion, and in other obvious ways convey the fact that the message we present comes from the written Word of God. People can be saved through the spoken word, and God is pleased to bless the spoken word of testimony (Romans 10:17). But it is important for children to associate the message with written Scripture. Remember, the Bible will be around and available to them long after you or I have left. The fact that we use the Bible and establish this pattern in their minds may be important in their own attitudes toward Scripture and their faithfulness in reading and studying it. In the final analysis, we teach as much or more by example as we do by precept.

After all, it is His Word that God has promised to bless (Isaiah 55:10–11), not necessarily our illustrations, cleverness, or cute expressions.

### Do teach the need, concept, and urgency of faith

At this point I must emphasize the necessity of understanding the key terms *faith* and *believe*. Few Christians have actually made an adequate study of these essential terms. In

> *Our goal as evangelists is to see chldren come to the point in which they call upon the Lord Jesus.*

the New Testament these two words have the same root: one is a verb, one is a noun. In essence they have the same meaning and refer to that firm and welcome conviction about Christ, His person, and His Work that results in obedient response. We must help children understand the difference between mere mental assent to facts and true biblical faith and belief. This is one of the areas where the evangelist must be a diligent student of Bible doctrine. If you cannot explain to a child in accurate, valid biblical terms the meaning of *faith* or *believe*, you will find yourself very limited in effectiveness.

### Do encourage the child to communicate with the Lord Jesus

Saving faith has its object in the Person of Christ. He is a living Savior and knows the inaudible thoughts and cries of our hearts. The child needs to understand that salvation comes through Christ, not the evangelist. If a child wants to be saved he or she must deal with the Savior. We must get out of the way and make sure that Christ is the focal point of our message and our method. If Christ is properly presented in communicating the gospel, it will be natural for the child to commune with Him.

Although salvation is not through prayer but through faith in Christ, it is biblically clear that faith involves receiving Christ and establishing a personal relationship with Him. It may be important in cases where the child has not prayed audibly to ask the child to tell you if he or she talked with the Lord Jesus. Ask the child to tell you what he or she said to Him. Since Scripture teaches that "everyone who calls on the name of the Lord shall be saved" (Joel 2:32; Acts 2:21), our goal as evangelists is to see children come to the point in which they call upon the Lord Jesus.

### Do inquire about and review what the child did and said in receiving Christ

This is not a matter of unduly prying into a child's private life but rather expressing interest in the child and making sure the expression of faith was biblical. At this point some misunderstandings may need to be cleared up through careful, patient Bible teaching.

### Do follow up

The Great Commission given by the Lord Jesus to His disciples (Matthew 28:18–20) makes clear that our responsibility is not only that of evangelism or the making of disciples but also baptizing and teaching.

One of the most significant things for an evangelist to recognize is that his presence with the child who has just trusted Christ is in the most crucial "moment of readiness" for the first aspects of follow-up. It is urgent that we immediately get the child back into an examination of the Scripture passage that we used in pointing him to Christ. Let that Scripture become the foundation for his assurance of salvation. Let us use these moments strategically and wisely and set a pattern of looking into God's Word for instruction and encouragement.

Proper follow-up always involves an emphasis upon the child's reading and studying the Word of God. There is no substitute for this in the Christian life. This may be accomplished and enhanced in a number of ways. First, there are booklets for children who have just trusted Christ. These encourage and illustrate simple ways of Bible study and review the essential ingredients of a growing Christian life. In addition to the study of the Word of God, children also need to learn the importance of a regular and disciplined prayer life, witnessing to others about their faith, dealing with sin in a biblical way, choosing proper Christian friends, and seeking fellowship in a local church where the Word of God is taught.

Another specific suggestion for follow-up is the use of correspondence courses. Such materials as the children's correspondence courses produced by Emmaus Bible College are highly recommended. This is a particularly effective alternative if the adult will not have personal access to the child.

Your own personal contact will be one of the most effective ways to accomplish this important task. Children are keenly impressed by efforts of adults to visit them and take time to talk with them. This gives the adult an opportunity to talk with the child and assess his problems as well as his progress and make a more specific attempt to meet his needs.

Sometimes the one who leads the child to Christ does not have exposure to him on a long-term basis. In such cases it is often possible to get the child's address and make contact with a mature and knowledgeable Christian who lives in the same area. Ask that person to step in and provide some follow-up ministry. It is important to let the child know either through a conversation, a phone call, or a letter that you have asked an adult to do that. This will help pave the way for a more receptive response from both the child and his family. It may take some questioning and searching to find such an adult, but asking a fellow believer to follow up has good biblical precedent (Philippians 2:19–23).

In light of the unique needs of children, it is particularly important to be concerned about their choice of friends. First Corinthians 15:33–34 stresses our responsibility to make the right choice of those with whom we closely associate. One effective follow-up is to encourage the child to establish the right kind of personal friendships as well as church fellowship. In fact, if a child moves into teenage years without establishing good Christian friendships and loyalty to a local church, it is unlikely that he will make it through adolescence without some serious or tragic spiritual default.

The development of a believer's prayer life and his witness for Christ are also vital aspects of biblical living that should be considered in follow-up. Each of these areas could be the subject for an entire study, and there is no thought of minimizing the importance of prayer, witness, and service for Christ in this brief reference. These will not necessarily and automatically become a part of the life of a child who trusts Christ. Children must be cultivated and taught, and it becomes our responsibility to be diligent in fulfilling all aspects of our responsibility.

This chapter is taken from *How to Lead a Child to Christ* (Chicago: Moody, 1987).

## Further Reading

Alice Chapin. *Building Your Child's Faith.* Nashville: Nelson, n.d.

Phil Phillips and Syvelle Phillips. *Helping Your Children Walk with God.* Nashville: Nelson, 1992.

Donald E. Sloat, *The Dangers of Growing Up in a Christian Home.* Nashville: Nelson, 1986.

# Sooner or later

You know, it never entered my mind that I might not succeed in building a full-size blimp in the backyard, and Dad never flinched at the idea.

"Just be sure to get the grass cut, and don't leave nails and boards lying around," he said, and he went back to painting the porch.

I had plenty of nails and boards. The previous summer's twenty-foot model of the *Titanic* hadn't quite gotten past the keel-laying stage, so behind the garage there was a sizable pile of two-by-twos bristling with nails. My brothers and I pulled out all the nails, pounded them straight on the patio, and put them to work holding the two-by-twos together again, only in a different shape.

### Blockbuster

What a feeling, driving in that first nail! It was the same feeling I had when we started building a mad scientist's lab in the basement – complete with a monster on a slab – so we could make a blockbuster movie with Dad's old Standard 7 spring-wound movie camera.

Or when we started making hot air balloons out of laundry bags and raining them down on the neighborhood . . .

Or when we bought two old lawn mowers at the Goodwill so we could use the engines to power the two airplanes we were building in the garage out of the two-by-twos that would soon become the keel for the *Titanic* . . .

Or when I built that robot – Well, actually the secret lab where I was going to build the robot . . .

Or when we made an eight-foot giant to wear on our shoulders so we could stalk the neighborhood and scare everybody (we made it out of the two-by-twos because it was more fun than the blimp) . . .

Or when we dug up the alley because we were going to build a World's Fair . . .

Dad never flinched. He never said, "It's a dumb idea" or "It'll never work" or "Remember the last project?"

No, he just let us use his tools and the same old nails and, as long as we put the tools back and didn't kill ourselves, he just watched.

### Unseen

Our old Tower portable typewriter really did belong to Mom even though I kept it in my room and used it more than she ever got the chance to, hunting-and-pecking out reams of stories, poems, and essays suitable for sticking on the refrigerator but which no one ever saw.

I hid most of my stuff. Too self-conscious, I guess. Whenever Mom got her paws on something I'd written, it would end up in the hands of friends and relatives. They'd all be reading it and praising it, and I'd be embarrassed.

But sometimes – not often, just sometimes – I'd purposely leave something on the dining room table so she'd see it. Maybe sometimes – not often, just sometimes – I liked being embarrassed.

And Mom never said a word about the typewriter.

I was going to be the future Walt Disney and learn to draw cartoons and make great movies. My folks bought me a huge drawing pad, two charcoal pencils, a book on how to draw heads, and a big gum art eraser.

I liked being a ham and making people laugh. My folks bought me a Jonathan Winters album, and I wore it out. Then I wore *them* out: "Hiya, honey. I'm Maude Frickert!"

I was going to be a great singer – I was a pretty good soprano anyway! Mom played the piano, and we all sang.

## Glue

I could make anything out of empty cereal boxes: a toy jetliner, a huge mansion for my rubber animals to live in, even a scale model of the 1962 Seattle World's Fair. Mom kept me well stocked with Wheaties and Cheerios boxes and Elmer's Glue,® and when I think of all the glue she had to wash out of my jeans . . .

You know, it has recently occurred to me:

My older brother is a missionary in a land hostile to the gospel. He's gotten one church well established, and now he's getting ready to plant another one.

My younger brother used to feel sorry for everything, even rocks he'd kick on the way home from school. He coupled that compassion with years of hard work, and now he's a licensed family counselor.

My sister used to dream about being an actress, a singer, and a poet. For a while, she was a teacher who acted, sang, and wrote poetry, but now she's pursuing a ministry in theater arts. She says it's something she's just got to try.

I finally got my own typewriter, kept banging away, and saw my first novel published when I was thirty-six.

## OK to dream

I think the four of us kids just assumed all along that it's OK to dream, to aspire, to try and fail, but then to try again. We don't whine much. We don't hear little phrases in our heads such as "That's a dumb idea," "It can't work," or "Remember that last project?"

No, we just keep building our blimps and airplanes and *Titanics,* pulling the nails out of the last dream's two-by-twos and building the next one. We were bound to succeed sooner or later.

Mom and Dad always knew that.

**Frank Peretti**

# Male and Female Differences in Children

## *Jim Brawner*

Children not only come in combinations of four general personality types (which all act differently at various stages), they also come in one of two genders.

It took coaching junior high track for me to realize just how opposite the opposite sexes are. For instance, I found that both sexes like to see the other gender in tank tops and shorts. But that's where the similarities end. Guys are there to show off for the girls and conquer. Girls are there to show off for the guys and relate to other girls.

You'll notice this most visibly during a high school football game. Upon a touchdown or other significant event, the guys will give each other "high five" and "low five" slaps, but generally remain pretty cool. Oh, they can show emotion too, but they generally save it for when they win the conference game or some other paramount event. They don't want to look foolish by celebrating every little score or tackle too much.

In contrast, the girls in the stands, those in the marching band, and especially the cheerleaders on the sidelines hug and scream at every turn of events. They chatter away about the assured victory. Only when the game's over and they are forced to go home do they stop their characteristic way of relating to their chums.

Thus we see a world of difference in the way the sexes relate. I mean, when was the last time you saw Lee Iacocca stand up at the end of labor negotiations and hug the other guy to celebrate finalizing the contract? Some of these differences are culturally learned, but many are innate.

## The image of God

No gender is more godly than another. That may seem self-evident, but stop and think about how different segments of our society treat the opposite sex, and you'll see my point. Radical feminists seem bent on destroying many of the traditional female traits. On the other hand, males seem bent on putting down females by implying that the male half of the population is more worthy than the other.

What does the Bible mean when it says that God "created man in his own image . . . ; male and female he created them" (Genesis 1:27)? One author writes that "God's character and personality are so wonderfully complex that He had to make two very different sexes to contain it all."[1]

In the Old Testament God is referred to in both male and female terms. He is spoken of as "Father" but also has the interesting title "El Shaddai," which, according to many scholars, literally means "the breast, the one who gives nourishment."

In Christ — who was fully God — we see a rough and tough person who clears out the Temple with tables flying and moneychangers running for cover, yet washes His disciples' feet. He calls the Pharisees "sons of vipers," yet weeps at the tomb of His friend Lazarus.

Although God's image is reflected by both males and females, most humans are born one

> *We see a world of difference in the way the sexes relate.*

or the other (unless you're the type featured in grocery store tabloids, akin to "Hamster Boy Born to Valley Girl"). Seriously, though, we must understand our little boys and girls to better relate to them.

## Any parent knows

As any parent of both gender children knows, girls are talkers, squealers, and screamers, and boys like to run, jump, and throw balls through windows. My brother Jerry, father of three girls and no boys, says, "Having grown up with two brothers and only one sister, it was a real shock to find my three daughters screaming at the drop of a hat. It drove me crazy for a while, but now I'm accustomed to it."

Also, girls tend to emphasize relationships, whereas boys emphasize action and power in their play. One girl who babysits a lot said, "Boys and girls may both play with cars, but the boys are content to make "vroom" noises, while the girls pretend that they are each driving a car, discussing where they'll go and who they'll visit." How true.

And one father who has both boys and girls marvels, "You know, I never had to teach my two sons how to make all those good boy noises − bang! vroom! aaugh! − they just started making them one day."

## Nature vs. Nurture

Back when June and Ward Cleaver were raising the Beaver, society provided clear sex role distinctions: dad brought home the bacon and mom fried it. Women wore dresses; men "wore the pants in the family." Real men were strong and rugged, whereas women were the

### *About the author*

*Jim Brawner, M.Ed., a U.S. national swimming official, is director of Kanakuk Kamp, a Christian sports camp in the Ozarks of Missouri. He is the author of* Connections: Using Personality Types to Draw Parents & Kids Closer (Moody) *and the father of three children.*

soft "weaker sex." Boys were made of snakes, snails, and puppy-dog tails, whereas girls were a blend of sugar, spice, and everything nice.

But all these artificial distinctions began to crumble when "Rosie the Riveter" went to work in factories to support the men who had left to fight in World War II. After the peace treaty was signed, many women continued in the work force.

At this same time the modern women's movement began pushing for equality − not only in the workplace, but in our culture as a whole. The more radical women of the movement declared that the sexes were "identical

> *No gender is more godly than another.*

> *Biologists are discovering that there is an inborn difference between males and females.*

from the neck up" and anyone who disagreed was a male chauvinist pig who wanted to keep women in submission by continuing the culture's "sexual stereotypes."

If parents have both a boy and a girl, they soon realize that there are bigger differences than just what color blanket they came home in. But what are biological and what are culturally learned differences?

Biologists and other scientists are discovering that there is an inborn difference between males and females — from the neck up, as well as down. And, although comprehensive research has not been completed in the entire field, some preliminary results are worthy of note.

### Physical differences

There are significant distinctions between males and females in addition to the material made clear by the charts in sex education classes. The following differences are observed in more than three-fourths of the adult men and women examined.[2]

An adult man pumps about 88 percent more blood through his veins than the average woman. In addition, drop for drop, females have about 20 percent less red blood cells than do males. This means that men have a greater capacity for oxygen, and thus energy and endurance.

Mens' bodies tend to be 40 percent muscle and 15 percent fat; womens' tend to be 20 percent muscle and 20 percent fat. Add to this the fact that men's bones tend to be heavier and larger than women's. Most men can out-lift, out-throw, and out-run most women.

But despite the apparent physical edge, a woman will outlive the average man by eight years. Women also age more slowly — even without Oil of Olay! Men age approximately 10 percent every year after forty years of age. Women age five times slower at a consistent 2 percent each year after child-bearing years. The brains of men deteriorate more rapidly than those of women.

Although chromosomes determine the sex of a baby at the split second of conception, at twelve weeks of gestation a male and female fetus look identical. At that point a male baby will begin producing androgen, which causes an amazing metamorphosis to a distinctive male body.

The higher level of androgen also tends to make boys more active. A study at Johns Hopkins revealed, however, that girls who were labeled "tomboys" had higher levels of androgen than other girls. Further proof came from UCLA, where researchers discovered that women who took male hormones to prevent miscarriage gave birth to girls who thought and fought like boys.

At the sixteenth week of a male's fetal development an even more amazing transformation takes place. At this time many of the nerve connections between the two hemispheres (sides) of the brain begin to dissolve, due to a surge of androgen. Because of this about 80 percent of males can use only one side of their brains at one time. Most females, however, can retrieve and store information on both sides simultaneously.

Research on stroke victims has revealed that mens' and womens' brains are physically different too. Because men cannot process data in both sides of their brains, a stroke tends to be more debilitating to a man than to a woman. Put in computer talk, in a stroke a disk sector of his brain has been damaged and he has no backup. The data is forever erased.

### Mental differences: it's in the hormones

As I pointed out above, there's quite a struggle going on in our society regarding sex roles. With some exceptions it is typically conservatives doing battle with more liberal scientists (both social scientists and hard science experts). But in recent years secular researchers – people with no axe to grind from a Christian viewpoint (often termed "religious bias") – have been finding solid evidence about male/female differences. And, although the body of research is still developing, there are some things we do know.

For example, child psychologists at the Gesell Institute for Child Development in New Haven, Connecticut, studied at length the behavior of identical boy and girl twins.[3] They videotaped their play and tried to filter out all the cultural factors that could possibly influence behavior. Although they could not totally rule out learned behavior, they found that boys would typically resolve their conflicts with playmates by pushing, shoving, or yelling, whereas girls would want to talk it out.

Among other possible explanations, they believe this reflects differing physical maturation patterns between boys and girls. Such patterns put girls ahead of boys in terms of language skills; boys are more motor-skills oriented at that stage. We'll see below that even when boys grow up to be men, and girls women, that this difference is still evident, though to a lesser degree. And that fact is evident to any observer, regardless of the observer's "religious bias."

A study described in *Scientific American* told of research done to track the effect that varying estrogen (the predominant female hormone) levels have on female performance abilities.[4] They were investigating whether the different hormonal mix that males and females undeniably carry could be the basis for gender differences.

The researchers found that when the women's estrogen level was at its highest (such as during ovulation during the monthly cycle), they performed significantly higher on verbal tests than during the rest of the month. Additionally, they performed most poorly on the spatial tests (tests where men usually

> *Don't fall into the trap of stereotyping your children by whether they came home from the hospital in blue or pink.*

excel) when the estrogen levels were high.

The significance of their findings? Put simply, when the maximum female factors are present (i.e., high estrogen levels), females perform better on the classically female-dominant tasks (verbal and fine motor skills). Conversely, when estrogen levels are lower, females' test scores on traditionally male-dominated skills (i.e., spatial tasks) are higher, more in the range of male test scores. So under maximum female conditions, females test out as more strongly female, and under minimum female conditions, they test out as more strongly male.

The researchers noted above have done further work that examines body mass among men and women, especially looking at differences between right-side and left-side formation and structure. Have you ever noticed that your right foot is bigger than your left, or vice versa? Well, they have found that most people have asymmetrical body mass – that is, the right side is larger than the left (or vice versa). And, terming their findings "amazing," they found that men tend to have larger and more developed right sides, and women left sides.

The scientists hypothesize, with some degree of certainty, that this gender difference may be linked with brain hemisphere dominance – that is, that men have larger right-side bodies because of their left hemisphere dominance (remember that the brain hemispheres control the opposite side of the body). And women, being right-hemisphere dominant, would have a corresponding left-side body development. Of course, the differences in mass are very small, but in the early stages of the research, the differences are statistically significant nonetheless.

Thus it seems there definitely is something inherently different about girls and boys. These results and more indicate that there is solid evidence available from a hard science viewpoint. They support the scriptural principle "male and female he created them" (Genesis 1:27). Research will probably continue for many more years on this, but there have been solid, statistically valid studies done on certain aspects of the male/female puzzle, and it's certainly legitimate to examine them.

# Boys and girls at camp

One scene that highlights boy/girl differences is when we have the camp session for seven- to thirteen-year-olds. Our camp is laid out so that the girls are on one side of our property and the boys are on the other. Only on special occasions do we bring them together.

On those nights we get together in an open-air roofed facility — actually, it's a basketball court by day — and have line dances, square dances, and the like — all under controlled conditions. But what I notice is how the preteen boys and girls approach the social function in very different ways.

The boys by and large either run off to the pool to swim, or they sit on the low wall surrounding the floor. The girls are so crazy about square dancing that they'll dance with each other if there are no boys willing. Thus we see the female predisposition with social activities, and the boys liking physical activity such as swimming. (Of course some fear of girls is mixed in on the part of the boys, but I believe the preferences are still exemplary of their distinct orientations.)

Another point of contact between the boys' camp and the girls' is what we call "goodie mail." It's a sort of inter-camp mail system where different campers can write friendship notes to each other. And of course that is a high point of the girls' day. But on the boys' side it is less ecstatic. In fact, the boy who receives a typically long and mushy note from a girl camper will receive his share of kidding.

The differences in how they communicate via this special mail system are interesting. The girls will write miniature novels, with poetry and the whole shebang.

The boys, in contrast, will just scribble a crude-looking note on a scrap of paper. Or they will go another route in communicating, such as sending a messenger instead of writing.

When boys and girls get a bit older and start to think about dating, things change a bit. Girls in the early years of adolescence are more prone to having crushes on boys, and they openly share their feelings, especially with their girlfriends. Some boys may have crushes, but they aren't as free about revealing their feelings.

I have found that at about age fifteen boys start openly courting girls, with victory clearly in their sights. They want to impress girls, and they go for it, with a date as the prize. Girls, on the other hand, tend to daydream about the ideal relationship with the ideal boy and are more covert in their style than the boys.

When parents have a girl of this age, they should approach discussions of relationships with boys from a feelings orientation, yet keep in mind that much idealization is going on. Help her see that she has to deal in fact and not feelings, as well as be realistic. Just because Tom smiled at her today in the hall as she walked past doesn't mean he is dreaming about her all day long.

# "You hurt my feelings"

I have also noticed a difference in how boys and girls (and even men and women) handle hurts and other interpersonal conflicts. Boys tend to blow up quickly when angry, then cool down quickly, much like a summertime cloudburst. Girls, on the other hand, tend to remember for a long time how someone wronged them or hurt them. They can remember every word, every bit of body language at the time of the infraction, every bit of the social setting in which it happened. Their remembrance pattern more closely resembles a long, sustained winter drizzle. Since relationships are important to girls — and since their brains are wired differently from boys — they tend to have the memory of an elephant when it comes to hurts.

We need to keep that in mind when we want to communicate with them after they've been hurt by us. The Bible's advice not to "let the sun go down while you are still angry" (Ephesians 4:26) is all the more important.

## Better or worse

Perhaps nowhere else do we see the highly charged political atmosphere (as one researcher called it) come to the fore than in the male/female realm. In other words, some folks get highly upset whenever male/female differences are discussed. I think that is usually due to misunderstanding regarding what is meant by "different" — they think that this term necessarily implies that one gender is better than the other.

But that is not my meaning. In the beginning, God created us as different genders on purpose, with oneness in a marriage relationship as one of His primary purposes in bestowing such diversity (Genesis 2:18, 24). During our youth (and here's the significance for parents), we need to be nurtured in male- and female-appropriate ways so that we can grow up to be the types of male or female God intends for us to become.

But in a sense, we're incomplete without opposite-sex relationships. We're one part of a puzzle looking for that complementary other puzzle piece, which is usually found in a marriage partner. So even though we're very different from the opposite gender, that

# And a child shall lead them

Years of traveling with three children, homemaking, writing, recording, and everything those roles demand had left me depleted. It had become difficult to take the children with us on the road because of school, yet they seemed to need our family together more than ever.

When we were gone, much of the responsibility for keeping things on an even emotional keel fell to our eldest, Suzanne, then fourteen. It was time to leave once again, and I went as usual to each of the children's rooms to tell them good night.

**Failure**
Suzanne was last, and as I began to pray with her, I was overwhelmed with the sense of failure I felt as a singer, the pull of my heart to stay with the children, the incredible fatigue from rarely getting anything finished, the deep desire to write and go back to school, the frustration of not feeling "good enough" at anything. The dam of restraint broke and the tears came in torrents. "I can't go –" was all I could manage.

I felt the small, strong hands of my daughter lifting my face to hers. "You must," she said softly. "If you don't go, who will say to the people what God has given you to say? Don't worry about us. We're going to be just fine. Amy and Benjy and I – we're called to let you go. And you must go."

And so it was that at one of the crossroads of my life, a time of discouragement and defeat, my daughter became my big sister in the kingdom.

**Gloria Gaither**

This reflection appeared in the May 1987 issue of *Fundamentalist Journal*.

difference is OK because it's part of the Creator's master plan. It is beautiful to see how in a marriage relationship — or in a family setting — the strengths and weaknesses of each sex can complement each other.

# Pink and blue blankets

See why God created two genders — and why we need each other? Don't fall into the trap of stereotyping your children by whether they came home from the hospital in blue or pink. There are few "blanket" statements that we can make about gender differences.

Remember that a full one-fifth of males do not have predominantly one-side-of-the-brain thinking. Many girls are as aggressive as the stereotypical boy. And much of what constitutes male and female behavior and roles is largely a product of our unique cultural setting.

So don't cage in your children. There are general principles that fit most children, but remember you're raising unique, one-of-a-kind kids who carry in their souls a portion of the image of God. And that diversity was intended from the beginning.

This chapter is taken from *Connections: Using Personality Types to Draw Parents & Kids Closer* (Chicago: Moody, 1991).

1. James Watkins, *Sex is Not a Four-Letter Word* (Wheaton: Tyndale, 1991), 182.
2. Norman Geschwind, "Proceedings of the National Academy of Sciences," *USA '79*, 1982, 5097–100.
3. Janice T. Gibson, "Are Boys and Girls Really So Different?" *Parents* (September 1990): 157.
4. "Profile: Viva la Difference — Doreen Kimura Plumbs Male and Female Brains," *Scientific American* (October 1990): 42.

## Further Reading

Jim Brawner. *Connections: Using Personality Types to Draw Parents & Kids Closer.* Chicago: Moody, 1991.

# The Joys and Struggles of Adoption

*Christine Wyrtzen*

Orange and yellow clowns decorate the walls. The smell of fresh paint lingers. A white, satiny finish on the wood trim glistens with hope and promise. Everything is in order. The changing table seems on alert, and the appropriate powders and lotions have been put on standby. A yellow gingham diaper bag hangs decoratively on the wall, containing only the best diapers. No generic brands in this room.

The dresser drawers are in perfect order. Scented drawer liners, cut to exact size, line the bottoms. Piled on top are an array of items fit for a little king or queen: undershirts, drawstring nightgowns, terry stretch suits, bonnets, and pinafores exude the aroma of Ivory Snow® and lie impeccably folded. Triple-matted, cross-stitched samplers bear the sentiment of blissful parenthood.

Yet something is missing. The absence is stark. The door is open just enough to reveal a woman face down on the floor, groaning in disappointment and despair. The helpless ache for a baby can be heard in each sob.

This is the story of adoptive parents. I know, for I was the woman on the floor. Ron and I represent one of three couples, according to statistics, who will face infertility. Nothing has challenged our faith more than the grief of wanting children. And nothing has brought us more joy than the process of adoption.

### About the author

*Christine Wyrtzen is a recording artist, author, and broadcaster. She is coauthor of* Lessons on Love from Critter County *(Standard).*

*One of three couples will face infertility.*

# The inability to conceive

The inability to conceive is a terrible blow to most women. I quickly learned the sense of loss that overcomes a woman who desperately wants and needs to be a mother but cannot conceive. My desire to be a mother had been a passion since childhood. When I was ten, our family took care of a baby for several weeks. She was the neglected product of an underprivileged home. Penny became a member of our family. She was a highlight of my childhood. Like most little girls, I often visited a fantasy world where my dolls became real. With Penny, I was a "real" mommy.

Ron and I mourned our loss, our inability to conceive, for a time, but we reached a point where we decided that it made little difference whether we had biological children or were blessed through adoption. In that we may have been atypical, but we had lots of love to give and were ready to make a life-long commitment to any child God would give to us to raise.

# Frustrations

We proceeded head-long into the adoption process and were soon confronted by a new set of frustrations. Some agencies predicted a five-year wait. One, however, assured that we would be parents within a year. Once we were screened, our home study completed, and the required paperwork completed, I decided that a one-year wait would be similar to being pregnant. That was the point at which we created the special room described above. Each time we walked by the freshly decorated room, we enjoyed a wonderful sense of anticipation. We were certain that any day the phone would ring and we would hear the news of the birth of our first child.

The days turned into months – then years. Three Christmases passed without a child to bring holiday cheer – four years in all. How painless to see that in print now, but quite another thing to have endured it for seven childless years.

After grieving on the nursery floor, I quit subjecting myself to the sight of the room. The fresh paint gave way to discoloration and the freshly washed clothes turned musty. We turned the heat off and left the door closed for months at a time. It's mocking emptiness was simply too painful to acknowledge.

If you have chosen to pursue adopting and are enmeshed in the difficult waiting period, it may help you to know that, while painful, it is part of the process. Each adoptive couple I know shares some version of the same story – that of unbearable waiting.

# Fulfillment

Late one day in June 1979 we were contacted by a pastor who told us of an unmarried girl in his church who was due to deliver soon. Were we interested in pursuing that option? We responded with a resounding "Yes!" and contacted a lawyer who handled the delicate details.

We were eating supper one night when we were called and informed that the birth mother was in labor. We paced like cats, beside ourselves for the rest of the evening. Just before midnight we learned we were the parents of a nine-pound, healthy baby girl. The door to the nursery was swung wide open, and the baby clothes washed once again. Three days later we were handed our little girl while standing under an old oak tree near our lawyer's office. It was as though the branches above us applauded as they swayed in the summer breeze. Ron and I had waited years to experience this moment, which was now beyond description. My empty arms were full. We named our daughter Jaime Susannah.

# Adopting again

As months of fulfillment passed, we began thinking about adopting again. We put in our names at several agencies. Waiting was easier this time since we were reveling in the joy of parenthood with our beautiful daughter. Three years later an agency informed us that our son had been born. Ryan Dean Wyrtzen came home three days later.

Ron and I have found that parenting has been highly underestimated. The joy of investing and giving unselfishly brings incredible reward. Yet I would not be honest if I did not admit that adoption brings its own set of challenges.

# Why suffering?

Questions regarding God's sovereignty and human suffering come to play in the years of waiting. Infertile couples watch as their friends and acquaintances plan their families and have children according to their own schedules. To complicate it further, these hurting, childless adults watch teenage pregnancy rates escalate out of control and ache with the knowledge that precious children they would give anything to nurture and love are being aborted by the thousands. Studies have shown that for every baby aborted, there is a couple waiting to adopt.

Infertile couples often ask, "Why does everyone have a baby but us? Can God not trust us to be good parents? When this world desperately needs families who will try to raise servants of God, why are we childless?" The suffering, childless couple feels worthless.

We endured that additional pain. Our answers are not pat ones, designed to send you away assuaged. Your ache will still be there and needs to be continually acknowledged. However, it is true that God allows the broken places in our lives and uses them to give Himself a platform where He can develop intimacy with us. Pain provides God a powerful stage from which He can speak to yearning hearts.

The ache of barrenness brings greater joy when a couple finally walks through the door

> *The initial shaping of the child's emotional make-up takes place in the womb.*

of parenthood. Each day becomes a priceless gift with the child. It is only human nature that what once has eluded us then becomes an even more precious possession.

Scripture tells us that children are a "gift from God," and nothing underscores this fact more strongly than adoption. It might seem easier to claim ownership and rights to a child conceived naturally. He is your flesh. But when each of our children was placed in our arms, though we were totally unrelated to their physical development, we were vividly reminded that they were a gift, an ongoing loan from God.

# Feelings of rejection

A second major struggle related to adoption involves the self-worth deficiencies most adopted children bring with them. Within even the most loving and nurturing of homes, the adopted child will often experience nagging rejection conflicts. No amount of unconditional love from the adoptive parents can erase the feelings and questions the child harbors from the womb. This issue is left out of most preadoption counseling and needs to be addressed. It is critical that adoptive parents be made aware that the initial shaping of the child's emotional make-up takes place in the womb. This understanding prevents adoptive parents from assuming too much responsibility for the painful emotional symptoms that eventually surface.

We have just emerged from a painful stage with Jaime. She is twelve at the time of this writing. For the first nine years of her life, she suffered unexplainable fears. She came to us with an uncontrollable fear of men. No amount of talking, praying, and nurturing from safe men in her life could heal the anxiety. The men she trusted most were her daddy and grandfathers, but attempts to leave her with other trustworthy men brought hysteria. This fear became obvious when she was only a couple of months old.

She has also suffered from "separation anxiety," an overreaction to being separated from me. Leaving her in the nursery at church was always traumatic. Starting school was equally hard, though Ron's sister, whom she loved, was her teacher. Though my concert schedule takes me away from home only two weekends a month, the good-byes were extremely difficult. Once I was gone, however, she adjusted well.

Preadolescence naturally saw these fears resurface, and we were motivated to find the origins. Time with a biblical, Christian counselor proved life-changing for Jaime. The choices her birth parents had made were discussed. Her feelings of rejection by her birth mother were gently exposed, and she has been able to deal with those. She was encouraged to keep a journal, communicating any anger and her questions.

Ron and I were encouraged to take the blame off ourselves. We had gone through the endless hypotheticals: If only we had prayed more, learned more, handled her differently, and so on. It was a rocky eighteen months, but Jaime emerged beautifully. Today she is open about her struggles and equally communicative about how God's grace has healed most of the brokenness.

# Prebirth legacies

A third major struggle is also one not discussed enough outside the counseling office. Each of us, adopted or not, carries generational "bents" that can be either godly or evil. Prayerfully removing those that are ungodly is critical. In adopted children in particular, it is imperative that these legacies be broken to allow the child the freedom to grow in Christ. Otherwise, he or she will be drawn toward the handicaps of ancestors and have to constantly work against harmful, driving forces they do not understand.

We believe that Jaime's fear of men, for instance, was due to prebirth legacies. It was only when prayer was offered to break these generational ties that Jaime started to experience freedom. The following guidelines explain the process:

*(1) Orally acknowledge the power of Christ's blood to defeat any generational lines of evil.*

*(2) Command the following to be permanently broken:*

*Ungodly blood lines and ties*

*Ungodly inheritances and legacies*

*Curses and ungodly blessings*

*(3) Bring the above to the Father and ask Him to declare them null and void and of no further binding effect in the physical or spiritual worlds.*

*(4) Ask the Father to seal these areas so the person will no longer be vulnerable.*

*(5) Ask God to sever Satan's power to carry out, through his evil forces, all assignments and commissions related to these generational items.*

Ron and I continually ask God to help us discern what issues are generational with our children and what are simply choices they are making out of their free wills and natural bents toward sin. When we agree that symptoms reveal something ancestral, we review the above steps.

I trust this is a message of hope and encouragement. Though I have been vulnerable about our three greatest struggles, the pleasures of raising Jaime and Ryan have far outweighed any concerns. Adopted children have unparalleled capacities to understand the spiritual application of being "adopted sons of God" far earlier than most children. Their point of brokenness is the very door that allows God to meet them at a very tender age.

Orange and yellow clowns have now given

# Almost never knew you

Good night, Sweetheart. I love you.
Oh, I can't believe how fast you're
growing up. It was so much fun to see
the look on your face when you got
what you wanted for your birthday today!
I know what it's like to get what you
always wanted. I waited so long for you.
I felt helpless because someone else had
to give you life before I could have you.
I can't imagine what my life would be like
without you. I'll never forget the day
you came home to me. Oh! What a special
day that was!
It wasn't long ago you were placed within my
arms.
Time stood still before you came.
Little did I know that though I never carried you
I could be your mother just the same.
Now I see growing within your eyes
A depth that goes beyond a baby's cry.
You've brought so much to my life.

I almost never knew you. I almost never loved
you.
I almost never heard you call my name.
I would've missed the joy and laughter
And all the love thereafter,
Cause you filled my empty arms when you
came.

She must have known what you had to give
When she chose to let you live.
Cause you've brought me such delight
That only comes when two hearts unite.

I almost never knew you, almost never loved
you.
I almost never heard you call my name.
I would've missed the joy and laughter,
And all the love thereafter,
Cause you filled my empty arms when you
came.
Yes, you filled my empty arms when you came.

way to soccer tournaments and drama workshops. But the joy of their births still rings and reverberates throughout our home. Our empty arms have been filled with hugs of love. We are grateful for the two young mothers, our heroines, who decided to give our children the gift of life. In honor of them, I share the lyrics to a song I wrote for our children, a celebration of their lives and the choices of two courageous young women.

## Further Reading

Vicky Love. *Childless Is Not Less*. Minneapolis: Bethany House, 1984.

Kay Marshall Strom and Douglas R. Donnelly. *The Complete Adoption Handbook*. Grand Rapids: Zondervan, 1992.

Martha Stout. *Without Child: A Compassionate Look at Infertility*. Wheaton: Shaw, 1990.

# What? Call a Shrink?

*Grace Ketterman*

Sharon's dark eyes glistened. Her mouth drooped. Her shoulders slumped, and her unkempt appearance summarized how she felt about herself and her life. Concerned friends had asked me to evaluate her. The tears, the posture, the sad expression, her quiet voice, and slow speech told me Sharon was suffering emotional pain. Sharon herself said life was not worth living. She even had a suicide plan.

I urged Sharon's parents to seek counseling, carefully listing the signs of her serious depression. To my amazement, her father exploded into rage. He railed at me and threatened to sue me (I've not yet understood for what). He denied the severity of Sharon's problems and refused to provide the help she so sorely needed. Fortunately, others rallied to her, and she made it through that crisis.

On the other hand are those parents who seek psychiatric consultation when their children become involved in something so common as excessive sibling rivalry. Between these extremes, there is a broad spectrum of children's needs and parents' responses. Most parents genuinely want what is in the best interests of their children. They just don't know if a given period of distress is a minor crisis, a stage of development, or a major psychological problem for which they need professional help. If you have wondered the same, here are the signs that may tell when you and your child need professional help.

### About the author

*Grace Ketterman*, M.D., is the medical director of prevention programs at Crittenton in Kansas City, Missouri. She is the author of Depression Hits Every Family *and* Mothering: A Complete Guide for Mothers of All Ages *(Oliver-Nelson), as well as* Understanding Your Child's Problems *(Revell)*.

# Symptoms of a major psychological problem

**(1) Your child's behavior is strange and very different from other children his age**

There are several diagnostic categories in which this is the case. Autism and schizophrenia are the best-known entities. Afflicted children consistently and noticeably live in a world of their own. More intense and persistent by far than the daydreamers or imaginative children, these youngsters perceive life very differently from most. They see strange things and hear voices no one else can verify. They may withdraw in the silence and isolation of their strange experiences. Autistic children react to life's frustrations with rage. They have great difficulty learning speech, and social skills are missing.

These children can be greatly helped by structure, medication, and guidance. They may well need periods in treatment centers to establish the exact program each needs. Be sure you find a physician and counselor you trust and then work faithfully with them. Even children with such severe disorders can learn to live productive, useful lives when they have ongoing professional supervision.

**(2) Your child is severely depressed over a long period**

Most serious depression is seen in early adolescence and beyond. We are, however, seeing more depression and even suicide in younger children. There are several signs of serious depression.

*A change in emotion or mood.* Most children become moody occasionally — some more than others. They pout and whine or yell and bang about for an hour or an evening, but soon they forget all about the problem and are happy again. The depressed youth does not recover so quickly. His sullen or melancholic mood persists over days. If your child's moodiness lasts more than a week, you may need professional help.

*Changes in eating and sleeping habits.* Once again, such changes are common in perfectly healthy young people. Growth lags and spurts, physical activities, and various illnesses account for such normal variations. In the depressed child, the changes are more pronounced and prolonged. Depression can cause either overeating or loss of appetite. Similarly, it may result in excessive sleep or the inability to sleep. Most authorities agree that parents need not be alarmed unless such changes last at least two weeks and are accompanied by other symptoms.

*Changes in social habits.* Depressed youngsters may not feel able to focus on good appearance. They do not pay attention to hygiene or proper attire. They often choose dull colors and commonly wear black or dark brown. They refuse to attend social events and prefer to mope alone. Some young people confuse parents by becoming silly or clownish. They are trying to avoid the inner world of despair through external giddiness. Interestingly, this group typically has "accidents," and minor injuries during their show-off periods.

*Changes in academic or job performance.* Children who are seriously depressed have difficulty concentrating and remembering. Schoolwork and grades inevitably suffer. One young woman worked part time in a bank. During a bout of severe depression, she made many mistakes in figures. Since peoples' money is so important, she finally lost her job — not due to a lack of ability, but due to her problem of concentrating. Her depression needed help.

In some depressed young people, there is a heroic effort to compensate for failure in school. They study extremely hard and may even temporarily improve in their academic achievement. When such extreme efforts fail to make them feel better, however, they may become even more depressed.

*Precious treasures are given away.* When depression becomes extreme, young people often plan to commit suicide. In preparation for this, they give away cherished belongings. Music albums, jewelry, books, or almost any sentimental item may be given to friends for no apparent reason. Friends need to understand that such gestures are often a serious sign of impending self-destruction. They need to be instructed about seeking help for a friend who may give some treasures to them. Be sure your children can always talk with you about such concerns.

*They write notes alluding to death.* Young people considering suicide, or depressed enough to wish to die, often leave notes about. They may describe their wishes or plans. Often they read poetry or listen to music (so plentiful in today's world) that glorifies death or suicide.

*Alcohol and drug abuse.* As chemicals usually temporarily make their users feel better, seriously depressed young people are likely to abuse them. Friends or amateur dealers introduce them to a substance that initially improves their mood. The discovery of such an "easy" road to relief from despair may quickly enslave a vulnerable youth.

*There is a pervasive inability to experience pleasure.* The seriously depressed youth does not feel like laughing. The silly jokes, so common among youngsters, do not seem funny. In short, they do not find wholesome pleasure or enjoyment in anything, nor do they expect to ever enjoy life. They frankly see no tomorrow and have no plans.

*Spiritual health suffers.* In their despair, youth who are seriously depressed find that their faith falters. They wonder where God is and how He can allow such pain. They suffer serious doubts and often stop their personal devotions.

According to my experience and that of other child experts, these signs and symptoms are the major indicators of truly serious depression. If your child evidences four or five

> *If you are in doubt about your child's emotional health, seek consultation.*

of these, he or she is likely suffering from major depression and needs psychiatric help.

If it were my child and she evidenced even one or two of these signs over a period of two weeks, I would seek an evaluation. Though I am trained to help others, I would not try to assess the problems of my own children. A parent's emotions can so easily cloud their judgment. And in the case of a child's mental and emotional health, we dare not take chances. If you are in doubt about your child's emotional health, seek consultation.

### (3) Your child's behaviors are seriously antisocial

We are seeing increasing numbers of young people and children who behave in worrisome ways. They are physically aggressive and even kick or hit parents and teachers. They act like bullies from the early grades on.

As they reach adolescence, their troublesome conduct worsens. It may drive them to stealing, cheating, and lying. In one study (Search Institute, Minneapolis, Minn.), about 60 percent of junior high aged youth said they saw nothing wrong with such behaviors if they did not get caught.

Young people who are lonely may become involved in repeated sexual encounters. They see so much sex on television and in movies, it is easy for them to be deceived by the excitement, glamour, and apparent intimacy of sex. They easily rationalize away the risks of such casual and promiscuous activity, and it becomes a habit.

Skipping school, refusing to do or to turn in school work is another sign of a serious conduct disorder. School, with its abstract reasoning and futuristic focus, is meaningless to these hedonistic students. They are bent on finding power and momentary pleasure — now. School is simply not fun!

Conduct disordered youth show little respect for their parents, others, or themselves. They are rude, rebellious, and may even be abusive of their parents and siblings.

Drug and alcohol abuse by these young people is different from depressed youth. Here, chemicals offer ever new and changing patterns of excitement. They offer a chance to reach the deceptive pinnacle of power and pleasure. The approbation of similar peers is part of this culture.

Spiritually, many youths living in such a destructive pattern are in grave danger. Since they feel so powerful, they have little need, so they think, for God. In fact, they are easy prey for the cults and outright Satan worshipers who have invaded our culture. Finding power from a negative, destructive, and deceptive source can feed their egos. It is extremely difficult to get such young people to even consider a relationship with God.

# Guidelines for seeking professional help

If you have a child who evidences bizarre behavior and seems to experience the world and himself differently from peers, seek help. If you have a youngster who evidences emotional distress that is severe and prolonged, look for someone to counsel you. And if your child is showing increasing evidence of disobedience, disrespect, and rebellion, run for aid. Here are some guidelines to help you find the right sort of help.

> *It is imperative that the whole family be involved in the process of discovering what's wrong.*

Children can suffer severe depression.

## (1) Find a professional who shares your faith

When you call a counselor, do not be afraid to ask if he or she is a Christian. In some communities, Christian therapists are sorely lacking. Seek someone, then, who will at least be in sympathy with your beliefs.

## (2) Find a counselor who understands family counseling

It may seem that your child is (or has) the problem. We often discover that he or she is only the "presenting" problem. Often there is sibling rivalry. There may be inconsistencies between parents. Commonly these days parents are too permissive, though they can also be too strict and harsh. One may lean toward too much compassion and excuse making, allowing the child to manipulate to get her way. It is imperative that the whole family be involved in the process of discovering what's wrong and setting things straight.

### (3) Keep your mind open regarding medication

In my opinion, we use medicines too much in treating children. But there is also a highly valid place for medication.

A child with schizophrenia or autism can be relieved of his often horrifying hallucinations by proper medicine. Over time the dosage will vary and many youngsters will learn to recognize the buildup or decrease in stress that will enable them to help regulate the dosage.

Depression can certainly be relieved by medication. To deprive a child of the benefits of such a prescription would be cruel. But as the child improves and learns to think positively, react calmly, and practice self-control, it would be foolish to continue medication – at least in many cases.

Be sure your counselor works at both the cognitive (thought) level and the physical.

### (4) Practice your own faith

Studies have shown that healthy families are strengthened by spiritual values practiced at home.

In children and adolescents, emotional, psychological, and behavioral problems are common. It is reassuring to know that there is qualified help available. If your child is a source of concern, do not hesitate to seek advice.

---

### Further Reading

Gary Collins. *Can You Trust Psychology?* Downers Grove, Ill.: Intervarsity, 1988.

Grace H. Ketterman. *Understanding Your Child's Problems.* Tarrytown, N.Y.: Revell, 1989.

Paul D. Meier. *Christian Child-Rearing and Personality Development.* Grand Rapids: Baker, 1979.

# The Challenge of Traveling with Kids

*Annie Chapman*

The station wagon stopped. A bunch of kids jumped out and frantically unpacked and set up tents, stakes, sleeping bags, everything needed to make the camp site their home away from home.

In no time the camp was fully functioning and everyone, even the youngest, had done his part. A neighboring camper told the father, "I can't believe how your kids pitched in to set up camp."

"Well," the dad replied, "you see, I have a system. No one goes to the bathroom until camp is set up."

That dad had learned that traveling as a family can be difficult and that one must develop techniques to inspire cooperation.

We are a family who, in essence, takes family vacations for a living ("without any of the fun stuff," our teenage son would add). For more than a decade we've been packing up and going somewhere as a family nearly forty weekends a year, ministering through music concerts, marriage seminars, and church services.

We usually leave on Thursday or Friday and come home Monday. That leaves Tuesday to unpack, catch up on the mail, grocery shop, and do laundry. Wednesday is usually spent getting ready to leave again. Why put up with a schedule like this? Why sleep in motels where the mattresses have been slept on by many strangers before us?

I recall one night after a hard day's traveling and singing, as we all lay quietly awaiting

## About the author

*Annie Chapman has been in a nationwide music ministry with her husband Steve since 1974. They have coauthored three books:* Married Lovers, Married Friends, Gifts Your Kids Can't Break, *and* Smart Women Keep it Simple *(Bethany House). They have two children.*

the blissful sleep we needed, my husband Steve broke the silence. "I wonder who slobbered on this pillow last night?"

The moans and groans of the kids reminded us again of the ever-present question: "Why do we do this?" Our wander lust was satisfied years ago. Traveling is now a necessary ill rather than an exciting thrill.

Why eat restaurant food prepared by someone you cannot prove washed their hands? Why require our children to sacrifice team sports, friends' birthday parties, slumber parties, Sunday school in their own church, and no pets? Why climb into airplanes built by the lowest bidder, or travel in abused rental cars that could leave us stranded anywhere? Why endure comments like, "From the balcony you looked young and pretty; up close I see that you're not."

Why? We feel called to a ministry of encouragement to families, and traveling happens to be a part of that. We believe the kingdom of God is being attacked, one family at a time, and whatever we can do to ward off the enemy, we will do it.

That calling came in 1980 when Steve stepped out of a music group that had kept him on the road as many as twenty-one days a month. Because of our decision to travel as a family, our home became not only a house on a street in Nashville, Tennessee, but anywhere we are together.

Like the innovative dad at the campground, we have had to develop ideas to make our lives sane and manageable. Whether you travel as a family only once a year or so, or have become a regularly mobile family, perhaps some of what we've learned will prove helpful.

# Traveling with younger children

Think back to the last trip you took with your small children. Maybe it was a one-hour trip to Grandma's house or maybe a transcontinental trek to Yellowstone National Park. Regardless of the distance, I'm sure you were bombarded by the irritating refrain: "How much longer?"

The question is universal, and so is the response "We'll get there when we get there. Now don't ask again!"

> *We believe the kingdom of God is being attacked, one family at a time.*

Traveling with small children can, however, be a wonderful experience for both child and parent. Here are some suggestions:

## (1) Don't expect children to be content without your assistance

Children are different. Some entertain themselves beautifully, filling hours with quiet, creative play. (Personally I've never met one of those!) Other children need assistance, suffering very short attention spans.

We started traveling when Nathan was three and Heidi a babe in arms, and we traveled almost exclusively by van. Long hours cramped into a $5' \times 5'$ area were challenging. I would carefully select the toys, books, and tapes to take along. The activities that kept their attention best were noted and kept in the van to be used only on long trips. But no matter how interesting, even the new toys and books would eventually lose their luster, and the "I'm bored" blues would start. That was my signal to set aside the book I wanted to read or the handiwork I was enjoying to enter into their world for a while.

Conflict comes when the children sense that mentally I am not with them. Of course, this does not exist only in crowded vans. Even at home I might be on the phone, excluding the children from my life. The results are similar. When the children are neglected, they become even more insistent for attention.

The only solution is to set aside my "stuff" for a while and read them a story, or have them tell me a story, or play a rousing game of "Go Fish." We even tried playing "Hide and Seek" one day in the van. It sounded something like this: "One, two, three, here I come, I see you." It's not much fun when there's no place to hide. After a while, though, they would be ready to play on their own once again.

### (2) We made provisions for the long hours of boredom

It is unrealistic to expect children to be happy if they're bored. During one twenty-one-day trip when the children were five and two, traveling four thousand miles in an unair-conditioned van from Tennessee through Texas and Arizona, we discovered some entertaining ideas. (It's amazing what you can come up with, right before you lose your mind.)

We stopped along the way and made the sacrificial purchase of a small television that could be played through the 12–volt system of the van. Later we added a VCR. Bible story videos, a few Disney films, and "Little House on the Prairie" episodes were added. The children enjoyed the break in routine, especially when we had to travel at night and it was too dark to read or play.

We've also made good use of audio tape player and headphone sets. The children tended to enjoy the same tape over and over and over and over. We enjoyed that tape all we possibly could the first time. A choice would have to be made. It was either the same tape, or Mom and Dad. Not certain what the children would decide, we opted for headphones, which secured our place in the van.

### (3) We made traveling fun by providing special treats

Keep goodie bags on hand to reward the children for special accomplishments like memorizing a Bible verse, finishing a book, or reciting a poem.

Try a coupon system. Coupons can be redeemed for a back rub or a tummy tickle or a long distance call to Grandma or Grandpa, a friend, or another relative.

Make sure, especially for the young child, that the reward can be enjoyed immediately. A $50 saving bond for their college education is

**With attention, travel can be made fun.**

wonderful, but a stick of gum now would mean more.

One idea we used was a five-day policy. Whenever we were out for an extended period, every fifth day we would allow the children to select a toy, a book, a game, a hair ribbon, or whatever. If what they wanted cost more than we had allotted, they could save up their toy stop money till the next fifth day. The children enjoyed this so much that if it was time to come home and they were almost to the next fifth day, they would beg us to stay out on the road. Do I have to tell you that request was never granted?

The five-day policy was a privilege that could be forfeited if behavior warranted. A side benefit was that the policy eliminated the need on the children's part to nag for toys, because they knew their day was coming.

## Traveling with older children

One of the most common questions asked our teenage children is "Do you like traveling with your parents?" If you have been around teenagers, you know that such a question is a risk. Their answer could be anything from,

"Yes," to "I hate life."

Both responses are honest. Our kids do not know any other way of life. They are, however, aware that this way of life has cost them some fun. As they have gotten older we have tried to make traveling as painless as possible.

One way is to not require them to travel all the time. Whenever there's a special event at school or church, we do everything possible to provide care for them at home. Steve's parents have been a great help when special situations arose.

When the kids do travel with us, we try to connect them with peers at our destination. Whenever possible we'll call ahead to see if there are youth events at the church where we'll be ministering. There may be a youth pizza party after the concert, or the host family may invite a family with children the same ages as ours. We understand the social needs of teens.

We also encourage them to bring along music, tapes, and books to make the long, monotonous hours of travel more bearable. They have also been allowed to bring a friend when we were traveling by ground.

Remaining a strong, united family is our primary goal. Another goal is to fulfill the work we feel called to do on behalf of other families. The two goals would be in conflict if we did not take our children with us as much as possible. They have been a tremendous blessing to us by their willingness to uproot their own world to be a part of our work. We appreciate them more than they will ever know.

# Traveling as a couple

In our zeal to make our travels enjoyable for the children, we have discovered a hazard to the health of our marriage. We're not just Mom and Dad; we're also husband and wife. We make a special effort to be alone, just the two of us.

There's an old hymn we used to sing in West Virginia entitled "If We Never Meet Again, This Side of Heaven." We're convinced it was written by a couple who traveled with kids who shared one motel room night after night.

Now that the children are older, we gladly find it necessary to ask for two motel rooms. This is to the advantage of the children and us. (At least Steve has been happier!)

There are many wonderful aspects of traveling together: the fabulous places we've seen and the world-changing people we've been privileged to meet. But there is one thing that can rob us of the joy of being together: murmuring.

That was the terrible sin that kept the Israelites wandering the desert for forty years. And it is the same hideous sin I have committed countless times during our years of wandering the country.

I did not feel like a sinner. I felt like a victim. When a flight was delayed or canceled, I took it as a personal assault, and I let someone know it. When the hotel lost our reservation, or overbooked us right out of their computer, I felt it my responsibility to teach them that they cannot do the public (me and mine in particular) that way and get away with it.

I openly criticized food set before us. How else would a restaurant ever learn to please the public if we mutely allowed them to serve up such fare? I did not feel like I was sinning, but I was. Just like the Israelites who murmured about the lack of water, and the lack of food, and then the sameness of food, and then the water again, I had fallen into the dastardly sin of murmuring. Exodus 16:8 says that their murmuring was not against Moses but against God Himself.

An attitude of ingratitude is at the core of murmuring. In murmuring in the desert, the Israelites were saying, "You are a helpless, impotent God who does not take good care of those who follow you."

One weekend trip started with all of us feeling under the weather. We made it through our first concert, but the next morning we woke up with a bad case of the flu.

We arranged for a Saturday night concert replacement, but the pastor wanted us to come for Sunday, sick or well. Against our better judgment we decided to try it. Who were we to deny God an opportunity to perform a miracle?

When an airplane engine died, we assumed we would as well, but the pilot manhandled the plane back to the ground. Glad to be alive, we temporarily forgot our flu for the next five hours in a little airport.

We finally arrived at our destination, having gotten worse with each hour. We were put up in a Bed and Breakfast with the bedroom on the fourth floor and the bathroom down the hall. Dinner was down a steep embankment to McDonald's. As I cried and complained to God, I was indignant about feeding my sick children Big Macs.

Nathan ended up in the hospital emergency room, and we humiliated ourselves through two lip synched concerts. We finally made it back to Nashville and remained very ill for the next week.

I murmured a lot that weekend, and obviously it would not take much to get me started again. There was a lot to murmur about, but I made the situation worse by my cry-baby, wimpy attitude. I kept saying, "Oh God, please get me out of here." My prayer now is, "Oh God, don't let me fail the next test so badly."

Murmuring robs us of opportunities to see God at work, especially in those situations when we are most needful of His intervention.

I have been working on my tendency to murmur. When we arrived at a hotel recently at midnight, after a hard day's traveling, they had overbooked. When they sent us to another hotel, I wasn't even tempted to do bodily harm to the clerk. Ah, progress!

The traveling Steve hates most is flying. He often says, "I wish they wouldn't call airports 'terminals.'"

He is also uncomfortable with the overuse of the term *final*. He detests when they ask, "What's your final destination?" or when they announce, "We're making our final approach."

Those sick airline phrases remind us, however, of the deepest desire of our heart. We look forward to the journey's end. We want to be home. But as long as we must, we'll travel.

---

### Further Reading

Carol Van Klompenburg and Joyce Ellis. *When the Kids Are Home From School.* Minneapolis: Bethany House, 1991.

Kathy Peel and Joy Mahaffey. *A Mother's Manual for Summer Survival.* Pomona, Calif.: Focus on the Family, 1989

# Releasing Your Grown Child

*James C. Dobson*

Several years ago, we explored this topic by conducting an informal poll of the Focus on the Family radio listeners. I asked them to react to this question: "What are the greatest problems you face in dealing with your parents or in-laws, and how will you relate differently to your grown children than your parents have to you?" An avalanche of mail flooded my offices in the next few days, eventually totaling more than 2,600 detailed replies.

## 2,600 replies

We read every letter and catalogued the responses according to broad themes. As is customary in such inquiries, the results surprised our entire staff. We fully expected in-law complaints to represent the most common category of concerns. Instead, it ranked fifth in frequency, representing only 10 percent of the letters we received. The fourth most commonly mentioned problem, at 11 percent, related to sickness, dependency, senility, and other medical problems in the older generation. In third place, at 19 percent, was general concern for the spiritual welfare of un-Christian parents. The second most common reply, representing 21 percent, expressed irritation and frustration at parents who didn't care about their children or grandchildren. They never came to visit, wouldn't baby-sit, and seemed to follow a "me first" philosophy.

That brings us to the top of the hit parade

of problems between adults and their parents. May I have the envelope please? (Drum roll in background.) And the winner is, the inability or unwillingness of parents to release their grown children and permit them to live their own lives. An incredible 44 percent of the letters received made reference to this failure of older adults to let go. It was as though some of the writers had been waiting for years for that precise question to be asked. Here are a few of their comments:

## Becoming independent

1. *"Mother felt my leaving home was an insult to her. She couldn't let go, couldn't realize I needed to become an independent person, couldn't understand that I no longer needed her physical help, although I did need her as a person. Quite unintentionally she retarded my growth by 35 years."*

2. *"One of the greatest problems is to have my parents see me as an adult, not as a child who doesn't know the best way to do things. As a child, I played a specific role in my family. Now as an adult, I wish to change my role, but they will not allow it."*

3. *"Our parents never seemed able to grasp the reality of the fact that we had grown from dependent children to capable, responsible*

> I don't need a mother anymore!

## About the author

*James Dobson, Ph.D., is founder and president of Focus on the Family. His many best-selling books include* Parenting Isn't for Cowards, Hide or Seek, The Strong-Willed Child, Love Must Be Tough, *and* Love for a Lifetime (Word). *He and his wife, Shirley, have two grown children.*

*adults. They did not recognize or appreciate our abilities, responsibilities or contributions to the outside world."*

*4. "I am 54 years old but when I visit my mother I am still not allowed to do certain things such as peel carrots, etc. because I do not do them correctly. Our relationship is still child-parent. I am still regularly corrected, criticized, put-down and constantly reminded of the terible things I did 50 years ago. Now we are not talking about major criminal acts, just normal childish disobedience during the pre-school years. I was the youngest of five and the only daughter and I still hear, 'I would rather have raised another four boys than one daughter.' Pray for me, please. I need Jesus to help me forgive and forget."*

We received literally hundreds of letters expressing this general concern. The writers wanted desperately to be free, to be granted adult status, and especially, to be respected by their parents. At the same time, they were saying to them, "I still love you. I still need you. I still want you as my friend. But I no longer need you as the authority in my life."

# A personal experience

I remember going through a similar era in my own life. My parents handled me wisely in those years, and it was rare to have them stumble into common parental mistakes. However, we had been a very close-knit family, and it was difficult for my mother to shift gears when I graduated from high school. During that summer, I traveled 1,500 miles from home and entered a college in California. I will never forget the exhilarating feeling of freedom that swept over me that fall. It was not that I wanted to do anything evil or previously forbidden. It was simply that I felt accountable for my own life and did not have to explain my actions to my parents. It was like a fresh, cool breeze on a spring morning. Young adults who have not been properly trained for that moment sometimes go berserk in the absence of authority, but I did not. I did, however, quickly become addicted to that freedom and was not inclined to give it up.

The following December, my parents and I met for Christmas vacation at the home of some relatives. Suddenly, I found myself in conflict with my mom. She was responding as she had six months earlier when I was still in high school. By then, I had journeyed far down the path toward adulthood. She was asking me what time I would be coming in at night and urging me to drive the car safely and watching what I ate. No offense was intended mind you. My mother had just failed to notice that I had changed and she needed to get with the new program herself.

Finally, there was a brief flurry of words between us, and I left the house in a huff. A friend picked me up, and I talked about my feelings as we rode in the car. "Darn it, Bill!" I said. "I don't *need* a mother anymore!"

Then a wave of guilt swept over me, as though I had said, "I don't love my mother anymore." I meant no such thing. What I was feeling was the desire to be friends with my parents instead of accepting a line of authority from them. My wish was granted by my mom and dad very quickly thereafter.

Most parents in our society do not take the hint so easily. I'm convinced that mothers and fathers in North America are among the very best in the world. We care passionately about our kids and would do anything to meet their needs. But we are among the worst when it comes to letting go of our grown sons and daughters. In fact, those two characteristics are linked. The same commitment that leads us to do so well when the children are small (dedication, love, concern, involvement), also causes us to hold on too tightly when they are growing up. I will admit to my own difficulties in this area. I understood the importance of turning loose before our kids were born. I wrote extensively on the subject when they were still young. I prepared a film series in which all the right principles were expressed. But when it came time to open my hand and let the birds fly, I struggled mightily!

# Fear

Why? Well, fear played a role in my reluctance. We live in Los Angeles where weird things are done by strange people every day of the year. For example, our daughter was held at gunpoint on the campus of the University of Southern California late one night. Her assailant admonished Danae not to move or make a noise. She figured her chances of survival were better by defying him right then than by cooperating. She fled. The man did not shoot at her, thank God. Who knows what he had in mind for her?

A few days later, my son was walking his bicycle across a busy road near our home when a man in a sportscar came around the curve at high speed. Skid marks later showed he was traveling in excess of eighty miles per hour. Ryan saw that he was going to be hit, and he jumped over the handlebars and attempted to crawl to safety. The car was fishtailing wildly and careening toward our son. It came to a stop just inches from his head, and then the driver sped off without getting out. Perhaps he was on PCP or cocaine. Thousands of addicts live here in Los Angeles, and innocent people are victimized by them every day.

Such near-misses make me want to gather my children around me and never let them experience risk again. Of course, that is impossible and would be unwise even if they submitted to it. Life itself is a risk, and parents must let their kids face reasonable jeopardy on their own. Nevertheles, when Danae or Ryan leave in the car, I'm still tempted to say, "Be sure to keep the shiny side up and the rubber side down!"

What are *your* reasons for restricting the freedom of your grown or nearly grown children? In some cases, if we're honest, we need them too much to let them go. They have become an extension of ourselves, and our egos are inextricably linked to theirs. Therefore, we not only seek to hold them to us, but we manipulate them to maintain our control. We use guilt, bribery, threats, intimidation, fear, and anger to restrict their freedom. And sadly, when we win at this game, we and our offspring are destined to lose.

Many of the letters we received in response to our poll were written by young adults who had not yet broken free. Some stories they told were almost hard to believe in a culture that legally emancipates its children at such a young age. Consider this excerpt from a young lady with very possessive parents:

*I'm 23 and the eldest of 3 children. My parents are still overprotective. They won't let go. I have a career and a very stable job but they will not allow me to move out on my own. They still try to discipline me with a spanking using a belt and hold me to a 10:00 P.M. curfew. Even if it is a church activity, I must be home by 10:00 P.M. If it's out of town or impossible for me to be home by that time, I'm not allowed to go. I have high Christian moral standards and they trust me, but they are just overprotective.*

Can you imagine these parents spanking this twenty-three-year-old woman for her minor infractions and disobediences? Though I do not know the girl or her parents, it would appear that they have a classic dependency problem occurring commonly with a very compliant child. No self-respecting strong-willed individual would tolerate such dominance and disrespect. A compliant girl might, while harboring deep resentment all the while.

In a sense, this twenty-three-year-old is equally responsible for her lack of freedom. She has permitted her parents to treat her like a child. First Corinthians 13:11 says, "When I was a child, I talked like a child, I thought like a child, I reasoned like a child. When I became a man, I put childish ways behind me." What could be more childish than for a woman in her twenties to yield to a physical thrashing for arriving home after 10:00 P.M.? Of course, I believe young adults should continue to listen to the accumulated wisdom of their parents and to treat them with respect. However, the relationship must change when adolescence is over. And if the parents will not or cannot make that transformation, the son or daughter is justified in respectfully insisting that it happen. For the very compliant child, that tearing loose is extremely difficult to accomplish.

## Two bad alternatives

Parents who refuse to let go often force their sons or daughters to choose between two bad alternatives. The first is to accept their domination and manipulation. That is precisely what the twenty-three-year-old girl had done.

Instinctively, she knew her parents were wrong, but she lacked the courage to tell them so. Thus, she remained under their authoritative umbrella for a couple of years too long. She was like an unborn baby in the tenth or eleventh month of pregnancy. Granted, the womb was safe and warm, but she could grow no more until she got past the pain and indignities of childbirth. She was overdue for "delivery" into the opportunities and responsibilities of adulthood.

To repeat our now familiar theme, it is the very compliant child who often yields to the tyranny of intimidation. Some remain closeted there for forty years or more. Even if they marry, their parents will not grant emancipation without a struggle, setting the stage for lifelong in-law problems.

The other alternative is to respond like a mountainous volcano that blows its top. Hot lava descends on everything in its path. Great anger and resentment characterize the parent-child relationship for years, leaving scars and wounds on both generations. The strong-willed individual typically chooses this response to parental domination. He isn't about to let anyone hem him in, but in the process of breaking free, he loses the support and fellowship of the family he needs.

This chapter is taken from *Parenting Isn't for Cowards* (Waco, Tex.: Word, 1987). Used by permission.

**Further Reading**

Jay Kesler. *Parents and Teenagers.* Wheaton: Victor, 1984.

Vern C. Lewis and Bruce Narramore. *Cutting the Cord.* Wheaton: Tyndale, 1990.

Jerry and Mary White. *When Your Kids Aren't Kids Anymore: Parenting Late-Teen and Adult Children.* Colorado Springs: NavPress, 1991.

# Learning to Achieve Adulthood

*Henry Cloud*

Phil entered his boss's office with an awful feeling in the pit of his stomach. He didn't know why, since he had been through performance reviews many times before. Rationally, he understood that his boss liked him, but he nevertheless felt afraid.

In the midst of his runaway thoughts, he found himself imagining ways in which his performance wouldn't be good enough or in which he himself would somehow be disapproved. The inner turmoil was almost unbearable, yet no matter how he tried to get rid of those feelings, he couldn't. He had tried memorizing verses on fear during the preceding week, but even that didn't seem to help.

Phil got more discouraged as he thought of other situations where similar feelings overtook him. When he went to the elder board meetings at church, he would almost break out in a sweat. He would sit at the table and have all sorts of good ideas, but he was afraid to say them, fearing that someone would disagree and think his ideas were stupid.

As he sat in the board meetings, he would look at the individual members and try and figure out why they seemed so powerful to him, but it made no sense. He was as accomplished as they, at least on the outside, and he should have felt as though he had a right to be there. But inside, his feelings of inferiority persisted. He had a recognizable fear of being "one-down" to the rest of the men. Secretly, he was afraid they might find out.

The same fears would overtake him in social situations as well. When he played golf with his buddies, he would start to think that they were in some way better than he. Some of his friends would occasionally express strong opinions with which he disagreed, but he found himself afraid to express that disagreement. He'd just nod and go along with them. Sometimes that made him feel ashamed, even wimpy. He just didn't feel like a man around other men. He felt more like a little boy.

If you can identify with Phil, you know what it is to feel like a "little person in a big person's world." The scenario Phil experienced is a predictable one for people who grew up in dysfunctional families, even for outwardly successful Adult Children of Dysfunctional Families (ACDFS). In a word, they haven't grown up.

God has outlined a system for development, including a critical link in the chain of recovery. I call it achieving adulthood, becoming an equal with other adults.

## The path

Normal development is a process. In a home, authority is vested in the parents. They are the authorities, the experts in living. Children naturally look to their parents for teaching in all areas of living, from finding food to driving a car. It is a long and painful process, but when it is over, a young adult should feel reasonably comfortable in assuming an adult role and

## About the author

*Henry Cloud, Ph.D., is codirector of the Minirth-Meier Clinic West and has a private practice in California. He is the author of* When Your World Makes No Sense *and coauthor of* Secrets of Your Family Tree *(Moody).*

exercising authority over his or her life. He should also have reached the point where he feels equal to other adults as siblings under God (Matthew 23:8–10).

There are advantages to assuming an adult position in life. A fully adult person comes out from under a "one-down" position in relation to other adults. He or she can think and reason for himself. He can choose what to believe and what values to adopt. He can decide which job or career he likes or is best suited for.

As he matures sexually, he can choose appropriate sexual expression and a mate. He can pursue, develop, practice, and hone his talents. He can establish mutual friendships with other adults, and he can experience the

joy of establishing a community of his choice that reflects his preferences. He can choose hobbies and vacations that are to his own liking.

*Adulthood is the phase in life characterized by independence of choice and expression.* Paul gives us insight into this important developmental passage when he describes the bondage of childhood as compared to human adulthood and becoming a child of God:

*What I am saying is that as long as the heir is a child, he is no different from a slave, although he owns the whole estate. He is subject to guardians and trustees until the time set by his father. So also, when we were children, were in slavery under the basic principles of the world. (Galatians 4:1–3)*

A child is not free. He or she is under the authority or expertise of parents and is, in a real sense, practicing for adulthood. But when the child becomes an adult, he can truly "own" his own life and be his own boss. Ultimately, that is what gives him the freedom to surrender to the authority of God. An adult is the master of whom he will serve, because he decides things for himself.

Compare this freedom to the feeling of being under someone else's rule. You must gain "permission" to have an opinion, make choices, hold beliefs, choose your church — and so on. It is not a pretty picture, but it is the world in which ACDFs often live.

# Problems

It would be nice if everyone grew up in a family that allowed for the kind of development I have just described, a family that supported one's effort toward growth. But not everyone grows up in such a family. Some people grow up in dysfunctional families that do the opposite: they keep the children always in a childish position and send them into adulthood still feeling "one-down" to other adults. That sort of treatment is a foundation for failure to achieve equality with the adult world.

Let's look at some of the symptoms of feeling "one-down" to other adults:

### Extreme need for approval
When an adult constantly needs the approval of other adults, that usually means he is stuck in some childish stage of development. He is always looking up to the people around him as though they were parents who held judicial power to certify him as acceptable. But no matter what level of approval he attains, it is never enough.

### Extreme fear of disapproval
An extreme thirst for approval is the motivator of the one-down person's performance. The Bible teaches that we are to be motivated by the grace and acceptance of God and others. But if we feel as if we are constantly one-down to all of the parent figures around us, then we will constantly fear this disapproval and condemnation. That pattern will yield paralysis life-wide and stunt growth.

### Constant and unrelenting anxiety
The one-down person experiences constant and unrelenting anxiety. This symptom is not surprising when one considers that the person living in the one-down position sees himself as always subject to criticism and disapproval. And that in turn means that, from the one-down person's perspective, every other adult has the power to judge him unacceptable. What a scary way to live!

### Avoidance of risk and fear of failure
If we feel one-down to others, we will avoid taking the risks necessary for growth. We can only learn by taking risks and practicing (Hebrews 5:13–14; Matthew 25:26–27), and Jesus commands us to use our talents. But if we are afraid of the opinions and criticisms of others, we have given them parental power in our lives and have to avoid their judgment at all costs. Judgment would be too much for us to bear.

### Inferiority and superiority feelings
If we are stuck in a one-down position in relation to other adults, instead of feeling like equal siblings under God with differing talents (Romans 12:3–8), we will always be comparing ourselves with others to see if we measure up. Invariably this system fails to give us the confidence we need, and we end up feeling inferior to our imagined picture of perfection in others.

On the other hand, if we are particularly aggressive, we may have a tendency to look at others as inferior and try to become a parental authority over them, constantly judging and criticizing. Neither extreme is what God has in mind for maturity.

### Extreme feelings of competition
Some try to overcome the feeling of being one-down by constantly competing with others. Their goal is to overcome everyone and end up king of the hill. They may win the battle, but they will lose the war, for all their relationships are characterized by power struggles. People don't feel close to them and therefore maintain their distance, because they don't trust them.

### Powerlessness
Children are by nature "under" the power of adults. That's OK for a child, but as developmental processes take over, this attitude needs to be shed. If a person fails to get rid of it as he grows older, as an adult he will tend to resist expressing assertiveness with other adults. He will be passive in relationships and conflicts and often will feel like a victim in relation to his peers. He will have little sense of direction in his life.

### "Different is wrong" thinking
Adults naturally differ on many things, such as opinions, tastes, and thoughts. People who still think of themselves in the childish position believe that their thoughts, opinions, and tastes are subject to being judged by the

parent figures around them. If their opinions differ from those parent figures, they see themselves as automatically "wrong."

### Rules-dominated thinking
People who think of themselves as children do not experience the freedom to be governed by principles. Jesus was slow to give rules about anything, but He had a great many principles.

### Impulsiveness
A child is kept in check by parental structures, or what the Bible speaks of as the law. But the problem with the law is that it actually has the effect of leading to greater lawlessness. It produces more rather than less passion, more rather than fewer sinful impulses (Romans 5:20; 7:5). The person under the parental commandment of the condemnation of the law ends up sinning more. He is subject to powerful, almost compulsive behaviors such as overspending ("I just couldn't help myself"), overeating, and the like. He feels the "should" of the law and rebels against it. This is the sin-guilt cycle.

### Hatred of authority
Many who have been crushed by strict authority figures during childhood have not been able personally to identify with the expertise of adulthood. Being an adult means having a certain amount of expertise in various areas; you aren't perfect, but you certainly have adult-level talents and strengths. Instead of acquiring this attitude as they grow up, some ACDFs resent all authority and rebel against it, always trying to find freedom through rebellion.

### Depression
It should be clear by now why this is a depressing way to live. If one constantly feels inferior, guilty, and put down, it is difficult to be happy. In addition, feeling one-down naturally brings with it a good deal of unresolved hurt and

> ## *Boundaries define what we think, feel, want, do, choose, and value.*

anger, which in turn sets a person up for depression in adulthood.

### Passive-aggressive behavior
Passive-aggressive behavior is asserting one's will in an indirect way. Instead of being honest about our aggressive urges, we cloak them in actions that are superficially neutral. We are conveniently late to an appointment with a person with whom we're upset. Perhaps we resent our supervisor on the job, so we struggle with procrastination, never seeming to get to the tasks at hand. Or we might exert an overabundant amount of control in relationships.

Passive-aggressive behavior is a frequent symptom resulting from feeling one-down. The loss of power felt in the one-down position leads to covert attempts at restoration to power through resistance.

### Person worship
When someone is still looking at other people as parent figures, he tends to inappropriately idealize them. He will follow them as though they were mini-gods and forget who the real God is. He has failed to make the transition from being under man (his parents) to being under God, as seen in Matthew 23:8–10:
*But you are not to be called "Rabbi," for you have only one master and you are all brothers. And do not call anyone on earth "father," for you have one Father, and he is in heaven. Nor are you to be called "teacher," for you have one teacher, the Christ.*
Some people caught in this syndrome may worship a pastor or other spiritual leader instead of God, in the name of honoring their leaders. In reality, such a practice is a modern-day form of idolatry.

# How does it happen?

If it is God's plan that we all grow up into functioning adults, what goes wrong in a dysfunctional family to prevent that? Let's explore some of the patterns that keep people from achieving adulthood.

## Lack of proper development

There are stages to normal development, and there are prerequisites before a new level of maturity can be approached. If a child does not know how to attach emotionally to others, he cannot form the peer support groups that allow him to separate from his family at the age-appropriate level and thus achieve adulthood.

It is important in adolescence for a teen to develop deep attachments to friends and other people outside his home in order to prepare for leaving home. If a teenager does not have skills to form these close and supportive relationships, leaving home and becoming an adult will be impossible for him. Appropriate relationships provide the resources for growth through the entire process, and this stage is no different.

Boundaries are important elements of adulthood, for they teach us a basic sense of responsibility and ownership of our lives. We need to be able to be separate people and become our own people apart from others, thus having our own identity. Boundaries are the cornerstone of this identity formation. Without them, it is impossible to become an adult.

Boundaries define what we think, feel, want, do, choose, and value. The ability to stake out positions in these areas is part of the transition to adulthood and must be well-developed if an individual is to keep on moving toward adulthood. If he does not have this capacity, he will not come out from under a one-down opinion of himself, for he will not be able to distinguish his thoughts and feelings from someone else's.

## Authoritarianism

The Bible teaches that parents are to be authorities in the home who "grow up a child in the way he should go," to paraphrase Proverbs 22:6 (see also Deuteronomy 6:6–9). The goal is for parents to impart God's ways to the children and get them ready for independence. Developing such independence in a child will require the parent gradually to shift power from himself to the maturing child.

The principle of exercising authority through empowering subjects is seen in many places in the Bible. God the Father gave Jesus all authority and power to accomplish the goals He wanted Jesus to accomplish (Matthew 28:18). When God made Adam, He empowered him by giving him important responsibilities. Adam was to be responsible for the whole earth, to rule and subdue it (Genesis 1:28). There was a real delegation of power from God to Adam.

## Authority figures

The earthly family is to be the same way. The parents, as authority figures, are to teach the children how to gain expertise in living and then to become authorities over their own lives. Parents build this expertise in their children through gradually giving over responsibilities to them.

There is a difference between an *authoritative* style of parenting and an *authoritarian* one. In the authoritarian home we do not see a biblical view of authority. The authority figure is dogmatic, dominated by black-and-white thinking, and rigid, domineering, and controlling. These characteristics of his behavior keep his children powerless, prohibit learning, and stunt meaningful growth.

Authoritarian parenting has been linked in research to many behavioral problems and all sorts of immaturity in children. The New Testament warns the father to avoid provoking his children to anger, causing them to lose heart (Ephesians 6:4; Colossians 3:21). The authoritarian ruling style does not empower

**Parents need to encourage their children to develop their talents.**

the child whatsoever. Rather, it keeps the child powerless, stifling his maturity and setting the stage for later episodes of aggressive rebellion or for a passive death of the spirit. In contrast to this authoritarian style, the authoritative parenting style positions the parent as an expert in living who passes his expertise on to his children, preparing them for adulthood.

## Lack of practice

Hebrews 5:14 tells us that we mature as we practice. That means that there must be the freedom to fail. Homes that are critical of failure do not produce learning in the child, yet achieving adulthood is practically impossible without learning. Children growing up in a hypercritical atmosphere tend to avoid risk-taking for fear of the consequences.

One young adult told me that as a ten-year-old boy he built a tree house he was very proud of, but his father came home and chewed him out because the angles in the roof weren't "architecturally correct." Every time he tried something new, his father berated him over the particular way in which he did not do it perfectly. Eventually, he gave up trying. As an adult he was horribly afraid of trying to learn new skills on the job or in his personal life because the threat of failure was too great.

## Lack of resources

Some parents do not look for emerging talents in their children and fail to provide them with the resources they need to develop their talents. God has given everyone talents and abilities, and parents need to provide their children with the resources for developing them.

> *A home atmosphere might be loving (good) but controlling (bad).*

There are parents who withhold resources even when they are available. Being too poor to provide resources is one thing, but withholding support that is possible financially is quite another. What is involved here are specific kinds of refusals: not allowing a child to attend workshops, clubs, or join sports teams; refusing to buy necessary sports equipment; refusing to help with the purchase of costumes for dramatic productions at school; and so on. In the healthy family, if a child shows some ability, the parent tries to provide the setting and tools needed to develop that skill.

Invariably the child will do some shopping around to find his niche or area of expertise and interest. Too many parents give up at this stage. When a child wants to try a new skill, they say, "No, I won't allow you to play baseball. Remember when you were going to learn to ski? I sent you on that church trip and spent all that money, and you haven't been skiing since." Now I'm not advocating reckless spending of money. Instead, I'm encouraging a bit of freedom for kids who are trying to find their niche. That will normally involve some false starts. That's OK. No one knows what he is going to wind up liking without trying it out first.

## Permissiveness
The extreme opposite of the authoritarian parent is the overly permissive parent who establishes insufficient authority in the home and provides little in the way of limits. Such a parent does not provide an adequate structure for the child to learn right from wrong or to learn to be an authority as an adult later in life (Proverbs 19:18). There is nothing wrong with parents being the boss. Indeed, that is

necessary, for parents really do know more about life. What's more, God desires it. But He does not advocate dictatorship.

## Inconsistency
The inconsistent style vacillates between authoritarianism and permissiveness. It sets up a split in the child between impulsiveness that knows no limits and guilt that knows *only* limits.

Many parents are in conflict over their own sense of authority. As a result, they act out both sides with the child. When they do this, the child never develops a consistent authority structure within himself. He is either impulsive or guilty, just like the home structure. The result is chaos, both in the family and within each personality.

## Lack of respect for personal differences
In the authoritarian home compliance is the norm. But in reality, people are different from one another. They have different tastes, opinions, and talents, to name but a few. In some homes this difference among individuals is punished, unnoticed, or in some way devalued. That keeps the child from developing an adult identity.

The child in such a home fears his difference from his parents' choices. He may not want to be a professional like Dad; he may not want to be a missionary like Grandfather; he may not like sports and instead prefers music. There may be many differences he will want to express. But he knows that expressing those differences will not be accepted in his home. Children like this sometimes have to become "black sheep" in order to avoid conformity and fusion with others. Their differences need to be accepted.

## Imbalance of love and limits
Developing authority over one's adult life comes from an internalization of the style of parents who are balanced in love and limits. As children observe their parents, they take

their balance into their own souls. Parents who balance love and limits, research tells us, have children who are independent, outgoing, and social.

On the other hand, when there is an imbalance of love and limits, problematic combinations develop in homes. A home atmosphere might be loving (good) but controlling (bad); or loving (good) but permissive (bad); or controlling (bad) and unloving (bad again). All of these parenting styles produce authority problems in children.

The Bible tells us that there should be standards and limits in a home but also grace and love. This combination is like God's very nature, which is sometimes described as being composed of justice (limits) and mercy (love).

## Denial of sexuality

Achieving adulthood includes learning about our God-given sexuality. Homes that exclude sexuality from normal existence prohibit development into healthy adulthood. Here, as elsewhere, balance is important. Homes that repress any sexual aspects of the personality do not allow the child to grow into adult sexuality, whereas permissive homes sometimes overwhelm a child with sexual impulses. Some homes are so Victorian that even mentioning sex is a moral sin, whereas others have virtually no sense of decency or modesty.

Sexuality must be balanced in the home for a little person to incorporate that aspect of his or her personhood into existence, and thus become a "big person." Homes that avoid or repress sexuality cause teens to fear their sexuality and thus avoid adulthood. Permissive homes, on the other hand, force children into adulthood much too early, causing equally grievous problems.

## Convictions of the heart that prevent achieving adulthood

Some attitudes of the heart can stifle our move to adulthood. Consider whether any apply to you or to your upbringing.

### Distortions about God

- *God is dogmatic about everything and does not like me to question things; such questions represent a lack of faith.*
- *God is a rigid parent who will crush me if I disagree with Him.*
- *God wants me to be a clone of my spiritual leaders and authority figures and to do everything their way.*
- *God does not allow me freedom in the gray areas of Christian conduct, such as entertainment options; in fact, I doubt whether there even are gray areas in God's view.*
- *God will punish me when I try to learn new things and don't execute them perfectly.*
- *God does not like me to have my own opinions; having my own opinion would be rebellion.*

### Distortions about others

- *Everyone is always critical and disapproving of my actions and thoughts.*
- *No one allows me to fail and thus learn to do better.*
- *Others will hate me if I disagree with them.*
- *Others will like me better if I am compliant to their wishes, demands, and plans.*
- *Others never fail like I always seem to be doing; they seem to know everything.*
- *My leaders are perfect; they have no weaknesses; their beliefs are better than mine; they know what I should do better than I do; they are always right.*

### Distortions about ourselves

- *I am worthless if others don't approve of me.*
- *I should never have tried that; I really messed it up; I am a miserable failure.*
- *I have no right to my opinions; they are usually wrong anyway.*
- *My beliefs are the only right ones.*
- *I know what is best for him or her.*
- *I should always do what I am told.*
- *My sexual feelings are bad.*
- *I shouldn't feel angry/disappointed/sad/lonely (and so on).*
- *I will never measure up to him or her.*

# New attitudes and activities

In order for us to achieve adulthood and grow past a dysfunctional background, we must challenge old ways and practices. That will require new skills.

*Confess to God and to others your need to become an adult (Matthew 5:3; James 5:16).* God and His family (the church) feel OK about your inadequacies in this area; they do not expect you to be all grown up all at once. Find a family of believers who will accept your present state of maturity and encourage you to adulthood by gently pushing you back onto the playing field of life when you skin your knees.

*Develop a theology that allows for the concept of practice.* You are about to embark on a road of learning; there is no way for you to know already what you need to learn. Give up the need to be already there, and get onto the practice field. The only way to gain expertise is through practice.

*Find your talents and pursue them.* God has given you certain talents and abilities, and He wants you to develop them. In fact, He will be displeased if you fail to try to develop and use them (Matthew 25:14–29). He is on your side in this endeavor (Romans 8:31–32).

*Become aware of your own opinions and thoughts.* Adults think for themselves. You should listen to counsel from teachers and experts (Proverbs 11:14), but it's OK to develop your own expertise in important areas so that you don't constantly need parent figures to make your decisions for you. This point applies to both husbands and wives as they relate to one another. Yes, the husband is the head of the home, but that does not mean that wives are to abrogate responsibility for thinking for themselves. (Husbands may also be in danger of failing to think for themselves; independence of thought, so long as it is genuine independence and not running roughshod

over others or an exercise of arrogance, is necessary in all adults.) Pray for guidance and wisdom (Psalm 32:8). God wants to teach you in many areas, and He will guide you to the information you need. Gather lots of data from the experts, but then identify what you believe. That will keep you from being a groupie or a cult member.

*Respectfully disagree with authority figures when you have a different opinion.* This sort of assertiveness is the only way to get into a dialogue, which is where we learn. The authority figures we are talking about here include God. If you disagree with Him about something, tell Him. Job and David did (Job 10:1–22; Psalm 22:2). That was the beginning of dialogue and learning for them. This capacity for dialogue needs to appear in a marriage, too; wives and husbands need to learn how to respectfully disagree with one another when their opinions differ. In terms of people in general, you may be surprised that even the authorities can learn something sometimes and change their position.

*Dethrone people whom you may have put on pedestals (1 John 5:21).* If you have set anyone up as perfect, you have set him up as an idol. Try to see him or her more realistically and as a brother or sister instead of a parent. Your goal in this is to achieve brotherhood with men and establish the Fatherhood of God (Matthew 23:8). Here again, wives who enthrone their husbands (or husbands who enthrone their wives) need to think through what it means for them as adults to place someone in such a position.

*Submit freely to those in roles of authority over you.* Acting like a rebellious child in relation to authority (e.g., government or church) is to be controlled by your compulsive reaction. Submission proves our freedom; rebellion against authority proves our childish state. The equality-minded adult is able to submit to the God-ordained role as to God and does not feel as though he is somehow giving in to a person (Romans 13:1). There is a deli-

**Respectfully disagree with authority figures if you have a different opinion.**

cate equality involved in balancing the need to submit freely to those in authority and the need to dethrone people one has put on a pedestal. Wives, particularly, can find this process difficult. They need to remember that it is a process.

*Treat others as equals.* Do not parent them; yet do not allow yourself to be controlled or judged by them either. To do the latter is to put yourself or them under the law. In the free/gray areas, make up your own mind, and allow others to do so also (Colossians 2:16–19). Here again, wives and husbands need to see their spouses as equals and not as parents or as children.

*Give up your rigid thinking and don't succumb to the black-and-white thinking of others.* Appreciate the things that we cannot know for sure (Romans 11:33–36). That is to allow God to be God and us to be human. Give up the need to have certainty and rules for everything. Worship God, not rules.

*Deal with sexuality.* If you are afraid of your sexual feelings, get in a setting where it is safe to talk about them, and accept them without shame. Remember, shame is a product of the Fall (Genesis 3:10). Marriage is a wonderful opportunity often ignored by Christian couples to talk about sexual feelings. Sexuality is something you talk about in marriage, not just do. Sexuality is good when it is practiced under God's guidelines; He made it.

*Take responsibility for your life.* When you were a child, you were under the rule of stewards and managers, typically parents (Galatians 4:1–3). But as an adult, you are no longer under their responsibility. You are not the steward of your life. This holds true for married people as well as for singles. Marriage is a partnership, a yoking of two walking along together, but there comes a point when each of the partners must assume responsibility for his own life. In fact, it is a misunderstanding on this very point that leads to the enabling behavior exhibited by spouses married to persons caught up in compulsive disease. Accept responsibility, for with responsibility comes freedom and fulfillment.

*Look at every adult around you as an equal.* These adults — and they include your spouse — may have very different talents and experiences, but you are equal to them in terms of worth. Learn to cherish your differences instead of being judged by them or by being proud (Romans 12:3–8).

*Realize where you disagree with your parents.* The Bible tells us that we are to examine our actions and to avoid blindly doing things according to the "tradition of the elders" instead of according to God's ways (Matthew 15:1–3). Distinguish your plans and views from those of your parents.

*Pursue your dreams.* Share your dreams with God, and allow Him to shape them (Proverbs 16:3). Then go for it!

This chapter is taken from Dave Carder et al., *Secrets of Your Family Tree* (Chicago: Moody, 1991).

## Further Reading

V. Gilbert Beers. *Best Friends for Life: Building Lifelong Relationships with Your Children.* Eugene, Ore.: Harvest House, 1988.

Pat Holt and Grace Ketterman. *Choices Are Not Child's Play: Helping Your Kids Make Wise Decisions.* Wheaton: Shaw, 1990.

Charles R. Swindoll. *You and Your Child.* Nashville: Nelson, n.d.

# ADJUSTING IN THE LATER YEARS

# Sending Your First Child to College

*Jay Kesler*

Leaving a son or daughter at college has to rank with the other traumas of parenthood — childbirth, personal commitment to Christ, weddings, and the birth of the first grandchild. Being the president of a small liberal arts college, I now have a ringside seat to observe hundreds of parents going through this experience. It's an excellent replacement for the hackneyed definition of mixed emotions (watching your mother-in-law go over a cliff in your new car).

## Mixed emotions

There is shared excitement over this new chapter in their life — pride at having been accepted, apprehension at the prospect of competing with others, concern over the new strains on the family budget, wonder at the new level of personal freedom and unregulated schedule, a nagging fear of sexual dangers, date rape, and statistics about the new morality (which seems strangely like the old immorality).

On the return trip home in the nearly empty car, we bombard ourselves with questions about compatibility with new roommates. Where will they put all those clothes? Will they fit in? Can we keep up? Did I see a boy with an earring? What do those slogans on the t-shirts mean? Do the kids really understand? Who is going to control the decibel level of the music? Did my son seem withdrawn? Will he make friends? If she falls in love with someone from another state or, God

### About the author

*Jay Kesler, Ph.D., is president of Taylor University and has written* The Family Forum, Parents and Children, *and* Parents and Teens *(Victor).*

forbid, another country, will we lose contact forever? We've never felt so alone or so helpless — so impotent to intercede, protect, and monitor.

Each year we have a commitment service at Taylor University with freshmen and their parents where we try to face these emotions together and, through a one-hundred-year-old ritual, join those who have gone before in

**There is shared excitement when a child enters college.** ▶

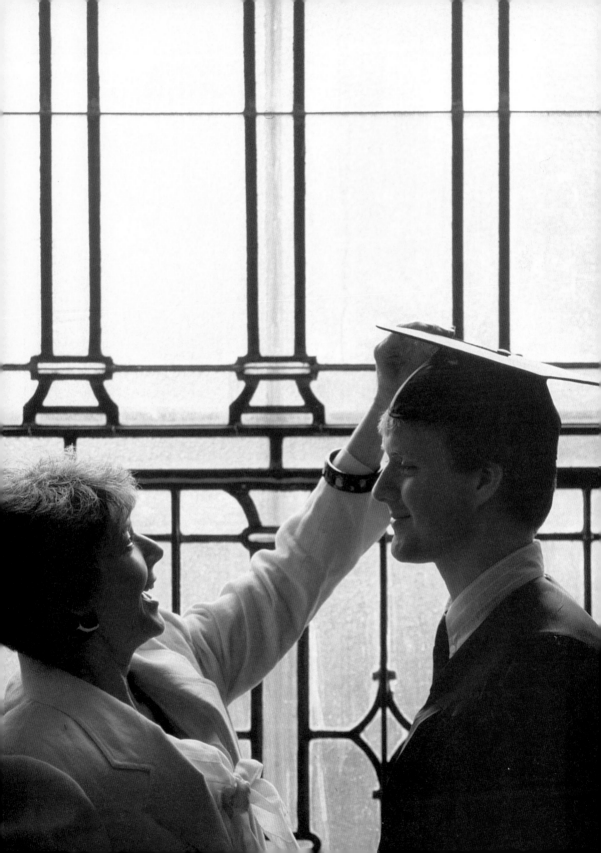

"casting these cares upon Him." As we sing hymns, read Scripture, and participate in responsive readings, we make promises to one another and to God to make this milestone one more step in the process of Christian faith. In a most literal sense we are "giving of our best to the Master," for His task of preparation for a life of intentional service.

Of course, college is not a word that wholly describes the experience. There are many kinds of colleges with many different approaches in many different environments. I remember, for instance, my first week at a secular university in contrast with the one that freshmen have at a Christian college. After my parents had left for home, I was exposed to a series of all-male fraternity "smokers" at which sophisticated (or so I thought) upperclassmen introduced us to the manly pursuits of smoking, alcohol, and blanket parties. When parents leave their children at a Christian college, there are certainly conversations about freedom, independent living, and student methods of circumventing rules, but attending a picnic with chorus singing, testimonies, and communion is very different from experiencing a coed dorm.

## A Christian college

If you are sending a son or daughter to college, I would offer several pieces of advice. First, assess the essential stance of your son or daughter in relation to their world. Does he or she tend to absorb the two or three feet around them, or do they tend to change those they meet. If a child is rebellious, secretive, deceptive, evasive, dishonest or double-minded, as hard as this is to accept, he will probably be the same in a magnified way when he is away at college — unless something intervenes. That something in a Christian college is the combined commitment of administration, faculty, staff, and peers to provide a positive environment in which the Christian gospel is aggressively implored. Not

all respond, but the overwhelming majority are permanently marked for good by this experience.

## A secular college

The something for which parents pray at a secular college might be the influence of a campus ministry such as InterVarsity or Campus Crusade, the witness of another Christian in the dorm, or the persistent voice of the Holy Spirit using the contrast between the libertine environment of the university and memories of loving parents, secure home, and consistent values. Hundreds of vacillating young people are brought to mature Christian commitment on secular campuses each year by this cause-and-effect method. Many who want to be free but not that free, wild but not that wild, and with a kind of fear for their own well-being, seek a "shelter in the time of storm." Some unfortunately spend some years, even a lifetime, struggling with these issues. Thus, my bias toward Christian education.

My purpose here is not to argue the relative merits of Christian higher education over secular environment. However, it is important to understand that these are truly formative years. It is during this period that the basic structure of the mind will take place. It is during this period that young people develop their worldviews. I encourage parents to enter into mature dialogue with their sons and daughters. Try to escape concern for the minutia that necessarily dominated your concerns during their youth, i.e., personal hygiene, clothing, eating habits, and music, and begin level conversation.

By "level" I mean to begin treating your son or daughter as a fellow adult and attribute to them the same respect that you afford other adults. Discuss values, ideas, convictions, and beliefs. Allow them to question, postulate, and struggle, but do not be afraid to share the compelling logic of your convictions as well as your opinions. Tell them how you reached your conclusions, including the pain of getting to your present state of growth. Rather than sitting at home wringing your hands, engage God in prayer over them and begin a more mature chapter of parenting, that of intellectual and spiritual interchange between loving adults.

## Telephone and letters

I encourage the use of the telephone on a limited basis. A weekly call at a prearranged time can be a valuable exchange of chit-chat and mutual assurance. Expect them to be homesick and encourage them to hang in there until the first planned trip home. Usually after the first weekend or two home, the student will begin to look forward to the return to school where his own routine is established and a new independent life has begun.

Though we cannot, as parents, help but feel a sense of rejection, we must remind ourselves that the goal of parenthood is fostering independence. Students unable to break from parents have not yet reached maturity. Be complimented by both the struggle and pain of the break because it indicates a strong bond and the desire for independence. It means you have done a good job of preparation. They feel capable. This is a tribute to your parenting skills.

As much as possible replace the telephone with letters. They are more thoughtful and permanent and can be saved and reread when necessary. Perhaps you have never put your deepest feelings into words or have felt too self-conscious to say certain things face-to-face. A well-reasoned, caring letter can convey more than a hundred phone calls.

Express your own faith in a most reasoned and careful way. Assure them of your love, and don't be afraid to confess your fears and concerns. This gives them an opportunity to write their assurances to you and to expose the convictions of their hearts. Let them tell

> ## *College is a time to question.*

you why they think they can handle certain challenges and experiences and then give them chances to do so.

## The influence of college

Keep in mind that college is a time to question. It is through this process that people learn. Professors, both Christian and secular, are "people who think otherwise." This is not because they are trying to destroy faith or because they have no convictions of their own; it is because they want students to think through their own opinions and develop personally satisfying positions based on sound reasoning.

In secular settings sometimes professors can be convinced atheists and sometimes they are biased and unfair; however, it has been my experience that by debating my Christian bias with them, I have grown stronger, not weaker, in my faith. This will be especially true if pastors, Christian friends, and parents are close enough to share in the struggle and provide strength and encouragement.

Your son or daughter will change in college; however, it is a valuable thing when they trade externally imposed standards for internally established convictions of their own. This is the process of working out their own salvation with fear and trembling (Philippians 2:12).

Many parents are intimidated by their child's college experience. Don't be. You have arrived at your place in life through a personal set of experiences and exposures. Share them, test them with your son or daughter. Iron sharpens iron, and, of course, there is always the possibility of a parent adjusting an opinion based on the experience of the child. This should not be ego-threatening if both believe that ultimately God is the source of truth and

> *There is growth for parents in letting go.*

that together both have learned more of His world or word.

In the final analysis, sending your first child off to college is a gigantic step of faith. Not to feel apprehension would require inordinate self-esteem. We naturally question, however, so allow me to offer some assurances.

## Four assurances

First and foremost, *have faith in God.* He cares for your children more than you do. He will never leave you or forsake you (or them). The Holy Spirit never sleeps nor can He be kept out of the deepest recesses of the human heart. He is working in all circumstances of your child's life, even when you are unaware or unable to help. Remember, "the prayer of a righteous [parent] is powerful and effective" (James 5:16).

Second, *have faith in yourself and in the strength of your home.* All of the lessons and advice, even those that to this point have been unheeded, are in the back of your child's consciousness. They will surface to provide guidance, strength, and, when necessary, conviction in times of need.

Third, *prepare yourself for the very natural sense of loss.* Until the nest is empty, many parents are unaware of how much of their time, energy, and emotional capital is invested in their children. Many tell me that they begin the process of rediscovering each other. This can become a wonderful time of refocusing on the love and romance that initially brought you together. Let's face it — part of the sadness at your child leaving home is the realization that you are growing older. This accounts

for the universal parental emotion at hearing someone sing, "Sunrise, Sunset." We now have opportunity to develop our mature life without some of the distractions and demands of dependent children.

Finally, *be confident of the process.* Maturation is normal. You honestly would not like to live with the consequences of arrested growth. Thirty-year-old sons and daughters living at home do not evidence healthy families. There is growth for young people in going away and developing independence, but there is also growth for parents in letting go. After all the emotions and adjustments have been processed, the result is most rewarding. We are allowed to see the fruit of our labors manifested in self Oregulating young adults committed to Christ with the advantage of educational and life experiences their grandparents only dreamed about.

I also get to preside over graduation ceremonies, and I'm able to see the truth of what I've attempted to express here. When I see the parents posing with smiling graduates in caps and gowns, I see signs of growth and looks of accomplishment on the faces of those parents as well.

### Further Reading

Robert Kachur, ed. *The Complete Campus Companion.* Downers Grove, Ill.: Intervarsity, 1987.

Alice and Steve Lawhead. *The Ultimate College Student Handbook.* Wheaton: Shaw, 1990.

Ronald Nash. *Choosing a College: The Christian Parent and Student Guide.* Nashville: Wolgemuth & Hyatt, 1989.

Greg Spencer. *A Heart for Truth: Taking Your Faith to College.* Grand Rapids: Baker, 1992.

# Happily Empty-Nesting

*Dennis and Ruth Gibson*

When the first snow storm arrived one winter, Dennis went in to the garage, looking for his favorite snow shovel — a lightweight one with a convenient handle. He looked on the garage wall where he stored it and could not see it. He invited Ruth to come out and help him, and she could not see it either. So he cleared the driveway with a heavy, clumsy shovel, muttering that some thief must have made off with the good one.

An hour later, upon leaving for work, Dennis took one last look in the garage and saw that snow shovel exactly where it was supposed to be. We had trained ourselves to overlook it all summer long, and now, when we needed it, our eyes could not see it.

What a parable of taking our loved-ones for granted! After the youngest chick leaves the nest, we shift from the roles of Mom and Dad back into the roles of husband and wife. To really get somewhere in this journey of happily empty-nesting, we recommend that you become a BIKER. That means doing the following:

*B* – *Balance solitude and companionship*
*I* – *Invest in each other*
*K* – *Keep channels of communication open*
*E* – *Eliminate irritations*
*R* – *Rejoice in your freedom from parenting*

### About the authors

*Dennis and Ruth Gibson are founders and directors of Wheaton Counseling Associates. Dennis Gibson, Ph.D., is a licensed clinical psychologist and author of* Vitality Therapy *and* The Strong Willed Adult *(Baker).* **Ruth Gibson** *is a widely sought speaker and is the author of* Chipped Dishes, Zippers and Prayer, A Memory Sampler, *and* Say Yes. *Together they wrote* The Sandwich Years *(Baker) and cohost the weekly television program "Positive Living." They have three adult sons.*

## Balance solitude and companionship

One day while we were visiting the Pacific Ocean, our oldest son Steve gave us a little surfing experience. First, he put Ruth face-down on a long board and, standing in water about waist-deep, he gave the board a shove toward shore at the right moment. Ruth caught the wave and had a good ride, squealing in delight. Then it was Dennis' turn.

Steve coached Dennis that to get a good ride, he needed to inch forward to keep the tip of the board down. Upon catching a wave Dennis hunched forward, and the tip of the surfboard plunged to the bottom of the sea, flipping Dennis and filling his nostrils with sand and salt water.

He came up spluttering, "Steve, what happened?"

Steve said that he had leaned forward too much and needed to keep his weight back. As Steve launched him on a second wave, Dennis edged back too much, and the wave passed underneath, leaving Dennis with no thrill at all.

"Steve, what happened?"

Steve explained that this time Dad had leaned back too much. To skillfully ride a surfboard, you have to play the board like a musician plays a fine instrument.

The third time Dennis experienced a marvelous miracle. A surge of power rose up beneath him as the wave caught that long board and propelled it toward the shore. What an exhilarating experience of the power of the sea! Now we know why our three sons love surfing so much.

The key to success in the empty-nest marriage is like that in surfing. To experience the power and joy the relationship can give requires balance. Each partner needs time alone to be refreshed with favorite activities. Each also needs time for companionship. Marriage is a covenant of companionship. "The Lord God said, 'It is not good for the man to be alone'" (Genesis 2:18).

An accordion makes music by coming together, pulling apart, and coming together again. Both movements are necessary, like inhaling and exhaling. So it is with time alone and time together. The key to balance is talking it over and making these arrangements mutually.

We need also to balance roles as husband and wife with our roles as parents of now-adult children, *and* perhaps also toward our

> *We need to balance roles as husband and wife with our roles as parents of now-adult children.*

elderly parents who need us more and more to care for them as their abilities decline (see *The Sandwich Years* [Baker, 1991]).

# Invest in each other

A man and his wife reached the low point of their marriage. On a trip to Florida, the man looked out the hotel room and noticed his wife beside the swimming pool right below their window. He thought of pouring a pitcher of hot coffee on her because of how she had been treating him. Instead, he recalled the biblical instruction to do good to those who mistreat us (Matthew 5:44–45) and to give a cup of cold water in the name of Jesus (10:41). So, as an act of obedience to God, he lovingly prepared a cup of tea and carried it downstairs to his wife — not because he *wanted* to, but because his Master instructed such a thing. With tears of joy, he tells audiences today, "As I carried that cup of tea down the stairs to my wife, I fell in love with her again."

Scripture teaches two powerful principles of mental health illustrated by this story: "It is more blessed to give than to receive" (Acts 20:35) and "Where your treasure is, there your heart will be also" (Matthew 6:21).

Many people say, "If I did something loving to my spouse when I don't *feel* loving, I would be hypocritical." Not so! Hypocrisy means that we do not live by the principles we profess. God never instructed us to be true to our feelings, but true to His instructions. So, when we go against feelings that do not correspond with God's directions, far from being hypocritical, we are being obedient to God, our highest authority. Our feelings do not merit our allegiance. They are fickle dictators.

This godly man probably benefitted more than his wife did from his kind action toward her. By investing in her the treasure of his loving time and action, he came to prize her. We can love those whom we don't like. Love is a decision!

# Keep communication channels open

When we go to our dentist, he teaches us to floss our teeth. He explains that flossing once every twenty-four hours breaks up colonies of bacteria before they can group together and form plaque. In a similar way spouses can prevent a hardening of heart from accumulating between them by following the scriptural injunction: "Do not let the sun go down while you are still angry" (Ephesians 4:26). That means building into your routine some daily checkpoint in which you address such questions as, "Is there any unfinished business between us?" Or, "Can we be friends again even though we still have this issue we haven't worked out yet?" A good daily time for using this "mental floss" is just before going to bed. Another might be at any time you pray together, such as when giving thanks at a mealtime.

Norwegian immigrants to the Midwest a century ago built this biblical principle into the very furniture of their houses. You can see an example at a tourist attraction called Little Norway in southern Wisconsin. In the corner of the master bedroom is the "Sorry Chair." This fixture consists of a small, flat, unpadded triangle of wood in a corner attached to the two walls near the marital bed. If either

> *We can love those whom we don't like. Love is a decision!*

**Each partner needs companionship.**

spouse felt hostility toward the other at the end of a day, before either of them could crawl into bed *both* had to sit on that hard, cramped Sorry Chair until they said, "I'm sorry." What a great tradition for (a) *requiring* close physical contact between two persons who want nothing to do with each other; and (b) making it a greater agony to remain stubborn than to apologize and forgive.

Suppose you often let several days go by without clearing up the loose ends of aggravations with your spouse. One tradition you can adopt is to celebrate your wedding anniversary every month. We were married on June 18, so on the eighteenth of *every* month we reaffirm our love to each other and each invite from the other an uninterrupted statement of how each candidly thinks we are doing as a couple. We also follow the rule that the first words out of the listener's mouth must be, "Thank you for telling me how you see things."

We also borrow a concept from Marriage Encounter. We start our "state of the union" words by telling an endearing quality we appreciate about our partner. For example, if Ruth is about to tell Dennis her concerns about how things have been going, she may begin by saying, "An endearing quality that I treasure about you is your devotion to doing whatever you undertake with a high degree of excellence." That is a loving way to compliment a perfectionist!

# Eliminate irritations

One rainy night Ruth was criticizing Dennis's driving: "Aren't you going too fast? You're too close to the car in front of us. Don't you think you took that turn a little too sharply?" Dennis felt harassed and resentful.

He suggested that we try to use the principle of relabeling. "I am having a hard time viewing what you are doing right now as anything other than criticism, and what seems to me like unjustified criticism at that. I am finding it very hard to feel friendly toward you. Can you help me to see it any other way?"

Ruth answered, "Maybe I can give you an I-message" (rather than starting with "You" and delivering an attack). "I feel frightened when the roads are slippery and our car starts to get close to the one ahead. I'm scared that we might get into a crash. I would like it if you would slow down and keep a bigger space between our car and the one ahead of us."

A light flashed in Dennis's mind. The new label for Ruth's criticism was "request." Yes, her words and grimaces could be labeled "criticism," but to regard them also as "a request" freed Dennis from bitterness and defensiveness.

As long as he labeled Ruth's words and actions as only "criticism," he was stuck with either giving in like a spineless wimp, or blowing up in anger to show Ruth who's boss. The

instant he saw her as also making a request, he thought of himself as a gentleman who likes to be a gracious host to anyone who rides in the front seat of his car. He realized that he could bring peace of mind to his dearest loved one simply by moving the ball of his foot a quarter inch. The remarkable thing was he *wanted* to!

As Romans 12:2 says, we are transformed by the renewing of our minds. Seeing things from a different slant makes *us* different. If you are currently into such a negative attitude toward your spouse that it will take more than a Sorry Chair or a monthly anniversary celebration to fix it, consider what you would miss about your spouse if he or she were suddenly to die. This perspective may help you to decide that the dirty socks he leaves lying around or the lengthy phone calls she makes to the kids are a small price for the harmony you purchase by choosing not to say anything about them.

# Rejoice in your freedom

It was inconvenient to drive the kids around. It was time consuming to teach them manners over and over. Going to their events kept you from doing other things you would have liked to do. In the empty-nest years we tend to reminisce only about the delights of the child-raising years. But now we get the chance to be husband and wife again, like we were before the first child came along. Resume the adventure!

When our youngest son was just months away from leaving home we joked a lot about how we would get along without him. One evening we were clowning about Dennis as an eternal athlete and Ruth as the perennial cheerleader. We were hamming it up quite a bit, so our son shook his head in mock dismay and said, "Well, at least you two weirdos have each other."

That statement said a lot. In the truth spoken in jest our son was saying that because

Mom and Dad have each other as husband and wife, he is free to leave the nest and make his own life, knowing that the nest will be intact for his occasional visits. He need not handicap himself by having some kind of disabling problem that gives Mom and Dad something to work together on, lest they split up for lack of a parenting project to share.

To make sure we continued to walk in the Spirit during our empty-nest years, each of us decided to become a BIKER. We **B**alance, **I**nvest, **K**eep channels open, **E**liminate irritations, and **R**ejoice.

## Further Reading

Frank B. Minirth, Brian Newman, and Robert Hemfelt. *Passages of Marriage.* Nashville: Oliver-Nelson, 1991.

Cliff Schimmels. *And Then There Were two: Empty Nesting After Your Kids Fly the Coop.* Wheaton: Shaw, 1989.

# Romance and Communication in the Later Years

*Howard and Jeanne Hendricks*

During the frenetic madness of World War II we were two teenagers who spied each other in the hubbub of a large city and decided to pursue a friendship. After five college years, which separated us most of the time, we sealed our devotion with marriage vows and now are more enraptured with each other than ever. How can such a phenomenon occur in a society where 50 percent of all first-time marriages end in divorce — and where researchers say that probably only six marriages in a hundred are truly fulfilling?

"How do you two do it? What's your secret? What do you know that we don't?" These kinds of questions spout constantly, so from our own dog-eared, long-tested, and much-mended by-laws of matrimony, here is our code for tenured care and feeding of romance and good companionship. Everyday do-ables.

To define terms more precisely, we do not equate romance with infatuation. Our ecstasy is not "foolish and unreasoning passion" as the dictionary speaks of it. Nor does it fit the original meaning of romance, as "a long, fictitious tale of heroes and heroines." It is simply a love affair, an old-fashioned, for-real, heart-to-heart connection.

## Communication

Communication, in our personal glossary, covers a multitude of messages. We are partners who gave ourselves to each other in every respect. To be sure, there are distinctly male and female flanks, but they are blended in a single-purpose venture.

Nothing we have to say concerns money — we have had it both ways, with and without — or health, which in our case has been up and down. Nor family. We have ridden a roller coaster, having lost three children before birth and done our share of wrestling in order to rear four independent, strong-willed originals into adulthood.

Our formula, in fact, does not start with us at all. It took shape in God's Research and Development think tank. Only divine insight could have thought of putting together two such unlikely halves from very opposite families of Philadelphia and developing them into one compatible whole. There is no plausible human explanation. To begin, we have a lot to laugh about.

## Humor

Humor has always been a part of our communication, but it gets better as memories pile up. On the steamy night of our wedding, for example, the candles wilted and bent over and "just ruined our pictures," but they have provided chuckles ever since.

Someone has said, "There is nothing so unromantic as a seasick bride." Well, this one, dressed in a crisp white linen suit, had to use an airsickness bag on the first leg of the honeymoon. Not funny to the embarrassed groom, but hilarious in the rearview mirror of older years.

When money was scarce and we were using cast-off furniture, it was "interesting" to

> *Only six marriages in a hundred are truly fulfilling.*

experience the bed falling apart as the old slats quit and our mattress dropped us to the floor in the midst of an amorous embrace.

One of the beauties of aging is the ability to see yourself in the comic strip while it is being written. Recently we sat with 250 people in an air-conditioned plane waiting to take off on a one-hundred-degree day. Uniformed mechanics, brandishing tools, marched back and forth, each with that I'm-the-answer-to-your-prayer look. The just-a-few-minutes delay stretched to more than two hours. We snacked and watched the parade with amusement; only in an affluent society could we afford such shenanigans.

Or consider a recent spectacle of the two of us, dressed for dinner, heading out on the interstate. On an overpass where two traffic arteries merge, our car, without warning, like some stubborn mechanical mule, refused to budge another inch. No hint of impending trouble, plenty of gas in the tank, but nothing! It was rush hour; we were on the inside lane, and along with the honking hordes behind us were the flappable fans of the Texas Rangers baseball team, whose game was scheduled to begin in an hour. We were blocking the route to the stadium. Friendly executive types paused to assure us they would call for assistance on their car phones. Irritated truck drivers dragged their eighteen-wheel rigs within inches of our steel skin and blasted us with horns and dirty looks.

We felt both temperature and anxiety rising. Finally we reminded the Lord that He had two children stranded, now for more than thirty minutes, in the middle of a summer afternoon traffic gridlock with no visible means of escape.

Lest we forget that He has a sense of humor, there appeared at our rear bumper an

### About the authors

*Howard Hendricks is distinguished professor and chairman of the Center for Christian Leadership, Dallas Theological Seminary. He has coauthored* Husbands and Wives *and* The Christian Educator's Handbook on Teaching *(Victor), as well as* Living By the Book *(Moody).* **Jeanne Hendricks** *is a homemaker, writer, and speaker. They have four children and five grandchildren.*

ancient pickup, ornately painted in pastels and carrying a row of wildly gesticulating Mexicans in the front seat. They beeped their musical horn and pointed to a push plate on their front end. Perhaps they were the Hispanic angelic corps dispatched for salvage operations such as ours. We found neutral and started our perilous journey, crossing five lanes of whizzing wheels until we coasted to a curb-side phone. Our thumbs-up was met with a Latin chorus of "Bravo!" as the colorful crew rattled off. We could almost hear our guardian angels chuckling.

## Caring

Somehow God never signed the prenuptial agreement we had carefully prepared and asked Him to bless, calling for schooling and part-time jobs for both of us until such a time as we felt ready for a family. Our message seemed to have been lost in the heavenly translation, and anniversary number one found us stealing kisses in a hospital room. We had a newborn daughter in an incubator (infant ICUs having not yet been invented) and the new mommy was weak and sick. Already we had learned that real romance can flourish without frills and scented lace. We were just glad we had all survived.

A half dozen major surgeries and a life-threatening chronic disease have taught us to watch out for each other. "Two cabbage heads," we tell our aging selves frequently, "are better than one." Did you take your pills?

> *If the Lord can forgive our sins unconditionally, then we can forgive each other.*

Did you check the suitcases through to the final destination? Got the umbrella? Such questions are not pestering irritations but code words of a protective TLC. A special look, a tidbit too profound for words: I love you so much that I don't want anything to go wrong for you.

## Forgiveness

Life has a way of scratching the polish off romantic notions. She plans an intimate dinner; he calls at the last minute to announce a delay. He forgets the anniversary; she sulks icily on her pity pot. She throws away the old

**As seniors we have a sense of history, so we relax.**

jacket; he blows his cork in the predawn rush to go fishing — after all, it was there three years ago.

Many misunderstandings seem to erupt in the crunch of travel. With chagrin he remembers when he slammed the door in anger and dashed to the airport to catch a plane for a speaking engagement in California. There in the hotel room, preparing to recommend the Christian life to others, his conscience reminded him of his own ruptured relationship. Picking up the phone, he called Dallas to say, "I'm sorry, darling. Forgive me." And she did.

She confesses to occasional conflict in the cockpit —

He: *OK, you've got the map. Which way do we turn?*

She: *I dunno. Can't find the cross street — that way I guess.*

He: *Naw! Look at the sun. What good's the map if you can't read it? I know where I'm going. Just tell me the street.*

She: *Oh, admit it! You don't have the foggiest idea where you are! You are the most bullheaded . . .*

Now it's her turn to ask forgiveness.

Communication is alive and well; it just isn't always warm and cuddly. Nor does it have to be. But it must be constantly tuned in to the wave-length of the partner. We have found that the hard core of our kinship is bedrock acceptance. Patience we are still learning. But one thing we have gotten down pretty well: We are two imperfect people. If the Lord can forgive our sins unconditionally, then we can forgive each other. "Love is patient, love is kind . . . keeps no record of wrongs" (1 Corinthians 13:4–5).

# Contentment

The elegance of seniorhood is that we have a sense of history, so we can relax. We predated television, penicillin, polio shots, and the pill. We grew up before pantyhose and automatic gearshifts. We married before electric blankets and fought for privacy before daycare centers and two-bath houses. We could rarely afford babysitters, so the kids learned early that daddy and mommy loved to hug each other. They never doubted that we were madly in love — and still are.

"Godliness with contentment is great gain" (1 Timothy 6:6). So wrote the apostle Paul. The truly romantic and communicating marriage must meet at a point outside itself. For us our Lord is that focus, our dependable North Star. We discovered early that the two of us are like a seesaw, up and down, unless we are stabilized and balanced by His presence.

Our honeymoon has become ancient history and our marriage has been through the meat grinder of modern family dilemmas, but the secret to our romance and communication is the foundation. We set our sights on each other with total commitment, and together we fastened our future on our God and Savior Jesus Christ. His book tells us, "He who began a good work in you will carry it on to completion" (Philippians 1:6). The credit line has His name on it.

---

## Further Reading

Win Couchman. *"Don't Call Me Spry": Creative Possibilities for Later Life.* Wheaton: Shaw, 1990.

Frank B. Minirth, Brian Newman, and Robert Hemfelt. *Passages of Marriage.* Nashville: Oliver-Nelson, 1991.

H. Norman Wright. *Holding on to Romance.* Ventura, Calif.: Regal, 1987, 1992.

H. Norman Wright. *Romancing Your Marriage.* Ventura, Calif.: Regal, 1987.

# Tips For New Grandparents

*Stephen and Janet Bly*

> *No one gave us any clue on how to manage suddenly becoming a grandparent.*

A full day of shopping in the city and a forty-mile drive home left us both bushed. After unloading the car, we slipped off our shoes and collapsed in the living room. That's when the phone rang. It was our oldest son Russell calling from the hospital. Lois, his wife, was about to face a Cesarean for the two-week-early delivery of our first grandchild.

"Dad, can you come down?" the frantic voice prompted.

So back down the mountain another forty miles we hurried. Not that we could do anything — Just sit, wait, pray. It was Russell's turn to be the dad. Lois was the mom. The child born would not be our child, yet would somehow seem as though it should be.

It was a foretaste of the strange and wonderful transition of grandparenting. That Valentine's Day in 1990 Zachary Nathaniel Bly entered our family, our world, our hearts, and we began the tenuous balance of keeping the proper distance in our new role.

People had given us tons of advice before we had our own children. Everyone had opinions about how to be a good mother or a good father. But no one gave us any clue on how to manage suddenly becoming a grandparent. It would have been nice if some seasoned grandparents had pulled us aside and told us.

### About the authors

**Stephen Bly** *serves as pastor of Winchester Community Church in Winchester, Idaho. He has written eleven books and has also coauthored eleven books with his wife, Janet, including* How to Be a Good Mom, Be Your Mate's Best Friend, *and* How to Be a Good Grandparent (Moody). **Janet Bly** *has written four books, including* Managing Your Restless Search (Victor) *and* Friends Forever: The Art of Lifetime Relationships (Aglow), *and speaks at women's conferences and retreats as well as family and writers' seminars. The Blys have three sons and two grandchildren.*

# You won't feel like a grandparent

*"You won't feel like a grandparent."* Yes, our son was twenty-six years old. But that never felt right, either. We still had to remind ourselves that we were not thirty or thirty-five anymore, not even forty. But now this son of ours was all grown up and had a child of his own. People started calling us "Grandpa" and "Grandma," and we darted our heads quickly around looking for *our* folks.

We were only a few moments older when we heard the news, "It's a boy!" Our bodies had not suddenly accelerated in age. After all, we were a long way from retirement. We still had a child at home ourselves. But we immediately entered the realm of a new generation.

When Zachary was born everyone in the family shifted titles and roles. Our children became parents. Siblings became aunts and uncles. Aunts and uncles and grandparents became "greats." We are all working through the shock of adjustment.

Meanwhile, our conversation is constantly peppered with stories about Zachary. We carry six pictures of him in our wallets. We never pass the infant section of the department store without an urge to stop and buy something.

# Your children need you the most

*"During those first few months your children will need you more than your grandchild does."* But Zachary's parents didn't seem to notice our uncertainties about grandparenting. They were too busy struggling as new parents. The only one in the family confident about what he should do at any given moment was Zachary.

Russell called us at 1:30 a.m. one day to ask

It's grandparents' privilege to spoil their grandchildren.

us how to get the baby to stop crying. We groggily reviewed the obvious. "Change the diaper. Feed him, burp him, rock him, walk him."

"But we've done all of that!" Russell moaned.

"Well," we added, "just put him in his crib in a comfortable position, turn out the lights, close the doors, go to bed, and stuff two pillows in your ears."

"But how long do they go through this, keeping you up at night?" Russell persisted.

We looked at each other, smiled, glanced at the clock, and told him, "To the grave, son, to the grave."

# Two sets of grandparents

*"You are not your grandchild's only set of grandparents."* They are out there somewhere. They will find the cutest outfit you

have ever seen. They will buy the most perfect birthday present — something you never even thought of. They will send homemade cookies that are the envy of the preschool. They will call, and you will have to watch your grandchild run to the phone shouting "Grandma! It's my Grandma!" Besides, they will have different ideas about life and children and how to do things.

This sharing a child that's almost like your own takes getting used to. But in our case it is not a matter of competition but an opportunity for sincere gratefulness. Zachary has two more sets of ears to listen to his hurts. Two more sets of eyes sparkle with pride. Two more voices echo those infamous words, "Peek-a-boo!" Two more sets of feet lead him around the amusement park. And two more souls offer up prayers for his daily safety. Grandparenting is a team effort.

# Get acquainted quickly

*"The most important thing you can do for this new grandchild is to get acquainted as quickly as possible."* Much is said about the importance of "bonding," having those hugs and coos and touch as soon after birth as possible. But not all grandparents have the opportunity to watch as the nurse cleans and wraps the newborn through the nursery window. Not every grandparent nurses Mom and baby the first precious days of life. But any grandparent, with effort, can "catch up."

A close study of photos, frequent calls and questions, assessments from other close observer friends and family, even videos can help establish intimacy and smooth preparation for the first time you will be together.

In between grandparent visits our daughter-in-law keeps a small magnetic box on the refrigerator, low enough for Zachary to reach, which holds each of the grandparents' pictures. He can grab them, look at them, and yes, even mangle them a bit, any time he wants. He's getting better acquainted that

way with the long-distance grandparents, so they're not strangers each time they come.

# How available are you?

*"Let your kids know exactly how much time you can offer them."* We live right next door to Zachary and his parents. On September 26, 1991, when Zachary was just nineteen months old, sister Miranda arrived. Mom and Dad needed even more help to relive the chaos. But the close-by grandparents also need time for work. We are full-time writers in our home. We are here but not always available. We let our kids know what hours each week or month we will volunteer to baby-sit. That way they know we truly do want to help, but we are also up-front about our time (and energy) limits.

That does not mean we are not open to emergency interruptions. But the parents need to know when they are not imposing to ask, and the grandparents do not have the uncomfortable feeling that they are being taken advantage of.

# Spoiling your grandchild

*"Do not be afraid to give your grandchildren a little better than they deserve."* The very first question we were asked after Zachary was born was, "You aren't going to spoil that baby, are you?"

Of course we are. We're the boy's grandparents. It's our obligation — and privilege.

It finally hit us one day why grandparenting is so great. The pressure's off. We are not the sole, responsible disciplinarians for Zachary and Miranda. We can get away with spoiling them once in a while. As long as their parents are doing their jobs, we can relax with the pure joy of fun with these kids. But that does not mean giving them an unreal view of the world, or being foolish with our money, or violating their parent's instructions.

For us, spoiling means giving them a little

better than they deserve – doing all the things for the grandchildren we never had time or means to do for our own children. Zachary gets a two-mile walk in the stroller most every day to see the ducks, caterpillars, and big trucks at the state park. Miranda's first dress will be a very impractical, heirloom-type, white-lace-and-pink-ribbons model.

## Grandparents are unique

*"Remember that your role in their life is unique."* The love and affection shown to a grandchild by this particular grandmother and this specific grandfather cannot be made up by anyone else. Other grandparents can love them with all their hearts, but they can't love them with your heart. Only you can do that.

You have a different world of experiences than the others. You have different talents and skills and interests. You have different dreams for their life. They need you!

## Setting an example

*"Allow them to fully impact your lifestyle."* Grandchildren are one more reason to keep plugging along, faithful and fruitful in this sin-sick world. It's one more reason to evaluate our life's investments and priorities.

"I never got riled up much about causes before," one new grandma admitted to us, "until my first grandchild arrived. Then it hit me that I cared what kind of world she would be living in. The far-off future mattered because she mattered. That's when I got involved."

## Prayer

*"Start immediately a regular time of prayer for your grandchild."* Our prayer list has gained two more permanent members. Those names will remain as long as our minds stay clear enough to reach out to a loving and powerful God.

We pray for their health, for their physical development, for their social adjustment, for their intellectual progress, and even for future friends, future mates, and, of course, for their salvation and growth in the knowledge of God.

When Zachary and Miranda are old enough, we will tell them that we pray regularly for them. That's when we can ask their own requests and needs.

## Sensitivity

*"Be sensitive to your children who do not have kids yet."* "It seems we don't count anymore," one son told us. "Only the couples with the kids get the parents' attention."

"That's not true," we said in shocked response.

"OK," he continued, "what would be your reaction if Russ and Lois and the grandkids moved twelve hundred miles away and we moved next door instead?"

Ouch. "We'd want you *all* close by," we lamely countered.

Proverbs 17:6 states that "Children's children are a crown to the aged." Grandchildren are meant to be our crown. Our symbol of honor. Our reward. Our delight. They are bright jewels intended to put a sparkle in our thoughts and wealth in our hearts for years.

Zachary was only thirteen months old and had not begun to speak. But he could, of course, communicate. As we entered his house it was obvious he was mad at his mother.

"He pulled the toilet paper completely off the roll for the third time this afternoon, so I finally locked the bathroom door," Lois explained.

Tears streamed down his chubby cheeks. The weight of the world's injustice seemed to be crashing in on him. Nothing was going right. Nothing would ever be right again. Then, suddenly, he looked up and saw us at the door.

"Oh!" he screamed. He ran down the hallway with arms outstretched, jumped into our arms, heaved a big sigh, and laid his head against our shoulders.

All was at rest. Everything would turn out OK. Grandma and grandpa were here.

Maybe that was the first time Zachary let us know that we had a special, unique place in his life.

It wasn't the last.

Welcome to grandparenting!

### Further Reading

Stephen and Janet Bly. *How to Be a Good Grandparent.* Chicago: Moody, 1990.

*Promises for Grandparents.* Wheaton: Shaw, 1990.

# Index

All feature photographs
courtesy ZEFA (UK); except
pp. 31–32, 113, 183, 217
(Peter Wyart); p. 170 (Clifford
Shirley); p. 223 (Tim Hansel)
Illustrations on pp. 255, 261 by
Julia Pearson